EXPLORING
TWENTIETH-CENTURY
MUSIC

EXPLORING TWENTIETH-CENTURY MUSIC

Otto Deri
City College of the City University of New York

HOLT, RINEHART and WINSTON, INC.
New York   Chicago   San Francisco   Atlanta   Dallas
Montreal   Toronto   London

PREFACE

In all phases of music history a certain amount of time has had to elapse before radical innovations were found acceptable. This time lag appears to be greater now than in any other period, notwithstanding the spectacular progress made in musical communication during the twentieth century. Music composed more than fifty years ago—works written around 1910 by Schoenberg, Webern, and Bartók—has not become part of the average listener's experience. The aim of the present volume is to provide an orientation that will make the new music more accessible to the listener of contemporary music.

A study of the history of musical taste reveals that, in any given period, the principal cause for the listener's resistance to musical innovations stems from his reluctance to break away from familiar listening patterns. When the listener approaches twentieth-century music with previously established auditory habits, his failure to comprehend the new musical universe will be nearly total, for the music of our century is built upon entirely new premises which demand a perceptual approach that is totally different from that of previous eras. Without a reorientation of his listening habits and esthetic attitudes, the listener will rebel against the innovations and against the innovators who have caused his frustration; the new music will remain incoherent and chaotic. Consequently, musical innovations must be met with a willingness to listen and to learn.

For this reason the musical attitudes and perceptions of the listener have been the primary concern of this book. Such a consideration served as the basis for the selection and organization of the material presented, as well as the amount of space devoted to each subject. Unavoidably, the objective of all-inclusiveness had to be relinquished in favor of selectivity.

This book is designed either for a college course or any course of study in twentieth-century music. The reader, it is assumed, may or may not be specializing in the field of music. It is also assumed that the reader has a minimal fund of knowledge concerning the materials of music—at least the equivalent of an introductory course in music.

The book is divided into three major sections. The beginning of Part I briefly summarizes the main cultural events of the twentieth century and their impact upon the artist and the arts in general. The reader is made aware of the fact that music is not an isolated phenomenon, evolving independently from the other arts, but is influenced by the intricate and subtle interplay of external forces that reflect the cultural milieu at a given time in history.

The main body of Part I (Chapters 2–6) examines the elements of music (melody, rhythm, harmony, texture, and form)—their historical role and function as seen from the vantage point of the present century. Here, the aim is to help the reader make the necessary transition from previously established patterns of listening to a new auditory integration. Each musical element is viewed separately in the historical context of the last 200 years. This time limitation seemed advisable for two reasons: first, the music from 1750 to 1900 developed along fairly consistent lines; and second, the music of the classic-romantic era is familiar to the majority of listeners.

In each chapter the element under discussion is viewed in its evolution from the classic-romantic era to the twentieth century. The relationship and interdependence of the elements are kept in mind, although each element is traced in a separate chapter. For example, how the relationship between melody and harmony underwent considerable change before the twentieth century is shown; similarly, the diminishing role of melody and harmony is brought into focus at a time when rhythm had assumed a dominant position in the structure of the new music.

Throughout the text emphasis is placed on actual listening experiences and the specific events that occur within a composition. Approximately 300 examples accompany the text to facilitate this objective.

The changes that occur in perceptual values are examined in terms of their expressive intent rather than from a purely technical point of view. The reader is constantly reminded that a new musical language has become necessary because the old idiom was found to be inadequate for the expression of musical thoughts by the twentieth-century composer. The expanded range of expression in the new music often necessitates a reorientation in the esthetic attitudes of the listener—a reorientation that may involve his basic notions concerning the nature of music.

In addition to the reorientation of esthetic, perceptual, and expressive values, the reassessment of the meaning of basic concepts is frequently necessary, as all too often the fixed meaning attached to these concepts proves to be too narrow for the role they have assumed in twentieth-century music. Some of the basic concepts concerning the elements of music are also reviewed because of the ambiguous nature of musical terminology.

In the last chapter of Part I (Chapter 7), new compositional procedures such as serialism, chance, and electronic music are discussed. Here, too, historical continuity is stressed and links with the musical past are established at novel points of departure. On the whole, the attainments of the avant-garde receive only cursory treatment since they are too close in time and are largely unfamiliar because of infrequent performances and the unavailability of scores and recordings, for critical assessment to be of much value.

Part II (Chapters 8-14) focuses upon the music of specific composers. The works of those who paved the way for the new music—the forerunners—are presented in Chapter 8. The remaining chapters are devoted to a detailed examination of the music of Stravinsky, Bartók, Schoenberg, Berg, Webern, and Hindemith. Although the space allotted these composers outweighs that normally allocated in standard textbooks, it is the author's belief that as the leading figures of the first half of the twentieth century—both in terms of the greatness of their music and the influence they exerted on younger composers—they merit extended treatment. These are the composers who endeavored to express what had not been previously stated and whose works owe their existence to a new order of sounds. It is felt that a detailed study of their music will offer more insight to the reader than an examination of the music of composers whose art was built on the traditional level of experience, however successful or appealing it may have been.

Each of the six composers is considered in a separate chapter; a biographical sketch projects the composer against his environment and a profile of his personality is drawn. Esthetic beliefs and attitudes, based on the composer's writings, are also brought into focus. Stress is also placed on the musical influences that shaped the composer's formative years. The major content of each chapter, however, centers upon the development of the composer's style by delineating the main characteristics of his principal works. Selected compositions are also analyzed.

Part III offers the reader a glimpse of the European and American musical panorama—an overview of the contributions of various countries to twentieth-century music. In assessing these contributions, the musical standing of each country is defined and the main achievements of its major composers are summarized.

If this volume is used as a textbook, it is expected that the examples and the works discussed will be heard. The general reader is urged to provide listening facilities for himself, as this volume will be of little value unless accompanied by repeated hearings of the musical selections. The reader who wishes to build a record library of contemporary works will find a suggested list of recordings in the discography.

Particular thanks are due to my colleagues in the Music Department of the City College of the City University of New York, who were often used as sounding boards for various ideas. I am also indebted to Miriam Gideon, who read parts of the manuscript and made valuable suggestions, and to Mrs. Virginia Red for her critical reading of the text. I also wish to express my thanks to Melva Peterson, music librarian at City College, for her able assistance. I am grateful to Joan Cenedella, whose editing helped to soften the Hungarian accent of the text.

New York, February 1968   O.D.

CONTENTS

PART I

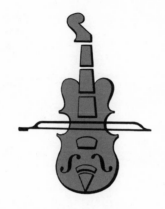

MATERIALS OF
TWENTIETH-CENTURY MUSIC

INTRODUCTION

The peculiar heroism of modern artists is chiefly manifested in their unflinching attentiveness to the world's and the self's chaos as revealed to them by the contents of their own mind

—YEATS

THE ARTIST AND HIS ENVIRONMENT

Generally, an artist's work will mirror to some extent the cultural climate in which he lives. This mirroring may vary in specificity; sometimes the work of art merely reflects such general qualities as the state of equilibrium or tension of a particular culture, while in other instances the correspondence is more specific. For instance, the dominance of religious thought during the Middle Ages manifested itself as the central subject matter in art and music. When religion ceased to be an all-embracing interest, the artist also widened the range of his subject matter to landscape and portrait painting. An instance of even more specific parallelism can be established between Couperin's elegant, highly ornamented clavecin style and the dress and manners of the court of Louis XIV.

There are, however, many factors which make it difficult for the cultural historian to establish clear-cut correlations between the artist's work and his environment.

There have always been artists whose contributions are out of phase with their era. While some such as Rachmaninoff and Sibelius in the twentieth century have clung to the traditions of the preceding period, others have anticipated the next phase as did Berlioz in the early part of the nineteenth century. There are also the artists who reflect elements not apparent in their environment, elements that have been suppressed or forbidden by society.

Contradictory correlations between the artist's style and his environment may also occur due to the polarity of psychic life, a phenomenon called by Nietzsche *Anderstreben*[1]. As a result of this urge, the artist may undergo sudden reversals in his style development. Renan once commented that "the more a man develops, the more he dreams of the opposite pole."

Opposite tendencies existing in the same period are often to be understood, according to Curt Sachs, as a bipolar resistance against some tenet of the preceding era. Thus, the fact that in the nineteenth century the epigrammatic style of some of Schumann's piano pieces and the colossal tonal frescoes of Berlioz appeared simultaneously should be understood as a common reaction to the judicious, well-balanced proportions of the earlier classical style.

The consistency of stylistic tendencies of the arts in a given period is further weakened because the rate of change is different in the various arts. Architecture, for instance, has moved at a slower rate in its history than painting. The style of architecture remained comparatively stagnant. While painting moved swiftly through a variety of styles reaching impressionism around the middle of the nineteenth century, architecture still adhered to much earlier traditions. Music, on the whole, moved at a slower rate compared to literature or painting, possibly due to its nonverbal, essentially nonrepresentational nature.

STYLE EVALUATION AND

TIME PERSPECTIVE

Another phenomenon concerning style evaluation—significant for our

---

[1]*Anderstreben* — the urge of the suppressed part of consciousness to assert itself.

examination of the music of the twentieth century—is the unevenness in our perception when dealing with distant past, recent past, and the present. It seems the further we go into the history of past centuries—and this is true for political and art history as well—the narrower our perception becomes, just as objects seem to get smaller when seen from a vehicle in motion. Toynbee has said that from the distance of 300 years it is difficult to comprehend the motives that prompted nations to wage war against each other. It seems as the time distance increases, our perception becomes less differentiated. This anomaly in our perception is borne out by Table I which contains a tabulation of the duration of stylistic periods in music as seen today.

Table I

Style	Time	Duration
Romanesque	800–1100	300 years
Gothic	1100–1400	300
Renaissance	1400–1600	200
Baroque	1600–1750	150
Classical	1750–1810	60
Romantic	1810–1900	90

The tabulation indicates that as we proceed toward the present, the stylistic eras become increasingly shorter. One should not, however, exclude the possibility that the accelerated rate of stylistic change may also be due, at least in part, to the increased tempo of social change. Be that as it may, it should be kept in mind that the diversity of the present is more acutely perceived than diversities of the past. Thus, today, we tend to look upon the Brahms-Wagner controversy, which reached its climax in 1860, more in terms of clashes of personalities than in terms of irreconcilable musical philosophies, as was held at the time. On the other hand, the numerous "isms" registered in our century support the theory that we are apt to magnify our present currents.

Despite the anomaly in our time perception and the lack of homogeneity of one stylistic period, despite the dialectics of style development which brings about the coexistence of one tendency with its opposite, and despite the uneven rate at which the styles of different arts evolve, there seems to be a common, spiritual denominator, Zeitgeist,[2] in every period which sets the dominant tone for that era. Thus the minuet does capture the essence of the courtly, somewhat artificial,

[2]Zeitgeist — the spirit of the time.

formal atmosphere of its period, and one even assumes a correspondence between the formal delineations of this dance and the strict social stratification of the period. Correspondingly, one feels that the changed social atmosphere of the nineteenth century, wherein a newly emerged social class learned how to enjoy life, is well captured in the free-flowing waltz.

THE SPIRIT OF THE TWENTIETH CENTURY

The closing decades of the nineteenth century brought a false sense of security and prosperity. The storm warnings of a few philosophers and writers such as Nietzsche, Dostoievsky, Zola, and others were unheeded on the whole, and man enjoyed the improved conditions of a materialistic culture.

The opening decade of our century saw some unrest and conflict, though limited to only a few participating nations. World War I began in an optimistic atmosphere: perhaps for the last time in the history of mankind soldiers marched to their recruiting stations singing spontaneously, cheered by the population.

The disillusionment came in 1918. The tremendous price in human life—more than ten million soldiers died in the war—failed to settle the issues that led to the war. The losing nations were bent on revenge, and with the Russian Revolution a new separation between the East and West began.

The decades following World War I saw unprecedented technological progress, new upheavals in social stratification, and increased spiritual emptiness. The role and radius of the individual shrank; he became more and more lost in the mass movements of management and labor. Modern civilization made a near-robot of the working man. His life forces had no meaningful outlet or field of action. Whatever he accomplished at the small station of his life was devoured by the giant organization of which he was an infinitely small part. The realization of the futility of his personal efforts in his work resulted in general passivity. Even entertainment became mechanized through the new mass media. The nearly complete automatization of the individual in an over-mechanized society was predicted by Oswald Spengler in his *Decline of the West* and best portrayed and communicated by Chaplin in *Modern Times*.

This trend towards automatization was also accompanied by a spiritual vacuum in which man found himself. The ideas and values that formed the core of man's thinking in the past centuries were destroyed by the machine age, which offered nothing in the place of the old theological-humanistic foundation.

In the 1930s the principles of national socialism and fascism served as temporary magnets: the "little man" was highly susceptible to the paranoid dreams of his leaders. For a while, at least, it seemed possible that the "super race" would bear out the dreams of Nietzsche and Spengler. The defeat of Hitler in 1945 put an end to this possibility, but not before millions died in the battlefields, in bombed cities, and in concentration camps. Nevertheless, it soon became apparent that World War II also failed to bring real peace. With the beginning of the atomic age, the complete destruction of our civilization became a distinct possibility. A new nihilism swept over the world; "human predicament," "absolute zero," "wasteland of futility" were the catchwords. In Erich Fromm's words, "In the nineteenth century the problem was that *God was dead;* in the twentieth century the problem is that *man is dead.*"[3]

THE ARTS AND THE ARTIST IN THE TWENTIETH CENTURY

The tumultuous events of the twentieth century had a profound effect on the artist. Because of his heightened sensibilities, he felt the destruction and the horror of the wars even more keenly than the average person; the drabness of the mechanized life along with the prevailing spiritual emptiness placed him in a tenuous position. He felt both isolated and unwanted. It is interesting to observe how similarly this isolation is expressed by a leading scientist and an outstanding painter. "The artist often has an aching sense of loneliness," writes Oppenheimer,[4] the physicist, "for the community to which he addresses himself is not there; the traditions and the culture, the symbols and the history, the myths and the common experience which it is his function to illuminate, to harmonize, and to portray, have been dissolved in a changing world." Klee,[5] the great modern painter, also sees the artist as one cut off from human roots, from the participating life of the community. "We have found the parts but not the whole," he writes. "We still lack the ultimate power, for the people are not with us" (*Uns trägt kein Volk,* in his words).

[3] Erich Fromm, "The Present Human Condition," *Perspectives USA,* **16** (Summer 1956), p. 75.

[4] Robert Oppenheimer, *Prospects in the Arts and Sciences,* Concluding Address, Columbia University Bicentennial Meeting, December 26, 1954. Published in *Perspectives,* **11** (Spring 1955), pp. 9–10.

[5] Paul Klee, *On Modern Art* (London: Faber & Faber, Ltd., 1948), p. 55.

PLATE 1. MAX BECKMANN: *Blind Man's Buff,*
1945 (triptych: center panel, 90″ x 80″; left panel,
42½″ x 74½″; right panel, 42½″ x 74½″)
The Minneapolis Institute of Art, Minneapolis. Gift
of Mr. and Mrs. Donald Winston

**PLATE 2. ARNOLD
SCHOENBERG:** *Self
Portrait,* 1910
The Bettmann
Archive, New York

The lack of orientation and the feeling of displacement made itself strongly felt in the arts. In the visual arts erratic, swiftly changing "isms" (dadaism, futurism, and so on) followed each other in restless succession. The emphasis was on distortion, decomposition, and dehumanization. The human body was broken down into its geometrical components by the cubists. Other artists such as Léger and de Chirico introduced half-human, half-mechanical forms as subject matter, symbolizing man's plight in the machine age. In music, electronic devices threatened to eliminate the human element in performance.

MAIN TRENDS IN THE VISUAL ARTS

The gulf separating the modern artist from his environment is clearly shown by the *antirealistic* quality, which is the most prevalent tendency in twentieth-century art. It takes on one of the following three modalities:

Expressionism   In this style the significance of the object is de-emphasized by the artist, who is more concerned with his innermost feelings aroused by the object. In other words, the true meaning of the object lies in the *meaning* and *values* that the artist attaches to the object, the reveries it evokes. Promptings from the deep layers of the artist's consciousness make themselves felt, in which process meanings may become more and more tenuous. In accordance with these attributes, expressionism does not attempt to represent reality faithfully, but "subjectifies" and intensifies the experience. Van Gogh is considered as the forerunner of this movement, which has Kokoschka, Rouault, Beckmann, Nolde, and others in its ranks. An example of expressionistic art is shown in Plate 1.

Plate 1 shows highly individualistic symbolism portraying a nightmarish mixture of horror, lust, and anxiety.

The close parallelism between expressionism in the visual arts and in music is illustrated by a painting of Arnold Schoenberg (Plate 2), the leader of expressionism in music, who in the pre-World War I years was closely allied to a group of avant-garde painters.

An increased emphasis on the visionary and an even greater leaning toward a fantasy world is known as *surrealism*, a branch of expressionism. Chagall and de Chirico are the two best known exponents of this style, illustrated by Plate 3.

As can be seen from Plate 3, the surrealist artist's imagination is so powerful that it transcends all boundaries of reality, producing images suggestive of the arbitrariness of the dream world.

It is also evident that both the expressionist and the surrealist were influenced by the discoveries of psychoanalysis. The unconscious,

PLATE 3. MARC CHAGALL: *I and the Village,* 1911 (75⅝" x 59⅝")
Collection, The Museum of Modern Art, New York. Mrs. Simon Guggenheim Fund

hitherto repressed, yielded new source material for the artist. Furthermore, due to the new psychological insights, the symbolism of ancient and primitive art was perceived now in a totally new light.

Abstractionism   The same goal, namely to turn away from the objects of the physical world, can be achieved in a different way. The abstract painter, also, as a point of departure, uses a real physical object, but instead of drawing on the inner processes of fantasy elicited by the object, he "abstracts" the values which lie in the potentials of the *material* he is working with. In this style the content or experience presented is overshadowed by the structural matter. Abstractionism started with cubism around 1910, led by Picasso and Braque. Their aim was to reduce form to its geometrical essence. In this style, in general, the artist's approach is intellectual as compared to expressionism. Consciousness of design, relations of proportions and textures are in evidence; values of color, line, and shapes are woven into richly varied patterns. In the process, the reality of the object, which once served as a point of departure, is more or less disregarded depending on the degree of abstraction. The transformation may be so complete that hardly any physical similarity with the object remains. Plate 4 exemplifies abstract art.

In Plate 4 the geometrical element is obvious as well as is the arbitrary rearrangement and decomposition of the perceptual values which were characteristic of the real object.

Nonobjective Painting (sometimes called pure abstraction)   In this approach the artist does not employ a physical object as his original subject. It consists of the juxtaposition of geometrical shapes, such as circles and triangles, and intuitive ordering of line and color creating a "cosmic rhythm." Kandinsky—whose friendship with Schoenberg will be discussed later—and Mondrian were the leaders of this movement. Plate 5 shows an example of nonobjective art.

In summing up the characteristics of the three approaches under discussion, it can be seen that all three avoid, although in different ways, the representation of reality. The first, expressionism, focuses on the inner processes of the subjective mind, while the second, abstract art, is concerned with the possibilities offered by the material. The third, nonobjective art, shuns representation altogether.

Regardless of which of the three alternatives is chosen, the task of the perceiver will not be an easy one. The innermost feelings of the expressionist artist may be so personal and divorced from reality that communication becomes extremely tenuous. In abstract art, the decomposition of the material may assume such proportions that the expressive intentions may become highly problematical. Finally, in nonobjective art, the esthetic experience, according to the followers of this movement, depends on a special ability on the part of the viewer to res-

PLATE 4. JUAN GRIS:
Guitar and Pipe, 1913
(25½″ x 19¾″)
Collection, The
Museum of Modern
Art, New York. Gift of
the Advisory
Committee

**PLATE 5. WASSILY
KANDINSKY:** *Geometrical
Forms,* 1928 (19″ x 11″)
Philadelphia Museum of
Art, Philadelphia. The
Louise and Walter
Arensberg Collection

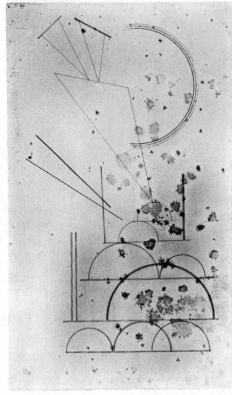

onate with the "spiritual vibrations" emanating from the painting. The stylistic distinctions in actual appearance are not always as clearly delineated as it would follow from the above descriptions. For instance, the dividing line between expressionism and abstract art is often very thin; the term *abstract expressionism* suggests a possibility for the reconciliation of the two tendencies. Furthermore, painters are often claimed by more than one school: Klee, as an example, is claimed by all of the aforementioned groups.

Finally, two avant-garde movements, with diametrically opposed objectives are part of the twentieth-century picture. One, called *perceptual abstraction* or *op art,* resembles superficially the approach of the nonobjective artists in that this movement also renounces physical objects as models of representation. Where the nonobjective painter by his arrangement of line, color, and shape hopes to communicate with the viewer by virtue of some mystical rapport, the op artist shuns any appeal to emotions. Instead, based on careful research in visual perception, using often complicated mathematical calculations, the op artist wishes to fascinate the eye without involving the viewer as a person. Depersonalization is now complete; the canvas, realized by careful permutations of the spectrum, merely exists as a generator to the perceptual response of the eye (see Plate 6, p. 15).

In contradistinction to this carefully calculated scientific approach stands the school of the so-called action painters who produce their works by various techniques based on chance procedures.

MAIN TRENDS IN LITERATURE

The withdrawal of the writer from the realities of the outside world is in evidence in literature too, even though there are writers who fight for the conscience of the world. Nevertheless, the typical protagonist of the modern novel is the non-hero and the dominant themes seem to be alienation and estrangement. The counterpart to nonrepresentational painting is seen in the paucity of content in literary forms. In poetry, for instance, epic writing, the most content-oriented, is out of fashion. In novels, the trend is also away from the story that is highly plotted. More often the stream-of-consciousness type of writing is used, stressing personal associations and symbolic connotations rather than a chain of events.

Expressionism is a stylistic movement found in literature too, exemplified by the earlier writings of Joyce and Kafka. The latter's *The Trial,* for instance, is filled with dreamlike eerie events which, although they seem to lack causal relationship, evolve with a terrifying inevitability.

In drama, the playwright of the movement known as the *Theater of* _the Absurd_ often depicts a fantasy world not dissimilar to that of the surrealist painter.

MAIN TRENDS IN MUSIC

Since the main body of this volume is devoted to the study of music of the twentieth century, comments at this point will be only in the nature of a preview.

Two points need clarification in particular; first, in what over-all way is music affected by the _Zeitgeist_ of the twentieth century; second, can one detect, and to what extent, a common denominator between the trends in music and those which were said to characterize the visual arts?

The outstanding similarity between music and the other arts in the twentieth century is in their isolation from the community. Klee's words, _"Uns trägt kein Volk"_ ("We have no support from the community"), hold true for the composer of advanced music to an even greater extent than for the creative artist in other fields, as opposition by the general public to new music is greater than to modern painting or literature. Today, compositions written more than half a century ago, for example Schoenberg's _Pierrot Lunaire_ or Webern's early music, are rejected by a majority of listeners.

Due to the abstract nature of music, the question of representation or attitude concerning the physical objects of the world would not be a fruitful approach. It is to be assumed, however, that modern music, like the other arts, also reflects the tensions and anxieties of modern life. Thus the harshness of the sound in the new music, and the distortion, dissolution, and pulverization of its elements—a trend observed in the visual arts too—can be interpreted as the expression of the modern composer's alienation. This is where the listener's re-education must start; he has to realize that music does not have to have a pleasing surface beauty—a premise upon which the music of the last 500 years was based—and its aim is not necessarily relaxation. Beyond this esthetic reorientation listening habits have to be revised, too, because the premises upon which predictability was based in earlier music have lost their validity. Thus, tonality, the most important principle of musical coherence, has been renounced in a good deal of contemporary music.

A new order also pervades melodic, rhythmic, and textural values. For these reasons, the study of contemporary music must be a course in _ear-training_ in the widest sense of the term. It is for this goal that Part I of this book centers on melody, rhythm, harmony, texture, and principles of organization. The purpose will not be to delineate _rules_, but rather to acquaint the listener with the new modes in which these perceptual values appear, underlining also the composer's aim in expressiveness.

PLATE 6. RICHARD ANUSZKIEWICZ:
Corona, 1965 (18″ x 18″)
Courtesy Sidney Janis Gallery, New York

Correspondences between the arts can be observed in terms of stylistic categories too; the counterparts of both expressionism and abstractionism are observable in music. Expressionism in music is applied usually to the compositions of the Schoenberg school dating from the years preceding World War I. The emphasis here is on subjective inner processes, often touching upon previously repressed realms of the psychic life. The equivalent of abstractionism can be seen in neoclassicism which emphasizes form consciousness and reflects the composer's interest in the control and manipulation of the materials of his art. The works of Stravinsky, composed between World War I and II, exemplify this style.

The close relation between music and the visual arts is also borne out by the parallel tendencies of the avant-garde. The totally organized music of the serialists, in whose works every note follows a prearranged order (see Chapter 7) is linked by some to the calculated approach of the op artist, while others relate it to the earlier nonobjective style. Furthermore, chance music, whose basic premise is that the choice of notes should depend on such chance events as the tossing of coins or matches, shows some parallel tendency with action painting.

The application of the same stylistic labels in the different arts raises grave questions. Despite the difficulties and oversimplifications involved, efforts to seek a unity of the arts are worthwhile and instructive. The student of contemporary music should take a global view of the arts for they have one feature in common: their relevance to modern man's problems. Such a global view should make the study of contemporary music less forbidding to the layman. He should realize that in studying modern music, he is not on completely new ground; rather, he is exercising his imagination on another segment of his contemporary environment. It has been often stated that a study of modern art helps us to adjust to modern life. According to one of the leading Gestalt psychologists: "Art, psychologically considered, is not an idle play of our emotions, but a means of helping us to find our place in the world."[6]

---

[6]Kurt Koffka, "Problems in the Psychology of Art," *A Bryn Mawr Symposium, 1940.*

MELODY

The role of melody is one of the most controversial aspects of contemporary music. Many critics and countless listeners claim that the new music is "tuneless," that is, devoid of melody. Henry Pleasants, summing up the "European musical tragedy" of the twentieth century, writes:

> Composers denied those very lyric faculties of music which prompt people to express themselves musically and which make the musical expression of others intelligible. Preoccupied with harmony and instrumentation, they forgot that the musician's primary purpose in life is to *sing*.[1]

[1] Henry Pleasants, *The Agony of Modern Music* (New York: Simon and Schuster, Inc., 1955), p. 161.

The equation of melody with singability raises the fundamental question: what is melody? Unfortunately, the number of treatises dealing with melody is very small compared to the hundreds of volumes written on harmony. It seems as if it were tacitly admitted that melody is the fruit of some mysterious native endowment whose sources lie deep in the unconscious, and that it therefore defies strict conceptualization, whereas harmony being less elemental and more man-made, and more recent too, lends itself better to systematization.

Another reason for the paucity of writings on the subject could be that it is somewhat artificial to isolate the melodic component for discussion. It is inextricably tied to rhythmic considerations and often also closely linked to harmonic procedures. Despite this close interdependence, the melodic style of a composer, or that of a historical period, is in itself a subject well worth exploring. Because of its controversial nature an examination of the melodic component is an absolute necessity for the student of contemporary music.

THE CONCEPT OF MELODY

According to the definition in *Webster's Seventh New Collegiate Dictionary* melody is (1) "a sweet or agreeable succession or arrangement of sounds: TUNEFULNESS (2) a rhythmic succession of single tones organized as an aesthetic whole. . . ."[2]

Obviously, both definitions are formulated according to the view current in the nineteenth century, as if the original Greek meaning of the words *melos* (song) and *aoidos* (singer) still prevailed, thus suggesting that melody necessarily should be tuneful or singable. Should anyone apply these characteristics of melody to the music of the twentieth century, he would conclude that our new music shows a dearth of melody. This intolerance toward the new music can also be explained by the fact that the listener is conditioned to eighteenth- and nineteenth-century music and to the resultant narrow generalization as to what music (melody) should be like.

Neither is Webster's formulation of melody as an "aesthetic whole" usually applicable to modern melodies. It is particularly the problem of wholeness, the unit or pattern quality of melody, that divides the theorists. Those who object to the pattern theory argue that pattern is a relative matter, that after a sufficient number of hearings *any* succes-

[2] By permission. From *Webster's Seventh New Collegiate Dictionary* © 1967 by G. & C. Merriam Co., Publishers of the Merriam-Webster Dictionaries.

sion of tones will be experienced as a pattern. On the other hand, Gestalt psychologists emphasize the point that melody is a *whole,* and as such it is more than the sum total of its parts. This wholelike quality becomes apparent, they claim, when we memorize a melody: instead of memorizing single tones, we automatically aim at larger units. Critics of modern music claim that it is devoid of melody because no patterns or units are observable.

It is obvious that the concept of melody needs broadening. This need was recognized by Abraham[3] who conceived of melody as a musical line that has significance. Significance is preferable to pattern because the significance of a musical line may often be felt before its Gestalt quality is grasped.

Another instance in which critics decry the absence of melody occurs when the melodic pattern is shaped by rhythmic forces rather than by pitch differences; this happens in both traditional and modern music. Undoubtedly, this was the basis upon which Stravinsky found Beethoven's melodic inventiveness deficient. The Russian composer claims that Beethoven spent his whole life imploring the aid of this gift he lacked. The validity of such criticism brings again the definition of melody to the foreground. According to Stravinsky, melody "is the musical singing of the cadenced phrase"; to this he adds:

> I am beginning to think in full agreement with the general public that melody must keep its place at the summit of the hierarchy of elements that make up music. Melody is the most essential of these elements . . . because it is the dominant voice of the music.[4]

The question brought up by the quotation is whether one should believe that Beethoven lacked the "gift" of inventing melodies, such as Stravinsky had in mind, or whether he used his driving terse statements that are often considered melodically "unpromising" by preference and choice. This case also shows the extent to which music criticism depends on preconceived notions concerning the elements of music. Ironically enough, the same criticism concerning the lack of melodic gift was also leveled against Stravinsky by a number of writers.

For all intents and purposes, the concept of melody should be viewed in a broader sense than is suggested by the definitions based upon earlier musical traditions. Its meaning is established by the significance of the horizontal component in music. Also, melody does not necessarily depend on singability.

---

[3] Gerald Abraham, *This Modern Music* (New York: W. W. Norton & Company, Inc., 1952), pp. 75-76.

[4] Igor Stravinsky, *Poetics of Music*, translated by Arthur Knodel and Ingolf Dahl (New York: Vintage Books, Inc., 1956), pp. 42-43.

MELODY AND SCALES

In different cultures and at different times melody appeared within a variety of scale systems. It should be emphasized that any scale system is a generalization, formulated by the music theorist ex post facto. In other words, the scale system is not a *norm*, according to which melodies are invented, but the reverse holds true: the generalizations about scales are based on the empirical evidence of the music of a given period. Thus, the seven-tone scale with the major and minor modalities was the result of a slow process and it was not until its practices were established that the theorist codified its rules.

The twentieth-century composer in a search for new melodic and harmonic solutions often resorted to other scale systems than the well-known major and minor modes of the diatonic scale. Among these the oldest is the pentatonic (5-tone) scale, upon which the folk music of geographically distant cultures was built for thousands of years:

EX. 2/1 Pentatonic Scale

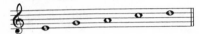

An old pentatonic melody from the Turkestan region of Central Russia is cited.

EX. 2/2 Pentatonic Melody

There is a renewed interest in the pentatonic scale in contemporary music, particularly in the works of Debussy, Ravel, and Bartók. The opening measures of Bartók's "Evening in Transylvania" are built on this scale:

EX. 2/3 BARTÓK, *Hungarian Sketches,*[5] "Evening in Transylvania,"
opening

[5] Copyright 1932 by Karl Rozsnyai and Rózsavolgyi & Co.; renewed 1960. Renewal assigned to Boosey & Hawkes, Inc. Reprinted by permission of Boosey & Hawkes, Inc. and Editio Musica, Budapest.

The Whole-Tone Scale   The whole-tone scale (Ex. 2/4) originated in the music of the Far East and consists of six equidistant steps, the significance of which will be examined in later chapters.

EX. 2/4 Whole-Tone Scale

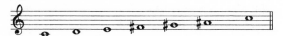

The sound of this scale will bring the music of Debussy to mind, although it was used by Mussorgsky, Liszt, and other composers before Debussy.

The Modes   The medieval modes also reappeared in the music of the twentieth century, and were favored particularly by Debussy, Ravel, Vaughan Williams, Bartók, and Kodály. The modes often suggest an archaic mood. The opening of Bartók's *Rumanian Dance* No. 2 (Ex. 2/5/a) is set in the Dorian mode; Example 2/5/b shows the Dorian mode upon which the melody is built.

EX. 2/5/a BARTÓK, *Rumanian Dance No. 2,*[6] opening

EX. 2/5/b Dorian Mode

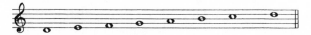

SCALE—KEY—TONALITY

Often *scale* and *key* are used mistakenly as synonymous concepts. It should be kept in mind that scale is the more static and narrower concept, meaning merely the stepwise arrangement of the seven tones built on one or another selected tone as a starting point. Key, on the other hand, is a broader and more functional concept implying a frame of reference, revolving around and gravitating to its center. The sense of centeredness is known as tonality. It is a powerful organizing principle in music, both melodic and harmonic, and it became one of the

[6]By permission of The Béla Bartók Archives, New York.

strongest pillars of form in the classic-romantic era. The tenuous presence of tonality in twentieth-century music and its occasional renunciation (atonal music) are the most disturbing features of modern music
for the average listener.

One more concept requires clarification here, that of *chromaticism:*
if notes are employed in a melody (or in the harmonic structure) which
are not part of the particular tonal frame of reference in which the
melody is set, these notes are called chromatic. Chromatic notes usually
have some tension-creating effect or at least are experienced as somewhat unexpected. In some instances their function can also be that of
ornamentation. In Example 2/6, the opening measures of Beethoven's
"Eroica" Symphony, the C sharp represents chromaticism:

EX. 2/6 BEETHOVEN, *"Eroica" Symphony,* first movement, opening

MELODIC STYLE IN THE CLASSIC-ROMANTIC ERA

The purpose of an examination of the melodic component in the
classic-romantic era, as stated earlier, is to demonstrate that the peculiarities of twentieth-century melody are the result of a gradually changing conception concerning the role and nature of melody. It should be
added that the change in melodic thinking was the result of a gradual
change in the over-all esthetic outlook.

While a distinction is made between the styles of classical music
(comprising generally the works of Haydn, Mozart, and a controversial
amount of Beethoven) and romantic music (music of the nineteenth
century after Beethoven), the reader is warned not to read into these
distinctions differences of an antithetical nature. The dividing line
between the two styles is ambiguous as is shown by Beethoven's controversial position. Furthermore, the early romantic composers (Schubert,
Mendelssohn) had many features in common with the classical tradition, while Mozart often showed signs, particularly in his melodic style,
of foreshadowing romanticism. It should be remembered that every
stylistic category is an oversimplification because every work of art has
more facets than can be described by a label. Categories of styles can
often be considered as necessary historical dividing lines whose boundaries are frequently highly controversial. Artists often resist such labels,
as Debussy unsuccessfully tried to shed the label of *impressionism.*

Notwithstanding the dangers inherent in these generalizations, it can still be maintained that classicism is characterized in all the arts by a distinct form consciousness, and by a tendency toward the universal rather than the personal. Also, a firmer control over emotions is in evidence than in works of the romantic era. On the other hand, the romantic artist is more concerned with subjective statements which are often presented in an emotionally less restrained manner. His interest often lies more in color than in considerations of design, and he is also prone to break away from traditional modes of expression. Youthfulness and often a Dionysian intoxication mark the romantic temper.

In an over-all view, it will be observed that the three basic elements of music (melody, rhythm, harmony) are differently interrelated in the two styles under discussion. In the classical style the three elements appear judiciously balanced compared to the music of romanticism, in which one or the other element tends to be exaggerated. Melody, in the classical style, is closely integrated with the other two elements, while the romantic composer often gives it a preferred position.

Melody, more specifically, will be examined in the two styles from the following points of view:

1) Shape and range of melody, intervals, chromaticism.
2) Inner organization, punctuation, paragraphing.
3) Vocal thinking.

1. Since the classical composer was primarily interested in the architecture and in the logical elaboration of his melodic ideas, it suited his purposes—particularly in movements in sonata form—to invent terse melodies, or rather motifs, with sharp profiles which carried in themselves latent possibilities for later development. Particularly the opening melodies in first movements of symphonies, sonatas, and chamber-music works show this sharply etched quality. The melodies usually avoided the extreme ranges of the instruments.

The intervals most frequently found in the typical classical melody are scale steps and the notes of the common chord. An examination of the opening themes of the first movements of Beethoven's nine symphonies will show that every one is built either on scalelike progressions or on the notes of the tonic triad.

The reader familiar with the music literature of this period should have no difficulty finding examples of his own. But he should also look for exceptions. It would be tempting to say that the cited tendency has the quality of lawfulness. This, however, would be misleading; there are many melodies built differently. One can only state that the described tendency was dominant in that period.

In the nineteenth century a gradual change took place in melodic thinking. In fact, it was so gradual that it would be beyond the scope of this volume to document all of the gradations. The trend, in general, was toward wider range, wider and more unusual skips, and more chromaticism. Also, asymmetry in phrase structure was increasingly favored, often coupled with rhythmic complexities. The resulting expressive values shifted toward restless gestures instead of classical balance, toward longing rather than fulfillment, and, on the whole, toward a more subjective communication.

Schubert's opening melody from the first movement of his String Quartet in A minor is representative of early romanticism. Although this melody at first suggests classic equilibrium, as it unfolds it assumes an increasingly romantic flavor. The widening span of intervals, the rise in dynamics, and the change in modality should be noted.

Numerous examples could be listed, melodies composed between 1830–1845 by Weber, Mendelssohn, and Schumann, to document the earlier mentioned tendencies. It is not claimed that *every* melody represents a movement forward on the same path, but the examination of large enough samples shows the trend of the melodic style. The opening of Schumann's String Quartet, Op. 41, No. 3, composed in 1841, exemplifies the suggested change:

EX. 2/7 SCHUMANN, *String Quartet in A Major,* Op. 41, No. 3, first movement, opening

The falling fifths, the vocally conceived embellishments, increased chromaticism, and veiled tonality contribute to the romantic sentiment of the Schumann example.

Around midcentury Liszt and Wagner broke further away from the classical tradition and gradually paved the way for a completely new conception of melody. The two melodies in Examples 2/8 and 2/9 show ambiguous tonal thinking, unvocal skips, chromaticism, and irregular structure.

EX. 2/8 LISZT, *Faust Symphony,* first movement, 5 mm. after Study letter G

EX. 2/9 WAGNER, *Tristan und Isolde,* Act II, Scene 2, piano-vocal
score, p. 161

...das Seh - nen hin zur heil' - gen Nacht, wo ur - e - wig, ein - zig wahr..

In the last decade of the nineteenth century Richard Strauss added to these features, extending the melodic range even further. A well-known instance of this is found in the virtuoso treatment of the violin in the opening of *Don Juan* (Ex. 2/10) where the violinist has to cover almost the entire range of the fingerboard in the three opening measures.

EX. 2/10 STRAUSS, *Don Juan,*[7] opening

During this period the influence of folk music added fresh flavor to the melodic style. Examples of the folk influence can be found in the symphonies and Slavonic dances of Dvořák, and in the works of Smetana and Grieg.

2. Turning now to melodic organization, more often than not melodies in the classical period were symmetrical–based on a four + four measure plan. The *proposition* stated in the first four measures (antecedent), was answered by the second four measures (consequent). Example 2/11 contains one of countless examples:

EX. 2/11 MOZART, *Piano Sonata in A Major,* K. 331, opening

Example 2/11 constitutes a full musical sentence divided into two halves by a colon or semicolon, with the full cadence coming at the end of the sentence. This delineation is easy to perceive and to predict even for the beginner. Melodies with a less symmetrical design are somewhat less obvious:

[7]Reprinted with permission of the publishers, C. F. Peters Corporation, New York.

EX. 2/12 MOZART, *Symphony No. 40 in G Minor,* K. 550, Minuet, opening

The non-German composers, with Berlioz among the first, took the initiative in breaking with the traditional mode of *punctuation.* The main theme of the *Symphonie Fantastique,* composed in 1830, is an early example of irregular phrase structure and the absence of predictable paragraphing:

EX. 2/13 BERLIOZ, *Symphonie Fantastique,* first movement, mm. 72–78

The music of Liszt and Wagner shows the same tendency toward a freer type of melodic organization as seen in Examples 2/8 and 2/9. Listeners conditioned to the traditional melodic organization objected to the new melodic patterns which did not follow the path of well-established musical expectations. Quite some time passed before audiences realized that the "new" melody could also be meaningfully perceived if the necessary adjustments were made in one's mode of listening.

3. The over-all melodic thinking in every period is also reflected in its vocal writing. In the classical period the melodies of Haydn and Beethoven were conceived instrumentally rather than vocally. Neither composer was particularly attracted to art song or opera, and with the exception of Haydn's masses and oratorios, neither of them achieved his best in the sphere of vocal music. However, Mozart's entire melodic thinking was vocal; the term "singing allegro" was first applied to his melodies. At times, his vocal parts contain larger skips and bolder chromaticism than his instrumental melodies for dramatic motivation.

In line with the increased interest in melody during the nineteenth century, there is a change in the treatment of the voice, as seen in the songs of Schubert and Schumann. Many of their melodies both instrumental and vocal, are characterized by lyric tenderness. The most important change in the vocal writing of the period, however, began with Wagner. The conception of the unending melody was associated with his style. His vocal parts often assumed a declamatory character. Contemporaneously in Russia, Mussorgsky designed vocal melodies that were conceived according to the inflections of the Russian language rather than to the standards of the *bel canto*.

In *Pelléas et Mélisande* (Ex. 2/14) Debussy brought the *parlando* (speaking) vocal style to a point from which it was only one more step to Schoenberg's *Sprechstimme*.

EX. 2/14 DEBUSSY, *Pelléas et Mélisande,*[8] Act I, Scene 1, piano-vocal
score, p. 18

MELODY IN THE TWENTIETH CENTURY

The melodic component in twentieth-century music is hard to define; it will be much easier to determine its nature in the *negative*. The new melody—thinking of the music of Stravinsky, Bartók, Schoenberg, or other composers who write in an advanced idiom—will usually *not* have a symmetrical structure; the intervals will *not* be based on the major or minor forms of the triad or on the steps of the diatonic scale; it will not have the punctuation (cadences) as known from eighteenth- and nineteenth-century music; and it will *not* be readily singable. Often the melody lacks any total center.

In the affirmative, it is difficult to generalize with regard to intervals and range. Compared to nineteenth-century melody, the new melody uses even larger skips or will favor very narrow intervals. In other words, modern melody has a bipolar tendency, and in either case it veers away from earlier traditions. Concerning specific intervals, the seventh, the ninth, and even larger intervals are used frequently along with the fourth. Augmented intervals appear with great frequency, particularly the augmented fourth (tritone). In other instances, small intervals (half steps and whole steps) are used exclusively, resulting in some form of irregular chromaticism. A few composers, such as Hába, Bloch, and Bartók have attempted to divide the half step into quarter steps (microtones). Thus far, however, the Western ear has failed to adjust to these differentiations.

[8] Permission for reprint granted by Durand et Cie., Paris, France, copyright owners; Elkan-Vogel Co., Inc., Philadelphia, Pa., agents.

Intervals relatively seldom used are the third and the sixth, the favorite melodic intervals of earlier centuries. On the whole, melodies with larger skips will have longer phrase lengths, while melodies with narrower intervals are more likely to be broken into smaller units separated by rests. In music with narrow intervals and short phrases, the melody will generally be dominated by rhythmic forces, as is often found in the music of Stravinsky.

To illustrate some of the characteristics of modern melody, Example 2/15 features an atonal melody with wide skips and an irregular structure.

EX. 2/15 SCHOENBERG, *Third Quartet*,[9] first movement, mm.
62–68

However, irregular designs and large skips are not inevitable features of the new melody. Schoenberg, for instance, occasionally wrote melodies with symmetrical formation and average-sized intervals (Ex. 2/16). In this example the atonal setting gives novelty and tension to the conventional-looking melody.

EX. 2/16 SCHOENBERG, *Piano Concerto*,[10] first movement, opening

Melodies of smaller intervals are often found in the music of Bartók; the fugal opening of the *Music for Strings, Percussion, and Celesta* is a well-known example (Ex. 10/12) of a melody built on small intervals, as is the main motive of the Fourth Quartet (Ex. 2/17).

---

[9] Quoted by permission of Mrs. Gertrud Schoenberg and Universal Edition, publisher of first edition.

[10] Quoted by permission of G. Schirmer, Inc. and Universal Edition, publisher of first edition.

EX. 2/17 BARTÓK, *Fourth Quartet*,[11] first movement, m. 7

Melodies that derive interest more from their rhythmic character than from their intervallic profile will be discussed in the next chapter. Stravinsky's *Rite of Spring* demonstrates one of this type.

EX. 2/18 STRAVINSKY, *The Rite of Spring*,[12] "Spring Rounds," mm. 53–56

Singability is often problematic if the tonal feeling is tenuous, regardless of how broad an arch the melody may otherwise have. Seemingly, the opening of Sessions' First Quartet has all the requirements of a singable melody, although vocalists may think otherwise.

EX. 2/19 SESSIONS, *First Quartet*,[13] first movement, opening

In vocal writing there is a definite trend toward declamation and a percussive treatment of the voice. Increased declamation manifests itself in Schoenberg's *Sprechstimme,* a vocal device employed in *Pierrot Lunaire* (Ex. 2/20). *Sprechstimme* is recitation in which the pitch line is merely approximated, but the rhythmic values are rigidly controlled.

EX. 2/20 SCHOENBERG, *Pierrot Lunaire*,[14] "Der Dandy," opening

Mit ei - nem phan - ta - - - sti-schen   Licht ...

An extremely free use of the voice may be observed in a song by Webern:

EX. 2/21 WEBERN, *Geistliche Lieder,* Op. 15,[15] "Morgenlied," mm. 3-5

... mit   hel - lem Schein   lässt sich   sehn   frei gleich wie   ein   Held

— und   leuch-tet in die gan - ze   Welt.

To illustrate the percussive use of the human voice, an excerpt from Stravinsky's *Oedipus Rex* is quoted:

EX. 2/22 STRAVINSKY, *Oedipus Rex*,[16] Act I, Scene 1, 4 mm. after Study No. 11

E pes- te, Oe - di - pus,   Oe - di-pus, ser-va nos,   Oe - di-pus, Oe - - -

In the total picture of melodic style, the influence of folk music maintained itself in some countries (Hungary, Russia, and England) while it diminished in others (Germany, France, and Italy). In the coun-

---

[14] Quoted by permission of Mrs. Gertrud Schoenberg and Universal Edition, publisher of first edition.

[15] Copyright by Universal Edition, Vienna. Used by permission.

[16] Copyright 1927 by Russischer Musikverlag; renewed 1955. Copyright and renewal assigned to Boosey & Hawkes, Inc. Reprinted by permission.

tries in which avant-garde tendencies are particularly strong, the influence of folk music has noticeably weakened.

In certain avant-garde styles there is a trend known as athematic writing, sometimes called *athematicism,* that eliminates any semblance of a theme or motive. Instead, a single note, a timbre, an interval, or a chord may assume referential meaning. The stress on timbre differences in a melodic line is known as *Klangfarbenmelodie,* a device often used by Webern (see Chapter 13).

In summary, melody is still one of the basic elements in most twentieth-century music although its appearance and character have changed. Whether or not one subscribes to the opinion that melody has declined in the twentieth century will depend largely upon one's conception of the term. Naturally with the increasing emphasis on rhythm, melody is not as dominant as it was in the nineteenth century. The new melody has an irregular and often unpredictable outline. The intervals are seldom those that will easily accommodate the human voice; melodic lines frequently display a succession of very large skips or an irregular alternation of narrow steps. Among the favored intervals are the seventh, the ninth, and larger intervals, in addition to augmented intervals, particularly the tritone. Often the melody is more dependent on its rhythmic energy than on the interest of its contour. In vocal writing, a new device, *Sprechstimme,* appears as a natural outcome of Wagner's and Debussy's approach to the voice. Finally, some composers, particularly Stravinsky, have drawn on the percussive potential of the human voice.

No amount of reading about modern music will be as helpful in establishing a rapport with the new music as firsthand aural contact. As a preliminary step a few examples are listed below which can be sung with the aid of the piano.

In the first exercise it is suggested that one intone three successive ascending whole steps:

EX. 2/23 Three Ascending Whole Steps

In order to sing this pattern without difficulty, one may have to overcome the mental set established by the usual scale pattern, that is, C–D–E–F. Once Example 2/23 is mastered, one should practice the interval from the lowest note (C) to the highest note (F sharp), to secure the tritone in one's memory.

The next example (Ex. 2/24) is a melody based on the tritone.

EX. 2/24 BARTÓK *Second Quartet,*[17] second movement, opening

Allegro molto capriccioso
Violins I & II

The melody appearing in Example 2/25 will also aid the "uncondi-tioned" reader in understanding the melodic deviation from well-established patterns.

EX. 2/25 BARTÓK *Fourth Quartet,*[18] last movement, mm. 16–18

Allegro molto
Violins I & II

One may gain vocal control over successive fourths by singing the next example (Ex. 2/26).

EX. 2/26 BARTÓK, *Concerto for Orchestra,*[19] first movement, opening

Andante non troppo (♩ = ca. 73-64)
Cellos & Basses

p *legato*

RHYTHM

One of the most striking features of the new music is the novel emphasis on the rhythmic component. The acceleration of the tempo of life: racing motors, breaking the sound barrier, the total impact of the complex sounds produced by modern civilization seem to have penetrated the consciousness of the composer. As a result, he has turned to a new exploration of the time element in music.

THE CONCEPT OF RHYTHM

The definition of rhythm is nearly as controversial as that of melody. In raising the question of what rhythm is, Curt Sachs writes: "The answer, I am afraid, is so far just a word: a word without a generally accepted meaning. Everybody believes himself entitled to usurp it for an arbitrary definition of his own. The confusion is terrifying indeed."[1] Another treatise on rhythm cites fifty definitions of the concept.

Rhythm, even when dissociated from music, has more than one meaning. Rhythm is discussed whenever a change is perceived. The change may occur as a temporal event, such as the periodic changes in nature (for example, day to night, or the succession of the seasons), but one also refers to the rhythm of a painting or of a wallpaper design. In the latter instance, one alludes to the recurrence of lines and shapes. In still other cases, one refers to the rhythm of bodily movements.

In music, the term is often defined as the alternation of stressed and unstressed beats. Rhythm has also been called "the pattern of time" and "organized fluency." The meaning of the concept has also changed from country to country, and from culture to culture.

The issue is further beclouded by the colloquial use of the term: we hear of students who play *without* rhythm, or of others who do not play *rhythmically*. One even hears references to the "slow rhythm" of a piece or to a rhythm that gets faster in a composition.

It is obvious that the term is used with different shadings and has different levels of meaning.

It is proposed that rhythm in its broadest sense should be considered as the articulation of *time* in music, that is, how the musical sounds are related in time. In accordance with this broad meaning it should be possible to think of musical rhythms existing on the periphery of the esthetic experience. Furthermore, the pattern quality should *not* be thought of as an *absolutely* necessary feature of the concept. Thus any succession of musical sounds will always imply some kind of rhythm, since the tones will be either equal or unequal in time; in both cases time relationship, or rhythm, is established. In other words, there is no music without rhythm.

Given this enlarged meaning to the concept, the recurring and vexing question of the patternlike aspect of rhythm is bypassed. Avoided also is the conceptual dilemma that arises when we hear someone play a harmony exercise on the piano at a very slow and arbitrarily uneven speed. According to almost any definition of rhythm, such a sequence

[1] Curt Sachs, *Rhythm and Tempo* (New York: W. W. Norton & Company, Inc., 1953), p. 12.

of chord progression would be without rhythm, because no alternation between stressed and unstressed beats could be perceived and no pattern observed. On the basis of the proposed broad definition, one would ascribe some kind of rhythm to such a harmony exercise, even if it lacked a pattern and barely reached the threshold of esthetic quality. It is granted, of course, that time relations in music usually do form some kind of pattern.

In connection with the problem of pattern perception, it should be mentioned that Gestalt psychologists have repeatedly proven in their experiments that we *tend* to hear patterns, even if there is *no* pattern contained in the stimuli. According to them, even the mechanical ticking of a metronome is heard as if stressed and unstressed beats alternate. Thus, one could generalize that in experiencing rhythm (time relation of tones), we *usually* group separate sounds into some kind of a structured pattern, although rhythm can exist in music above and beyond our awareness of such structured patterns.

RHYTHMIC GROUPINGS:

BEAT, MEASURE, AND METER

Beat, measure, and meter are subconcepts in the over-all area of rhythm. The meanings of these concepts are less controversial, and the terms will be employed in their usual sense: namely, the recurrent pulsations in music are recognized as the *beats* and the grouping of these beats is indicated by the *meter*. Thus, meter is the organization of the beat. Each unit, described by the meter, forms a *measure* or bar. It is assumed that the reader has some familiarity with the construction and notation of the standard meters.

It is considered important that the listener be aware of the organization of the beats when he listens to music. The point is not to intellectualize the musical experience, but to become aware of the *bodily* or physical response to the rhythmic stresses. It is held important that even the layman should have a consciousness, or at least some awareness, of the beats, somewhat akin to the kind of consciousness a person has who is just about ready to dance. He will not verbalize, "So this is a $\frac{3}{4}$ waltz, or a $\frac{4}{4}$ foxtrot," but will let the music run through his body before he actually engages in dancing. After some practice, the same awareness of the grouping of the beats can be achieved in listening to forms of music other than dance music. When the process of identifying the beat becomes difficult, it is suggested that one first seek out the accented beats only. When these have been perceived, the next step is to count the beats from one accented beat to the next. The perception of the complex rhythms of twentieth-century music will be discussed later.

Before turning to an examination of the various rhythmic devices, it should be pointed out that meter regulates only the *relative* time values within a measure. $\frac{4}{4}$ meter would indicate the value of four quarter notes, or their equivalents, in a group. The meter, however, does not suggest how *slow* or *fast* these quarter notes should be; only that they be of even duration. Thus, another determinant is needed, that of the absolute speed. This is conveyed by the tempo indication in a general way, and by a metronome signature in a specific way.

RHYTHMIC DEVICES

The following rhythmic devices will be discussed: 1) syncopation; 2) displaced accent; 3) cross-rhythm; 4) polymeter; and 5) changing meter.

SYNCOPATION

Syncopation is an ancient rhythmic device, one that is frequently employed in folk music. Despite its readily recognizable character, it is one of the least clarified of musical concepts.

In most textbooks and musical encyclopedias syncopation is defined as "the shifting of the accent to the weak beat." This obvious misinformation has been handed down from one source to the next, although upon brief reflection the inadequacy of the definition is apparent. In simply shifting the accent to the weak beat, we gain merely displaced accents, not syncopation, as can be seen from the following example.

EX. 3/1 Displaced Accent

Even the *Harvard Dictionary of Music*[2] accepts this misconception of syncopation and cites the opening of the third movement of Brahms' Fourth Symphony (Ex. 3/2) as an example of syncopation:

[2] Willi Apel, *Harvard Dictionary of Music* (Cambridge: Harvard University Press, 1946), p. 726.

EX. 3/2 BRAHMS, *Fourth Symphony,* third movement, opening

The Brahms excerpt produces stressed weak beats, but not syncopation.

What, then, is syncopation? A clue can be found in the etymology of the word. "Syncope" in Greek means "a cutting up," thus indicating a clash, or cutting across. In a typical syncopated rhythm, we will find a clash which is caused by the tone that enters between beats, thereby "cutting up" or negating the pulsation of the primary beats. In other words, syncopation is a rhythmic device in which the recurring beats (real or implied by a pre-established pattern) are negated by another musical line. The syncopated tone will enter where there is no change in the pulsation; the pulse itself is ignored (Ex. 3/3)

EX. 3/3 Syncopated Rhythm

In Example 3/3 one can see that the first note of the melody coincides with the first pulsation. The second note of the melody, however, as can be seen even visually from its spatial position in the notation, anticipates the second pulsation. When the second pulsation occurs, the quarter note of the melody negates it by "cutting across." The last eighth note follows after the second pulsation. The example quoted in the *Harvard Dictionary* is not a syncopation because the negation of the pulsation is missing.

Syncopation should be considered as a rhythmic irregularity which often creates tension.

Another type of syncopation is the off-beat syncopation; here again is an instance of noncoincidence between pulsation and another line in the music (Ex. 3/4).

EX. 3/4 Off-beat Syncopation

Even the proposed definition of syncopation does not provide a satisfactory answer in every case. For instance, a question might be raised about the tied G in Example 3/5. Does this constitute syncopation?

EX. 3/5 Negation of beat by tie

Although the quarter note (G) is tied over to the first eighth note of the next measure where the pulse is negated, the G on the third beat appears on the pulsation itself, which is contrary to the definition. This type of rhythmic occurrence is a weak cousin of true syncopation.

DISPLACED ACCENT

Another tension-creating rhythmic device is the displaced accent. This device temporarily disrupts the rhythmic flow. In the classical period, displaced accents were used like seasoning, in small amounts (Ex. 3/6), while in the twentieth century they have become frequently used rhythmic devices.

EX. 3/6 MOZART, *String Quartet in G major,* second movement,
              mm. 3–6

Displaced accents can also be combined with syncopations, an example of which may be found in the intricate Scherzo movement of Beethoven's String Quartet, Op. 18, No. 6.

CROSS-RHYTHM

A cross-rhythm is a superimposition of different rhythmic values, such as two against three or three against four, which results in some form of clashing, as seen in Example 3/7.

EX. 3/7 HAYDN, *Piano Sonata in C Major,* first movement, m. 10

Cross-rhythms were used with moderation in the classic-romantic era, but are abundant in twentieth-century music.

POLYMETER

Polymeter (Ex. 3/8), sometimes called multimeter, and incorrectly, multirhythm, is the superimposition of two different meters.

EX. 3/8 STRAVINSKY, *Petrouchka,*[3] m. 38

In Example 3/8 the differing meters are superimposed in such a way that, regardless of the different values contained in the measures, the bar lines still coincide and the duration of both measures is the same. There are cases, however, where polymeter is employed so that bar lines do not coincide, as in the Scherzo movement of Ravel's Piano Trio (Ex. 3/9).

---

[3] Copyright by Edition Russe de Musique. All rights assigned to Boosey & Hawkes, Inc. Revised edition copyright by Boosey & Hawkes, Inc., 1947. Reprinted by permission.

EX. 3/9 RAVEL, *Piano Trio*,[4] second movement, 4 mm. after
Study No. 10

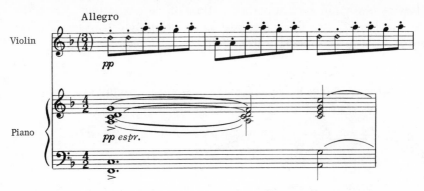

Composers of the twentieth century have rediscovered this device that was used in primitive music and also in the Renaissance. A passage from a fifteenth-century song (Ex. 3/10) demonstrates the early use of polymeter.

EX. 3/10 Fifteenth-Century Song

CHANGING METER

Changing meters within a movement are used with great frequency in twentieth-century music; East-European folk songs served as one of the main sources for this practice.

A distinction may be made between two types of changing meters in twentieth-century music. There are those that are used purely as rhythmic effects to create complete rhythmic ambiguity. Often the purpose of such rhythms is to provide hitherto unsuspected possibilities to a dancer. A typical example would be the "Sacrificial Dance" from Stravinsky's *Rite of Spring*. The meter changes in every measure $(\frac{3}{16}, \frac{5}{16}, \frac{3}{16}, \frac{4}{16}, \frac{5}{16}, \frac{3}{16})$ with bewildering swiftness resulting in frenzied excitement. The second application of changing meter is one that gives a special inflection to the melody, such as that found in Example 3/11.

[4] Permission for reprint granted by Durand et Cie., Paris, copyright owners; Elkan-Vogel Co., Inc., Philadelphia, Pa., agents.

EX. 3/11 BARTÓK, *Concerto for Orchestra,*[5] fourth movement,
          mm. 4–8

Focusing again on the perceptual aspect, the listener's awareness of the metric structure of the melody in Example 3/11 is necessary, if he is to fully appreciate its curiously tenuous and light quality. In the example from *The Rite of Spring,* however, where the metric changes serve the purpose of an over-all rhythmic effect, the exact clarification of each metric change would probably add very little to the understanding of the music. Nevertheless, it will increase the meaningfulness of the experience if the listener knows that swift metric changes occur.

Pianists are fortunate in having Bartók's *Mikrokosmos,* a collection of pieces, in which similar rhythmic devices are presented for the student, along with other problems of modern music. Number 126 of Volume 5 is a fine study in changing meters. It is also imperative that string and wind players be exposed to such problems early in their studies.

RHYTHMIC STYLE IN THE CLASSIC-ROMANTIC ERA

In describing the rhythmic style of a period, one must, of course, go beyond an examination of rhythmic "devices." One has to consider the role rhythm has played as a shaping force in the architecture of the music and its position with regard to melody and harmony.

Speaking in this larger sense, one could generalize that rhythm was a more vital force in the classical period than in the post-Beethoven era of the nineteenth century. Nevertheless, some of the rhythmic experimentations that paved the way for the twentieth-century rhythmic language took place in the second half of the nineteenth century.

If we group Haydn, Mozart, and Beethoven together, Mozart's style seems to be more deeply rooted in his melodic invention, whereas Haydn and Beethoven used rhythmic motives more often as an element of form-building. Not only did they use sudden accentuations (both on stressed and weak beats), syncopations, and cross-rhythms more often than did Mozart, but there is a rhythmic pulsation in their motives which lends a unique character to their music. For instance, the opening motive of Beethoven's Fifth Symphony does not contain any rhythmic device, yet it has a compelling profile; it is the rhythmic quality rather than the melodic contour of the motive that pervades the total architecture of the movement.

The rhythmic propulsion of Beethoven's opening motives is often enhanced by a pause. There are countless examples of this effect in Beethoven's sonatas and string quartets.

In the romantic era, although Chopin, Berlioz, and Schumann often employed novel rhythmic complexities, their music, on the whole, was more melodically and harmonically oriented. Rhythmic intricacies were signs rather of capriciousness and whimsy than of dynamic motivation. These subjective, rhapsodic moods were often enhanced by tempo fluctuations within the movement—a practice almost unknown to the instrumental style of the eighteenth century.

The trend toward the complexities of twentieth-century rhythmic style can easily be traced. On the whole, most of the commonly used contemporary rhythmic devices were present in nineteenth-century music, but usually as exceptional occurrences. Thus, we do find, though infrequently, an unusual meter such as $\frac{5}{4}$ in the third movement of Chopin's C minor Piano Sonata or $\frac{7}{4}$ in Liszt's *Dante Symphony*. Toward the end of the century $\frac{5}{4}$ meters became more widespread, particularly in Slavic music. Irregular meters were not easily accepted at first: the noted Viennese critic, Hanslick, found the $\frac{5}{4}$ meter of the second movement of Tchaikovsky's Sixth Symphony irritating and incomplete.

Complex cross-rhythms can be found in Chopin's Etude in F minor (Ex. 3/12), in addition to the many other examples in his oeuvre.

EX. 3/12 CHOPIN, *Etude*, Op. 25, No. 2, opening

Schumann was also fond of cross-rhythms: Example 3/13 is an interesting instance of rhythmic clashes.

EX. 3/13 SCHUMANN, *Carnaval,* "Eusebius," opening

Schumann's music is likewise marked by a paradoxical combination of original rhythmic features alongside foursquare, repetitive treatment of rhythmic groupings.

Brahms, whose rhythmic style is the most original in the nineteenth century, was greatly influenced by Schumann. Although Brahms was considered a conservative, tradition-bound composer by his contemporaries, it is becoming increasingly evident from our vantage point how much Brahms contributed to twentieth-century musical thinking. This is particularly true in the field of rhythm. Brahms, as a rule, avoided the 4 + 4 regular phrase structure and also the regularity of pulsation. His phrases run across the bar line with great frequency and cross-rhythms are among his favorite devices. A particularly interesting example of polyrhythm can be found in his *Paganini Variations* (Ex. 3/14):

EX. 3/14 BRAHMS, *Paganini Variations,* Op. 35, No. 2, Variation VII

Brahms is perhaps the only composer of the nineteenth century who placed rhythm in the service of musical architecture, following the orientation of the classical composers. The reader can find interesting manipulations of the opening rhythmic motive in the last movement of his String Quartet Op. 51, No. 2, in the course of which the motive appears in ever new rhythmic guises.

We can also see in his music a new use of changing meter. In earlier music, if a change of meter occurred, it did so usually at a sectional delineation within the movement. Beethoven, for instance, introduces a change of meter at the beginning of the Trio section in the Scherzo movement of the Ninth Symphony. Also in the slow movement of that symphony metric changes occur at the opening of new variations. Brahms, however, uses the change of meter more organically: in the first movement of his Third Symphony, for instance, the meter changes from $\frac{6}{4}$ to $\frac{9}{4}$ when the second theme is introduced, in order to broaden the flow of the music. Frequent instances of displaced accents should also be noted in this movement, and in Brahms' music in general.

As a result of folk influences changing meters appear with increasing frequency around the turn of the century; the reader can find examples in the works of Dvořák, Mahler, Richard Strauss, and others.

RHYTHM IN TWENTIETH-CENTURY MUSIC

As stated earlier one of the most striking features of the new music is the novel emphasis on the rhythmic component. The eruption of rhythmic forces occurred around 1910 in Stravinsky's early ballets and in Bartók's *Allegro Barbaro,* shocking the musical world with savage East-European and Asiatic rhythms. This event was preceded by a curious lull, represented by Debussy's refined, understating style.

The rhythmic style of the French master brings to the foreground again the definition or meaning of the term, *rhythm.* Those who think of rhythm as a "life-giving force," or as "the pattern of accented and unaccented beats," or as the "movement in music," will conclude that rhythm in Debussy's music has relinquished its characteristic nature. According to a critic, "timeless passivity" pervades Debussy's music, which he describes as having reached the "nadir of rhythmical life." Close examination will reveal, however, that rhythm is used with great subtlety, often deliberately concealing the obvious pulsation. The brief, orchestral prelude to *Pelléas et Mélisande* contains a surprisingly varied rhythmic texture. In the *Afternoon of a Faun* a number of interesting features occur; one, shown in Example 3/15, illustrates Debussy's rhythmic inventiveness.

Debussy also employs changes of meter with great finesse; for example in the restatement of the opening section of the Scherzo movement of his String Quartet the $\frac{6}{8}$ meter of the opening section changes to $\frac{15}{8}$. Applying the suggested definition of rhythm as referring to time relation, we will not be forced into disparaging value judgments when examining a rhythmic style so rich in nuances. Furthermore, those who consider only the obvious and easily perceptible pulsations as a sign

EX. 3/15 DEBUSSY, *Afternoon of a Faun,*[6] m. 31

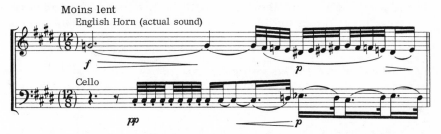

of rhythmic life would have to judge a march by Sousa as rhythmically richer than a composition by Debussy.

Debussy's avoidance of the obvious regularity of the pulsations was also favored by Stravinsky, who appeared on the scene a few years later. The two composers differed only in their means: while the French composer often deliberately concealed all pulsations, sliding across bar lines, Stravinsky *destroyed* the regularity of pulsations by placing accents on weak beats or by continually changing meters.

The shock value of the early works of Stravinsky had far-reaching effects on composers on both sides of the Atlantic. As significant as these rhythmic effects were, it would be erroneous to believe that the contribution of rhythm to twentieth-century music is limited to the savage poundings of *The Rite of Spring* or to the swiftly changing meters of the "Sacrificial Dance." In addition, rhythm has re-established itself in our new music as a *form-generating* process, somewhat similar to the role it occupied in the classical period. Even if it is not always easy to demonstrate, close examination will often reveal that the organization of a modern composition is based upon a complex pattern of rhythmic events (see Berg's "Hauptritmus" in *Wozzeck* in Chapter 12). It should be mentioned, parenthetically, that some avant-garde composers build their compositions on the periodic recurrence of specific rhythmic values—rhythmic row (see Chapter 7).

Nevertheless, Stravinsky's early works served as the standard source of reference for the rhythmic idiom of the new music. A study of the "Infernal Dance" from the *Firebird Suite* (1908) will show an abundance of syncopations, displaced accents, cross-rhythms, in addition to meter changes.

In *Petrouchka,* the rhythmic language is even more advanced. Examples of polyrhythms are numerous; in measure 38, Ex. $\frac{3}{8}$, $\frac{7}{8}$ and $\frac{3}{4}$ meters appear superimposed. Later, in Tableau 3, an ingenious superimposition of $\frac{3}{4}$ over $\frac{2}{4}$ is employed, signifying that the clumsy Moor is unable to keep up with the Ballerina's swift steps.

[6]Permission for reprint granted by Jobert, Paris, France, copyright owners; Elkan-Vogel Co., Inc., Philadelphia, Pa., agents.

The Rite of Spring contains the *locus classicus* for displaced accents: the regular pulsation of the eighth notes is disrupted by accents on the weak beats (Ex. 3/16):

EX. 3/16 STRAVINSKY, *The Rite of Spring,*[7] "Dance of Adolescents," opening

Allegro

In the "Jeu de Rapt" unusual cross-rhythms occur: at measure 45, groups of 3, 4, 5, 6, and 7 notes are fitted into the same beat by five woodwind players.

Another typical rhythmic device employed by Stravinsky, and later adapted by many followers, is the restatement of the same motive on different beats in subsequent bars. For example, in the opening of *Petrouchka,* the dotted rhythm appears irregularly on different beats in the first few measures.

EX. 3/17 STRAVINSKY, *Petrouchka,*[8] opening

The documentation of so many novel rhythmic devices drawn from Stravinsky's work is not accidental. One may safely say that he alone revitalized rhythm, even though the bold rhythmic novelties of the early works were sublimated in his later compositions.

Next to Stravinsky, Bartók contributed most to the new rhythmic idiom. He incorporated the rhythmic peculiarities of Hungarian, Bulgarian, Rumanian, other East-European, and even North-African folk songs into his style (see Chapter 10).

A rhythmic device, often used by both Stravinsky and Bartók, is the *ostinato,* that is, the persistent repetition of a rhythmic figure. The measure quoted in Example 3/18 is reiterated in eight successive measures.

EX. 3/18 BARTÓK, *Sonata for Two Pianos and Percussion,*[9] first
movement, m. 195

In comparing the rhythmic styles of Stravinsky and Bartók, several writers have expressed the view that it was Stravinsky who influenced Bartók. Without resolving this question, it is suggested that the similarity in the rhythmic styles of the composers may lie in their common Asiatic ancestry. Be that as it may, Bartók and Stravinsky represent a musical invasion from the East, at the same time that Western-European music was invaded on a "second front" by jazz with its African rhythms. Curiously, Stravinsky anticipated some of the features of jazz, such as complex syncopations over a regular beat and the new emphasis on brass instruments. After World War I, when American jazz bands appeared in Europe, a number of composers attempted to draw from this new idiom, among them Milhaud, Honegger, Ravel, and Křenek. The novelty, however, quickly wore off and little jazz influence is traceable in European music after 1930. Jazz had a more lasting and subtler influence on American music.

Composers of the Viennese atonal school (Schoenberg, Berg, and Webern) remained unaffected by the Afro-Asian rhythmic influence. Although rhythmic irregularities and complexities are abundant in their works, changing meters and displaced accents are used more sparingly, particularly by Schoenberg and Berg. Of the three, Webern shows the greatest rhythmic intricacies. Nevertheless, the rhythm in their music does not have the ritualistic quality and savagery which is found in the music of Bartók and Stravinsky. In Example 3/19 a complex cross-rhythm is cited from Alban Berg's *Lyric Suite:*

EX. 3/19 BERG, *Lyric Suite*,[10] third movement (*Trio Estatico*), m. 76

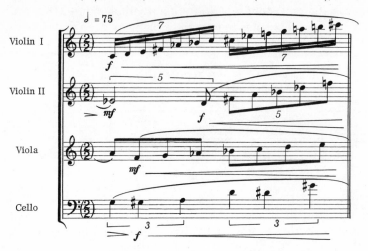

American music is particularly rich in rhythmic inventiveness; in Example 3/20 a cross-rhythm by Griffes is shown:

EX. 3/20 GRIFFES, *The White Peacock*,[11] opening

An unusually complex combination of cross-rhythms and cross-accents occurs in Elliott Carter's Second Quartet (1959).

It was an American composer, Charles Ives, who first experimented with superimposition of *tempi* in his *Unanswered Question:* the strings maintain a steady slow tempo, while other sections of the orchestra play at an increasingly faster speed. The performance of this work requires two conductors.

Elliott Carter invented a device he calls *metric modulation*. The term *modulation*, borrowed from a harmonic principle, refers to the process in which metric formations are changed gradually, resulting in varying

EX. 3/21 CARTER, *Second Quartet*,[12] fourth movement, m. 597

rates of fluctuations in the pulsation. Often it is achieved by the acceleration of the pulsation of one voice that may or may not influence the other voices. The subtleties of Carter's rhythmic style are naturally inexpressible in traditional notation.

Of the recent rhythmic experiments, Blacher's technique with variable meters should be pointed out, wherein metric groupings follow a prearranged arithmetical progression; for instance, a progression such as 2-3-4, 3-4-5, 4-5-6 will result in the following metric groupings:

EX. 3/22 Technique of Variable Meter

Another arithmetical approach to rhythm is used by Messiaen; basing his technique on Hindu rhythms, he varies rhythmic values by a special kind of augmentation or diminution. Augmentation here does not mean the doubling of the time value, but rather the addition of fractional values. Thus, if augmentation takes place by one-fourth of the note values, then the following changes would result:

[12] Quoted by permission of Associated Music Publishers, Inc.

EX. 3/23 Original Value Augmentation by One-Fourth

Original   Augmented by One-Fourth

The devices used in the experiments of Ives and Carter are related to the rhythmic experimentation of Stockhausen, particularly in his *Zeitmasse* for woodwind quintet (1957). In some instances different metronome indications are superimposed; at bar 202 the oboe's eighth notes equal 64, while the English horn's eighth notes equal 80, against the bassoon's 112. Stockhausen writes notes more closely together when they are to be played *accelerando,* and more widely apart when they are to be played *ritardando.* Other novel tempo indications used by Stockhausen are *schnell-verlangsamen* (quickly slowing down) and *langsam beschleunigen* (slowly quickening); in both cases the composer indicates the rate at which these changes should be carried out. At times some players quickly slow down, while others increase their tempo slowly. A new rhythmic indication in avant-garde music is also found in the proportional markings; for instance, 5:4 means five note values are to be played in the time of four.

Although it is difficult to generalize about the diverse nature of twentieth-century music, and therefore about its elements, there are certain over-all tendencies that characterize the new rhythmic style. As a result of irregular pulsation, and changing meters, and the like, the single beat has been emancipated. The modern performer seldom thinks of the single beat as a member of a unit that makes up the measure, occupying therein a privileged (accented) or relegated (unaccented) position. The rhythmic element has become so flexible and irregular that the meter signature is often a convenience merely for the conductor and not for the player. The often quoted "tyranny of the bar line" has been eliminated, if it ever existed. In a musical sense it really did not, as even the four-measure phrase of the classical masters demanded phrasing across the bar line. Only the unimaginative, mechanical performance suffered from the strait jacket of the bar line.

In summary, rhythm occupies a more dominant role in the music of the twentieth century than it has undoubtedly ever occupied in the history of Western music. The main features, irregularity and unpredictability, are not unlike the characteristics found valid for modern melody. Contemporary composers have shown a great fondness for changing meters, polymeters, displaced accents, and many types of cross-rhythms, all tension-creating devices that often have a jolting effect upon the listener.

The following exercises are presented so that the reader may concretely experience the rhythmic style of the twentieth century. The task is to beat the basic pulsation and intone the note values.

The first exercises (Ex. 3/24) were written by the author; they are to prepare the reader for the ones that were derived from Stravinsky's *Les Noces* and *L'Histoire du Soldat* (Ex. 3/25).

EX. 3/24 Rhythm Exercises

EX. 3/25 Rhythm Exercises

HARMONY

Compared with melody and rhythm, harmony is the most recent and the most intellectual element in music. Its evolution has been largely a conscious, reasoned process, whereas in the development of melodic and rhythmic styles unconscious promptings seem to have played a considerable role. The intellectual factor in harmony is demonstrated by the existence of harmonic *systems,* a required study for the music student, in which man-made rules and principles are articulated, whereas the rules of melody and rhythm are less susceptible to systematization.

The harmonic procedures in twentieth-century music are extremely complex and as yet not codified. For this reason, and also assuming that the reader does not have an extensive background in theory, the discussion in this chapter, and in subsequent discussions dealing with composers' harmonic styles, will focus on harmonic *principles* rather than on procedures.

THE CONCEPT OF HARMONY

Harmony consists of chord progressions, a chord being three or more tones sounded simultaneously. It should be emphasized that harmony consists of chord *progressions* and not of chords, since no harmonic meaning can be attached to a single chord, taken out of its context. A G–B–D chord, for instance, is harmonically so ambiguous that it is meaningless. Only from the context in which it appears can we judge whether it is the tonic triad in G major, the dominant in C major, or the subdominant in D major.

THE FUNCTION OF HARMONY

In the classical and romantic periods the function of harmony, more often than not, was to give background, context, or added meaning to the melody. By using an analogy from the visual field, borrowing the terminology from Gestalt psychology, one could say that melody is to harmony as *figure* is to *background*. If the background (harmony) is changed, as in the visual field,[1] the figure (melody) will assume a new meaning. Examples 4/1/a and 4/1/b illustrate this point: the tiny melodic fragment is harmonized in two different ways:

EX. 4/1/a

---

[1] Experiments in the visual field show that one's perception of the dominant color will depend on the color of the background.

EX. 4/1/b

The harmonic contrasts are less sharply drawn in Example 4/1/b, lending a somewhat mellower quality to the melody. Such differences are more telling in a real musical context, such as the various harmonizations of the Bach choral melodies. Finding different harmonic solutions to the same melody has always intrigued composers (see a contemporary example of three different harmonizations of the same melody in Example 10/21).

HARMONIC TENSION AND RESOLUTION

It was stated that the function of harmony is to provide background, added meaning to the melody. In addition to this purely *musical* role, chord progressions also induce tensions and resolutions. These could be considered harmony's *psychological* potential. The inexperienced listener is often unaware that the powerful expectations he experiences are created by a harmonic buildup. The way a composer deals with the pattern of harmonic tensions and resolutions defines his harmonic style. Wagner's harmonic style, for instance, is characterized by tensions that often remain unresolved for long periods, musically portraying the lack of fulfillment in human relationships.

In musical terminology, chords that demand resolution are called dissonances, while chords that sound more stable, representing a point of repose, are consonances. Acousticians have attempted to give a scientific theory of consonances and dissonances, based on the ratio of frequency of vibrations. According to this theory, the simpler the ratio of the frequency of vibrations between two tones, the more consonant the interval will be, and increasing complexity in the ratio will lead to increased dissonance. Some theorists (among them Hindemith) explain the whole harmonic evolution on an acoustical basis, using the overtone series as their point of departure.

Since there is nothing *absolute* about the harmonic meaning of any chord, and since harmonic meanings will always depend on the musical context, that is, what happens in the music before and after, any scientific system that attaches fixed values to intervals or chords will have limited musical validity. What makes such a scientific theory musically vulnerable is that the *same chord* may be experienced as inducing tension in one situation and as a resolution in another context. For example, in the opening of the Prelude to Act I of Wagner's *Tristan* (Ex. 4/2), the final seventh chord is felt as a resolution on account of the preceding higher tension, whereas exactly the same chord creates tension in Example 4/3, demanding some kind of resolution:

EX. 4/2 WAGNER, *Tristan und Isolde,* Prelude to Act I, opening

EX. 4/3 Chord Sequence

There is an additional variable present in judging dissonances, namely, the listener's past experience. The inexperienced ear will be shocked by a chord that is completely acceptable to a listener who is familiar with advanced harmonic idioms.

Judgments regarding dissonances have also varied from one historical period to the next; in the not too distant past, for example, the chord of the dominant seventh was found quite harsh.

It is interesting to note that the ear will often tolerate a new and hitherto unused dissonance if there is some extramusical, dramatic justification for its introduction. A number of Richard Strauss' dissonances were accepted on this basis. According to the usual historical process, a dissonance used at first for dramatic reasons soon becomes part of the harmonic language, divorced from its dramatic associations.

Harmonic rules, on the whole, are not immutable. Thus, at one time chromaticism was inadmissible, and dissonances could be used only if prepared for. In other instances it is not the rule that changes, but the musical motivation, which created the rule, loses its validity. For instance, the taboo concerning parallel fifths existed in a period when the writing was aimed at achieving clarity and independence of voice-leading. However, in a musical style where the composer's aim in using parallel fifths is to create certain sonorities the earlier rule will not apply.

TONALITY

The concept of tonality was defined as a tonal frame of reference and considered an organizing principle in melodic thinking (see Chapter 2). This same principle is also employed for organizing chord progressions, that is, harmony. Thus we can conceive of tonality as referring to the melodic line in which the gravitational center rests on a *tone* (tonic), or as referring to the harmonic framework, in which case the gravitational center is based on a *chord* (tonic chord).

Tonality, built on the major-minor key system, was of paramount significance in more recent Western music not only as the pillar of the melodic-harmonic framework, but also as the most important organizing principle in the architecture of music. It was tonality that unified the simplest folk song as well as the four-movement symphony. It organized the outer form of the symphony (a common or related key linked the four movements together), as well as the form of single movements. It is the evolution of tonality and its eventual dissolution in the twentieth century that has been the central topic of the history of harmony in the last four centuries.

HARMONIC STYLE IN THE CLASSIC-ROMANTIC ERA

In the classic-romantic era melodic-harmonic thinking was unified by the principle of *tonality*. The harmonic tonality, the tonal feeling that pervades the chord progressions, solidifies and underscores the horizontal, that is, the melodic tonality. Every phrase, every sentence, and even larger units of musical organization gain meaning and coherence through the specific tension system inherent in tonal harmonies.

In order to see the interdependence between melody and harmony, let us return to Example 2/11 on page 25. The melody by Mozart exemplifies a musical sentence, composed of two four-measure units. In Example 4/4, the harmony is added and it can be seen how much the chord progression reinforces the melodic articulation.

The feeling that a colon or semicolon exists at midpoint was mentioned when the melody was examined in its linear existence. Now it can be seen how the inconclusive harmonic cadence supports that feel-

EX. 4/4 MOZART, *Piano Sonata in A Major*, K. 331, first movement, opening

ing, and how the final cadence contributes to the firm conclusion of the sentence. It was the tension and resolution pattern of the harmonies —implied also in the melody—which made the musical thought intelligible.

The experience of tonality, derived from the chord progressions, and the role of tonality in musical organization have been compared to the role of perspective in painting by several writers.[2] In painting, too, every detail of visual organization such as line, shape, proportion, and even color, will be governed by the rules of perspective. Both tonality and perspective will be perceived by the ear or eye, consciously or unconsciously, as fixed, basic values, and any deviations from these organizational principles are experienced at first as leading toward disorientation and incoherence.

The history of harmony reveals trends parallel to those observed in the history of melody. The use of scale steps and triadic outlines in the melodic idiom of the eighteenth century were accompanied by triadic chords, leaning heavily on the tonic-dominant relationship. Although chromatic harmonies were also used—occasionally quite boldly —these chords more often had the function of surprise and embellishment rather than the weakening of the feeling of tonality. Even in the eighteenth century, however, there are isolated cases of veiled tonalities (for example, the introduction to the first movement of Mozart's "Dissonant" Quartet in C major, K. 465, or the introduction of Beethoven's

[2] See Mark Brunswick, "Tonality and Perspective," *Musical Quarterly*, **29**, No. 4 (October, 1943).

String Quartet, Op. 59, No. 3). In both cases the feeling of tonality is suspended temporarily in order to give the keys an even greater radiancy, once they assert themselves, shining through the nebulous harmonies. Such exceptions fit into the pattern of artistic evolution: what was first an exception with a unique purpose becomes absorbed into a later style and accepted as the standard mode of expression. The same cautious beginning, followed by gradual acceptance, characterizes the use of passing notes, suspensions, appoggiaturas, and anticipations, terms used to describe a melody which, with regard to its harmonic environment, is ornamented, delayed, accentuated or anticipated as required.

Sometimes harmonic devices of the eighteenth century are used again in the nineteenth century, but with different musical motivation. The pedal point, the sustaining of a note (or chord) in one part, is a case in point. All three masters of the classical period often employed the pedal point, particularly the dominant pedal. The purpose of this device was to build up intense expectation which would be resolved finally by the appearance of tonic harmony. The pedal point was also used in the late nineteenth century, but with a different purpose. Instead of creating expectations, it was used with the intention of creating a clash in tonality; while the pedal point preserved a modicum of the prevailing tonality, the superimposed harmonies shifted toward different harmonic regions and could not be analyzed in terms of the same tonality. The following example bears out this point:

EX. 4/5 STRAUSS, *Don Quixote*,[3] Variation VII, m. 7

[3] Reprinted with permission of the publishers, C. F. Peters Corporation, New York.

Returning to the evolution of harmonic procedures during the nineteenth century, increased chromaticism—a trend also found in the melodic idiom of the century—is strongly in evidence. Numerous examples of chromatic harmonies can be found in the works of Chopin, Mendelssohn, and Schumann. The boldest harmonist before the middle of the century was probably Berlioz, whose music at times abandons all tonal feeling. With Liszt and Wagner chromaticism shifted more and more from its earlier embellishing function to a role of greater harmonic consequence, as is seen in Example 4/6:

EX. 4/6 WAGNER, *Tristan und Isolde,* Act II, Scene 1, mm. 27–29

Wagner's *Tristan* has often been cited as the most important single work on the road toward the dissolution of tonality. Schoenberg[4] called this harmonic stage *extended tonality*.

Increased chromaticism was not the only device that weakened tonality. The nineteenth century also witnessed an increasing dissociation between melody and harmony; composers started to use chords merely for their sonorous value and not as background to melody. Thus a phenomenon occurred somewhat similar to the emancipation of the *beat* discussed in the previous chapter. Now harmony seemed to gain self-sufficiency; chords appeared in an independent role and not merely as subordinated members of a larger harmonic unit. Again, Wagner was among the first to take the initiative. The Prelude to Act I of *Das Rheingold* is a typical example of the use of chords and chord outlines merely for atmospheric effect. Thus the background became the figure!

The weakening of tonal feeling was also achieved by avoiding the juxtaposition of tonic and dominant harmonies, which once served as the basic harmonic axis for the construction of small and large musical units. The decline of tonality thus had far-reaching consequences beyond mere harmonic considerations. The well-known cadential punctuation of symmetrical phrases, based on tonic-dominant sequence, now seemed obsolete. Moreover, the antithetical key areas of the tonic and the dominant, which previously served as pillars of the basic musical forms, unifying the total architecture of extended compositions, were not used any more as the sole principle of musical design.

HARMONY IN THE TWENTIETH CENTURY

The composer who contributed most to the founding of the new harmonic language was Debussy, considered by many as representing the dividing line between nineteenth- and twentieth-century music. In his music, clear-cut tonic-dominant relations are avoided and distinct major-minor key feelings are weakened or entirely abandoned.

Debussy, in his search for new harmonic solutions, reintroduced the medieval modes, thereby opening up possibilities beyond the tonic-dominant sphere. His use of the whole-tone scale (see Chapter 2), had far-reaching harmonic implications. Looking again at the whole-tone scale (Ex. 4/7), one can see that the vertical use of the first, third, and fifth degree of the scale will result in an augmented chord, instead of the tonic triad derived from the seven-tone scale.

[4] Arnold Schoenberg, *Style and Idea* (New York: Philosophical Library, Inc., 1950).

EX. 4/7 Whole-tone Scale

As only augmented or altered chords could be gained from the whole-tone scale, tonic-dominant juxtapositions were successfully bypassed.

Debussy introduced other harmonic innovations, such as series of sevenths or ninths chords, sliding in progressions of whole steps or half steps and in any direction. Often the meaning of otherwise unambiguous chords was made ambiguous by added notes.

Scriabin, like Debussy, broke with the traditional way of cadencing in his piano sonatas. The later sonatas of the Russian composer are particularly interesting and border on atonality. His chords are often built on the interval of the fourth, a common practice in later twentieth-century music.

In this free harmonic system cadencing becomes a matter of relativity; any progression that is more final than the preceding progressions could serve as a final cadence:

EX. 4/8 SCRIABIN, *Piano Sonata, No. 9,*[5] ending

The most decisive change in the harmonic evolution—the final break with tonality—was achieved by Schoenberg. The last movement of the Second Quartet (1908), to which a mezzo soprano voice is added, is considered the first atonal composition. The opening words (Ex. 4/9) of the text in the last movement of the quartet (*Ich fühle Luft von anderem Planeten*—I breathe air from another planet) are appropriate to the opening of a new musical world (see p. 62).

Although almost every note of the vocal line in Example 4/9 is doubled in one of the string parts, the accompanying harmonies do not suggest any key feeling. Even though the vocal line in itself may point to F major or D minor, the chords rule out any such assumption.

[5] Edition Russe de Musique, Berlin. Boosey & Hawkes, Inc., New York.

EX. 4/9 SCHOENBERG, *Second Quartet,*[6] fourth movement, mm. 21–25

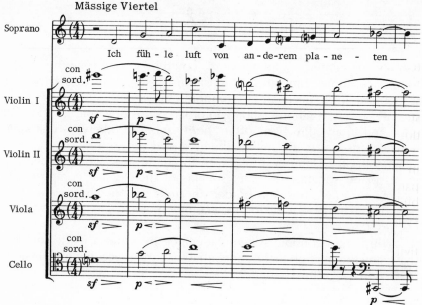

ATONALITY

Atonality, a highly controversial term in contemporary music, has two usages; in the first sense it merely refers to music that lacks a tonal center. Sometimes the term *free atonality* is used to describe this harmonic state, considered by Schoenberg as a transitional phase. He felt the need later to introduce a new means of structural organization to replace the abandoned principle of tonality. This search led to the method of twelve-tone composition (see Chapter 7). In its second meaning atonality is used with reference to twelve-tone music. This usage of the term is not recommended because twelve-tone compositions that are tonal do exist.

The controversy concerning atonality centers on two issues: 1) the term itself; and 2) the musical validity of atonality. Oddly enough the term was first criticized by Schoenberg himself. He stated in his autobiographical sketch: "In this period I renounced a tonal center—a procedure incorrectly called *atonality*."[7] He was later quoted as having said, "I regard the expression *atonal* meaningless. Atonal can only signify something that does not correspond to the nature of tone."

[6]Quoted by permission of Mrs. Gertrud Schoenberg and Universal Edition, publisher of first edition.

[7]Arnold Schoenberg, "My Evolution," *Musical Quarterly,* **38**, No. 4 (1952).

He suggested the term *pantonal* instead, implying that his new music is the synthesis of all tonal relationships.

Sessions regards the term atonal as:

> . . . at best a temporary slogan of doubtful usefulness. If it is taken literally in the sense of its derivation, it implies music in which the tones have no relationship to each other—an impossibility; and it is in any case an evasion of the real issue of what is actually heard in the music. It is also a negative term, which defines nothing and describes nothing. . . .[8]

A few years later his attitude toward the term mellowed. He writes:

> What is often called "atonality" was a very gradual development—so gradual, in fact, that, aside from the literal meaning of the term itself, it is impossible to define with any precision whatsoever. It is in other words impossible to show exactly where tonality ends and "atonality" begins unless one establishes wholly arbitrary lines of demarcation in advance.[9]

George Perle is also reluctant to give a fixed meaning to the term. Atonality, he claims, "precludes by definition the possibility of a statement of self-consistent, generally applicable compositional process."[10]

The term, however, is accepted by Persichetti, and is defined as "loosely applied to music in which a definite key feeling has been weakened or lost, and to music in which no key gravitation ever existed."[11] It is in this sense that the term is usually used in current theoretical writing.

The semantic argument seems unimportant in view of the vitriolic attacks leveled at the musical style itself.

CRITICISM OF ATONALITY

It comes as no surprise that Pleasants is in the front ranks of the attackers. He calls the fight for harmonic emancipation "a long lusty crusade for the privilege of committing harmonic suicide . . . Composers suddenly discovered that emancipation brought them, not freedom of musical speech, but inability to speak musically at all."[12]

---

[8] Roger Sessions, *Harmonic Practice* (New York: Harcourt, Brace & World, Inc., 1957), p. 408.

[9] Roger Sessions, "Problems and Issues Facing the Composer Today," *Musical Quarterly*, **46**, No. 2 (1960), p. 164.

[10] George Perle, *Serial Composition and Atonality* (Los Angeles: University of California Press, 1962), p. 9.

[11] Vincent Persichetti, *Twentieth Century Harmony* (New York: W. W. Norton & Company, Inc., 1961), p. 261.

[12] Henry Pleasants, *The Agony of Modern Music* (New York: Simon & Schuster, 1955), p. 104.

Constant Lambert[13] felt that atonality destroys one's sense of concord and discord. He claims, therefore, that counterpoint becomes meaningless, and that our sense of form becomes mechanical and arbitrary.

Atonality is also severely attacked by Hindemith.[14] In his view, composers who attempt to eliminate tonality succeed to a certain degree in depriving the listener of the benefits of gravitation. He likens this "trick" to the "sickeningly wonderful merry-go-rounds" in amusement parks, in which the visitor is tossed around in circles and sideways in such a fashion that even the onlooker feels his inside turned into a "pretzel-shaped" distortion. He terms atonal music a "devilish gadget."

The noted theorist, Albersheim, also takes a negative view of atonality. He writes:

> Even if we understand today why such a radical turn of style took place, we are just as clearly aware that atonality is not the positive achievement of a new order in music, but first of all the conscious abrogation of the hitherto prevailing order and the subsequent unleashing of chaotic and destructive trends. . . .[15]

Schoenberg's early atonal works drew sharp condemnation from Tovey,[16] who writes disparagingly about Schoenberg's style in which chords of fourths are "piled up." Tovey finds Schoenberg's fathering such theories as disconcerting as imagining Einstein telling fortunes on Bond Street.

Tovey's conservatism, voiced in the *Encylopedia Britannica,* is evident in musical lexicons too. The latest edition of Grove's *Dictionary of Music and Musicians* (published in 1958) contains a discussion of harmony and tonality that lags almost half a century behind events. There are only two musical examples of more recent vintage than the numerous examples drawn from Wagner's music.

The above presentation of viewpoints of atonality may give the reader the impression that favorable comments have been purposefully omitted. The fact is, however, that this style of writing, labeled by Gerald Abraham as a state of "musical anarchy," has but few protagonists.

Among the few commentators who took a positive stand is Křenek. Although not strictly a Schoenberg disciple, Křenek's lucid mind realized the irrationality of the attacks on atonality. He also points out that the term "atonal" was not invented by the composers who made use of the

---

[13]Constant Lambert, *Music Ho!* (Baltimore: Penguin Books, Inc., 1948), p. 209.

[14]Paul Hindemith, *A Composer's World* (Garden City: Anchor Books, 1961), p. 65.

[15]Gerhard Albersheim, "The Sense of Space in Tonal and Atonal Music," *The Journal of Aesthetics and Art Criticism,* **19**, 1 (1960), p. 27.

[16]Donald Francis Tovey, Musical articles from the *Encyclopedia Britannica* (New York: Oxford University Press, 1944).

device. In his view the term was coined by a Viennese critic in his panic and dismay upon hearing the first works of Schoenberg that were free of tonality. Křenek examined the usual points of criticism raised against atonality one by one and provides answers for each with impeccable logic. He concedes that certain attractive features that were unique to tonal music had to be relinquished, but he points to the important gains made in terms of a new expressiveness. He summarizes:

> . . . Perhaps the artistic worth of atonal music is uneven; I do not wish to propagandize in any way; but its human and historico-cultural value is definitely in the open and can be clearly ascertained. Atonality has given speech to the individual, liberating him from delusive chains and seductive illusions. By intensifying the expression of personal emotion to the utmost, it has demonstrated the loneliness and alienation of humanity as clearly as possible.[17]

Although atonality as a generalized musical stylistic conception has mostly met with sharp rebuke, there are compositions written in this style that have received lavish praise by critics and musicologists. Alban Berg's *Wozzeck* ranks highest among these works. Although there are some sections in the opera that are clearly tonal, the major portion of the work is written in the atonal style. It should be mentioned here that Berg uses tonality and atonality as a means of expression: thus, when Maria, the unfortunate, depraved heroine, turns to the Bible as her only source of security, the music becomes tonal. The effectiveness of mixing tonal and atonal styles holds out the possibility that in the future a reconciliation may occur between the two modes of writing; atonality will merely represent the equivalent of earlier dissonant regions, whereas tonality will bring the feeling of resolution, represented earlier by consonance. Whatever the future may bring, *Wozzeck* has been performed in all the major opera houses of the world and is considered a masterwork. One may question how a system that is "devilish" and "destructive" can produce such an unquestionably great composition. Also, Schoenberg's *Pierrot Lunaire,* another product of "free atonality," is gaining increased recognition. Could it be that the death sentence of atonality was rendered too hastily or that it was not based on sufficient evidence?

OTHER HARMONIC SOLUTIONS

Only a minority of twentieth-century composers have been identified with the "free" atonal style. Some have tried it, only to abandon it later; others have searched for new ways of treating tonality. Most of them

---

[17]Ernst Křenek, *Music Here and Now,* translated by Barthold Fles (New York: W. W. Norton & Company, Inc., 1939), pp. 141–166.

have agreed that the possibilities of a harmonic system built on the tonic-dominant axis have been exhausted. In general, these composers have maintained a modicum of tonal feeling, while attempting to find a more subtle, tenuous, and often disguised sense of tonality than has been used in preceding eras.

One group of composers, among them Bartók and Hindemith, has kept some conception of a tonic, freely using all the twelve half steps of the scale. It would be incorrect, however, to state—as some writers do—that these composers used the chromatic scale. The term chromatic may lead to misunderstanding, since in the harmonic context of such composers the distinction between diatonic and chromatic is no longer valid. The seven notes of the diatonic scale do not enjoy a preferred position, and the chromatic notes do not have their earlier auxiliary status. In this type of tonal thinking (called *pantonality* by Rudolph Reti[18]), a composition is no longer *in* a key (suggesting functional harmonies and major or minor keys), but rather *on* a key. Often the superiority of a tonal center is extremely tenuous and it may be negated through long portions of a movement, emerging only at the end.

These novel harmonic procedures that obviated the rules of the old harmonic system seemed arbitrary because the theorist lacked the tools to explain them. The man who undertook to provide the foundation for the new harmonic system was Paul Hindemith.

In his theoretical treatise, *Unterweisung im Tonsatz* (*The Craft of Musical Composition*), he set out to codify the rules of the new harmonic style that recognized a tonal center and the equivalence of the twelve steps of the chromatic scale, relinquishing the differentiation between major and minor keys. In the Introduction to his *Unterweisung*, he described the need for the new system:

> The discovery, in the last century, of the extreme limits of power and subtlety in the effect of musical tone extended the boundaries of the tonal domain at the disposal of the composer into hitherto undreamed-of distances. New combinations of tones came to be recognized, and new ways of bending a melodic line were discovered. . . . Blinded by the immense store of materials never used before, deafened by the fantastic novelty of sound, everyone seized without reflection at whatever he felt he could use. At this point instruction failed. . . . Confidence in inherited methods vanished; they seemed barely adequate now to guide the beginner's first steps. Whoever wished to make any progress gave himself unreservedly to the New, neither helped nor hindered by theoretical instruction, which had simply become inadequate to the occasion.[19]

[18] Rudolph Reti, *Tonality, Atonality, Pantonality* (New York: The Macmillan Co., 1958).

[19] Paul Hindemith, *Unterweisung im Tonsatz* (Mainz, 1937). English translation: *The Craft of Musical Composition* (New York: Associated Music Publishers, 1942), pp. 2–3.

As Hindemith's system is the only one which attempts to find a rationale for twentieth-century harmonic practices, it merits more detailed consideration.

HINDEMITH'S HARMONIC SYSTEM

Hindemith embedded his harmonic system in the "laws of nature," a view assailed by his critics. He turned to the science of acoustics for his point of departure, considering acoustical phenomena as "the mirror of the life of the spirit." In tying himself to the immutable laws of nature, he became vulnerable to criticism on the following three grounds: 1) He ignored the historical approach that clearly shows that the rules of harmony are not immutable, and that there is nothing absolute about man's perception of the elements of music. 2) By imposing the lawfulness of natural science on the elements of music, he ignored the fact that one's perception of music is always functional. In other words, human perception does not judge chords *singly* as having fixed values, but according to the context in which they appear. 3) By committing himself to tonality as the equivalent of the force of gravitation, he rejected all atonal and polytonal music as inherently worthless and "contrary to nature." As a result of this commitment, Hindemith also rejected Schoenberg's method of composition with twelve tones, which he considered as a phenomenon that "springs up like epidemics of measles, and disappears just as enigmatically."

The fallacy inherent in considering nature as the lawgiver to the art of music was pointed out by Norman Cazden in a scathing criticism of Hindemith's entire system. Cazden writes:

> Among such doctrines [nature theories] Hindemith's dealing with Nature appears less informed than some, less cautious and also less modest than many, about as inaccurate and as contradictory as most, and more dogmatic and fallacious than we have any reason to tolerate.[20]

Perhaps the following passage from *Unterweisung im Tonsatz* will corroborate Cazden's criticism and also show Hindemith's peculiar way of thinking in which the scientific and the mystical form a curious blend:

> In the Cortian organ it (the ear) literally possesses a minute frequency meter, each tiniest part of which is attuned to a certain vibration rate, and responds to a certain wavelength. When vibration combinations in the simple ratios of $1:2$, $2:3$, or $3:4$ strike this organ, they excite particular parts of its harmoniously designed structure, which distills from the feeling of correctness the most intense pleasure. The basic fact of

[20] Norman Cazden, "Hindemith and Nature," *Musical Review,* **15** (1954), pp. 288–306.

our hearing process reveals to us how closely related are number and beauty, mathematics and art.[21]

In spite of its vulnerable scientific foundation and its erroneous approach to acoustical matters—mercilessly exposed by the reliable Cazden—the system does have some practical value.

Hindemith took the overtone series as his point of departure and by using rather complex mathematical calculations he derived a grouping of the twelve chromatic tones in the following succession, called Series 1.

EX. 4/10 Series 1

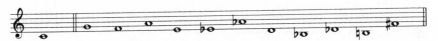

This series has no relation to the sets or tone rows, similarly employing the tones of the chromatic scale which appear in twelve-tone compositions. In Series 1 Hindemith shows the arrangement of the twelve tones of the chromatic scale merely in the order of their alleged relationship to the tonal center, represented by the first pitch in the series. Thus the farther a note is to the right of this series, the weaker its relationship to the key note C.

Two more items need to be pointed out: first, that the same series could be set up beginning with any of the remaining eleven chromatic steps, and secondly, that Series 1 does *not* show the relationship of the notes to *each other*.

In Series 2, Hindemith arranges the relation of intervals to each other. Series 2, derived from combination tones[22]—an entirely arbitrary procedure according to Cazden—appears as follows:

EX. 4/11 Series 2

The intervals in this table possess the greatest clarity on the left and become less "pure"—to use Hindemith's terminology—as one moves from left to right. In accordance with the modern view, Hindemith does not distinguish between consonant and dissonant intervals, but takes a relativistic view of the concepts.

---

[21] *Unterweisung im Tonsatz,* pp. 23-24.

[22] A combination tone is the term applied to a third tone that is heard when two relatively loud tones are sounded simultaneously.

Based on the premises of Series 1 and 2, Hindemith proceeds to set up a classification of chords, consisting of six groups. The six groups are labeled by Roman numerals, and Arabic numbers make further sub-divisions possible. Thus, Group I contains major and minor chords, notated I_1 in root position, and I_2 in the first inversion. Hindemith considers the chords of Group I as the most "valuable" chords, and those of Group VI as the least valuable. To give another example of the classification: Group III contains chords with seconds, sevenths, or both; III_1 again indicates chords where the root and the bass tone are identical, and III_2 denotes a chord in which the root is above the bass tone. It is also assumed that chords with higher Roman numerals produce greater tension than chords with lower numerals, from which distinction Hindemith derives the concept of *harmonic fluctuation*.

Added to this framework is a list of rules which recommend certain practices and discourage others. Exceptions are possible in order to achieve specific expressive goals.

Whatever flaws the system may have in its foundation, its merit is that it allows the classification of any imaginable chord. Also, as a practical musician, Hindemith was versatile enough to design tension values that have some generally accepted validity. Thus, using his chord classification, aside from atonal music, it is possible to analyze chords and harmonic values in the music of any period.

Concerning the validity of the rules, Landau's study[23] further weakens the value of Hindemith's system. Landau sampled Hindemith's own music (his chamber works from 1917–1952) and investigated the extent to which it followed the rules laid down in *The Craft of Musical Composition*. The results show that in the works composed during the time that Hindemith worked out his system, and in the period immediately following, the composer digressed the least from his own rules. In his earlier periods, however, and in the period from 1942–1946 certain rules were *excessively* violated. In fact, one specific rule was violated 565 times in the works studied. In Landau's summary the combined violations of all rules amount to 807. Since the total number of measures studied was 774, Hindemith violated his own rules approximately once in every measure! Thus, Hindemith's theory of harmony is not supported either by the "laws of nature" or by his own music.

Landau concluded that the application of the theory to practice is something less than might have been expected, considering that the theorist and the composer are the same person. Nevertheless, Landau, who is a less severe critic than Cazden, ends on a positive note:

> Hindemith's theories . . . although they may have fallen short of their purpose, are valuable as a guide to other theorists. It is no fault of

[23] Victor Landau, "Paul Hindemith, a Case Study in Theory and Practice," *Musical Review,* **21** (1960), pp. 38–54.

Hindemith that the ways of art, including his own, defy the theorist's passion for system and order and remain a mystery.[24]

In conclusion, no other theorist has used Hindemith's system as a guide.

PANDIATONICISM, BITONALITY, AND BIMODALITY

Another novel approach to tonality is an essentially diatonic treatment of harmonies that favors superimposition of diatonic harmonies with different functions. This procedure is often called *pandiatonicism*. Frequently the tonic and the dominant chords are sounded simultaneously, producing strong dissonances. In Example 4/12 pandiatonicism is exemplified.

EX. 4/12 COPLAND, *Sonata for Violin and Piano,*[25] first movement, coda

Stravinsky and some American composers, particularly Copland, are fond of this harmonic style.

Superimposition of different diatonic harmonies may result in establishing two simultaneously unfolding tonalities, that is, *bitonality*. Bitonality, can also be produced, of course, by harmonic practices described earlier.

The composer whose name is most often associated with bitonality, and even with polytonality, is Milhaud. *Polytonality,* that is, the simultaneous use of more than two tonalities, exists mostly on paper because the ear is unable to register three or more streams of simultane-

---

[24]Landau, p. 54.

[25]Copyright 1944 by Aaron Copland, copyright owner. Reprinted by permission of Boosey & Hawkes, Inc., sole publishers and licensees.

ous tonalities. In Example 4/13 an instance of bitonality is shown; the right hand plays in C major, while the left hand plays in A major:

EX. 4/13 MILHAUD, *Catalogue de Fleurs,* "Les Crocus,"[26] beginning

The simultaneous appearance of the major and minor modes (bimodality) is also often in evidence in twentieth-century music:

EX. 4/14 BARTÓK, *Second Quartet*[27] first movement, 4 measures
before study n. 21 (partial score)

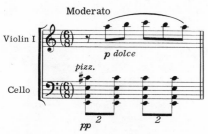

In summarizing the harmonic language of the twentieth century, it is obvious that profound changes have taken place. The most drastic change is the abandonment of tonality, which resulted in the collapse of the whole traditional harmonic system, giving rise not only to new harmonic conceptions, but also to an entirely new mode of musical organization.

It is somewhat paradoxical that the process leading to the dissolution of tonality has been a gradual one, yet the ear has refused to go along with the process, as borne out by the strong repudiation of atonality. The striking success of a few atonal works, however, indicates that this style has more promise than most music theorists today would grant.

Composers who have retained a feeling of tonality have expanded the concept of key center. Superimpositions of chords or of tonalities resulted in harsh dissonances and in an extremely tenuous sense of key center. The listener who misses the singability of melodies and looked in vain for the regularity of rhythmic pulsations is also deprived of the secure feeling derived from a strong sense of tonality. The lack of tonal feeling in the music demands a great change in the listener's attitude and nothing can re-educate the listener more successfully than repeated listenings to new works.

The thought arises whether the trend toward atonality is similar to the tendency of distorting reality found in the visual arts and diagnosed by Sedlmayer[28] as the "loss of center." Here, too, it was claimed that basic beliefs in order, unity, and harmony were shattered. One also wonders whether the superimpositions of clashing musical values observed both in the field of rhythm and harmony can be brought into relationship with the spiritual conflict that preoccupies the mind of modern man.

[28] Hans Sedlmayer, *Verlust der Mitte* (Salzburg, 1948).

TEXTURE

Texture refers to two aspects of musical "lines": 1) the *density* of the lines, that is, the number of lines and their relationship; 2) the *quality* of the "lines," that is, sound and instrumental color.

DENSITY OF TEXTURE

There are three types of density: a) *monophony,* a melody without accompaniment, such as a Gregorian chant; b) *ho-*

mophony, a melody with a subordinated accompaniment; and c) _polyphony,_ two or more independent melodies sounding simultaneously.

The type of texture of a composition is a highly important and revealing stylistic feature. A discerning ear will be able to identify the stylistic period of a composition solely on the basis of texture.

POLYPHONY—HOMOPHONY—COUNTERPOINT

From the above definitions it would seem that polyphony and homophony are clear-cut, absolute concepts. Although the basic meaning of each concept is unambiguous, music in reality is not always composed in such a way that the texture would unequivocally qualify as one or the other type. Polyphony and homophony are _over-all_ stylistic distinctions; therefore, whether a composition is written in one or the other style can be determined only on the basis of an examination of the entire work. Only a minority of compositions are pure types of homophony or polyphony. For this reason, it is preferable to think of these textures in terms of a _continuum;_ on one end is pure polyphony, such as a Bach fugue, with three or four independent musical lines, while on the other end is pure homophony, exemplified by Saint Saëns' _The Swan_ in which _one_ main melody appears throughout the piece in the context of a subordinated harmonic accompaniment. Between these two extreme poles falls a considerable portion of music literature.

While the terms polyphony and homophony are used to describe the over-all texture of a composition, the term _counterpoint_ is used to refer to a more specific occurrence.

Unfortunately, in musical terminology these concepts are often applied loosely: in most textbooks no distinction is made between _polyphony_ and _counterpoint._ Musical dictionaries usually attach two meanings to counterpoint: first, it means the art of combining melodies. It is in this sense that we speak of the discipline of counterpoint, a required subject in the music student's curriculum. Second, it also means a melody that is "added" to another melody. Thus, counterpoint is closely related to _melody._

Since polyphony refers to a texture in which two or more melodies appear simultaneously—and counterpoint also means a combination of melodies—there is obviously a certain overlapping of the meaning of the two concepts. The concepts will become clearer, however, if we remember that polyphony implies a _global_ picture of the texture of a composition, whereas counterpoint is the instance, or technique, through which polyphony manifests itself. It follows then that a composition written in the style of polyphony will always entail counterpoint because polyphony manifests itself through a combination of melodies, that is, through counterpoint.

What is harder to understand is that a work in the homophonic style can also tolerate some counterpoint. Homophony, as defined earlier, means a style of writing in which one melody predominates, accompanied by subordinate, harmonic lines. Yet, few extended compositions consistently adhere to such a texture; sooner or later, the composer, for the sake of variety, will introduce a counterpoint. Even such a distinctly homophonic texture as that of a Strauss waltz contains some counterpoint, but such a texture will not be considered polyphonic because of a few instances of counterpoint.

The argument may be summed up in the following way: pure polyphony, meaning an over-all style of employing two or more independent musical lines, *always* implies counterpoint. In the homophonic style, however, which is based on the predominance of one melody, counterpoint *may* occur, but the occasional appearance of counterpoint in the homophonic texture does not make it polyphonic.

This somewhat ambiguous terminology is paralleled by uncertainties in perception. Whether or not a texture is homophonic often hinges on the relative musical dependence or independence of the accompanying voices. As long as the case is clear-cut, as in *The Swan,* the perceptual problem is a simple one. The purely harmonic texture is unequivocally homophonic. Often, however, a harmonic texture, such as a choral melody harmonized in four parts, may contain such interesting voice-leading in the individual parts that the question arises whether these parts could not be looked upon as independent melodies. Actually, much eighteenth-century instrumental writing, although called homophonic, shows a good deal of independent part-writing, such as we find in later Haydn or Mozart string quartets. Although the main process here is a *harmonic* one, contrapuntal independence is often used to set the harmonic process into dynamic motion. Reluctantly, in lieu of a better term, we call this style homophonic. Conversely, in a Bach fugue, while the main process is *linear*—combined musical lines move simultaneously—harmonic considerations regulate the flow of the independent lines often more by implication than in an overt way. Thus, often it is a matter of emphasis whether the *horizontal* or the *vertical* aspect is more apparent.

Contrapuntal Devices: Imitation, Canon, and Fugue Already in the very early history of contrapuntal writing the freely moving parts often reflected each other. One line would *imitate* the other, as can be seen in this excerpt from a thirteenth-century manuscript:

EX. 5/1 *Montpellier manuscript,* cited in *Polyphonies de XIII*^e
Siècle (ed. Rokseth, 1936)

The exact "imitation" of a motive was only one of many contrapuntal devices; the appearance of a melody could be varied in a number of ways. The most important among these are augmentation, diminution, inversion, and retrograde. Example 5/2 shows the opening of Bach's *The Art of Fugue;* in Example 5/2/a its inversion can be seen (the intervals turned upside down); Example 5/2/b shows its augmentation, that is, the note values are twice as long as the original values and Examples 5/2/c its diminution, the note values halved. Finally, in Example 5/2/d the backward motion (retrograde) of the melody is shown:

EX. 5/2 BACH, *The Art of Fugue,* opening

EX. 5/2/a Inversion

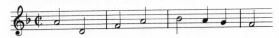

EX. 5/2/b Augmentation

EX. 5/2/c Diminution

EX. 5/2/d Retrograde

Out of imitation grew the *canon,* a more elaborate form of imitation; in a strict canon one voice begins a melody, followed by another voice that imitates the melody note for note. Canon may be employed either as a device applied to a smaller section of a composition or as a self-contained form.

The employment of the canonic principle on a larger scale and with greater freedom led to the fugue. The fugue is a composition, usually for three or four voices, whose purpose is the contrapuntal elaboration of the opening melody (subject). In this process imitation, canonic, and other contrapuntal devices discussed earlier are used. In contrast to the strict canon, the fugue subject is combined with another melody (countersubject) or melodies.

Fugal writing can be applied to a part of a composition or it can be sustained for an entire composition. Opinions differ as to whether the fugue is a texture or a form. Actually, neither term is quite satisfactory because it is not as predetermined as the other musical forms (such as rondo or variation form), but it represents a more dynamic process than the term texture would imply. Therefore, it is preferable to consider the fugue as a special manifestation of the canonic principle.

THE EARLY HISTORY OF TEXTURE

Prior to 900 A.D. Western music was limited to the expressiveness of a single line. However perfect these lines were, whether plain song or a folk song, their development was limited. In Rubbra's formulation, "the perfection and completeness of their expression put an unbroken circle round them, preventing any change except in the direction of a proliferation of ornament and decoration, as happened in the history of plain-song."[1] In the tenth century this circle was broken when, for the first time, melodic lines were combined. The combination of musical lines paved the way for the formation of larger musical units. This style remained predominant for about seven centuries.

As secular music grew in importance, a trend toward homophonic thinking became apparent. Around 1600 the birth of opera brought about important textural changes. In opera, personalized emotions and the need for a clear articulation of the text gave impetus to the rise of the homophonic style. Homophony gradually established itself after polyphony had reached fulfillment at the end of the Baroque era.

[1] Edmund Rubbra, *Counterpoint* (London: Hutchinson University Library, 1960), p. 12.

TEXTURE IN THE CLASSIC-ROMANTIC ERA

The break from strict polyphony in the seventeenth century was a gradual process. It was led by the Italian composers who, preferring lighter textures, stressed single melodies. In the North, however, the German composers adhered to strict polyphony.

The final break occurred in Austria around 1750, the year in which Bach died and the first works of Haydn appeared. At first Haydn and Mozart felt that homophony and polyphony were irreconcilable within the same movement, a notion suggested by some of their earlier quartets in which three homophonic movements are often followed by a fugue. Both masters, however, strove for a reconciliation of the two styles in their later compositions, in which rich contrapuntal lines enliven the essentially harmonic texture. Striking examples of Mozart's mastery of counterpoint can be found in his operas or in the last movement of the "Jupiter" Symphony.

The music of Beethoven shows the same trend toward the reconciliation of the two styles to an even greater extent. A comparison of the early and late quartets or piano sonatas will amply document this point.

In the years following the death of Beethoven composers were preoccupied with melodic and harmonic considerations. Harmonies became enriched with chromaticism, and in the second half of the nineteenth century harmonies were used for their sonorous values. The majority of romantic composers, with the exception of Brahms, were not outstanding in their mastery of counterpoint. The appearance of a fugue in some of the final movements of the works of Schumann or Dvořák usually marks the weaker moments of these composers.

One reason for the lack of affinity with contrapuntal thinking by romantic composers might well lie in the ideology of the romantic outlook. The aim of the romantic artist is to render a subjective account of personal feelings; for this expression homophony lends itself better than polyphony. One melody is naturally a more suitable vehicle for the expression of a subjective and intimate feeling than two or more melodies sounding simultaneously.

TEXTURE IN TWENTIETH-CENTURY MUSIC

Swing to polyphony

On the whole, twentieth-century music turned away from the melodic-harmonic, subjective expressiveness of the nineteenth century. One manifestation of this new trend was the reappearance of poly-

phonic textures, a stylistic feature evident in the music of the leading twentieth-century composers. Stravinsky, Bartók, Schoenberg, Berg,
Webern, and Hindemith—each in his own way—reveal *linear* thinking
in a majority of their works. According to Sessions, "The focal point
of the more advanced musical thought of today is polyphonic, and
more concerned with problems of texture and organization than with
harmony in the hitherto accepted meaning of the term."[2]

Terms used to describe the style of twentieth-century music, such
as neoclassic, neobaroque, and "back-to-Bach," however controversial,
also point to the revival of contrapuntal thinking.

Obviously, the harmonic evolution that took place around the turn
of the century, described in the previous chapter, created a new approach to counterpoint. Whereas in the earlier styles vertical relations
always implied functional harmonic movement, in twentieth-century
music the various strands of melody may run parallel, each on its own
plane, seemingly unrelated and independent. The novel combination
of melodies often results in augmented or diminished intervals, in
seconds or in sevenths. The term *dissonant counterpoint* is used for
this new way of combining melodies.

Example 5/3 from Schoenberg's *Three Piano Pieces*, Op. 11, illustrates
dissonant counterpoint:

EX. 5/3 SCHOENBERG, *Three Piano Pieces*,[3] Op. 11, No. 1,
mm. 25–27

Examples of twentieth-century contrapuntal writing can be found in
No. 8 ("Die Nacht") of Schoenberg's *Pierrot Lunaire*, or in the last movement of his Woodwind Quintet. The last movement of Hindemith's
Fourth Quartet, the second, fugal movement of Stravinsky's *Symphony
of Psalms*, and the first movement of Bartók's *Music for Strings, Percussion, and Celesta* furnish additional examples of the new type of
counterpoint.

[2] Roger Sessions, "Problems and Issues Facing the Composer Today," *Musical
Quarterly*, **46,** No. 2 (1960), p. 166.

[3] Quoted by permission of Mrs. Gertrud Schoenberg and Universal Edition, publisher of first edition.

Contrapuntal interplay occurs frequently between clashing *intervals;* in the last movement of Bartok's *Music for Strings, Percussion, and Celesta* a canon appears on the cluster of the second:

EX. 5/4 BARTOK, *Music for Strings, Percussion, and Celesta,* fourth movement, mm. 159–161

(partial score)

From the viewpoint of the listener's perception the fact that the twentieth century leans toward polyphonic textures creates an added difficulty. It is always easier to listen to music in which one melody enjoys a favored position in the context of functional harmony. Most listeners, nurtured on the music of the nineteenth century, are still attuned to this kind of writing. Contrapuntal music demands listening on several planes; such a division of the field of perception is always difficult. Strangely enough, it is often easier to distinguish the contrapuntal lines of twentieth-century music than those of baroque polyphony. In a Bach fugue, for example, because there is always a harmonic relationship unifying the horizontal lines, the listener may be less aware of the individuality of lines, whereas in the twentieth-century style, the single lines are set off sharply by the dissonant intervals.

QUALITY OF TEXTURE: SOUND

Musical lines are characterized not only by density but by color qualities as well. These qualities are determined by the character of sound, sometimes called tone color.

Even a monophonic texture is described fully only when the musical medium by which the tone is produced is known. The quality of the monophonic texture will naturally be different when produced by the human voice, a saxophone, or a viola. Likewise, in homophonic music, there is a decisive difference in texture when a violin melody is accompanied by a piano or by three other string instruments. The texture of a fugue will also sound different when performed by a vocal quartet as against a string quartet.

Sound values too will be affected by additional differences even within the same medium: for example, a middle C will have a different quality or timbre when sung by a soprano or a bass because the female voice is exploring its lowest range, producing a lusterless sound, whereas the male singer will execute the same tone brilliantly in his high register.

Additional determinants of tone color are loud and soft, vibrato and nonvibrato, pizzicato and arco, muted and nonmuted, legato and staccato.

Another textural factor is the size of a performing group: a Haydn symphony will sound light and transparent if performed by a small orchestra, and heavy-textured if played by the total complement of strings in the modern orchestra. The texture again will vary if the composer writes a single line for, say, all cellos as compared to 2-3 lines (*divisi*) for the same section, as happens so often in the music of Wagner and Debussy.

Obviously the quality of texture, that is, the *sound,* is a topic of vast scope. It encompasses the history of instruments from the crudest drums to the electronic production of sound, in addition to the consideration of all expressive means that affect sound production. It also includes the history of various performing media and their significance in various historical periods.

QUALITY OF TEXTURE IN THE
CLASSIC-ROMANTIC ERA

The history of sound values is closely linked to the evolution of the basic elements (melody, rhythm, and harmony) of music.

A glance at the history of sound will reveal additional findings: first, certain periods show preferences for certain sound media; second, some composers are drawn to one specific medium to the exclusion of all others. The first item is borne out by the popularity of art song in the nineteenth century, a period when a marked rapprochement between music and literature is evident. The second tendency—to center on one medium only—is exemplified by Hugo Wolf's complete preoccupation with art song, or by Chopin's exclusive interest in the piano as a medium for his compositions.

Contrastingly, one could also find a corresponding *lack* of affinity for certain media: composers who employed the large machinery of sound (Berlioz, Wagner, and others) did not express themselves in media in which sound is confined to a few instruments, as the string quartet.

An over-all comparison of the classic and romantic eras reveals a rather complex picture. Classicism shows a more consistent approach to sound. This period, governed by reason and restraint that kept melody, rhythm, and harmony in equilibrium, showed judiciousness in matters of sonority too. In the orchestra the separate groups were held in balance, while overemphasis of a single instrument was generally avoided. The orchestra depended on the sound image of the string tone for its main tone color. The woodwinds, although occasionally used brilliantly, occupied a secondary role. The number of instruments employed in the orchestra was not large, and the single instruments were used usually in their normal range. On the whole, transparency and clarity prevailed. Percussion instruments were used in moderation either to underline rhythmic accents or to achieve high points in dynamics. It should be noted that a number of instruments that existed in Haydn's and Mozart's time, such as the harp and trombone, were not included in the symphony and were considered admissible only when justified by dramatic motivation. Mozart, for instance, employed the trombone in *Don Giovanni* and the *Requiem* but never used the instrument in his symphonies. Insistence on clarity and restraint were responsible for this self-limitation.

Beethoven achieved a more massive and rugged sound than his predecessors, although he did not substantially enlarge the orchestra. This was due in part to his rhythmic effects (accentuations, displaced accents, and the like) and to a wide range of dynamics, which often resulted in violent contrast of moods and intensities. Another characteristic of his instrumental style, particularly in his late period, was his disregard for the performer. Difficulties, hitherto unknown, often strain the performer to the utmost. The raw and harsh sound of the *Grosse Fuge*, for example, approximates the textural qualities of twentieth-century music.

Composers of the post-Beethoven era are unified in their increased consciousness of sound. The new interest in sound values shows a bipolar tendency: while some composers (Berlioz, Wagner, and Richard Strauss) showed a preference for an overwhelming mass of sound, others aimed at sensuous sound on a small scale. Chopin and Schumann, for instance, discovered new possibilities in the sound of the modern piano, while a heightened expressiveness was also achieved in the use of the human voice.

As the woodwind and brass instruments underwent significant mechanical improvements, the orchestra accepted an increasing number of instruments in its standard complement. Along with more demanding parts, the new generation of players became more versatile instrumentalists. Among nineteenth-century composers Berlioz was most directly inspired by the sound of the instruments, and his treatise on instrumentation remains a valuable source book even today for the student of orchestration.

For a more complete understanding of the sonorous world of romanticism, one has to consider the over-all aims of this style. It was a youthful movement, full of personal feeling and yearning. Expressiveness and subjectivity were among its main tendencies, resulting in the overthrow of tradition and restraint. Accordingly, the classical poise of orchestral balance was swept away; single instruments became more prominent, singing forth with a new emphasis on melodiousness. The French horn opening of Schubert's great C major Symphony points toward the new emphasis on the sound of individual instruments.

Poetic, mysterious, and sometimes even grotesque effects were also sought as imagination often turned to the supernatural, as in the ghostlike effects in Weber's operas.

Sound often depicted elements of nature; the tonal portrayal of fire, water, storm, and forest spurred the composer's imagination. Interest in tone painting resulted in the employment of new instruments and novel instrumental effects; Berlioz, for instance, wrote for the shrill E flat clarinet and made use of the *col legno* effect, (playing with the wooden side of the bow), and other innovations.

In the first half of the century the woodwind instruments gained new prominence; in the second half, the brass choir was brought into focus, particularly by Wagner, whose orchestral sound was determined by harmonic motivation.

The end of the century witnessed huge orchestras that achieved unparalleled dynamic outbursts and frenetic climaxes. Tone painting also became more and more realistic with the tone poems of Richard Strauss. In this environment the linear writing and the traditional orchestral style of Brahms seemed out of date. Around the turn of the century the opulent, often bombastic, late romantic tendencies gave way to the subtle style of Debussy. Although he still employed a large orchestra in *Pelléas et Mélisande,* the textures are subtly drawn, usually with the help of only a few instruments. New effects and nuances were achieved by muted brasses and frequently by divided muted strings. Debussy was soon followed by Ravel, who treated sound with a subtle touch of virtuosity.

SOUND IN TWENTIETH-CENTURY MUSIC

The esthetic philosophy of the twentieth century had a profound effect upon sound. The new outlook, according to which music did not have to be pleasing to the ear, completely revolutionized the concept of sound. Furthermore, the new type of melody, the increased emphasis upon rhythm, and the total harmonic reorientation contributed their share to a novel instrumental and vocal style of writing.

Chronologically, as well as in order of importance, the revitalization of rhythmic forces which resulted in the emergence of the percussion instruments from their relative obscurity should be mentioned as an integral part of the new conception of sonorities in the twentieth century.

Through the music of Stravinsky and Bartók particularly, and also because of the jazz influence, the door opened to Asian and African rhythms, and along with these rhythms, to the sound of percussion instruments, which in their native ritualistic setting often assumed melodic significance.

As happens quite frequently in the history of the arts, an emphasis on one novel feature is accompanied by the decline of another. As the percussion instruments gained new recognition and woodwind and brass instruments also enjoyed renewed interest, the string sound ceased to maintain its dominance as the chief ingredient of the orchestral tonal image. This tendency is particularly evident in Stravinsky's works. A cursory glance at the scores of *Petrouchka, Le Sacre du Printemps,* or *L'Histoire du Soldat* shows that strings are utilized more for their percussive potentials than for their songfulness. If a string instrument is featured, as the violin solo in *Petrouchka,* the instrument is used with strident effect. In *Le Sacre du Printemps* the strings play an even smaller role; violins and violas are completely omitted in the *Symphony of Psalms,* while the Piano Concerto employs merely a wind orchestra.

Among other leading twentieth-century composers Bartók shows fondness for stringed instruments. His six quartets occupy a central position in his oeuvre. The strings, however, are seldom used with the old mellowness; effects of *sul ponticello, col legno,* and pizzicati that rebound on the fingerboard often suggest the sound of primitive folk instruments. Frequent use of harmonics, glissandi, and nonvibrato adds to the new world of sounds.

Instead of the strings, now the woodwind and brass instruments became the virtuosi of the orchestra and were featured also in various chamber music combinations. Well-known examples of this new virtuoso style can be seen in Bartók's *Concerto for Orchestra,* in Stravinsky's

Octet for wind instruments, or in Stockhausen's *Zeitmasse* for five woodwind instruments.

The piano is also used in a novel manner. While nineteenth-century composers made us almost believe that the piano was a singing instrument, composers in the twentieth century exploited the instrument's percussive potentialities, as may be seen in Bartók's *Allegro Barbaro.*

The percussion section grew not only in importance but also in the number of instruments and sound devices. The new sounds of the xylophone, woodblock, and slapstick were followed by the wind machine, the thunder stick, and the airplane motor.

One of the new favorites became the vibraphone, used by Berg, Boulez, and others. Another newcomer was the xylorimba, an enlarged xylophone.

For the first time, composers wrote for a combination of percussion instruments as did Varèse in *Ionization,* a piece for thirteen percussionists who play on more than twenty instruments. Orff and Chavez also wrote for percussion orchestra. In addition to the usual percussion instruments, Orff's *Astutuli* calls for five water glasses, wind machine, rattles, and the so-called *Steinspiel,* a high-pitched stone slab struck with a glockenspiel mallet.

Percussion instruments often formed part of chamber music combinations, too. In addition to the well-known examples of Bartók's *Sonata for Two Pianos and Percussion* and Stravinsky's *L'Histoire du Soldat,* there is the *Sonata for Piano and Percussion* of the American composer Peggy Glanville-Hicks; the Spanish composer Carlos Surinach scored his composition *Ritmo Hondo* for clarinet, trumpet, xylophone, and timpani. Percussion instruments were even featured in solo roles, as seen in Stockhausen's *Zyklus* and Elliott Carter's *Suite* for Timpani.

Despite the growth of the percussion section, the modern orchestra, after 1920, more often than not, is reduced in size, compared to the orchestras one finds in the early works of Stravinsky and Schoenberg. In the years following World War I, emphasis was placed on individual timbre rather than on large combinations of instruments. The so-called neoclassic style, the popular label for this period, favored dry and sober sonorities with lean, contrapuntal lines. In general, instrumental effects were frequently used to underscore the rhythmic component or to clarify contrapuntal lines, while the sound devices used earlier to enhance color and blended harmonies were seldom employed.

In the Viennese atonal school instrumental color was used to bring out eerie, tenuous psychological effects. Of importance is Webern's *Klangfarbenmelodie,* a device whereby a melody is presented in such a way that almost every tone is produced by a different instrument.

The Viennese atonal composers (Schoenberg, Berg, and Webern) and also Stravinsky in his later works often employed unusual instruments, such as the mandolin, guitar, and tenor saxophone, in combination with conventional instruments. Finally, "flutter tonguing," a special and rather novel sound often scored for the flute, but available on brass instruments too, should be mentioned. This curious sound effect is achieved by a rolling movement of the tongue.

Special use of the piano by the avant-garde, the "prepared" piano (see Chapter 16), should also be listed. By inserting various objects, such as thumbtacks and nails, between the strings of the piano, special effects can be obtained.

In summary, in twentieth-century music texture is decidedly more contrapuntal than in the preceding century. The sound aspect of texture is seldom based on sensuous beauty. As a consequence, the stringed instruments are rarely used in the traditional manner. Percussion instruments gained greatly in importance and the percussive potential of traditional instruments, particularly the strings and piano, is often stressed. The woodwind and brass instruments are featured with even more emphasis in contemporary scores, consolidating the gains made during the nineteenth century. Experimentation with new instruments, new sound devices, and the electronic production of sound (see Chapter 7) round out the panorama of new sonorities.

PRINCIPLES OF
MUSICAL ORGANIZATION:

Form

FORM AND FORMS IN MUSIC

Melodic phrases, rhythmic patterns, harmonic tensions and resolutions, and qualities of texture are the materials out of which a musical work is literally *composed* or put together. In other words, the composer achieves form and coherence by a judicious ordering of the elements of music. In a larger sense, then, *form* in music refers to all aspects of differentiation and punctuation that pertain to the organization of a composition. In a narrower sense, musical *forms* apply to specific principles of musical organization, as manifested in the sectional forms, rondo form, variation form, and sonata form.

In view of the far-reaching changes that have pervaded all the materials of music in the twentieth century, the crisis that

affected musical organization on all levels of construction can easily
be understood. The most important single factor responsible for this
crisis was the harmonic revolution that swept away the functional
harmonic system that was the pillar of musical organization in the
eighteenth and nineteenth centuries.

The emerging solutions, on the whole, up to about 1950, proved the
surprising durability of the traditional forms, which survived in the new
surrounding even though the premises upon which they were originally
built had lost their validity. With some exceptions, the innovations
that were introduced pertained to the organization of smaller units.
After 1950, however, the basic conception of musical form changed
so drastically that the resulting music seemed qualitatively different
from anything written in the last 600 years (see Chapter 7).

The survival of the traditional forms in the first half of the twentieth
century demonstrates their flexibility and resiliency. The multifarious
shapes in which they appear also expose the fallacy of the notion that
forms are fixed, ready-made molds into which musical material is
poured. As Rubbra aptly states:

> Much harm has been done in the teaching of music by using con-
> venient analytical concepts [such as sonata form] as "facts" that have
> an abstract structural validity. Forms are the courses that music takes
> under the impact of sociological and cultural forces. When these forces
> are spent or change direction, we can still write music that is labelled
> sonata, fugue or symphony, and which will still be such in essence, yet
> which, under analysis, will show marked structural diversities. In other
> words, the forms, that have developed in the history of Western music,
> although few in number, have no fixed shapes that can be measured and
> made available, like molds for a jelly. Rather are they like variants of
> archetypal ideas which are inexhaustible in potentiality, yet which always
> remain the same. This is the paradox of form.[1]

PERCEPTION OF MUSICAL FORM

The perception of musical form, that is, the grasp of the arrangement
of musical ideas, their sequence and relationship, is one of the most
important stumbling blocks to the understanding and enjoyment of
music both old and new. While the listener's ability to whistle the tune
of a composition, or to tap out its characteristic rhythmic pattern, indicates some grasp of a work, he will not really understand the music
unless the plan according to which the composition is designed is clear
to him. Since music happens in time, the reconstruction of the plan of

[1] Edmund Rubbra, *Counterpoint* (London: Hutchinson University Library, 1960), p. 56.

a composition places heavy demands on the listener. Of all the arts, music presents the greatest difficulty in form perception. A painting or a work of sculpture may be inspected in its simultaneous existence. The content of a novel, although it unfolds in time like a musical composition, is also more readily grasped than music because the delineations (parts, chapters, paragraphs) are visible and the meanings are made concrete through language. Moreover, should it be necessary, one can always turn back the pages and reread passages if memory needs refreshing. When listening to a symphony, however, this turning back is impossible, unless one listens to a recorded performance.

The particular difficulty in hearing form in music becomes obvious when compared to the task of perceiving form in the visual field. Here, an arrangement of figures, such as appears below, is immediately grasped:

Figure 6-1

No special training or undue concentration is needed to register the symmetrical nature of the design in Figure 6-1.

The recognition of a similar arrangement of musical values, however, is a decidedly more complex task. Since symmetry in music unfolds in *time,* the listener will have to grasp A (which in this instance stands for the first musical idea, and may be short or long, simple or complex) as a unit. Then, while he listens to B, the contrasting musical statement, the memory of A has to be maintained in order to grasp the relationship between A and B. In other words, B can be understood as a contrast to A only if the idea of A still exists in the listener's consciousness. Moreover, a firm grasp of A is necessary if the listener is to capture the moment when the composer reintroduces A, and thereby fulfills the symmetrical organization. Memory obviously plays an important role in the perceptual process. The task may be further complicated if the second A is altered (modified symmetry), a frequent occurrence in twentieth-century music.

Of course, one can merely listen to sound, which in itself is a source of esthetic pleasure. Such listening, however, does not rise beyond the sensuous level, and the listener will soon lose interest because the appeal of sound wears off after a while, as with all physical stimuli.

However, grasping a musical design such as symmetry implies more than the perception of the structural aspect. Understanding A as a musical idea and perceiving B as a new idea, related and often contrasted to A, inevitably entails the examination of those expressive values that are associated with the "content" of music. In music, form and content are inseparable. "Form is feeling" as stated by one writer, and according to Schoenberg, "It is the organization of music which makes the musical idea intelligible."

PRINCIPLES OF MUSICAL FORMS

Nearly all established musical forms can be derived from the following principles: 1) repetition and contrast, 2) variation, and 3) development.

These principles are not unique to music; they manifest themselves in the other arts as well as in one's daily existence. Some musical forms are based on one principle only, while in other forms one principle dominates, although another may also act. Thus, in a theme and variation movement in which the over-all design is built on the principle of variation, the effects of repetition and contrast may also be felt. Even more permeation is present in the sonata form; here, the over-all design of modified symmetry is based on repetition and contrast, while the middle section employs the principle of development. Because of such overlaps, a rigid classification concerning the derivation of musical forms is ill-advised. Allowing for this overlap of principles, one can generalize that most three-part forms and the rondo form are governed by the principle of *repetition* and *contrast,* the theme and variation form is built on the principle of *variation,* and the sonata form is the only form in which a whole section is governed by the principle of *development.*

THE PRINCIPLE OF

REPETITION AND CONTRAST

The principle of repetition and contrast can be observed in countless manifestations of life. Reference was made in the discussion of rhythm to periodic alternations, such as the cycle of seasons, the ebb and flow of the ocean, and the like. Whereas in the context of rhythm the discussion emphasized the periodicity of the mentioned occurrences, now the *form-giving* potential of changes and recurrences will be brought into focus.

The most frequently used design of recurrence is the three-part division in which the repetition recurs after a digression (A–B–A). In general, the return to an earlier phase seems to be a deeply rooted phenomenon in man's existence. Perhaps it is not too far-fetched to speculate that it is this reconciliation of opposites in man's inner and outer environment which is mirrored in the widely employed pattern of repetition-contrast-repetition in the arts.

In the visual arts the manifestation of symmetrical patterns has a more static quality compared to the temporal arts, and the arrangement of parts follows more closely the original meaning of symmetry. Thus, for instance, the facade of a Gothic cathedral, where the two sides carry flanking towers, can be cut into two equal halves by an imaginary central dividing line.

In the temporal arts, however, the concept of symmetry assumes a different meaning and is more related to the models cited previously. The dynamic quality felt in the temporal symmetry of music is perhaps due to the fact that since there is no simultaneous perception, the central dividing line—even an imagined one creating two equal halves —loses its meaning. No listener would ever perceive an A–B–A design in such a way that the first A, *plus the first half of B,* would constitute the first half of the perceptual unit, while the second half of B, plus the restatement of A, the second half, as it appears in the visual field, in view of the role of the central dividing line. In music the A–B–A design will always have a clear-cut ternary quality; B will be experienced as a digression from A, after which the restatement of A will gain new meaning.

Whether the shape is binary or ternary, the return harmonically is achieved by virtue of the gravitational force of the tonic. The idea of centricity in music has an ancient history, existing many centuries before the modern conception of tonality emerged. The Chinese likened the middle note ("chiao") to the center of the world, and the "sol" in "solfege" refers in Latin to the solar center. Curt Sachs mentions in his *Commonwealth of Arts* that a focal point, similar to our tonic, was present in the music of the primitives on the lowest level of civilization, and also, that this music contained well-wrought symmetry in answering phrases. The statement-contrasting statement-restatement sequence, based on the centricity of the tonic, is present in many folk songs of diverse civilizations and has become one of the foremost organizational principles in Western music. In the twentieth century, as centricity has become tenuous or nonexistent, the shape of music has been vitally affected.

Symmetrical Forms in the Classic-Romantic Era   The form consciousness of the eighteenth century manifested itself in movements of symmetrical structure marked off by strong lines of delineation based on a firmly established tonality. The minuet and trio form is the prototype for this kind of organization.

In the treatment of this design in the eighteenth century the large sections are carefully balanced, and the same tempo is maintained throughout. Contrast in B is achieved by a variety of means, through a change in texture, key, dynamics, instrumentation, or in articulation such as legato versus staccato.

In the romantic era a number of changes occurred in this form, most of them introduced or foreshadowed by Beethoven. Perhaps the most forward-looking is the scherzolike movement of the Fifth Symphony, where the second A is completely recomposed with different orchestration and dynamics. Furthermore, the movement does not have a clear-cut ending; instead, the coda builds to a tremendous climax on the dominant pedal point, leading directly into the last movement. This lack of separation between two movements constitutes an early example of fluidity or fusion in form, a tendency that characterizes later romantic musical architecture.

Signs of fluid organization can be seen in Beethoven's dance movements; often small connecting links appear between the large sections, such as at the end of the trio section of his String Quartet, Op. 18, No. 2, and also in the corresponding place in the Scherzo movement of his String Quartet, Op. 18, No. 6, thus smoothing the firm lines of demarcation.

While modified symmetry in a dancelike third movement was a bold innovation in Beethoven's time, it became accepted practice in the twentieth century. Meanwhile, more and more signs of fluid organization became apparent in the course of the nineteenth century.

Such connecting links are frequently found in the nineteenth century in minuet and scherzo movements; the linkage usually occurs at the end of the trio section, establishing a smooth connection with the restatement of the first A. Examples are numerous in Schubert's music, such as the Minuet of his String Quartet in A minor, the Scherzo of his String Quintet in C major, and the Scherzo of his great C major Symphony; an additional example of the same type is the bridge from B to A in the minuet of Mendelssohn's "Italian" Symphony.

The less formalized attitude of the romantic temper further manifested itself in the freer treatment of tempo; whereas in minuets of the eighteenth century the same tempo was maintained throughout, in the nineteenth century tempo changes within a dance movement are frequent. For example, in the Scherzo movement of Schubert's C major String Quintet, the A part is marked *presto*, while the B part changes to *andante*, establishing also a new meter. In the later nineteenth century such tempo changes became accepted practice; an examination of the dance movements of symphonies by Dvořák, Bruckner, and Mahler furnishes many examples. Brahms even went beyond this, occasionally welding together minuet and scherzolike sections into *one* dance movement, as in the third movement of his Second Symphony and in the third movement of his String Quartet in A minor, Op. 51, No. 2.

The history of codas attached to dance movements also shows a gradual line of development. In the minuets of Haydn and Mozart, codas almost never appear; since both composers used codas in other types of movements, one might assume that the use of codas was avoided by these two composers so as not to disturb the symmetry of the three balanced sections. Again, Beethoven appears as the first composer to break with the earlier practice by adding codas to his dance movements.

In contrast to the dance movements, the history of the three-part song form as applied to many slow movements shows from the start a less formalized treatment. The rule here was modified symmetry even in the eighteenth century; the second A was different, embellished often or intensified. In the nineteenth century such movements were subject to even freer treatment; Chopin's works offer a rewarding study for the variety of treatment of modified symmetry. Twentieth-century practices are sometimes anticipated, as for instance in the Mazurka in A minor, Op. 55, No. 1, where the second A returns in the "wrong" key (G sharp minor).

Fluidity and increased freedom also characterized the treatment of the rondo form in the nineteenth century.

Three-part Forms in the Twentieth Century   The twentieth century has witnessed a trend away from symmetrical patterns in the design of melodies, harmonies, and metric organizations. Due to the interdependence between small and large units in musical organization, it follows that the larger structures also reveal a preference for asymmetry or at least for strongly modified symmetry. In minuet and scherzolike movements *modified* symmetry is now the rule rather than the exception; examples can be found in the scherzolike movements of the Ravel and Debussy String Quartets, in the second movement of the Fifth Symphony by Shostakovich, in the dance movement of Prokofiev's Second Piano Sonata, and in the dance movements of Bartók's Fourth and Fifth String Quartets. Curiously, in some works in a very advanced idiom, such as Schoenberg's Septet, Op. 24, and his *Piano Suite,* Op. 25, we find instances of exact *da capo* restatements; such unmodified symmetry is found in the minuet movements of both named compositions and in the Gavotte of Op. 25.

Obviously, when the contemporary composer employs the traditional *da capo* treatment, the effect is not the same as it was in the eighteenth and nineteenth centuries because in the absence of tonality, or even in cases where a very tenuous tonality prevails, the return will not be experienced psychologically by the listener in the same way it was when the fulfillment of symmetry, that is, the return, also meant recapturing the home key.

In the twentieth century the perception of all forms built on repetition has become increasingly problematical, since in the absence of a strong sense of orientation given by tonality, the listener now has to depend more strongly on the retention of the melodic-rhythmic characteristics of the musical ideas. Since the melodies are seldom singable or predictable, and the metric organization is often extremely complex, the retention and identification of musical ideas, and consequently the perception of their arrangements, have become increasingly difficult. While in the past even the casual listener may have grasped the outer structure of a Mozart minuet after two or three hearings, it may require twenty or thirty hearings before the same sequence of ideas is recognized in a minuet by Schoenberg.

In twentieth-century treatment of the so-called three-part song form, as often applied to slow movements of symphonies, sonatas, string quartets, and the like, we often find extreme condensation, or merely hints at the theme, instead of repetitions. Such a hint occurs in the slow movement of Stravinsky's Piano Sonata: the return of A is signified by the restatement of the first two measures of the first A only, and the rest of the section is entirely recomposed. This process is known as "repetition by substitution."

Another division of sectional form can be seen in the arch or *Bogen* form, meaning the reversed return. In this arrangement the sections in an arch are reversed in order on each side of the central section. The design will be A–B–C–B–A. Honegger and Bartók are particularly fond of this form; a typical example can be found in the third movement of Bartók's *Music for Strings, Percussion, and Celesta* (see Chapter 10).

THE PRINCIPLE OF VARIATION
AND VARIATION FORMS

Little will be said about the musical application of the principle of variation, manifesting itself in theme and variation form, passacaglia, and so on, because these forms are fairly well understood even by the listener of limited experience. The significance of the variation principle in serial music will be discussed in the next chapter.

It is well known that the principle of variation is a rich pattern-forming device in life, and in nature in general. An obvious example drawn from nature is the difference in color, shape, vein, and size of leaves of the same tree; the fact that no two leaves are alike is a manifestation of the principle of variation.

In music, the most obvious form based on the principle of variation is the *theme and variation form.* The composer starts out with a theme (either his own or a borrowed one) and then composes a number of *sections,* called *variations,* in which the theme appears in ever new guises. In the strict variation form (favored in the eighteenth century), each variation is of the same length and has the same harmonic layout as the theme. As a rule, each variation is given to *one* modification, brought about by melodic, rhythmic, harmonic, or textural changes.

In the nineteenth century, as a result of diminishing form consciousness, the trend was toward *free* variation form, meaning an increased flexibility in the treatment of the theme. Each variation may be of different length and is not governed by the same harmonic plan. On the whole, there is much less resemblance between the theme and the variations than in the strict type of variation movement. Examples for free variation form can be found in the works of Schumann, Franck, and others.

In twentieth-century music the variation form is used by both tonal and atonal composers. Bartók, although adhering to traditional forms in general, rarely used the variation form. The slow movement of his Violin Concerto is one of the rare instances. Stravinsky employed the form more frequently; perhaps the slow movement of his *Octet* for winds is the best-known example. In the works of American composers, Copland's *Piano Variations* and the slow movement of Sessions' Second Quartet provide rewarding examples for study. The passacaglia, one type of variation, was particularly favored by Hindemith; the last movement of his Fourth Quartet is a characteristic example (see Chapter 14). The slow movement of Ravel's Piano Trio and Webern's *Passacaglia,* Op. 1, offer stylistically diversified illustrations.

In serial music, which is itself based on the principle of perpetual variation (see Chapter 7), the theme and variation form is frequently used. Examples can be found in Schoenberg's *Variations for Orchestra,* Op. 31 (see an analysis of that work in Chapter 11), in the slow movement of Webern's Symphony Op. 21, or in his *Variations for Orchestra,* Op. 30 (see Chapter 13 for an analysis of the last named composition).

THE PRINCIPLE OF DEVELOPMENT:

SONATA FORM

Development implies the process of growth, that is, the growth of live organisms. One uses terms such as child development, or developmental psychology, in referring to the process of growth or maturation. In music, development means the working out of musical ideas, and its most typical manifestation is found in the development section of sonata form.

Sonata form is a rather late development in the evolution of musical forms. It represents a new phase in musical thinking, based often on the duality of musical ideas as opposed to the one idea and one mood of the dances of the Baroque period. But what is even more important in sonata form is the design of key relationships. Its essence lies in the opposition of key areas in the exposition, followed by the free modulatory pattern of the development, and in the eventual reconciliation brought about by the recapitulation with the reaffirmation of the home key. Sonata form is a purely instrumental and a typically first movement form, although it is also employed in slow and last movements.

SONATA FORM IN THE CLASSIC-ROMANTIC ERA

The history of sonata form between 1750–1900 reflects the same tendencies that were outlined in the discussion of the elements of music. The classical composer, as a rule, used relatively simple material for his main theme, propelled by a strong rhythmic drive. The emphasis thereafter is on the unfolding, which follows a compelling logic often coupled with dramatic inevitability, rather than on songfulness. By contrast, the romantic composer's objective is revealed at the very outset, where more emphasis is given to melody and to sound values than to the logic of construction. This stress on the melodic-harmonic values lends a lyric and more static quality to the music, while rhythmic values are less in the foreground.

In the classical sonata form the ideas and sections are strongly delineated, whereas in the romantic style they are presented with considerable fluidity. Lines of demarcation between sections are less obvious. For instance, often the end of the exposition is hardly noticeable; instead of the breathing spell given by the double bar—usually distinctly felt in the classical style—the music often glides almost imperceptibly into the development section. Quite frequently the composer foregoes the tradition of repeating the exposition, as found in the later works of Beethoven.

The romantic composer, as might be expected, takes a freer attitude with regard to key relationships; the second group may enter in an unexpected, often distant key. Schubert, an early romanticist, already showed harmonic adventurousness by introducing his recapitulation sometimes in keys other than the tonic.

Other structural liberties were taken; in some instances the recapitulation was partially or totally omitted or, as another sign of nonconformity, new material was introduced in the development section. This latter device was also anticipated by Beethoven, and on very rare occasions by Mozart too.

It is impossible to enumerate all the digressions and innovations romantic composers achieved in this form or in the organization of the outer structure of the instrumental works called *sonatas.* However, two items concerning the sonata as a whole should be mentioned: first, the romanticist's predilection for fluid organization which led to the linking of movements together without a break, as occurs, for example, in Mendelssohn's Violin Concerto or in Schumann's Fourth Symphony; second, the application of the so-called cyclic principle, whereby the same theme recurs in subsequent movements of a composition. French composers, such as Franck and Debussy were particularly fond of this device.

One more word should be said about the musical processes which took place in the different sections of the sonata form. In the classical style, in accordance with its fondness for order and lucidity, the exposition was really expository in the sense that the main musical objective was the presentation of themes with hardly any attempt to elaborate them. Elaboration was reserved for the development section. The romantic composer, however, was unwilling to submit himself to such a restriction and we find early examples in Schubert's works, for instance, in the exposition of the first movement of his "Unfinished" Symphony, where the announcement of the secondary theme is followed by procedures which have developmental qualities. More than one critic has raised the question whether such a digression violates the spirit of sonata form.

Around the middle of the nineteenth century a group of composers (known as the neo-Germans) proclaimed that the abstract instrumental compositions in three or four movements had become obsolete. The sonata form, in particular, was the target of their attacks and new types of organization were sought. Gradually, more and more composers turned to writing symphonic music motivated by extramusical inspirations in which the form was dictated by the exigencies of the "program," such as a novel, a poem, or a painting.

One of the early examples of welding story and traditional form together is Berlioz' *Symphonie Fantastique* (1830). The composer's dilemma is obvious: whether to do justice to the title of the movement (Dreams, Passions, Reveries) or to fulfill the demands of the first movement form. Not much later Liszt introduced the tone poem, a one-movement symphonic form based on a program. This form was adopted and further developed in the last two decades of the century by Richard Strauss.

In the Lisztian tone poem a novel musical process, that of transformation of themes, occurs. This device, when compared to development of themes, is more integrative. The wholeness of the themes is maintained, and by changes applied to the whole theme, new "wholes" are created. In comparison, the developmental process is more analytical, illuminating the themes by laying bare their component parts; in the process of transformation the theme, as a whole, gains a new musical existence.

The difference between developmental process and thematic transformation is illustrated in the following examples. In the first, the main theme of the first movement of Mozart's Symphony in G minor, No. 40, K. 550, is given, and one phase of its development is shown.

EX. 6/1/a MOZART, *Symphony No. 40 in G minor*, K. 550, first
movement, main theme

EX. 6/1/b Mm. 160–162, development section

The second example demonstrates thematic transformation employed in Liszt's *Les Preludes;* Example 6/2/a shows one manifestation of the theme and Example 6/2/b one of its transformations.

EX. 6/2/a LISZT, *Les Preludes,* basic theme, m. 3

EX. 6/2/b Transformation of the theme

Around the turn of the century the symphony and the tone poem coexisted. In general the abstract forms of instrumental music showed a much greater appeal and durability in the twentieth century than the neo-Germans would have wished one to believe.

SONATA FORM IN THE TWENTIETH CENTURY

A survey of the contemporary literature, disregarding the avant-garde composers, shows a marked adherence to the sonata form. With the exception of Stravinsky, the major contemporary composers, Bartók, Hindemith, Schoenberg, and Alban Berg, frequently used the sonata form,[2] as do a host of more conventional composers.

Close examination, however, will show that the form has been considerably modified. As a result, it is necessary to broaden the concept of the form. Historically, the sonata form was originally based on the firm establishment of the major-minor key system and on the principles of functional harmony. It does not follow, however, that this form could not fulfill the needs of another stylistic period with a different harmonic orientation. The fact that composers find the sonata form suitable in a completely different harmonic climate only demonstrates its deeply rooted, almost archetypal significance. The presentation of contrasting or differing musical ideas, their development, and their eventual return, however tenuous or distorted the return may be, still satisfies some very deep psychological and symbolic need.

Generally, sonata form in the eighteenth and nineteenth centuries assumed a somewhat modified symmetrical arrangement, achieving centrality through the principle of tonality that resulted in the reconciliation of basically antagonistic harmonic forces. In the twentieth century the form still entails a contrast between musical ideas though it is not necessarily built upon the antagonistic values of functional harmonies. The outcome, reached after maintaining a semblance of ternary design, may be extremely tenuous, the ending of a composition may only hint at a tonal center, or it may offer no reconciliation or resolu-

---

[2]The problem of the employment of sonata form in atonal and twelve-tone music will be considered in the next chapter.

tion. The latter cases resemble the plots of some modern plays, such as Becket's *Waiting for Godot* or Pirandello's *Six Characters in Search of an Author,* where irresolution is resolution.

The novel approach to sonata form in the twentieth century shows two distinguishing features: first, a new harmonic approach; second, changes in structural processes. The new harmonic devices are numerous, such as new key relationships replacing the tonic-dominant axis; tonality built rather *on* a key than *in* a key; bitonal ramifications and even avoidance of any sense of tonality. Structural changes involve extreme condensations, distorting of motives, hinting at motives instead of restating them, and rearrangement of the order of the ideas in the recapitulation. Most modern sonata-form movements have an open structure throughout all three sections; thus the exposition (and recapitulation, too) will be governed by musical processes similar to those of the development. Among all the outstanding twentieth-century composers Bartók stands closest to the model of the classical composers, particularly to Beethoven, both in the presentation of his ideas, and in the use of connecting bridge sections that link musical ideas together.

While it is impossible to render a complete list of all the harmonic and structural innovations that have been applied to sonata form in the twentieth century, a few examples are offered to make the earlier points more concrete. Additional examples may be found in Eschman's interesting study.[3]

For a novel key relationship between main theme and second theme, Hindemith's Oboe Sonata should be cited; here, instead of a tonic-dominant pattern, a *half-step* relationship is established in the first movement. Thus, while the main theme is centered on G, the second theme appears on F sharp (one half step below) in the exposition, and on A flat (one half step above) in the recapitulation. In his Viola Sonata, Op. 11, No. 4, both the main theme and the second theme appear a whole step higher in the recapitulation than in the exposition.

The practice of using all twelve steps of a key, centering on one note, as mentioned in the chapter on harmony, is often used as a harmonic framework for sonata form. In this setting the chromatic notes no longer have an auxiliary function. Bartók and Hindemith often use this approach to tonality, varying considerably as to the emphasis placed on the central note. At times it will dominate from the outset, setting up a fairly strong sense of centricity, while in other cases the feeling of a tonal center emerges only at the end of the composition and is experienced as a hard-won reconciliation. Thus, the C emerges as the central tone at the end of the first movement of Bartók's Fourth Quartet, yet the movement could not be looked upon as being in C major or minor. There are cases also of bitonal setting, suggesting

[3] Karl Eschman, *Changing Forms in Modern Music* (Boston: E. C. Schirmer, 1945).

two tonal centers from the beginning of a movement, such as in the first movement of Bartók's *Sonata for Two Pianos and Percussion*.

Structural changes often consist of reversing the order of appearance of the material in the recapitulation; for example, in the recapitulation of the first movement of Bartók's Fifth String Quartet the material appears in reversed order and is also inverted. Similar instances of rearrangement may be found in works by Prokofiev, Hindemith, and others.

A more specific instance of a changed harmonic setting may be found in the first movement of Bartók's Second Quartet; here, the same melody receives a completely different harmonic treatment in the recapitulation as compared to the exposition. Example 6/3/a contains the setting of the exposition, and Example 6/3/b that of the recapitulation:

EX. 6/3/a BARTÓK, *Second Quartet*,[4] first movement, opening

EX. 6/3/b Recapitulation, 6 mm. before study no. 17

[4]Copyright 1920 by Universal Edition; renewed 1948. Copyright and renewal assigned to Boosey & Hawkes, Inc. for the U.S.A. Reprinted by permission.

In other cases the rhythmic shape of the melody is changed in the recapitulation, a device that has no precedent in sonata-form movements of the eighteenth or nineteenth centuries. Examples 6/4/a and b show the two versions of the main theme from the second movement of Bartók's *Music for Strings, Celesta and Percussion:*[5]

EX. 6/4/a Main theme in exposition, mm. 5–7

EX. 6/4/b Main theme in recapitulation, mm. 373–375

Among all twentieth-century composers Bartók preserves most strongly the essential qualities of sonata form (duality of ideas, their development, and eventual restatement). To demonstrate this point, a comparison of the first movement of Beethoven's Fifth Symphony and the first movement of Bartók's Fourth Quartet follows. Similarities in musical thinking of the two composers have been mentioned by several writers. The comparison also shows that sonata form does not have to deteriorate into thematic formalism—as claimed by some writers—if transferred to a nontriadic context.

First, the proportions of the two movements are outlined in the following chart.

Proportion of Sections of the First Movements of Beethoven's Fifth Symphony and Bartók's Fourth Quartet

	Exposition	Development	Recapitulation	Coda
	Number of Measures			
Beethoven	124	122	123	129
	(62)	(61)	(61)	(64)
Bartók	49	47	28	34

[5]Copyright 1937 by Universal Edition; renewed 1964. Copyright and renewal assigned to Boosey & Hawkes, Inc. Reprinted by permission.

In order to achieve equalization, the number of measures referring to the Beethoven movement are divided by two (numbers in parentheses) because the meter of this movement is $\frac{2}{4}$ while the Bartók movement is in $\frac{4}{4}$ meter. The fact that the metronome indication is slower for the Bartók movement is another factor to be considered when judging the size of the movements.

As seen from the preceding chart, the proportions of the exposition and development are surprisingly similar; in both works they are of almost equal size, with slightly longer expositions than developments in both cases. The drastically abbreviated recapitulation of the Bartók shows the modern composer's disinclination to follow strict symmetry and his preference for condensation instead of repetition. The Bartók coda, though shorter both in absolute and relative size than Beethoven's coda, stands in a similar proportion to the recapitulation as the Beethoven coda. Incidentally, it should be noted that in the Beethoven movement the coda is the longest section among the four subdivisions. The two codas are also similar in their dynamic levels: 120 measures of Beethoven's 128 are *forte* or *fortissimo,* and most of Bartók's coda is marked *marcatissimo* and *sforzato* with 25 of its 34 measures marked *forte* or louder.

A closer examination of the two expositions shows in both movements a dramatic, strong main theme with more emphasis on rhythm than on melody:

EX. 6/5/a BEETHOVEN, *Fifth Symphony,* first movement, main theme, opening

EX. 6/5/b BARTÓK, *Fourth Quartet,*[6] first movement, main theme, m. 7

The second theme in both works consists of a melodic, lyric, and soft musical idea:

[6]Copyright 1929 by Universal Edition; renewed 1956. Copyright and renewal assigned to Boosey & Hawkes, Inc. for the U.S.A. Reprinted by permission.

EX. 6/6/a Secondary theme of Beethoven's *Fifth Symphony,* first movement, mm. 63–66

EX. 6/6/b Secondary theme of Bartók's *Fourth Quartet,* first movement, mm. 16–17

The significant point is that, although melodically and harmonically the ideas represent a completely different musical style, the psychological confrontation of a strong, dramatic, masculine theme with a lyric feminine theme is characteristic for both works.

The key relationship between the main theme and secondary theme is the conventional one in the Beethoven with C minor turning to the relative major, E flat, at the entrance of the secondary theme. This key is then maintained throughout the exposition. The recapitulation re-affirms C minor, of course, although the second theme is presented in the tonic major (C major) in which key the recapitulation ends. It is only in the coda that the minor modality is recaptured and impressed on the listener.

The tonal framework of the Bartók is much more tenuous; the end of the movement suggests C as the focal point. Going backward from there, additional evidence for the centricity of C is suggested at the beginning of the coda (m. 126) where a canon starts, built on C in all four instruments. Additional evidence for the supremacy of the C is found in mm. 92–93, at which point the recapitulation occurs with the phrase leaning on C:

EX. 6/7 BARTÓK, *Fourth Quartet,* first movement, mm. 92–93

The first two notes of the movement (low C in the cello and E in the second violin) also suggest an orientation toward C, regardless of how short-lived the suggestion is.

Although the second theme is melodically pivoted around C sharp, D sharp, and G sharp, the lower instruments, particularly the viola (mm. 14–18), are anchored on C.

Beyond the suggested instances, there is no sense of C major or minor in the movement; after close familiarity, however, one gains the feeling that the C is a preferred tone, representing the tonal destination of the movement.

The tenuous centricity of C may explain the final outcome of the movement, although there are more important harmonic events to consider. These consist of two tone clusters, one made up of whole steps and the other of half steps, which often are juxtaposed. These two intervals are basic to the melodic-harmonic conception of the entire quartet.

The scheme of dynamics is also similar; in both movements the ratio of loud dynamics to soft dynamics is approximately 4:1. There is a difference in the dynamic devices, however. Beethoven often uses sustained crescendi, whereas Bartók prefers to change from soft to loud more abruptly without a transition. Based on evidence of other works, it might be said that composers of the twentieth century, more often than not, avoid long waves of crescendi. The reason for this is probably that such dynamic occurrences are usually associated with a certain type of expressiveness and clear-cut goal-directedness that run counter to purposes of the composer of the twentieth century. Additionally, the long waves of crescendi in nineteenth-century music were often supporting certain harmonic destinations (for instance, the dominant pedal point), which disappeared from the vocabulary of more advanced twentieth-century composers.

Although sonata form remains as a living force in twentieth-century music, a large portion of contemporary music follows a new kind of organization in first movements of larger works, for which neither terminology or analytic procedures have been codified. Stravinsky, for instance, often opens a movement with a terse rhythmic motive followed by an organizational method that could be called "additive," in the course of which new cells are derived from the opening motive, propelled forward by rhythmic forces. In such a case, it is difficult to distinguish the sections; the harmonic procedures also seem to be placed in the service of the manipulation of the motive instead of delineating sections by virtue of clear-cut cadences.

In some very recent music, new expressive forms are derived from transformations of timbre, densities, and registers. Associations of differentiated and undifferentiated pitch and texture as the basis of organization can be found in Carter's *Double Concerto for Piano and Harpsichord* (see Chapter 16).

The search for new forms is one of the most crucial questions of twentieth-century music, notwithstanding the fact that a large group of composers have adapted the traditional forms to their needs. A number of new approaches and experiments will be the subject of the next chapter.

NOVEL PROCEDURES IN MUSICAL CONSTRUCTION:

Serialism, Chance Music, and Electronic Music

SERIALISM

Serialism, or "serial techniques," represents a novel approach to composition. It implies a succession of one or more elements of music being ordered according to a predetermined plan. This approach has become one of the most important movements in the music of the twentieth century.

The first and decisive phase of serialism was initiated by Arnold Schoenberg, who, in the early 1920s, after a search of about twelve years, invented his epoch-making method of composition with twelve tones, a serialization of the twelve pitches contained in the chromatic scale. These twelve pitches appear and reappear throughout the composition in a predetermined order.

Although serialism regulates certain aspects of the musical construction, it does not automatically yield over-all compositional forms, at least not in the traditional meaning of the word. Actually, forms have to be superimposed on the serial procedures.

With regard to the twelve-tone method, at first it appeared to remain the exclusive property of its inventor and his two outstanding disciples, Alban Berg and Anton Webern. After World War II, however, when communications among the various musical centers were re-established, it became clear that the method had an unexpectedly wide appeal. Almost every country developed its own twelve-tone school, representing a wide spectrum of styles.

It also became evident that much wider possibilities were offered by serialism than was foreseen by its originator. Rhythmic values, intensities, and timbres—called parameters in the new terminology—were also subjected to serial procedures. On the international scene, Germany, Italy, and France were particularly active in the more advanced forms of serialism. England, on the other hand, was the least affected by the new movement. In the Soviet orbit, serialism was not accepted and performances of serial works were banned. In the past few years, however, there have been signs of a more liberal attitude.

It should be noted that even within the Western world an intense controversy surrounds serial music. The emotionalism of the attacks surpasses in bitterness even the Wagner-Brahms conflict of the nineteenth century.

FOUNDATIONS OF TWELVE-TONE MUSIC

The theoretical and esthetic foundations for the method were laid down in Schoenberg's essay *Composition with Twelve Tones*,[1] originally delivered in lecture form at the University of California. Now a historic document, it reflects not only Schoenberg's musical thinking, but also gives one a glimpse of the author's personality. Schoenberg feels that in the new method he brought a vision to life. This vision is likened to the creation of the Divine Model, although it is admitted that human creation has a hard path to travel from vision to enactment. As one reads the essay, one is impressed by the strength of conviction; the motto is the belief in the infallibility of one's inspiration. The writing

[1] Arnold Schoenberg, "Composition with Twelve Tones," *Style and Idea* (New York: Philosophical Library, Inc., 1950).

often has an almost biblical quality, as if it were a prophet's proclamation of new commandments.

One of the main points in Schoenberg's presentation is that twelve-tone music was created by *necessity*. His point of departure is the harmonic evolution that took place in the second half of the nineteenth century. He describes how Wagner's chromaticism and Debussy's nonfunctional harmonies progressively weakened the feeling of tonality. As a result of these developments Schoenberg in 1908 took the final step; in the last movement of his Second Quartet he renounced tonality altogether. No key center is established in this free, atonal style (see Chapter 4) and functional harmonic values cease to exist. On the surface it seemed that only a harmonic revolution had occurred; the new style, however, affected every compositional element. Atonal music had different melodic, rhythmic, and dynamic values, but more than any other feature, it was the organizational aspect of the music that was most critically affected. As was pointed out in Chapter 4, in tonal music small and large units rest on pillars created by triadic functional harmonies. Tonal music literally "progressed" due to the harmonic motion or progressions. Now without these harmonic goals, which furnished continuity as well as destination to the music, composition has become problematical. Suddenly the standard modes of structural differentiations (cadences, paragraphs, and sentences), were not at the composer's disposal. The crisis in achieving musical continuity manifested itself in the extreme brevity of the compositions written during this period. It should be mentioned parenthetically, that this extreme brevity was coupled with intense expressiveness, with the result that the term *expressionism* was used to describe this stylistic development.

From Schoenberg's account one learns that the period of free atonality was short-lived and was followed by silence for almost twelve years. During these years, the composer "laid the foundations for a new procedure in musical construction which seemed fitted to replace those structural differentiations provided formerly by tonal harmonies."[2]

The new method, the method of composing with twelve tones—dodecaphony—was invented to provide order and discipline for the anarchic state of free atonality. Schoenberg even went beyond these aims, however, claiming that the new method brought comprehensibility to atonal music.

Schoenberg asserts that the new laws and rules of the method were conceived "as in a dream." But, regardless of how convincing the dream was, he felt that he had to prove that the "new sounds obey the laws of nature."

Up to this point Schoenberg's argument shows some ambivalence.

---

[2]*Style and Idea*, p. 107.

On the one hand, he claims *historical necessity* for the emergence of his method; on the other, he presents its inception as a completely intuitive, creative act. Perhaps the stress on intuition was a premature defense against the anticipated attacks which were to accuse the composer of a cerebral and mathematical approach to music.

Schoenberg bases his claim for historical necessity on two considerations; first, that the motivic use of the twelve half steps of the chromatic scale was in the air in the second half of the nineteenth century; second, that during the same period attempts were already made to view the horizontal (melodic) and vertical (harmonic) aspects as a unified field.

For the first item illustrations can be found in the music of Wagner, Scriabin, Richard Strauss, and others. In Example 7/1 a motive from Wagner's *Tristan* demonstrates this point, in which all steps but one of the chromatic scale occur, without the repetition of any step.

EX. 7/1 WAGNER, *Tristan und Isolde,* Act I, Scene 1, mm. 26–27

Another example of a motive using the twelve half steps occurs in the fugue theme of Richard Strauss' *Thus Spake Zarathustra:*[3]

EX. 7/2 Mm. 1–4, p. 61 (min. score)

One can see from Schoenberg's first twelve-tone compositions that his thinking was influenced by such examples. In the fourth movement of his Septet, Op. 24, for instance, the twelve-tone motive appears melodically—in a continuous line in the voice and fragmented in the instruments—in a way similar to the purely horizontal method used by his predecessors. The difference between Strauss' and Schoenberg's treatment is that in Schoenberg the twelve-tone motive *recurs* throughout the movement retaining the same pitch order, but with great

---

[3] Reprinted by permission of the publishers, C. F. Peters Corporation, New York.

rhythmic freedom and an unrestricted use of any octave register. In Example 7/3, three melodic recurrences of the motive can be seen as they appear in the vocal line.

EX. 7/3 SCHOENBERG, *Serenade,*[4] Op. 24, fourth movement, mm. 6–14

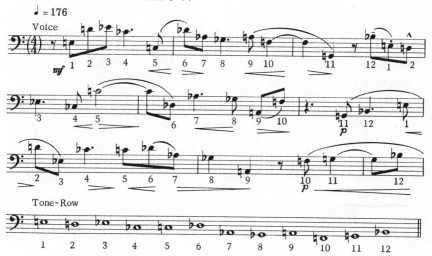

Concerning the historical antecedents of the second item—the unified melodic-harmonic field—illustrations can be found in the music of Scriabin and Brahms. In the former's late piano sonatas the "mystic" chord governs both melodic and harmonic events (see Chapter 8). Brahms' awareness of the "two-dimensional musical field" can be observed in Example 7/4 where the notes of the melody, played by the first violin, also appear in the accompaniment of the cello, but with different rhythmic values:

EX. 7/4 BRAHMS, *String Quartet in A minor,* Op. 51, No. 2, fourth movement, mm. 198–199

[4]Copyright 1925 and 1953 by Wilhelm Hansen, Copenhagen. By permission of the publishers and Mrs. Gertrud Schoenberg.

Schoenberg, however, went far beyond such an isolated instance of two-dimensionality; in his Piano Suite, Op. 25, a consistent two- (or more) dimensional use of the set can be seen. Melody, harmony, and contrapuntal lines are all derived from the same set throughout the five movements of the composition.

Summarizing Schoenberg's claim for historical necessity, it has been shown that both the motivic use of the twelve chromatic half steps and the unity of the melodic and the harmonic complex have occurred to other composers, but in a much more haphazard fashion.

There is even a possibility that composition with twelve-tone rows was anticipated by another composer. Contemporaneously with Schoenberg, Josef Matthias Hauer[5] invented a twelve-tone method. Since Hauer's method was much more limited, the priority of authorship is of no great significance. Hauer's twelve-tone rows were subdivided into two tone-rows (tropes), each consisting of six tones and used similarly to the older conception of scales. On the whole, Hauer's method lacked the scope and freedom characteristic of Schoenberg's formulations.

COMPOSITION WITH TWELVE TONES

The main feature of Schoenberg's method is the constant and exclusive use of one set of twelve different tones. The set (or tone row) contains the twelve tones of the chromatic scale arranged in a different order for each composition. A set of twelve tones appears in Example 7/5; it is the set upon which all five movements of Schoenberg's Piano Suite, Op. 25, are based.

EX. 7/5 Prime set of Schoenberg's *Piano Suite,* Op. 25

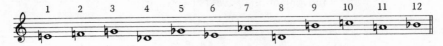

The first appearance of the set has been termed "original set," "basic set," "prime set," or *Grundgestalt* in German. In accordance with the terminology suggested by Babbitt, the term *prime set* (P) will be used.

Deeply steeped in the art of polyphony, Schoenberg applied certain contrapuntal devices (inversion, crab-forms) to the prime set, gaining three additional forms.

[5] Josef Matthias Hauer, *Zwölftontechnik* (Vienna, 1925).

EX. 7/5/a *Inversion* of the prime set (I)

EX. 7/5/b Backward, or *retrograde,* form of the prime set (R)

EX. 7/5/c *Retrograde inverted* form of the prime set (RI)

These mirror forms are not as arbitrary as they may seem to the reader who has a limited background in the history of music. Both Schoenberg and Rufer[6] emphasize the fact that these mirror forms were commonly used in the music of the fifteenth and sixteenth centuries.

In Schoenberg's new method, however, these various mirror forms were more than mere contrapuntal devices; they became an important part of his theory, the theory of multidimensional musical space. According to this theory, a musical idea, such as a tone row, may be allowed a change in its form of appearance in the field of perception. Whether a tone row appears horizontally (melodically), or vertically (harmonically), from left to right, from right to left (retrograde), upside down, or downside up (inversion), it retains its essential identity. In support of this theory, Schoenberg uses the analogy that an object, such as a knife, a bottle, or a watch remains the same knife, bottle, or watch from whichever side it is viewed.

In addition to the mirror forms, each set can be "transposed," that is, appear on any of the remaining eleven half steps of the chromatic scale; this way—four forms of the set in twelve transpositions—forty-eight sets can be realized. If a set appears in a transposition, an arabic index number will signify the level of transposition, employing half steps as a unit and using as a basis the first tone of the particular set that is to be transposed. Thus, R_3 means a transposition of the retrograde set, three half steps higher than the first degree of the R set. Using the example of the prime set of the Piano Suite, Op. 25, R_3 appears as follows:

[6]Josef Rufer, *Composition with Twelve Notes* (New York: Crowell-Collier and Macmillan Company, Inc., 1954).

Ex. 7/6 R₃ form of set

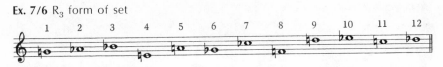

Any of the forty-eight derivations of the set may appear separately, or several forms of the set may be simultaneously combined.

RULES GOVERNING SET OPERATIONS

Horizontal and Vertical Use of the Set   The twelve tones of any of the forty-eight forms of the set may be used: a) purely as a melodic line; b) divided in such a way that some notes appear in the melodic line and others in chords, figurations, or contrapuntal lines; and c) all notes of the set may be grouped into one or several vertical aggregates (chords).

Repetition of Notes   The main rule concerning repetition of notes is that a note should not be repeated until its "turn" comes up again, that is, until after the other eleven notes have been used. This rule, however, has been misinterpreted even by Schoenberg's most authentic spokesman, Josef Rufer, who implies that a single note cannot be reiterated except under special circumstances. It is obvious from Schoenberg's music (see the six repeated B flats in m. 3 of Ex. 7/8/a) that he did not rule out the repetition of a single note with no other intervening notes. A reiterated note has no bearing on the pitch order and does not endanger the set structure. Often, a note is repeated to lend a salient rhythmic feature to a motive; as for instance in the second measure (Ex. 7/7) of Schoenberg's Fourth Quartet:[7]

EX. 7/7 First movement, opening

A note may also be repeated if otherwise, due to the limitations of the instrument, the sound could not be sustained for the desired length of time.

Use of Octaves and Their Doublings   Each note of the sets can appear in any octave register. The free use of octave equivalents often

---

[7]Quoted by permission of Mrs. Gertrud Schoenberg and Universal Edition, publishers of the first edition.

results in the characteristic, jagged melodic line found in Schoenberg's music. There are twelve-tone composers, however, who make less use of octave equivalence; for instance, Dallapiccola's style shows a rather consistent use of the same register, whereby his music is vocally less forbidding than melodic lines of Schoenberg or Webern. Another consequence of octave equivalence is that the original intervals may be replaced by their complementary intervals. Thus, a minor third

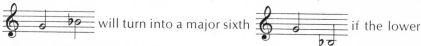 will turn into a major sixth if the lower

octave of the B flat is used.

Doubling of octaves should be avoided, according to Schoenberg, because the emphasis of doubling may inadvertently suggest a root or possibly a tonic chord. Such tonal suggestions seem completely alien to the basic premises of the method.

Keeping these rules in mind and the fact that any rhythmic value can be attached to the pitches of the sets as they appear and reappear, the reader can judge for himself the degree of freedom the method gives in forming a variety of musical ideas and shapes by studying Examples 7/8/a–e, which contain the opening measures of various movements of the Piano Suite, Op. 25:

EX. 7/8/a SCHOENBERG, *Piano Suite*, Op. 25,[8] Prelude, opening

EX. 7/8/b Gavotte, opening

[8]Quoted by permission of Mrs. Gertrud Schoenberg and Universal Edition, publishers of the first edition.

EX. 7/8/c Musette, opening

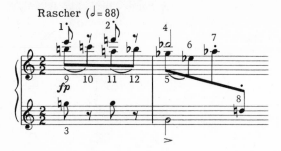

EX. 7/8/d Menuett, opening

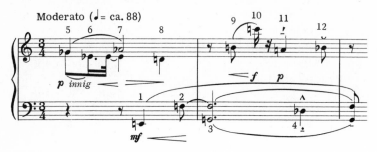

EX. 7/8/e Gigue, opening

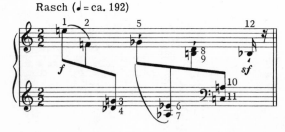

By sounding the openings of the various movements on the piano, the reader can also judge the validity of Schoenberg's analogy of the knife; in other words, is the identity of the set perceptible in the openings of the different movements?

More often than not, a composition will begin with the prime set; that this is not an absolute rule can be seen from Example 7/8/d, in which 5 and 6 are stated first.

Whether the prime set is used thematically, as a continuous melodic line with a sharp rhythmic profile, or whether the set is immediately broken up into its segments, will vary from composition to composition. Schoenberg was inclined to follow the first course, as seen in

Example 7/9, which contains the opening theme of the first movement of the Fourth Quartet.

EX. 7/9 SCHOENBERG, *Fourth Quartet,* first movement, opening
(partial score)

In Example 7/10, containing the second movement of Webern's *Concerto for Nine Instruments,* an immediate breaking up of the prime set is in evidence.

EX. 7/10 WEBERN, *Concerto for Nine Instruments,*[9] second movement, opening

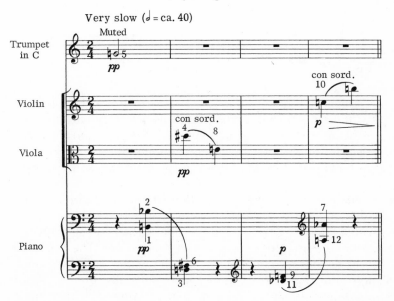

Webern's preference for the broken up patterns of the set, often referred to as pointillistic, was taken over by avant-garde serialists,

[9]Copyright by Universal Edition, Vienna. Used by permission.

members of the so-called Darmstadt School, who are sometimes labeled post-Webernites.

Intervallic Structure of the Set   The choice of intervals that make up a set is subject to careful consideration by the composer. At this point the composer has to decide on the matrix from which his vision will best be realized. The choice of intervals will determine both the melodic and the harmonic aspects of the work. Schoenberg's formulation, however, that the "set functions in the manner of a motive" is often quite misleading. Even Schoenberg himself at times breaks up his set at the beginning of a composition, as in the three four-part chords in his Piano Piece, Op. 33a.

In determining his set Schoenberg was very careful to avoid any sequence of intervals that would form triads or any intervallic structure that would establish a tonal feeling, since the raison d'être of the set was the organization of atonal music. Very soon, however, this original consideration appeared less cogent. Schoenberg's student, Alban Berg, for instance, constructed sets, which by using intervals that formed triads, achieved strong tonal feeling. The prime set of Berg's Violin Concerto demonstrates this point (Ex. 7/11).

EX. 7/11 Prime set

Another aspect of the intervallic structure of the set is the repetition of intervals; the repetition of certain intervals may facilitate the comprehension of the composition, particularly if the repeated interval is easy to grasp. In other cases, however, the repetition of a certain interval may be motivated by the intention to create specially dissonant harmonies.

Segmentation   The prime set is often so constructed that it naturally divides into patterns of subdivisions (segments). Thus, the set can be divided into two segments of six tones (hexachords), three segments of four tones, or four segments of three tones. The prime set of the first movement of Schoenberg's Fourth Quartet, seen in Example 7/9, falls into four segments of three tones. Generally, the division of the set into segments allows freer motivic treatment; it also makes contrapuntal devices (imitation and canon) more feasible than if the set were always treated as a whole. As expressed by Křenek: "The virtue of the twelve-tone technique does not lie in the mechanical omnipresence of the entire row, but rather in the unification of the design through tightly related motivic patterns."[10]

One way of naturally arriving at segmentation that has the quality of motivic unity is the symmetrical construction of the tone row. Webern was particularly fond of this device. In Example 7/12 the prime set of his *Concerto for Nine Instruments* is shown; here, the four segments of the set mirror each other.

EX. 7/12 Prime set

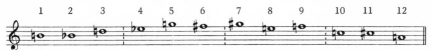

A special case of set construction known as the principle of combinatoriality was employed first by Schoenberg, but its theoretical implications have been developed by Babbitt.[11] Combinatoriality arises if the prime set is constructed in such a way that the first hexachord of one of its transformations—other than its retrograde—does not contain any pitch in common with the first hexachord of the prime set (the same applies, of course, to the second hexachord). An example can be observed in Schoenberg's Fourth Quartet, where the combination of P with I_5 achieves the conditions described above:

EX. 7/13

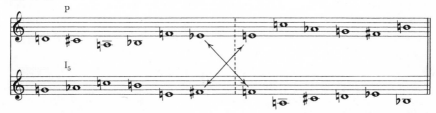

In Example 7/13 the first hexachords of P and I_5 encompass the total chromatic span, and the same is true of the two second hexachords. From this it follows that the pitch content of the first hexachord of P is identical with that of the second hexachord of I_5, the only difference being in the order of the pitches. (The same is true of the first hexachord of I_5 and the second hexachord of P). The most obvious advantage of the association of the two sets is that in vertical combinations the same pitch does not appear too close.

---

[10] Ernst Křenek, "Is the Twelve-Tone Technique on the Decline?" *Musical Quarterly,* **39**, No. 4 (1953), p. 521.

[11] Milton Babbitt, "Some Aspects of Twelve-Tone Music," *The SCORE and IMA Magazine* (June 1955).

CRITIQUE OF THE TWELVE-TONE METHOD

The twelve-tone method of composition is a subject of intense controversy. There is a small "in-group" closely allied with Schoenberg whose members believe in the "cause" with the fervor of cultists. Among them are Křenek[12] and Leibowitz,[13] both serial composers. Their writings, particularly those of Leibowitz, contain more idolatry and praise for Schoenberg's method and music than objective evaluation. Josef Rufer, a former student of the master, is another member of the group. His volume on twelve-tone music[14] is a detailed analysis of the method. Stuckenschmidt,[15] a German critic and Schoenberg's biographer, and Adorno, a musicologist, social scientist, and a former pupil of Alban Berg, are additional members of the group.

A positive but objective view of the method is expressed by both Babbitt and Perle,[16] American serial composers. Their writings contain valuable contributions to the literature of the twelve-tone method and to serialism in general.

The opposition, often no less dogmatic and partisan than the Schoenberg group, is represented by both a conservative and a radical wing. The conservatives attack twelve-tone music with the same vehemence with which they oppose atonal music (see Chapter 4). In their opinion the method is arbitrary, cerebral, and produces disastrous music. Of the conservatives Hindemith carries the greatest musical weight. He considers the music produced by the twelve-tone method a "nightmare," one of the "ugliest modern musical diseases." According to him, the twelve-tone method

> ignores the validity of harmonic and melodic values derived from mathematical, physical, or psychological experience; it does not take into account . . . many other facts either of natural permanence or proven usefulness. Its main "law" is supplemented by other rules of equal arbitrariness, such as: tones must not be repeated; your selected tone series may skip from one stratum of the texture to any other one; you have to use the inversion and other distortions of this series; and so on, all of which can be reduced to general advice: avoid so far as possible anything that has been written before.[17]

[12] Ernst Křenek, *Music Here and Now* (New York: W. W. Norton & Company, Inc., 1939).

[13] René Leibowitz, *Schoenberg and His School* (New York: Philosophical Library, Inc., 1949).

[14] *Composition with Twelve Notes.*

[15] H. H. Stuckenschmidt, *Arnold Schoenberg* (New York: Grove Press, Inc., 1959).

[16] George Perle, *Serial Composition and Atonality* (Los Angeles: University of California Press, 1962).

[17] Paul Hindemith, *The Composer's World* (New York: Doubleday & Company, Inc., 1962), p. 140.

In a brief digression from the survey of criticism, the attitudes of Stravinsky and Bartók regarding serialism will be considered.

For a long time Stravinsky was considered the polar opposite of Schoenberg in his thinking. In his later years, however, he became attracted to serial composition. Since 1950, most of his music is based on some form of serialism.

Bartók remained aloof from twelve-tone music; attempts by some writers to discern serial principles in his music seem to be far-fetched. Motivic unity and occasional correlations between the melodic and the harmonic dimensions are not enough evidence to label Bartók a serialist.

In the polemical writings concerning the twelve-tone method Schoenberg was seriously criticized by the avant-garde too. They felt that Schoenberg did not go far enough and that he adhered too strongly to traditional music. In the view of the avant-garde, particularly represented by the composers of the Darmstadt School (Stockhausen, Boulez, and Nono), Schoenberg has been by-passed and dethroned. Boulez notes that Schoenberg *IS DEAD* (italics his) not only physically, but also musically.[18] These composers did not understand how Schoenberg could be satisfied with the mere serialization of pitches, when rhythmic values, intensities, and timbres could also be serialized. Their criticism concerning Schoenberg's use of traditional forms, such as the sonata form, and his flirtation with tonality in his late style, will be discussed later in this chapter.

Disregarding the minority view of the avant-garde, it is not difficult to understand why the musical world was shocked by Schoenberg's method. In the first place, the romantic idea of inspiration and expressiveness was still too close to most musicians for them not to be shocked by the cerebral manipulations of the row techniques. Moreover, the method did not evolve gradually from established musical practices, but appeared suddenly as an emergency solution to *one* composer's musical crisis. Schoenberg started out with the rules, whereas in the history of music rules are usually codified *after* certain practices are crystallized.

The dispassionate student of contemporary music who is without any partisan involvement will be more interested in clarifying the theoretical premises of Schoenberg's method than in expressing one-sided praise or blind intolerance. One theoretical point in particular needs clarification: what is the nature and function of the tone row? Does the method have validity only according to Schoenberg's strictures, or is any approach to the method acceptable as long as the musical results are satisfactory?

[18] Pierre Boulez, "Schoenberg is Dead," *The SCORE and IMA Magazine* (May 1952).

The difficulty in answering the first question lies partly in Schoenberg's ambiguous theoretical formulations; the second question arose because the method opened up more musical possibilities than was foreseen by its inventor. Even the three Viennese "founding fathers" used the method in distinctly different ways, apart from the diversity found in the works of German, Italian, French, and American followers.

With regard to the nature of the tone row, Schoenberg held that, as a rule, it functions in the manner of a motive. Despite the motivic role he ascribed to the tone row, he repeatedly emphasized that the listener need not familiarize himself either with the construction or the sound of the row. These two thoughts are difficult to reconcile. If the tone row represents a certain configuration of notes whose purpose is to bring unity and comprehensibility to the music, why should the listener not familiarize himself with it? Familiarity with the tone row would seem as desirable as acquaintance with the *theme* in a theme and variation movement. Schoenberg's position would be more tenable if he did not consider the tone row as a motivic unit, but rather a "precompositional" element or a musical matrix, that serves as a basis for structural unity. Seen in this light, the use of the tone row would constitute a modus operandi that truly belongs to the composer's workshop. An examination of Schoenberg's twelve-tone works reveals his ambivalent attitude toward the function of the row, as has been pointed out.

It seems evident that if the tone row is used as a motive, then the listener should familiarize himself with it and seek out its salient intervallic characteristics, as should be done with any music in any style. If, on the other hand, the tone row is not used in the form of a melodic unit or configuration, but only as a source in the musical substratum, from which motivic cells are derived, then familiarity with the tone row will be of little help. A large number of repeated hearings, however, will probably lead to a conscious or semiconscious perception of unity.

In any case, whether the row is used more or less in the manner of a motive, it would be preferable to abandon the notion that the aim of the tone row (or in a larger sense that of the twelve-tone method) is to provide *comprehensibility*, as claimed by Schoenberg. The postulation of comprehensibility as one of the aims of twelve-tone music may be construed by hostile criticism as the failure of the method, since even after almost half a century, the majority of listeners still fail to comprehend music written in this style. Sometimes even the highly trained ear is unable to grasp the complex relationships that appear as a result of combining various forms of the forty-eight sets. Example 7/14 shows an instance of bewildering complexity; in this excerpt from the last movement of Schoenberg's Third Quartet the twelve notes of the set are divided among the four instruments.

EX. 7/14 SCHOENBERG, *Third Quartet,*[19] last movement, opening

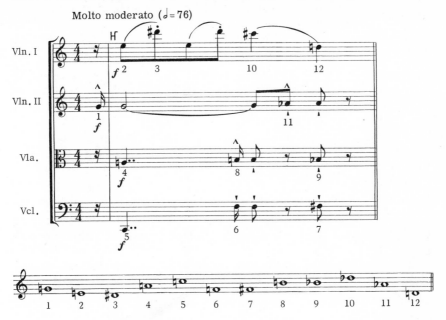

It should be obvious that such a web of voices cannot provide comprehensibility in terms of understanding and perception of the musical processes. It would be more modest and realistic to consider the method as a principle or technique of musical construction aimed at providing unity. The multidimensional use of the row also points more to its unifying role than to its Gestalt qualities. Schoenberg's analogy that a bottle remains a bottle whether viewed from one side or the other, or from above or below, seriously underestimates the complexity of aural perception compared to visual perception. A retrograde, inverted form of the prime set, combined with one of its transposed forms —keeping in mind that the rhythmic values may be freely modified— will hardly produce the kind of comprehensibility gained by looking at a bottle from above or below. Thus, Schoenberg's categorical formulation that the "employment of these mirror forms corresponds to the principles of the absolute and unitary perception of musical space" seems highly questionable.

The twelve-tone method, however, has validity as an organizational procedure that contains entirely new possibilities in achieving unity in musical construction. The processes entailed in operations with tone rows, as claimed by Schoenberg and others, stand closer to thematic

---

[19]Quoted by permission of Mrs. Gertrud Schoenberg and Universal Edition, publishers of the first edition.

transformation than to perpetual variation. Perle views the technique as a manifestation of the ostinato principle, while in another instance he also agrees with the idea of perpetual variation.

In the author's view it is misleading to think of twelve-tone compositions as having the characteristics of musical variations. Variation in music presupposes two criteria: first, that a theme should be subjected to modifications; second, that the treatment be sectional. In twelve-tone music, as a rule, neither of the two criteria is in evidence because the row often does not have the quality of a theme or motive and, furthermore, the various reappearances of the set are not delineated by any kind of paragraphing as occurs in any type of variation form. It is true, of course, that the *principle* of variation does manifest itself, but the musical process as such is perhaps closer to a subtle and perpetual thematic transformation. A comparison of the main theme of the first movement of Schoenberg's Fourth Quartet with that of the opening of the slow movement (Ex. 7/15 and 7/15/a) should make the point clear as to why the process of row operations stands closer to thematic transformation than to variation technique. In fact, the example reveals the kinship with the Lisztian type of thematic transformation.

EX. 7/15 SCHOENBERG, *Fourth Quartet,* first movement, opening

EX 7/15a Third movement, opening

The twelve tones of the row could be looked upon as a root rather than a theme (Křenek calls it "common denominator") from which musical life springs, pervading every aspect of the composition. In another formulation it could be said that the set contains certain precompositional conditions out of which the composer's vision will bring to fruition the final work of art. As stated earlier, the method represents a modus operandi and should not be taken, as unfortunately happens very often, as a modus vivendi. What should be understood is that the set, and operations with the set, do not furnish unity, per se; the method is merely a means toward achieving unity. As Roger Sessions has stated:

> Like any other technical principle it (serialism) yields nothing in itself; it is always for the imagination of the composer to discover what it can give him, and to mold it to his own uses. Like any other technical principle, it has to be thoroughly mastered, in terms of the composer's creative vision . . . . For this reason the young composer who has not grown up with it from the beginning . . . would be well advised to avoid it until he has become sure of his own musical identity, and can grow into it in full conviction and genuine musical maturity. It does not provide answers to all musical questions or in the last analysis to any; it is only a vehicle, and a means, which, let us reiterate, many composers find useful.[20]

The point is that the method does not work as a formula. In inept hands the method does *not* replace the structural differentiations once derived from tonality. Therefore, the twelve-tone method cannot be looked upon as conceptually comparable to tonality; however primitively and unimaginatively a composer may cast his work in a certain key, while the music may have little value, the key as an organizing principle will be evident to the listener. On the other hand, if a composer with the same shortcomings embarks on the twelve-tone method, the mechanical ordering of the twelve tones—even if all the rules of set operations are strictly followed—will not result in structural unity, but in chaos. Unfortunately, serialism can be used by the untalented. and unprepared composer as a device by which to overcome the greatest hurdle in composition, namely, continuity. The forty-eight forms of the set yield a vast pool of notes, and the rules for using these can be learned in a very short time. Thus the tone row and its manipulations can aid the unqualified composer who would otherwise be at a loss in making choices in nonserial music, where the continuity from one note to the next has to be dictated at all times by inner musical promptings.

[20] Roger Sessions, "Problems and Issues Facing the Composer Today," *Musical Quarterly*, **46**, No. 2 (1960), p. 167.

TWELVE-TONE MUSIC AND TONALITY

The twelve-tone technique is a method usually, but not necessarily, applied to atonal music as an organizational principle. Atonality and twelve-tone music are concepts of a different hierarchical order. Atonality is the broader concept and means a musical state of being, in which, in the absence of the gravitational force of tonality, there are strong centrifugal forces at work. The twelve-tone technique is a musical method invented for harnessing these unruly forces.

The basic premise of twelve-tone music, as formulated by Schoenberg, was that the twelve tones are related only to one another. This amounts to a definition of atonality as it implies that there is no central tone with which the twelve tones stand in any hierarchical relationship. In spite of this stipulation, the theoretical question as to whether the twelve-tone method can be applied to tonal music has been raised with increasing frequency.

Schoenberg felt one should not use the twelve-tone method for a community of tones that are in a state of equilibrium by virtue of the organizing principle of tonality. Since the invention of the method was motivated by the need to harness atonal music, it is in this light that one should look upon Schoenberg's original taboos concerning repetition of notes, that is their appearance "out of turn" or doubling of octaves. Such occurrences, it was feared, would create tonal suggestions, thereby disqualifying the music for the strenuous discipline implicit in the new method. The twelve-tone method was invented as a solution of a crisis and Schoenberg probably felt that the conditions of the crisis had to be maintained in order to justify the extreme solution. He was among the first to realize later that his early theoretical position was unduly rigid and, led by his musical instinct, achieved some reconciliation between twelve-tone music and tonal feeling in his later works.

A more intransigent view is taken by Adorno; according to him, the twelve-tone method is justified only "when it serves to introduce order into some musical content which is refractory to other methods of organization. Otherwise, the technique degenerates into an absurd system." Adorno later insists even more strongly on the same point:

> What is forgotten is that twelve-tone technique is without significance except insofar as it serves to bind together centrifugal, recalcitrant and more or less explosive musical forces. Unless accompanied by this corollary and contradiction, this technique has no justification and is a waste of time. In the case of a lot of music, relatively simple both in form and content, which is served up to us today dressed in

the twelve-tone fashion, it is merely a useless luxury and therefore esthetically wrong.[21]

Boulez focuses his criticism directly at Schoenberg and castigates the master for his return to tonal suggestions: "His return to tonality is considered further proof of inconsistency. Pseudo-thematic octaves, pseudo-cadences, strict canons at the octave return, as though we had arrived at a new method merely in order to recompose the music of the past."[22]

Roberto Gerhard, a former student of Schoenberg, takes a more moderate view in stating that:

> Our new musical language is in its early phase of development; promiscuity with elements of the older system at this stage could, therefore, only obstruct and delay its natural growth. But when it consolidates itself the time will come, no doubt, for the reintegration of many elements from the older system which for the present we must firmly discard.[23]

The British composer's view has a good deal of historical validity. The history of music at many points witnessed the introduction of new elements which at first seemed irreconcilable with the older style. It was seen in the discussion of texture (Chapter 5) that the style of homophony in its early phase seemed irreconcilable with polyphony. Yet, eventually a reconciliation of the two textures did take place in the later works of the classical masters. Likewise, in Berg's *Wozzeck*, tonality and atonality gained a musically valid and expressive reconciliation. Based on purely theoretical grounds, there is no reason to assume that the twelve-tone method and tonal music will have to remain separated. Berg's Violin Concerto is a convincing early example of a successful reconciliation between the new method and tonal feeling. Perhaps it would be safe to say that the method of twelve-tone composition does not lend itself as a means of organization for very simple musical ideas, just as a very slender musical theme would be out of place amid massive orchestral forces.

In summary, twelve-tone technique is a method that, as a rule, is applied to atonal music as an organizational principle. While the distinction between atonal and twelve-tone music has validity on the conceptual level, the human ear, at least in the present state of its development, is mostly unable to differentiate with assurance between free atonal and twelve-tone music. There are, indeed, very few listeners who could safely identify which movements of Alban

---

[21] Theodore Adorno, "Modern Music is Growing Old," *The SCORE and IMA Magazine* (December 1956), p. 22.

[22] Boulez, p. 21.

[23] Roberto Gerhard, "Tonality in Twelve-Tone Music," *The SCORE and IMA Magazine* (May 1952), p. 26.

Berg's *Lyric Suite* (see Chapter 12) are merely atonal and which ones are organized by the twelve-tone method. This fact once more brings up the question of whether the method of composing with twelve tones is an aid merely to the composer in dealing with his material or whether it facilitates the listener's experience if the tone row is brought to his consciousness.

TWELVE-TONE MUSIC AND TRADITIONAL FORMS

If the function of the tone row and its workings are correctly understood as a *procedure* in musical organization, it will be obvious that this procedure does not take care of the problem of musical form. The set operations yield the arrangement of the notes, allow the formation of motives, and regulate the interplay of contrapuntal lines, but they do not automatically take care of the over-all architectural design of the composition. A special design will have to be grafted upon the "lower" order created by the arrangement of notes.

Two main approaches to form can be discerned in the music of twelve-tone composers; in some works the traditional forms of tonal music (sonata form, variation form, and the like) are used while in other compositions new forms are employed that stem from the particular conditions determined by row operations. Upon closer examination of a number of twelve-tone works, it seems that if the tone row is used as a motive, then it is likely that traditional forms will be used, whereas the athematic approach to the row will result in new designs which are far from being codified. At times, some shape of modified symmetry can be discerned, as in the second movement of Webern's *Concerto for Nine Instruments*.

The survival of the traditional forms of tonal music is an interesting example of the durability of a musical thought process. The employment of the sonata form is particularly interesting, since the main function of this form in the eighteenth and nineteenth centuries was the reaffirmation of tonality. The main premise underlying the form was based on relationships between keys. Of what use, then, is the sonata form to the twelve-tone composer, asked the critics, if in the new music key relationships are nonexistent?

Křenek holds that "sonata form cannot thrive in atonal soil," although in another instance he states more tolerantly:

> Naturally it is possible having the means of atonality and the twelve-tone technique at hand, to build forms which in their general outlines imitate the appearance of the sonata. . . . But certainly it is questionable

whether such procedure would be in line with the real nature of the new musical language.[24]

According to Boulez, the weakness of the application of the sonata form to twelve-tone music is that the form is historically in no way connected with the new discovery. He also sees it as a paradox that Schoenberg pursued his experimental work in an "outworn code."

Babbitt is of the opinion that the transference of the external forms of triadic music to the twelve-tone context leads at best "to a merely thematic formalism and if one is seeking mere formalisms, there are certainly more ingenious ones than sonata form, rondo form, etc., for all that they might not possess this purely verbal identification with the hallowed past."[25]

It is difficult to predict what solutions the future will bring. It seems that the trend is toward the athematic (sometimes called extramotivical) approach to serial music, and as a result it is likely that new forms will emerge at a greater point of consolidation.

Another unpredictable variable is the extent to which tonal suggestions remain a force of attraction for twelve-tone composers. The more tonal values remain prevalent, the more likely it is that the "outworn codes" will continue to be used.

Other closed forms, such as A–B–A forms or variation form, are less controversial in their application to twelve-tone music because they depend less strongly on key relationships compared to sonata form.

In summary, it should be pointed out that Schoenberg's new method exercised a powerful influence on twentieth-century musical thought. The new method offered an ingenious and challenging mode of thematic development or transformation, creating a new kind of musical order. Composers experimented with tone rows consisting of twelve tones or less, writing atonally or with tonal suggestions using the traditional forms or inventing new ones.

NEW PATHS IN SERIALISM

Schoenberg's method of composition with twelve tones had a far-reaching influence. Many followers liberalized the method, while others proceeded toward an even more rigidly predetermined serialism by applying it to other elements such as duration, timbre, and intensities. This section will examine some instances of novel applications of the method.

[24] *Music Here and Now,* p. 183.
[25] Babbitt, p. 55n.

An unusual novel treatment of the tone row was introduced by Křenek in his Cello Suite where a fifth row is formed, a composite set, based on the four standard rows. Such a set, of course, has no structural validity viewed from the original premises; it is a completely arbitrary construct which cannot be detected as part of the substructure by either the eye or the ear.

Another digression from standard tone row procedures is the establishment of semi-independent sets in which one or more notes of the row are rearranged. This free use of the row was anticipated by Schoenberg too in his late works.

A number of additional free treatments of the row technique are cited in the first Appendix of Rufer's work,[26] cited earlier. Thus, for instance, Humphrey Searle, a British composer, uses several different tone rows simultaneously, while in the first movement of Mátyás Seiber's Second Quartet the first four notes of the series are repeated melodically several times by the first violin before other notes enter. In Seiber's Violin Concerto, *Fantasia Concertante,* the solo violin plays free passages against the strict twelve-tone background of the orchestra.

ROTATION

Rotation, according to Křenek's definition, is a procedure in "which the elements of a given series systematically and progressively change their relative positions according to a plan which in itself is serially conceived in that the changes occur in regular phases."[27]

In the same article Křenek cites one of his works, *Circle, Chain and Mirror* (1956–1957), as an example of rotation. The prime set is given in Ex. 7/16:

EX. 7/16 Prime set

The rotations are based on the following numerical operations: in the first derivation (Ex. 7/17) the first and the last note of the original set remained in their position, but the remaining pairs of notes appeared in the form of retrograde successions:

[26] *Composition with Twelve Notes.*
[27] Ernst Křenek, "Extents and Limits of Serial Techniques," *Musical Quarterly,* **46,** No. 2 (1960), p. 211.

EX. 7/17 First rotation

In the next rotation, the newly gained pairs appeared in their retro-grade forms.

EX. 7/18 Second rotation

The original tone row is recaptured through twenty-five additional rotations. The word *Circle* appears in the title of the composition be-cause of this circularity.

It is obvious that such manipulations of a tone row have no musical motivation. They have the nature of a musical game or number game, constituting an early manifestation of chance music.

In another use of the rotation technique Křenek rotated the tones in *Sestina* according to the various positions in which the key words appear at the end of each line of the poem.

Křenek admits that such rotations allow a large role to chance, but he claims that chance and inspiration are closely related because in-spiration, like chance, cannot be "controlled, manufactured, or pre-meditated in any way."

The analogy is vulnerable to criticism because inspiration is influ-enced, consciously or unconsciously, by the composer's total musical and nonmusical experience in life, whereas rotation is built on random manipulation of numbers or words. Oddly enough, however, Křenek prefers the "purity" of the rotation because inspiration is not really as "innocent" as it seems, but is rather "conditioned by a tremendous body of recollection, tradition, training, and experience. In order to avoid the dictations of such ghosts he (the composer) prefers to set up an impersonal mechanism which will furnish, according to the pre-meditated patterns, unpredictable situations."[28]

SERIALIZATION OF OTHER PARAMETERS

TOTAL ORGANIZATION

As stated earlier, rhythmic values, intensities, and timbre can also be serialized. Among these possibilities the serialization of rhythms has had

[28] *Musical Quarterly,* p. 228.

the widest appeal among the avant-garde. Tone rows of rhythmic values appear in the music of Boulez, Blacher, Messiaen, Babbitt, and others (see Chapters 15 and 16). Rhythmic tone rows are often correlated with pitch tone rows; in such cases the magnitude of the intervals may determine the rhythmic values. For instance, a larger interval will be associated with a larger rhythmic value, while a smaller interval with a correspondingly shorter rhythmic duration.

It is possible to order several variables simultaneously, leading to what is known as *total organization.* In total organization there is no demand made upon the composer's creativity or imagination. Musical ideas and their growth or development are replaced by the workings of the prearranged plan.

Sessions expressed doubt about the advisability of serialization of rhythmic values and found the serialization of dynamics even more objectionable since the latter does not represent absolutes. A pitch and a rhythmic duration represent absolute values, but dynamics such as *forte* or *piano* are relative terms and, therefore, their serialization is hardly feasible. Paradoxically, the astronomical orderliness often results in a chaotic listening experience. In total organization, to an even greater degree than in rotation, the composer abandons his role in shaping the materials of music, submitting to a mechanical order. It is the symbolic expression of a world in which free initiative disappears and man is the tool and the victim of forces beyond his control.

CHANCE MUSIC

It was seen how in totally organized music an element of indeterminacy manifests itself. The paradoxical relation between extreme rigor in planning and indeterminacy has been formulated by Rochberg as follows:

> While the stream of events in totally serialized music may be continuous in the sense that sound is always in motion, the discourse has lost its sense of direction, resulting in a type of planned indeterminacy.[29]

From 1950 on, indeterminacy or chance music, also called "aleatory" (from the Latin *alea* meaning chance, dice) music, became an important current in avant-garde circles. The term indicates that elements of chance are consciously introduced in music. This concept may operate on two levels: 1) the composer uses chance operations, such as tossing

---

[29] George Rochberg, "The New Image of Music," *Perspectives of New Music*, **2**, No. 1 (1963), p. 3.

coins or rolling dice, in the selection or ordering of his material; 2) the composer outlines the main course of his music—or at least states his basic ideas—but specific details are left to the performer's choice.

THE ROLE OF CHANCE
ON THE COMPOSITIONAL LEVEL

This new approach to composition is more than just a new technique. It is linked to a whole set of new assumptions made about music after midcentury. These new assumptions imply an entirely new conception of music, of its purpose and function. The previous notions concerning musical organization and continuity were questioned and replaced by new ideas. One of the notions concerned the emancipation of sound itself. The self-contained and self-sufficient role of sound was formulated by John Cage (see Chapter 16), the main spokesman for chance music.

> A sound does not view itself as thought, as ought, as needing another sound for its elucidation, as etc.; it has no time for any consideration—it is occupied with the performance of its characteristics: before it has died away it must have made perfectly exact its frequency, its loudness, its length, its overtone structure, the precise morphology of these and of itself.[30]

Perhaps even more to the point is the following:

> one may give up the desire to control sound, clear his mind of music, and set about discovering means to let sounds be themselves rather than vehicles for man-made theories or expressions of human sentiments.[31]

In view of these statements it is understandable that to the protagonists of chance music (Cage is their accepted leader), it does not matter where they turn for the source of their operation. While Cage derives his chance operations from the Chinese *I-Ching* (Book of Changes), the stochastic music of the Greek composer Xenakis is based on game theory of mathematical probability.

Cage's operations consist of tossing coins or marked sticks for chance numbers as described in the *Book of Changes*. The resulting compositions are "free of individual taste or memory in their order of events," according to Cage, a view similar to that of Křenek.

The feeling that traditions, the memory of the past in any form, are obstacles to be overcome by the artist has been expressed by modern painters and writers too, and is undoubtedly linked to existentialist

---

[30] John Cage, *Silence* (Middletown, Conn.: Wesleyan University Press, 1961), p. 14.
[31] *Silence*, p. 10.

philosophy. The American painter, Mark Rothko, for instance, mentions as examples of such obstacles "memory, history, or geometry, which are swamps of generalization from which one might pull out parodies of ideas (which are ghosts) but never an idea in itself."[32]

The reader who wishes to acquaint himself with the details of Cage's procedures is referred to the composer's account of the steps he followed in working out his *Music of Changes,*[33] where the charts are reproduced based on the tosses of the coins, which govern the order of pitch, duration, timbre, and the like.

If music produced in such a way is to be judged by conventional esthetic criteria, one would conclude that these works lack a syntax or grammar, continuity or any pattern of relationship, and as they are without expectations or goals, they do not qualify as music. Should these random samples of sounds become the music of the future, one's values would have to be re-assessed. As expressed by Meyer, this music challenges "our faith in a world of purpose and causality, time and prediction, choice and control, communication and morality . . . even man's place in the universe."[34]

THE ROLE OF CHANCE

AT THE PERFORMANCE LEVEL

The collaboration of the composer with the performer in the creative act has a number of historical precedents. For instance, in the Baroque period the performer was granted a degree of freedom in the realization of the figured bass even though the harmonic progressions were laid out by the composer. Also, in the cadenza of the classical concerto, the performer was entrusted with the improvisation of a section that had the function of an insert in the total work.

The recent aleatory compositions show a much wider degree of freedom given to the performer; such freedom may range from an improvised rubato in tempo or dynamics to the task of working out the actual architecture of the composition. Other choices left to the performer may be options to omit interludes or to reverse the order of movements.

The middle ground as to how much freedom should be given the performer, and the rationale for such freedom, is expressed by Boulez (see Chapter 15), the most articulate spokesman of the avant-garde. Boulez' point of departure is that Western music, with its predilection

---

[32] *Fifteen Americans,* edited by Dorothy Miller (New York: Museum of Modern Art, 1952), p. 18.

[33] *Silence,* pp. 57–60.

[34] Leonard B. Meyer, "The End of the Renaissance," *The Hudson Review,* **16,** No. 2 (1963), p. 186.

for the closed cycle, follows a single line of development that is always reproduced in an identical way. Therefore, classical Western works prohibit any active participation on the performer's part and rule out the element of surprise or personal solution in performance. By contrast, the music of the East, with its conceptions of elaborations, allows music to be "a way of being in the world, an integral part of existence." From this open system Boulez derived the concept of the "labyrinth," which he considers the most important notion in recent Western art:

> To me, the labyrinth notion in a work of art is like Kafka's idea in the short story called *The Burrow*. Everyone creates his own labyrinth; he cannot move into one that already exists because it is impossible to conceive of an architecture not related to his own secretion. One builds it exactly as the subterranean animal builds this burrow so admirably described by Kafka: resources are constantly shifted about so that everything can be kept secret, and new routes are forever being chosen to mislead. Similarly, the work must provide a certain number of possible routes, thanks to these very precise devices, with chance playing a shunting role at the last moment . . . . This notion of shunting does not belong in the category of pure chance, but in that of non-determinate choice, and this difference is fundamental; in a construction that is as ramified as works written today, there could not possibly be total indeterminacy, for such a phenomenon is contrary—absurdly so—to all organizing thought and to all style.[35]

Boulez carried out this idea of the labyrinth in his Third Piano Sonata where the main outline of the work is defined, but the performer has the task of choosing his own path by deciding on alternatives (such as omitting or inverting passages) offered by the composer.

Stockhausen gives chance a much greater role (see Chapter 15) in *Piano Piece XI* (1956). The score of this composition is printed on a 37 by 21 inch sheet that looks like an architect's blueprint. It contains nineteen short, separate musical fragments, accompanied by the following instructions:

> The performer looks at random at the sheet of music and begins with any group, the first that catches his eye; this he plays, choosing for himself tempo . . . dynamic level, and type of attack. At the end of the first group, he reads the tempo, dynamic, and attack indications that follow, and looks at random to any other group, which he then plays in accordance with the latter indications. "Looking at random to any other group" implies that the performer will never link up expressly chosen groups or intentionally leave out others. Each group can be joined to any of the other 18; each can thus be played at any of the six tempi and dynamic levels and with any of the six types of attacks. . . .[36]

---

[35] Pierre Boulez, "Sonate, que me veux-tu?" *Perspectives of New Music,* **1**, No. 2 (1963), p. 34.

[36] Reprinted in Karl Wörner's *Karlheinz Stockhausen* (Rodenkirchen, Germany: P. J. Tonger, 1963), p. 17.

It is difficult to critically assess a work such as *Piano Piece XI* because it will assume a different shape and order at every performance, depending on the performer's choices. It would be wrong, however, to say that the performer is improvising for he is merely allowing chance to take its course.

Other chance factors have been explored by Lukas Foss (see Chapter 16); in his *Echoi* (1961) for piano, clarinet, cello, and percussion, called "a work in progress," notes often appear without the staff lines and without stems, leaving the decision of establishing pitch or duration to the performer. Random aperiodic assortments of legato and staccato choices are suggested by new notational devices.

The various aleatory possibilities have an almost limitless range; some additional samples will be cited in Chapters 15 and 16.

ELECTRONIC MUSIC

Electronic music in its simplest terms means that sounds are produced electronically, then recorded on magnetophone tape. Following this, the sounds are rearranged and altered, then heard through loudspeakers. Thus, electronic music dispenses with the performer.

Electronic music did not erupt suddenly; it was preceded by a sequence of events, acoustical and musical, which finally led to the electronic production of sound.

The first important event in the prehistory of electronic music was the invention of the electronic tube in 1906. This was soon followed by the invention of electronic instruments, such as the theremin and the ondes martinot, both of which were played by moving the hand toward and away from a sensitive tube. Also, a movement known as *Bruitism* belongs to the antecedents of electronic music, The bruitists, a part of the Italian futurist movement, advocated noise as a replacement of musical sounds. The manifesto of Bruitism, published in 1913 by Luigi Russolo, distinguishes six families of noises. Although the movement did not create any compositions of lasting value, it affected the work of both Edgar Varèse and Henry Cowell (see Chapter 16) in the 1920s. Varèse's search for electronic sound, and his vision of it, is truly prophetic; he writes in 1936:

> Today with the technical means that exist and are easily adaptable, the differentiation of the various masses and different planes as well as these beams of sound, could be made discernible to the listener by means of certain acoustical arrangements. Moreover, such an acoustical arrangement would permit the delimitation of what I call "zones of

intensities." These zones would be differentiated by various timbres or colors and different loudnesses . . . . The role of color or timbre would be completely changed from being incidental, anecdotal, sensual, or picturesque; it would become an agent of delineation, like the different colors on a map separating different areas, and an integral part of form. . . .

Moreover, the new *musical apparatus* [my italics] I envisage, able to emit sounds of any number of frequencies, will extend the limits of the lowest and highest registers, hence new organizations of the vertical resultants; chords, their arrangements, their spacings—that is, their oxygenation . . . . The never-before-thought-of use of the inferior resultants and of the differential and additional sounds may also be expected. An entirely new magic of sound![37]

Another far-reaching influence of Bruitism may be seen in the *musique concrète* developed by Pièrre Schaeffer in Paris in the late 1940s. *Musique concrète* continued to explore noise in a more systematic way; the term refers to a procedure whereby any noise (thunder, raindrop, street noise, the sound of a brick slashed by a hammer, and so on) or sound was recorded on tape and then mechanically and technically altered. Some of the simpler techniques included certain manipulations with the tape, such as speeding up, slowing down, playing backwards, and montage (combining tapes). The electronic treatments included changing the timbre by filters and modulators, techniques also used later by the advocates of "pure" electronic music. Ussachevsky's early pieces, such as *Sonic Contours* and *Reverberation*, serve as adequate introductions to *musique concrète*.

The school of "pure" electronic music, led by Herbert Eimert and Karlheinz Stockhausen, started its experiments at the Electronic Studio of the Radio Station of Cologne in 1950. This group, strongly oriented toward Webern's music, approached electronic music with different purpose and motivation. They saw two chief reasons why scientific control over sound is necessary: first, totally organized music had become too complex for the human performer; second, the conventional instruments were too limited for achieving the subtle timbre differences they envisioned (see Chapter 13). Recently, however, as both schools have become interested in the mixing of electronic and nonelectronic sounds, the initial differences have disappeared.

Electronic music spread quickly; among the American pioneers are Vladimir Ussachevsky and Otto Luening.[38] With the help of the Rockefeller Foundation the Columbia-Princeton Center of Electronic Music

[37] Edgar Varèse, "New Instruments and New Music," a lecture given at Mary Austin House, Santa Fe, 1936; reprinted in *Contemporary Composers on Contemporary Music*, edited by Elliott Schwartz and Barney Childs (New York: Holt, Rinehart and Winston, Inc., 1967), pp. 197–198.

[38] Otto Luening, "Some Random Remarks on Electronic Music," *Contemporary Composers on Contemporary Music* (New York: Holt, Rinehart and Winston, Inc., 1967).

installed the RCA Electronic Synthesizer in 1960, and since then an increasing number of composers have familiarized themselves with the new method of composition. Yale University and the University of Illinois have also established electronic centers, and numerous electronic studios have sprung up all over the world. Luciano Berio and Bruno Maderna are active at the Milan Radio Station; Tashiro Mayuzumi in Tokyo; Henk Badings in Holland; and Serocki at Radio Warsaw.

The main characteristics of electronic music that seem to distinguish it from instrumental music were summarized by Stockhausen[39] in the following four points:

1) The correlation of the coloristic, harmonic-melodic, and metric-rhythmic aspects of composition. Stockhausen here refers to some of his experiments in which he succeeded in bringing all the different sound properties, which in earlier music had to be dealt with separately, under a *single* control. This point is supported by complex acoustical theories which have to be omitted in the framework of this discussion.

2) The composition and decomposition of timbres. Instead of the limited number of timbres of traditional music (muted, *sul ponticello*, pizzicato, and so on) in electronic music timbres of great variety can be produced. Gradations can be achieved far beyond the realm of instrumental music. Varèse mentions that "continuous, flowing curve" that traditional instruments could not give and which is obtainable by electronic means. A fascinating way in which timbres can be decomposed is the gradation by which a human voice can gradually lose its human quality by electronic manipulation. Such treatment provides a striking effect in Stockhausen's *Gesang der Jünglinge* (see Chapter 15). Completely novel effects may also be attained by employing electronic accompaniment to the live human voice, as in Babbitt's *Vision and Prayer* (see Chapter 16).

3) The characteristic differentiation among degrees of intensities. In electronic music a very large variety of dynamic levels with rich gradations can be achieved and *measured,* while in traditional music there are not more than six or seven levels which depend on subjective judgments.

4) The ordered relationship between sound and noise. This aspect of the sound continuum refers to the finely graded transition that can be established between noise and musical sound.

Stockhausen's four points do not exhaust the possibilities afforded by electronic music. He does not mention, for instance, the vast resources of sounds afforded by electronic music; instead of the 78–80 pitch levels, built on the half-tone division of the octave in earlier music, electronic music supplies an almost unlimited source of ex-

[39] Karlheinz Stockhausen, "The Concept of Unity in Electronic Music," *Perspectives of New Music,* 1 (1962), pp. 39–40.

tremely finely graded pitches. Also, the composer is liberated from the restrictions of the tempered system. Furthermore, rhythmic complexities may be realized that were impossible to execute by the human performer.

These broad possibilities raise many questions. First perhaps is the consistency of style. In conventional music the composer scored a work for a string quartet or woodwind quintet where the timbre limitations of the instruments insured a certain consistency in timbres and sonorities. In electronic music, however, there are no such safeguards; any sound or any timbre can be produced that may easily lead to incoherence, inconsistency, or even chaos.

Another important point raised by Babbitt[40] is the threshold of human perception. Whereas in the past the composer was mostly concerned with the capabilities of the performer, now the composer's problem is whether or not he has exceeded the perception of the listener. Again, conventional music has a safeguard in that the music is performed by a human being. This fact insures, at least theoretically, that the music will remain within the boundaries of human perception. Such a safeguard does not exist in electronic music; anything can be produced by the composer in dimensions above and below the threshold of human perception.

It is probably this unlimited freedom in the new medium that often hampers the composer. The solutions toward order and organization are numerous and diverse; in many instances, however, no semblance of order or organization is perceptible to the listener. Among the devices sometimes used the following can be cited: undifferentiated continuous sound textures are often juxtaposed to more clearly articulated sounds, and while one group of sounds may remain more or less constant, the other texture may undergo a kind of "development." In Babbitt's works, as for instance in his *Composition for Synthesizer,* recorded by the Columbia-Princeton Electronic Music Center, the composition is concerned with "the control and specification of linear and total rhythms, loudness rhythms and relationships, and flexibility of pitch succession." In other instances sound mixtures can serve as a "quasi row," and the mixtures may undergo inversion, transposition, and interpolation. The pattern of mixture of live sounds with electronic sounds, and their manipulation, can also be used as a principle of organization.

While it is much too early to assess the future of electronic music, one can already note a positive way in which it influences composers of instrumental music. The gradations of the sound continuum gained through electronic means has made a number of composers aware of the limitations of the traditional instruments. This realization prompted

[40]Milton Babbitt, "An Introduction to the R.C.A. Synthesizer," *The Journal of Music Theory,* **8** (1964), p. 2.

Henry Brant, for instance, to build violins, violas, cellos, and basses of various sizes. In this way a small, a medium-sized, and a large violin (or other instrument) will produce finer timbre differences than those achieved in the past. Another attempt to gain a finer timbre continuum can be seen in Ligeti's *Atmosphères,* where fourteen first, fourteen second violins, fourteen violas, ten cellos, and eight double basses *all* play different pitches in giant superimpositions of chords.

The elimination of the human performer, however, is a serious matter and may be seen as the climax in the progressive dehumanization of the arts, observed more than thirty years ago by Ortega y Gasset. Could it be that finally it will be the role of the machine to stir man toward new achievements in instrumental music?

PART II

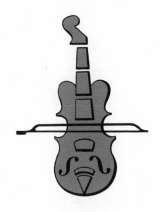

SIX LEADING COMPOSERS
AND THEIR FORERUNNERS

TRANSITION

    While in Part I *materials of music* were considered in terms of their function and role in twentieth-century music, in Part II the focus is on the *composers* themselves. The discussion in this part will center on six composers who are considered the most important figures of contemporary music, namely, Stravinsky, Bartók, Schoenberg and his two noted disciples, Berg and Webern, and Hindemith.

    Of the mentioned six composers, three (Stravinsky, Bartók, and Schoenberg) presented their first important works almost simultaneously (around 1910) to European audiences: it was around this time that Stravinsky's three early ballets *Firebird* (1909), *Petrouchka* (1911), and *The Rite of Spring* (1912) gained their first performances in Paris; that Schoenberg's Second Quartet (1908) ushered in atonality; and that Bartók's first major work, his First Quartet (1907) was premiered in Budapest.

In order to gain a deeper understanding of the significance of these six composers, the music of their immediate precursors who occupied the scene in the two preceding decades (1890–1910) will be examined in this chapter.

The first part of the chapter deals with the contributions of Mahler, Richard Strauss, Sibelius, and Scriabin; this section is followed by a more detailed examination of Debussy's significance, briefly touching upon the music of Ravel.

GUSTAV MAHLER (1860–1911) AND
RICHARD STRAUSS (1864–1949)

A comparison of the two composers will bring out superficial similarities and deep-seated differences. What is common to the two composers is their Austro-German background, and the fact that they both wrote for large orchestral forces which they conducted with great authority. Moreover, each, in his own way, had an unusual mastery of orchestral writing.

Despite their common origin, however, the two composers had different musical roots: Mahler was the heir to the symphonic tradition that was handed down from Beethoven. The Moravian-born composer was particularly affected by its Austrian flavor, reflected in the music of Schubert and Bruckner. By contrast, Strauss, born in Munich, was the descendant of the Berlioz-Liszt-Wagner lineage, which had little affinity for abstract symphonic forms, and turned toward freer orchestral essays based on extramusical inspirations.

In addition to these differences in musical ancestry, basic differences in the composers' personalities set the two men and their music apart. Undoubtedly, Mahler's more complex personality is at the root of his paradoxical musical idiom which is stylistically more problematical than Strauss' works, which, at any one given period, show a stylistically more consistent approach. The music of Strauss is never enigmatic; there may be a saturation of the texture with a large number of musical lines that cannot be heard singly, yet the composer's expressive aims are always unambiguous.

Mahler, on the other hand, may puzzle the listener even when his texture is lean and transparent. It is perhaps by virtue of this subtle expressiveness that Mahler stands closer to us after midcentury; his music often suggests man's loneliness and his search for identity, probing the deep layers of consciousness with a strange intermingling of tragedy and parody. In contrast to this passionate search, Strauss suggests the security of the successful bourgeois, speaking with the voice of the successful virtuoso composer. Even when his music depicts gruesome events, it has the character of a documentary presentation showing the keen eye (or ear) of an observer rather than the impact of a deeply felt participation.

Despite Strauss' greater outward assurance, it is Mahler who follows a straighter line in his development as a composer. He remains essentially on the same path, that of symphonic writing, composing songs between symphonic works, often with orchestral accompaniment. Furthermore, a growth in musical maturation may be observed as one examines the nine symphonies—a tenth was left incomplete—composed between 1888–1909. The only ambivalence Mahler demonstrates is the shifting back and forth from purely instrumental symphonies (first, fifth, sixth, seventh, ninth) to symphonies with solo voice and/or chorus.

By comparison, Strauss' choice of media shows a more diverse picture: after a brief phase of purely instrumental works (such as the early Cello Sonata, Op. 6, and the Piano Quartet, Op. 13), he found his medium in the tone poem, which he fashioned after the Lisztian model. While his earlier tone poems such as *Macbeth* (1886) and *Don Juan* (1888) are descriptive in the general sense, the later ones become increasingly programmatic, depicting events in sound, as for instance, the bleating of the sheep in *Don Quixote* (1897), Till's execution in *Till Eulenspiegel* (1895), and a family quarrel in *Symphonia Domestica* (1904). The size of the orchestra and the virtuosity demanded from the players far outrank any previous orchestral work. The extent to which Strauss raised the standards concerning the technical proficiency of the orchestral player is shown by the fact that "Orchestral Studies," based on the difficult passages from the composer's tone poems and operas, have been published for almost every instrument in the orchestra. There is hardly an audition today for an orchestral post in which the player's ability to play these passages would not be put to the test.

Mahler's knowledge of the instruments was just as acute, but he did not impose on the players tasks as strenuous and demanding as those found in Strauss' works.

After the turn of the century Strauss gradually abandoned the tone-poem form and devoted his time to writing operas and songs. His two most successful operatic works are *Salome* (1905) and *Elektra* (1908). One is inclined to predict that these two operas, together with *Der Rosenkavalier* (1911), will have greater durability than the tone poems, most of which already sound rather dated.

Salome and *Elektra,* although steeped in the Wagnerian style, have an authentic ring and a greater impact than the tone poems. In these operas, the tone painting points to psychological situations and is not as literal, as was true of the tone poems.

The later compositions of Strauss did not add much to his prestige. After *Der Rosenkavalier* he wrote a half dozen operas, songs, and some instrumental works with a considerably lighter texture, as in the Oboe Concerto and the Second Horn Concerto, which suggest a decline in the composer's creative powers.

Strauss' influence, although less profound than Mahler's is more tangible. His bold dissonances, introduced for dramatic purposes, were later incorporated by other composers in the more advanced harmonic language of the century. One such instance was quoted from *Don Quixote* (Ex. 4/5) in an earlier chapter; the following examples will further corroborate this point. In Example 8/1 a passage rich in tritones can be observed:

EX. 8/1 STRAUSS, *Elektra*,[1] Act 1, Scene 3, study no. 72

Example 8/2 illustrates a bitonal passage from the song, "Für Fünfzehn Pfennige":[2]

EX. 8/2 Ending

---

[1] Copyright 1909 and 1910 by Adolph Fürstner; copyright renewed 1937 by Fürstner Ltd. Copyright and renewal assigned to Boosey & Hawkes, Ltd. Reprinted by permission of Boosey & Hawkes, Inc.

[2] Quoted by permission of Fürstner Ltd. and Universal Edition.

Although Strauss was not an innovator in the field of rhythm, Example 8/3 from *Salome* shows an interesting, early instance of superimposition of different meters:

EX. 8/3 STRAUSS, *Salome*,[3] 3 mm. before study no. 228

Mahler's influence on contemporary music is manifold, but less obvious. In his use of unusual instruments, such as the guitar, mandolin, or the tenor horn, he was motivated by inner musical necessity and not by the intention of imitating sound. The unusual combination of instruments created unique moods which were to influence composers as diverse as Schoenberg and Shostakovich. The visionary *Ländlers* and marches find reverberations in Alban Berg's music and the deep expressiveness alternating with parodizing gestures can be linked to Schoenberg's middle period. The sparse scoring and distinct contrapuntal voice-leading can be viewed as a preliminary step toward later neoclassic thought.

As far as the contemporary position of the two composers is concerned, the majority of sources claim that Mahler has offered more to

[3]Copyright 1905 by Adolph Fürstner; renewed 1933. Copyright and renewal assigned to Boosey & Hawkes, Inc. Reprinted by permission of Boosey & Hawkes, Inc.

later twentieth-century musical thought than has Strauss. Copland[4] feels that Strauss represents the "final manifestation of a dying world."

Among contemporary composers only Bartók acknowledges indebtedness to Strauss (see Chapter 10), although he also pointed out in his later critical writing the German composer's shortcomings.

Mahler had the powerful support of Schoenberg, who in his *Style and Idea*, devoted a long essay to a defense of Mahler. All charges leveled at his music, such as vulgarity, childlike naiveté, and banality are refuted one by one. The ascendancy of Mahler's music is also suggested by the acclaim it received at the recent centenary celebration of the composer's birth, and by the increasing frequency with which his works have been performed since.

To become familiar with Mahler's music his *Kindertotenlieder* and his Fourth Symphony are recommended; among Strauss' tone poems, *Don Juan* and *Till Eulenspiegel* are suggested as good first listenings. These four works show the contrast between the realism of Strauss and the symbolic, spiritual mode of expression of Mahler.

JEAN SIBELIUS (1865–1957)

Among the various composers under discussion, it is Sibelius, whose oeuvre—seven symphonies and numerous tone poems (including the well-known *Finlandia*)—had the least effect on the subsequent generation of composers. Yet, his name is included in this section partly because of the composer's great popularity—enjoyed particularly in England—and partly because of the sharp controversy that surrounds his contributions. The divided opinions concerning this music which has been part of our concert repertory for about fifty years should serve as a reminder of how relative the criteria of music criticism are, and how little is known about the sociology and psychology of musical taste.

Curiously, the music itself which aroused the controversy is anything but provocative. One wonders how this brooding, somewhat dated music can be judged in such widely differing ways. Disregarding Finnish commentators who, of course, consider Sibelius a national hero, opinions are divided along national lines. English writers, joined in the 1940s by the American Olin Downes, were mostly responsible for building up the composer's image into a towering figure. They felt that Sibelius occupied a leading role among the composers of our cen-

[4]Aaron Copland, *Our New Music* (New York: McGraw-Hill Book Company, Inc., 1941), p. 36.

tury. According to Constant Lambert,[5] Sibelius is "the greatest orchestral innovator of our times" and "the most important symphonic writer since Beethoven." He stated in 1948, that "of all contemporary music, Sibelius seems to point more surely to the future." Compared to the twenty pages allocated to the Finnish composer in his book, less than one page is devoted to the discussion of Bartók's music, whose later works are considered "the musical equivalents of navel-gazing on the part of a philosopher."

In general, there seems to be a consistent trend according to which the idolization of Sibelius correlates to a high degree with a disparaging attitude toward the music of Bartók and Schoenberg.

Demuth,[6] another British author, sees Sibelius as a leading figure in contemporary music. In a separate chapter ("Composer in Isolation") he states that "his melodic processes and attitude to *form* are among the most remarkable of the century."

In strong contrast to the adulation of the English critics—among whom Cecil Gray should also be mentioned—devastating views are expressed by some French writers. Leibowitz,[7] for instance, concluded in an article entitled, "Sibelius, the World's Worst Composer," that his "originality resulted from his ignorance, incompetence, and impotence." Also Nadia Boulanger, the distinguished composer-teacher, who guided some of the most prominent American composers, dismissed Sibelius as a composer of no consequence. Likewise, in the Belgian Collaer's volume[8] on contemporary music, Sibelius receives merely a one-line credit.

German writers, too, show an almost total disregard for Sibelius; in Stuckenschmidt's voluminous history[9] of the music between the two wars, the name of the Finnish composer does not even appear in the index, whereas in Wörner's study[10] his life and works are summarized in two paragraphs. In the only Hungarian survey[11] of twentieth-century music, Sibelius' name is not even mentioned.

While the primary purpose here is not to express value judgments, it

[5] Constant Lambert, *Music Ho!* (London: Penguin Books, 1948), p. 224.

[6] Norman Demuth, *Musical Trends in the Twentieth Century* (London: Rockliff Corp., 1952), p. 258.

[7] René Leibowitz, "Sibelius, le plus mauvais compositeur du monde," *Aux Editions Dynamo* (Liège, 1955).

[8] Paul Collaer, *A History of Modern Music* (New York: Grosset & Dunlap, 1961; translated by Sally Abeles from *La Musique Moderne*, Elsevier, Brussels, 1955; copyright by The World Publishing Company).

[9] H. H. Stuckenschmidt, *Neue Musik zwischen den beiden Kriegen* (Berlin: Surkam Verlag, 1951).

[10] Karl H. Wörner, *Neue Musik in der Entscheidung* (Mainz: Schott's Söhne, 1954).

[11] Rezsö Kókai and Fabian Imre, *Századunk Zenéje* (Budapest: Zenemükiado Vállalat, 1961).

would be difficult to agree with the English critics who wish to elevate Sibelius to the position of a leading musical figure. The Finnish composer exercises his imagination on a local scene, creating a brooding, pastorale atmosphere with a good deal of fragmented motives, which rather frequently lead to predictable climaxes, using a fairly obvious harmonic scheme.

The music of Sibelius belongs to a bygone era; his Fourth Symphony, composed in 1912, seems out-of-step with the spirit of the period when compared to Schoenberg's *Pierrot Lunaire* (1912), Stravinsky's *The Rite of Spring* (1911), or even to the late works of Debussy.

ALEXANDER SCRIABIN (1872–1915)

Deeply steeped in mysticism and, like Mahler, seeking a solution concerning the final questions of human existence, Scriabin is often looked upon as Debussy's Russian counterpart. Actually, the resemblance is only slight, consisting mainly of the highly refined sensibilities characteristic of both composers and of their mutual interest in new harmonic procedures. Beyond these, the two composers differed in every other respect; socially, Debussy was extremely withdrawn, disdainful of the "people," whereas Scriabin could propagate his utopian ideas to the simple uneducated fisherman. Musically, Scriabin was drawn to abstract piano music (ten sonatas, preludes, dances, and so on). He was inspired at first by Chopin, rather than by Debussy, in whose oeuvre abstract instrumental works played a subordinate role. Furthermore, Scriabin's exalted, overwrought style, exemplified particularly by his two orchestral tone poems, *Poem of Ecstasy* (1908) and *Prometheus* or *The Poem of Fire* (1910), both showing traces of Liszt's influence, stand in sharp contrast to Debussy's restraint. Finally, the Russian composer's search for a synthesis between music, religion, and philosophy could never have been shared by Debussy, whose interest in music was central and all-involving.

What Scriabin had to offer to the subsequent musical generation was his intense expressiveness; the tension of inner musical forces often verged on the ecstatic—a mood to be recaptured later by Alban Berg in his *Wozzeck* and in the *Presto Delirando* of his *Lyric Suite*.

Even more important are his harmonic innovations. We find evidence in his later piano sonatas of an attempt to replace tonality by a rigid harmonic scheme, which can be considered the first explorations in serialism (see Chapter 7). In this system, a chord may serve as the foundation of a work, such as the famous "mystic" chord (Ex. 8/4) to his *Prometheus,* from which all melodic and harmonic material is derived:

EX. 8/4 SCRIABIN, *Prometheus,* "Mystic" Chord

Even such serial processes as segmentation and transposition are in evidence. In Example 8/5 two instances are given from his Piano Sonata, No. 7, which are based on a chord related to the mystic chord with the difference that D and D flat are used alternatingly. (In other sections of the work a G is also added to the basic chord.)

EX. 8/5 SCRIABIN, *Piano Sonata,* No. 7,[12] opening

EX. 8/5/a M. 196

Despite these harmonic innovations, Scriabin's music sounds somewhat lacking in differentiation and contrast; this is perhaps due to his dogmatic approach to the new harmonic framework and to an often monotonously symmetrical phrase structure.

[12] Edition Russe de Musique, Berlin. Boosey & Hawkes, Inc., New York.

CLAUDE DEBUSSY (1862–1918)

> *Debussy was the greatest composer of our period.*[13]
>
>   BARTÓK

The recent Debussy Centennial, celebrated all over the world, brought full recognition to the composer, who passed away almost unnoticed by most Parisians during the German siege of the city.

Seemingly, Debussy was born into a rich cultural era; his formative years coincided with the rise of the French symbolist literary move-ment led by such figures as Verlaine, Baudelaire, Mallarmé, Dujardin, Rimbaud, and others, and with the appearance of a group of painters—Manet, Monet, Renoir, Degas—commonly called impressionist. The fact was, however, that the works of these creative geniuses made little impact on the average Parisian. The period was marked by a materialistic outlook; the tone was set by the *nouveaux riches* of a utilitarian society and only a small intellectual elite cared for the arts. Thus, the artists lived in isolation on the periphery of society.

Perhaps none of the creative men experienced this isolation more acutely than the hypersensitive French composer. He soon discovered that people were corrupt and had vulgar taste. Therefore, nothing else remained for him but to withdraw into his ivory tower. As a result of these painful experiences, he became contemptuous of the common man. He wrote to a close friend, the noted composer, Ernest Chausson:

> Ah! If only the times we were living in were less depressing, if only young people could be expected to take an interest in anything but the latest form of bicycle! Of course, I have not the slightest intention of ruling over or shaping the tastes of my contemporaries, but, all the same, it would be nice to found a school of "neo-musicians" where an effort would be made to preserve intact the admirably symbolic qualities of music; where, in a word, people would learn once more to respect an art which has been defiled by so many hands . . . . The present state of affairs, of course, is due to the motto inscribed on all public monu-ments, "Liberty, Equality, Fraternity," words which at best are fit only for cab-drivers.[14]

Perhaps it was due to this alienation that he disregarded the usually accepted code of behavior in his private life, and antagonized some of his best friends with his arbitrary and self-willed actions.

---

[13] *Bartók Breviarium*, edited by Jozsef Ujfalussy. An interview with Bartók after Debussy's death. (Budapest: Zenemükiado Vállalat, 1958).

[14] Rollo H. Myers, *Debussy* (London: Duckworth, 1948), p. 55.

MUSICAL INFLUENCES

Debussy's works represent a mutation in the evolution of music. Even if certain influences, such as that of Massenet, can be detected in his early works, his first important orchestral essay, *The Afternoon of a Faun*, must have sounded strikingly novel at its premiere in 1893. This was the year when Tchaikovsky's Sixth Symphony was first performed; when Mahler was at work on his Second Symphony; and Dvořák's "New World" Symphony had not yet been composed.

In tracing musical influences, Wagner should be mentioned first. Debussy, like every other composer of the period, was deeply affected by the great German composer. However, after several pilgrimages to Bayreuth, disenchantment set in. In an article Debussy writes: "When Wagner takes from life he conquers it, places his foot on its neck and forces it to shriek the name of Wagner louder than the trumpets of Fame."[15] In the same article in comparing Franck's music to Wagner's he states: "There is none of the trickery (in Franck's music) so flagrant when Wagner performs a sentimental or orchestral pirouette by which he stimulates the attention of an audience wearied sometimes by a too continuous breathing of a rarefied atmosphere." In another instance, however, the most glowing tribute is paid to Wagner's *Parsifal*.

The most important lesson the French composer learned from Wagner —and in general from the neo-Germans—was that there are musical paths other than the abstract, instrumental, Austro-German symphonic style. This discovery led him away from the closed forms, and in particular from the sonata form, which was especially alien to Debussy's thinking. He also learned from Wagner that there is a freer form of musical speech from the one based on symmetrically balanced musical sentences with their antecedents and consequents, and that musical thoughts may be sustained over long stretches by delaying the harmonic resolution.

Next to Wagner the second most important influence upon Debussy was that of Russian music, encountered when as a young man he spent two summers as a tutor in Madame von Meck's house.[16] Here he became acquainted with the music of Glinka and Borodin, and later also with Mussorgsky. Thus, Debussy was the first Western composer in our times to inhale the fresher air of Eastern Europe; this current was soon to gain paramount importance in the music of Stravinsky and Bartók. At any rate, for Debussy this was a highly significant event: one may assume that the impact of Russian music enabled him to free him-

[15] Claude Debussy, *Monsieur Croche, the Dilettante Hater* (London: Noel Douglas, 1927), p. 120.
[16] Madame von Meck is known in the history of music as Tchaikovsky's patroness.

self of Wagner's overpowering musical personality. If Wagnerian influences can still be traced thereafter, as for instance in his masterwork, *Pelléas et Mélisande,* the influence shows itself rather in the reverse. Thus, the tremendous climax of the love duet in *Tristan* is replaced by the calm of Pelléas' confession ("Je t'aime"), which is enhanced by the silence of the orchestra. Even if traces of leitmotif technique can be seen here, it is employed with greater discretion than in the Wagnerian operatic scheme.

One more strain of influence exerted by various French composers, such as Satie, Chabrier, Ravel's early piano music should be mentioned in addition to a flavor obtained from Javanese and other Far-Eastern sources.

STYLE PROBLEMS

Had music historians taken to heart the warning of Wittgenstein, the great German philosopher, that "labels terminate thinking," they might not have been unanimously so quick in putting the label of *impressionism* on the French composer's highly original style. The term *impressionism,* first applied to the style of a group of painters, should be regarded with suspicion. In music this questionable label was first applied by the displeased, pedantic professors of the Paris Conservatoire in a warning to Debussy that "he beware of that vague impressionism which is one of the most dangerous enemies of artistic truth." Despite the composer's repeated protestations, the label was taken over by most writers rather uncritically. As a result, in most standard volumes on music history, the discussion of Debussy's music is almost inevitably adorned by a reproduction of a Monet or Manet painting, however little they may add to our understanding of Debussy's music.

In order to examine the issue more closely, we will consider the meaning attached to the term in painting. It did not represent the *credo* of a group, since it was coined almost accidentally by a critic who was provoked by the subcaption "Une Impression" (An Impression), of Monet's painting "The Rising Sun."

Nevertheless, impressionism gradually became known as an approach to painting in which the artist tried to capture the object as seen at a given moment. The aim of the artist was to capture this fleeting impression, together with its unique atmosphere, often caused by an unusual combination of light and shade. The resultant paintings, which more often than not depicted nature, showed a vivid color scheme with fine gradations and de-emphasized the plastic and formal aspects of the object. This generalization is narrow even for the mentioned members of the impressionists because the group represented a variety of orientations. Even so, it is perhaps safe to say that, *in general,* in most of the paintings color is highlighted and the preference was to leave the contours blurred; also, more attention is given to the temporary, fleeting appearance of the object than to its permanent characteristics.

Admittedly, some of these characteristics are applicable to the music of Debussy. He, too, often drew his inspiration from nature. His music frequently renders atmospheric qualities and subtle gradations. Perhaps for his early orchestral *Nocturnes,* especially for "Nuages" (Clouds), the term has some validity as Debussy himself admits a pictorial influence—that of Whistler's "Nocturnes."

However, there is nothing blurred in Debussy's art. His music is finely wrought and highly chiseled. Not since Mozart—who incidentally was Debussy's idol—was every note of a score so interdependent and carefully weighed as in this music. While it may bring about a trance-like state in the listener, the dreams are controlled by the master's guiding hand and conscious mastery. Despite its seeming elusiveness, the music has its own inexorable logic, often exasperating the musical analyst who, in a futile search for the well-known models (such as sonata form, rondo form, and the like) brands them all as "free forms" —surely a meaningless term.

As mentioned earlier, Debussy objected to the label of impressionism. That he did not seek to capture the fleeting, aural reality of his objects is clear from his words: "I have an endless store of memories which, in my opinion, are worth more than reality whose beauty deadens thought."

Listening to Debussy's orchestral *La Mer,* it becomes obvious that the composer's aim was not to portray the unique sound images of the sea, but to penetrate to the core, to the symbolic essence, of what the sea meant to him.

Likewise, in his opera, *Pelléas et Mélisande,* the characters are musically delineated in depth and are given a more lifelike existence than that rendered by Maeterlinck himself, conveying at the same time the timeless symbolism of the play. Already from the short orchestral Prelude to Act I, the listener is engulfed in a setting in which time and place play but a minor role.

The approach, to present the symbol rather than to state the object, has much in common with the symbolist writer's ideology. This is not to suggest that symbolism should replace impressionism as a stylistic label for Debussy's music, but to emphasize the point that there is a more valid correlation between literary symbolism and the French composer's style than between the usual associations with impressionism.[17]

[17] The minority view which rejects the label of impressionism is well expressed in Rollo H. Meyer's study on Debussy.

The symbolist writer, like Debussy, suggests rather than describes. Thus an indefiniteness is achieved, or perhaps rather an ambiguity; in any case, it is a tenuous quality, demanding imaginative participation on the reader's part. The poets were intrigued by the sensuous possibilities of words; vowels were associated with colors, and they talked about "orchestrating their lines." The word images were fraught with a complex chain of free associations; Dujardin, the poet, Debussy's friend, invented the "monologue interieur," laying the foundation for the stream-of-consciousness style of writing.

There were other signs which pointed to Debussy's affinity with symbolist poets rather than with impressionist painters. His interest in painting was slight, as one gathers from his letters from Rome. He never painted himself, but he wrote both poetry and prose. He was a frequent guest at Mallarmé's house and Pierre Louÿs, the poet, was his closest friend.

Before examining the traits of Debussy's music, one more style problem needs clarification. Is Debussy's art—or impressionism, as some would like to have it—a stylistically self-contained phase in the history of music, or is it a late manifestation of romanticism? The question is not an easy one to decide, since, as noted before, romanticism itself encompasses a complex musical idiom with contradictory tendencies. If sound consciousness is recognized as a common denominator of all romantic music, then the French composer's music belongs to it most decidedly. Additional common features are subjectivity in feeling and a tendency toward the unification of the senses.

Despite these similarities, however, Debussy's music also represents a countercurrent in the stream of later romanticism; his restraint, his understating style and economy of writing, together with his idiosyncrasy toward the closed forms, and his completely novel harmonic language, set him strongly apart from most of his musical contemporaries. For these reasons, one has to consider Debussy's position as marginal, representing a dividing line between the nineteenth and twentieth centuries. Nothing will express his marginal position better than if we refrain from pigeonholing his art. His style is as ambiguous as are the feelings aroused by his music. If one still wishes to generalize, he is more *anti-German* than antiromantic. Through him France gained a leading position in European music.

GENERAL CHARACTERISTICS OF
DEBUSSY'S STYLE

The most remarkable and novel aspect of Debussy's music is his harmonic style. It is characterized by the gradual abandonment of the

major-minor key system and the avoidance of tonic-dominant juxtapositions. Instead, modes, pentatonic and whole-tone scales (see Chapter 4) motivate melodic and harmonic motion. To understand Debussy's
preferences for these scales, one should not think narrowly of the
technicalities involved in these choices, but of the inherent psychological effects. One should keep in mind that the major-minor key
system with the tonic-dominant axis sets up a certain tension system
with very well-defined destinations and harmonic purpose. This is exactly what Debussy wanted to avoid. One gets the difference in feeling
in a condensed form if one plays on the piano in succession the seven-
tone scale, the Dorian mode, the whole-tone scale, and if one stops in
each case before the last tone. The urge to go to the tonic after the
leading tone of the seven-tone scale is considerable, and the tonic
sounds as if a destination had been reached. No such feeling is experienced when one recaptures the starting note, for instance in the whole-
tone scale. The point is that Debussy's harmonic world has a different
flow from the music of the preceding era; because there is no urgent
need to reach "destinations," the flow of the chords assumes a gen-
tleness, an unforced quality. Instead of sharply drawn functional harmonic progressions, harmonies—or perhaps one should say merely chords
—are presented, often merely for their sound values, with one unresolved
chord gently flowing to the next, without eliciting any need for the
resolution of these chords. Thus a chord has the same unfunctional
role in the texture as a word which is used for its suggestive quality
in the symbolist poet's lines. The frequent parallel motion adds to the
lack of inner tension; in Example 8/6, quoted from "Nuages," the
parallel ninth chords (Debussy's favorite chord) seem to follow each
other, without encountering any resistance:

EX. 8/6 DEBUSSY, *"Nuages,"*[18] m. 14

The feeling of dissonance ceases to exist in such passages, that is,
the urge for resolution disappears. Because of this, and perhaps also
because the listener does not have to anticipate expectations and their

[18] Permission for reprint granted by Durand et Cie., copyright owners, Paris, France;
Elkan-Vogel Co., Inc., Philadelphia, Pa., agents.

fulfilment, his consciousness will be loosened. As the ear is not concerned with the destiny (resolution) of the chords, it is easy to enter into a dreamlike state.

The loosening of consciousness is also aided by another feature, namely, Debussy's musical speech pattern. Unlike so much eighteenth- and nineteenth-century music, his mode of presentation of musical ideas is not rhetorical or discursive. The traditional, particularly German, musical speech was based so often on symmetrical phrases, with the antecedent-consequent groupings. Such phraseology, in addition to its harmonic goal consciousness discussed earlier, also has an implied musical meaning, inasmuch as the consequent is the musical answer or outcome of the antecedent. In an eight-measure sentence, after having heard the first four measures, the listener formed a definite expectation or prediction as to how the second half of the sentence would turn out. Again, such expectation was bound to keep him in a heightened state of consciousness, as compared to a musical language such as Debussy's in which music has a different kind of flow. Thus, whereas in the older music—with Wagner representing the turning point —there was a twofold expectation, one moving on the harmonic plane and the other on the phrase-content level, in Debussy's music no such inner mobilization of our sensibilities takes place. This uncommitted, free flow of music, in which a phrase depends much less on the cogency of the preceding phrase, contributes to the *suggestive* character of the music. This change in musical speech has its parallel in the stream-of-consciousness style of the symbolist poets which represented a similar departure from the earlier, strict rhetoric of the Alexandrines.

The composer's melodic style is equally subtle: Debussy seldom writes catchy tunes that can be easily hummed or whistled. In fact, in the later works the melodic style becomes increasingly fragmentary; the melodic material in *Jeux* (1913), for instance, suggests techniques that can be found later in the works of twelve-tone composers.

The rhythmic scheme is also refined; the significance of beats and bar lines seems to vanish (see Ex. 3/5).

Understatement also governs the range of dynamics; soft dynamics reign with fine gradations. An example of restraint in dynamics can be seen in the early *La Damoiselle élue,* a composition of approximately fifteen minutes' duration in which only four measures rise to *forte.*

Love for nuances and sensuousness also characterizes the French composer's approach to instruments. Muted and divided strings, frequent use of pizzicato, muted horns, and soft percussion sounds are some of the distinctive features of the composer's orchestral palette. His occasional use of a large orchestra does not produce a thick texture. On the contrary, in *Pelléas et Mélisande,* for instance, only a few instruments are chosen at one time, resulting in the sonority of a chamber orchestra.

Debussy's music is not aimed merely at entertaining the senses despite the utmost care given to the beauty of sound. His music represents a new phase in man's evolution, as it contributes to the refinement of the apprehending faculties of his consciousness. While the surface beauty of the music recalls the voluptousness of the period—and perhaps the eternal pleasure-seeking of the Mediterranean civilizations—there are often deeper allusions to the human dilemma. If Proust is right that man's memories are stored in negatives and that these negatives are developed—they come to life—through the illuminations of the great artists, then Debussy is one of the chosen few.

DEBUSSY'S WORKS AND INFLUENCE

Debussy was active in almost every branch of composition and his contributions had far-reaching effects in each field.

The composition of orchestral works is widely spaced in time and through them one may detect the main phases of his stylistic development. A good introduction to Debussy's music, in general, is his first orchestral essay, *The Afternoon of a Faun* (1893).

THE AFTERNOON OF A FAUN

The Afternoon of a Faun (Prélude à l'Après-midi d'un Faune) was inspired by Mallarmé's poem. A reading of the poem (see Appendix), followed by listening to the composition, reveals the subtle correspondence between the text and the music. The composition is by no means a musical synthesis of the poem, but a free interpretation thereof. In Mallarmé's words: "The score is an illustration . . . which would present no dissonance with my text. Rather does it go further into the nostalgia and light with subtlety, malaise and richness."[19]

Debussy's method of procedure is quite un-Straussian. There is no attempt to capture the sounds of reality. The outer structure of the composition shows a slight correspondence with the poem; the opening melody, suggesting the faun's awakening, returns at the end, as the faun curls up to resume his dreams. Despite this recurrence of the opening melody, it would be mistaken to view the work in the shape of an A–B–A design; the delineation of sections is avoided throughout.

The first six measures contain many of the essential features of the

[19] Quoted in Edward Lockspeiser's *Debussy: His Life and Mind* (New York: Crowell-Collier and Macmillan Company, Inc., 1962), Vol. I, p. 157.

composer's style. The opening flute melody (Ex. 8/7) moving between two fixed points (C sharp and G) captures the curious lethargy of Mallarmé's faun, awakening from his slumber:

EX. 8/7 DEBUSSY, *Afternoon of a Faun,*[20] mm. 1-2

Harmonically, no key center is felt and the phrases flow freely without establishing an antecedent-consequent pattern. The harp glissando (m. 4) is pure color—a delight to the senses—and the notes of the French horn bring relative calm. The ensuing silence is a typically Debussyan device. His pauses have neither the witty character of Haydn's unexpected rests, nor do they carry the rhythmic momentum generated by Beethoven's pulsating pauses. Debussy's silence is fraught with expectation. Larger boundaries of one's consciousness are stirred; the echoes of the past are tied to the intimation of the future.

The opening melody soon recurs in the oboe (m. 11), accompanied by tremolo, muted strings. Repeated statements of the same melody in a new harmonic and varied orchestral context lead via a transition passage to a sustained melody in D flat major at measure 55:

EX. 8/8 *Afternoon of a Faun,* mm. 55-58

Soon a *fortissimo* climax is reached (m. 70), followed by the opening melody in augmentation:

EX. 8/9 *Afternoon of a Faun* mm. 79-81

[20]Permission granted for reprint by Editions Jean Jobert, Paris, France, copyright owners; Elkan-Vogel Co., Inc., Philadelphia, Pa., agents.

With increasing fragmentation of the opening melody, the music gradually fades away, until the antique cymbals conclude the composition on a tone of elusive finality, not unlike the ending of the poem.

OTHER WORKS

In the orchestral works following the *Afternoon of a Faun,* the successive phases of Debussy's stylistic development may be detected. In the *Three Nocturnes,* written in 1898, some devices are applied which have been described as impressionistic. Strongly influenced by the sights and sounds of Nature, free-floating harmonies and muted orchestral effects create an almost impressionistic atmosphere.

Stronger contours and sudden changes in mood are found in the three symphonic sketches of *La Mer* (1905). Here the orchestral writing has a touch of virtuosity seldom encountered in the earlier works.

A new rhythmic vigor characterizes the *Images* (1908); this stress on rhythmic forces is apparent from the tempo indication *assez animé dans un rythme alerte mais précis* (fairly animated, in an alert but precise rhythm) of "Iberia," one of the pieces in this set.

In *Jeux* (1913), the last orchestral essay, one becomes aware of the long path the composer has traveled. The music of this ballet, commissioned by Diaghilev soon after the success of Stravinsky's early ballets, is lean and often fragmented. The motivic treatment is extremely complex, foreshadowing the "perpetual variation" technique of the twelve-tone composers. The sound consciousness is still present, sophisticated and tenuous, particularly in the introduction, pointing to Webern, or perhaps even to Boulez. Chords are often used as mere "vertical aggregates" as employed by serial composers. The organization of the piece is highly original, its continuity showing a resemblance to some of Stravinsky's scores.

In the abstract types of instrumental compositions, the early String Quartet (1893) and the three late sonatas (Cello-Piano, Flute-Viola-Harp, and Violin-Piano), composed in 1916–1917, should be mentioned.

The String Quartet occupies a prominent place in the modern chamber music repertory. It is an accomplished work, although a number of stylistic features appear less well integrated than in later compositions. Thus, the cyclic treatment is strongly suggestive of Franck, while the middle section of the slow movement brings to mind the liturgy of the Eastern Orthodox Church. The last movement is the least compelling, showing some inconsistency in style. What influenced later composers is the novel sound Debussy elicited from the four string instruments and the complete equalization of the four parts. The novel treatment of pizzicato in the Scherzo movement is particularly effective.

The late three sonatas merit close study; while in the earlier critical literature these works were always considered as evidence of the composer's decline, more recently there is a reversal in their evaluation. They are highly imaginative and concentrated; Example 8/10 from the second movement of the Cello-Piano Sonata shows the increasingly linear texture of the composer's late style.

EX. 8/10 DEBUSSY, *Cello Sonata*,[21] second movement, opening

The early piano works are his least adventurous essays. His approach to the instrument received considerable impetus from Ravel's piano works, whose influence is particularly noticeable in *Estampes* (1903) and to some extent in the two sets of *Images* (1905–1907). The two books of *Preludes* (1910–1913) and the *Etudes* (1915) are highly original works.

Debussy, like Chopin, expanded the pianist's horizon considerably. His music also demands perfect technical mastery to the point of virtuosity, which has to serve poetic ends. Unless the pianist has the mastery of the most refined pedal technique, and a highly sensitive ear for sonorities, the music will fail to come to life.

The two books of *Preludes* and the *Etudes* are a veritable compendium of twentieth-century piano problems, although less systematic and didactic than Bartók's *Mikrokosmos*. The scope of the music is vast, the expressive values range from highly condensed, intense epigrammatic essays, foreshadowing Schoenberg's *Six Piano Pieces,* to the percussive last study of the second book of *Etudes,* which points to Bartók's and Hindemith's *martellato* (hammering) piano style.

Turning to the vocal music, in view of Debussy's strong penchant for symbolist poetry, it should not come as a surprise that his songs, based on the poetry of Mallarmé, Verlaine, Baudelaire, and Louÿs, form the core of his music. His perfect understanding of and sympathy with

---

[21]Permission for reprint granted by Durand et Cie., copyright owners, Paris, France; Elkan-Vogel Co., Inc., Philadelphia, Pa., agents.

the poets resulted in the most unusual communion ever reached between words and music. The atmosphere of the poems is captured in the elusive, ambiguous harmonic idiom of the piano part, on which is grafted the perfect recitative of the vocal line. Perhaps of all the media in which he composed, this is the best avenue for the novice to enter Debussy's world, especially if he has a minimal command of the French language. Through the text he will gain insight into the meaning of the composer's harmonic devices, which play such a significant part also in his instrumental music.

The same qualities concerning the relationship of text and music are in evidence, only on a larger canvas, in his opera, *Pelléas et Mélisande* (1892-1902), his magnum opus. Due to limitations of space the work cannot receive the attention it merits. Let it be said, however, that after *Tristan* it represents the most important influence in recent operatic history. Alban Berg's *Wozzeck* would be inconceivable without *Pelléas*.

In general, Debussy's vocal style influenced a host of composers; his *parlando* conception of the vocal line anticipated Schoenberg's *Sprechstimme* and can also be felt in Bartók's Songs.

Debussy's influence manifested itself in two ways: in the first place, as has been pointed out repeatedly, the leading composers of the century, namely, Bartók, Stravinsky, Schoenberg, and Webern owe much to him whether such influence lies in the uniqueness of sonority, in the new way of treating form, in the novel approach to the human voice, or in the many other realms of composition. In the second place, there were composers of lesser stature who were more strictly Debussy "followers," trying to imitate his inimitable style. Among these, Delius (1862-1934), Respighi (1879-1936), De Falla (1876-1946), the American Griffes (1884-1920), and Loeffler (1881-1935) should be mentioned.

MAURICE RAVEL (1875-1937)

Ravel, who has more musical stature than the mere followers, may not be ranked with those composers who opened up creatively new ways of musical thinking. For this reason he receives only cursory attention in spite of his fine contributions to the music literature.

Ravel often suffers from a comparison with Debussy, although their musical personalities were quite different. What is most alike in their music is their harmonic style, namely their fondness for modal writing, and their preference for certain harmonic devices and progressions. The greatest difference lies in the basic approach to their art: Debussy, despite some Wagnerian and Russian influence, draws mostly on his inner resources and his main stimulus lies in his inner promptings. Ravel, on the other hand, takes much greater advantage of his musical environment, and those elements, whether they contain Spanish, Hebrew, Greek, jazz, or gypsy flavor, remain essentially unintegrated in his music.

The two French composers—although in a totally different way—stand in a similar relationship as do Mahler and Strauss. Debussy's art, as Mahler's, comes from the deepest layers of his consciousness, and perhaps for that reason it shows an inner consistency and a high degree of integration. Ravel is more like Strauss, which is not to imply that he was interested in the musical portrayal of specific nonmusical events as Strauss was, but that both of them lent a keen ear to their environment. An additional similarity between the two composers is their mastery of the orchestra; Ravel is less dazzling and less opulent than Strauss, but equally resourceful. His orchestration of Mussorgsky's piano work, *Pictures at an Exhibition,* is probably the most successful feat of orchestral transcription ever accomplished. A task such as this would never have attracted Debussy.

Surprisingly, in light of Ravel's superior treatment of instruments and tonal imagery, his orchestral works are not numerous. With the exception of *Rhapsodie Espagnole* (1907) all of his orchestral works were composed for ballet; best known among these are *Bolero* (1927), *Daphnis et Chloé* (1909–1912), and somewhat less frequently played is *La Valse* (1920). Two piano concertos (one for the left hand) should be added to his orchestral works.

Among his chamber music, his String Quartet (1902) offers an interesting comparison with Debussy's Quartet (1893). His all too seldom played Piano Trio (1914) is one of the most successful contributions to this genre—neglected in our century. Unusual sonorities lend interest to his Violin-Cello Sonata (1922).

The importance of his piano works has been mentioned; his *Jeux d'Eau* (1901) is more advanced in every respect than Debussy's works from the same period. The same is true of *Miroirs* (1905). With the *Sonatine* (1905) Ravel turned toward a more linear style.

In general, his melodic thinking is more incisive than that of Debussy, with great emphasis placed on dance rhythms.

SUMMARY

The six composers discussed in this chapter represent the transition from nineteenth-century romanticism to the contemporary era, ushered in around 1910 by the early works of Stravinsky, Bartók, and Schoenberg.

All six composers had strong ties with romanticism, although they differ significantly in the impact they exerted on the music of the new era.

Of the two Austro-German composers, Richard Strauss represents the more conservative outlook. Although he extended the harmonic vocabulary and enriched the orchestral palette, he is an end-of-the-road composer who brought musical realism to a climactic termination point. Mahler's art, by comparison, has a definitely forward-looking quality; his symbolism points to man's search for existence and his moods suggest the plight of the modern artist. His unusual instrumental effects, his attenuated sonorities, and his flair for irony and parody, may be linked to Schoenberg and particularly to the early works of Berg.

Sibelius' popularity ranks high among the composers of the transition period; the controversy surrounding his conservative music is a strange chapter in the history of more recent music. His influence on later twentieth-century music, however, is negligible.

The significance of Scriabin lies in his harmonic thinking, as it represents an important phase in the dissolution of tonality. His derivation of both melody and harmony from the same vertical arrangement of notes, foreshadows the two-dimensional musical space of Schoenberg. Scriabin's intense style also anticipates expressionism.

Debussy stands out as the most original and influential of the six composers. His entirely new way of weaving together brief fragmentary motives, his harmonic devices, such as the free treatment of dissonances, replacing the major-minor key system by use of modes and whole-tone scales, opened up entirely new avenues. Equally novel is his conception of sound, whose refined nuances, often reflecting Far Eastern influences, verge on the *Klangfarbenmelodie* device of the Viennese atonal composers. Novel, too, is Debussy's treatment of form which is characterized by a uniquely compelling continuity, a mixture, as it were, of the strictest logic and the greatest freedom. Finally, his *Pelléas et Mélisande* is a most important milestone in recent operatic history. One can state without exaggeration that Debussy exerted the most important single influence on a host of composers, including Stravinsky, Bartók, Berg, and even Webern and Boulez.

Next to Debussy, Ravel historically occupies a less important position, even though he significantly enriched the orchestral and piano literature with a number of masterworks.

• • • • • • •

The following diagram attempts to sum up the complex web of relations and lines of continuity which finally led to the music of the six composers who will be discussed in the following section of the book.

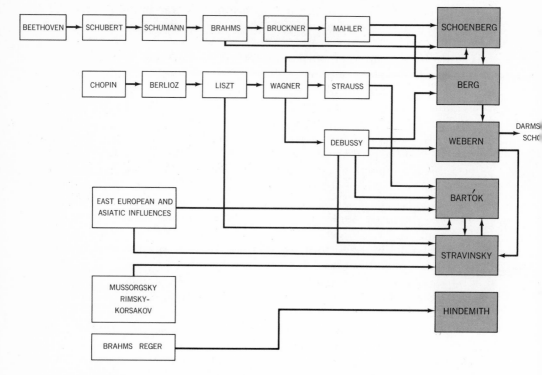

Admittedly, the chart is arbitrary and many important names are omitted; many additional connecting lines could be added. Even so, a number of points made in the present chapter become graphically visible; for instance, the different ancestries of Mahler and Strauss and the key position of Debussy. More importantly, the chart points up the significance of the East European and Asiatic influences on the music of Bartók and Stravinsky, which revitalized the rhythmic sense of the whole Western musical world. It also reveals that the Viennese atonal composers remained unaffected by such influences, showing them as the preservers of the Austro-German, or perhaps Central European, musical tradition.

IGOR STRAVINSKY
(1882–   )

*The Past is for us; but the sole terms on
which it can become ours are its subordina-
tion to the Present.*

EMERSON

Stravinsky has been a dominant force in the music of the
twentieth century. His life epitomizes the uprooted existence of
many leading contemporary composers, and his music embodies
nearly every significant tendency of the first half of the century.

A glance at the composer's output shows that environmental
forces were a powerful influence on his stylistic development.
The break with his native country after the revolution marked
the end of his so-called Russian period. A world citizen with
French naturalization papers, he now embarked upon a cosmopolitan course that, because of his adaptation of certain eighteenth-century practices, was labeled neoclassic.
World War II necessitated a new emigration; Stravinsky found

a haven in the United States and soon became an American citizen.

Among the many personal influences, the role of Serge Diaghilev, the director of the Ballet Russe, is of great importance. Diaghilev's aid and inspiration helped to make Stravinsky's early ballets a brilliant success.

While early in his career an older man gave impetus to the composer's creative work, in the late 1940s a young American musician, Robert Craft, attached himself to the composer, first as protégé and later as associate and spokesman for the older composer's music. Craft, a specialist in the music of Webern, was probably responsible for Stravinsky's turn to serial music, thus baffling the critics, to whom Stravinsky and the Viennese atonal school seemed irreconcilable opposites.

The events of Stravinsky's life and his esthetic beliefs will be outlined in conjunction with his stylistic development. The composer's writings will serve as the main source of material, beginning with the early *Autobiography*[1] (1935) and following with the *Poetics of Music*[2] (1939), a series of six lectures delivered at Harvard University. Additional material will be drawn from the five volumes[3] of conversations with Robert Craft, published more than twenty-five years after the *Autobiography*.

EARLY LIFE

Stravinsky was born in 1882 near St. Petersburg—today's Leningrad. The physical and psychological surroundings of his childhood emerge with much more depth from the Craft conversations than from the *Autobiography*. While Craft's probing questions may not always be very tactful (for instance: "What do you remember of your father's death and funeral?") he succeeds in eliciting a good deal of new material. For instance, all we know about the composer's father from the *Autobiography* is that he was a prominent bass singer at the Imperial

---

[1] Igor Stravinsky, *An Autobiography* (New York: Simon & Schuster, Inc., 1936; W. W. Norton & Company, Inc., 1962).

[2] Igor Stravinsky, *Poetics of Music* (New York: Vintage Books, 1956). Translated from the French by Arthur Knodel and Ingolf Dahl; copyright by The President and Fellows of Harvard College.

[3] Igor Stravinsky and Robert Craft, *Conversations with Igor Stravinsky* (Garden City: Doubleday & Company, Inc., 1959); *Memories and Commentaries* (1960); *Expositions and Developments* (1962); *Dialogues and a Diary* (1963); *Themes and Episodes* (New York: Alfred A. Knopf, Inc., 1966).

Opera; from the *Conversations* it is revealed, however, that he was impatient, authoritarian, and punitive. It also emerges from this source that as a child Stravinsky felt lonely and unloved by his parents. A touching association reveals that the cell of Petrouchka, the pathetic puppet, was based on the memory of his own room in his parents' house.

Regarding his musical studies, his progress was not spectacular. He was headed for a career in law when, in 1902, Rimsky-Korsakov accepted him as a student, on the condition, however, that he do remedial work in harmony and counterpoint. Harmony, incidentally, was a subject he intensely disliked.

His recollections of Rimsky-Korsakov are not entirely consistent in the two sets of sources. In the *Autobiography* he is remembered with respect and admiration as a "great teacher." In the more recent sources, however, either due to the passing of time or to Craft's insistent questioning, the teacher's stature diminishes considerably. Despite some faint praise, it seems to him in retrospect that the most important tools of composition he had to discover for himself.

What was extremely important, however, was that in his teacher's home he met the intelligentsia of St. Petersburg, among them Diaghilev, a second cousin, who at the time was the editor of an avant-garde literary magazine. Soon Diaghilev became the director of the Ballet Russe and commissioned the young composer to orchestrate two pieces by Chopin for the Ballet Russe, a test for bigger things to come.

DIAGHILEV'S INFLUENCE

Stravinsky's biographers usually see Diaghilev's influence merely as that of a powerful backer who launched the successful career of the young composer. A careful reading of the *Autobiography,* however, reveals that Diaghilev's influence was a much more profound one. Opening the pages of this volume at random, everywhere one encounters the ballet director's name. It seems as if Diaghilev, in the years when the early ballets were composed, assumed the role of a Svengali. One gains the impression that the Dionysian freedom and abandonment of the music of this period—later so strongly refuted by the composer—was at least partially due to the spell exerted by this demoniac, flamboyant personality. The frenzied, savage *Rite of Spring* was written at the height of their friendship, in 1912.

World War I caused the separation of the two friends. The composer settled in Switzerland for the war years where he conceived, with the collaboration of the Swiss poet Ramuz, *L'Histoire du Soldat.* The intense jealousy Diaghilev felt about the new work indicates the emotionally charged quality of their friendship.

The assumption that Diaghilev may have been a unique driving force behind Stravinsky's early primitivistic style is supported by the fact that the cooling off of their friendship coincided in time with the composer's gradual turning toward the classical, Apollonian ideal. Order, control, self-limitation—stressed frequently in the *Poetics of Music*— became the guiding principles.

As the years passed, the composer was increasingly reluctant to follow his extravagant friend's striving for "modernism at any price" and his search for something sensational. Nevertheless, Stravinsky experienced Diaghilev's death in 1929 with profound shock and in the *Autobiography* he cites "the terrible void created by the disappearance of this colossal figure." In the Craft volumes, however, Stravinsky comments rather on the negative aspects of the idol of his earlier years. The weaknesses of Diaghilev's character, his self-destructive vanity, his sexual pathology, and his absurd superstitiousness are now fully revealed.

OVERVIEW OF WORKS

The list of Stravinsky's works (see pp. 220–221) shows that the compositions inspired by story, by gestures, or by text, far outnumber those that were the product of abstract musical thought. Furthermore, the works belonging to the first category met with greater success—if frequency of performance is a measure of success. A glance at the list also shows, disregarding the ballet form, how little Stravinsky explores one medium after tackling it once. The early essays in string quartet form were never resumed; there is only *one* piano sonata, *one* piano concerto, *one* violin concerto, *one* mass, and so on. Although there are two symphonies—disregarding the Symphony, Op. 1, a student work—their setting and objectives are so different that it never occurs to anyone to refer to them as First and Second Symphonies.

It is easy to see why some commentators view Stravinsky's creative work as *problem-solving.* Once the demands of one particular set of circumstances were fulfilled, he moved to another medium. This illustrates Stravinsky's restless, curiously inquisitive musical mind, forever in search of new settings and new self-limitations. Perhaps this constant search for a new medium prevented a certain type of musical growth that often appears as the fruit of a composer's repeated efforts to gain mastery over one medium, as seen in Beethoven's stylistic development, reflected in his string quartets.

The one medium in which Stravinsky expressed himself repeatedly is in music for the ballet, and the only works that form a sequence and in which a thread of continuous growth can be observed are the three early ballets of the Russian period, all commissioned by Diaghilev: *The Firebird* (1909), *Petrouchka* (1910–1911), and *The Rite of Spring* (1911–1913) (often referred to by its French title, *Le Sacre du Printemps*).

Stravinsky's works will be examined in four sections: (1) the Russian period (1908–1917); (2) works from *L'Histoire du Soldat* to *Oedipus Rex* (1918–1927) (including a critical discussion of neoclassicism); (3) after *Oedipus Rex* to the *Rake's Progress* (1928–1950); and (4) serial works (1951–   ).

THE RUSSIAN PERIOD (1908–1917)

THE FIREBIRD

In *The Firebird,* Stravinsky is still very much influenced by the music of his teacher, particularly by *Le Coq d'Or,* a ballet also based on a Russian fairy tale. Both stories deal with the struggle between good and evil forces, and it is in the harmonic characterization that the younger composer adopted his master's scheme of depicting humans by diatonic harmonies and supernatural forces by chromaticism. Both works frequently employ the interval of the tritone, and the younger composer skillfully assimilates his teacher's oriental exoticism. In addition to the Russian flavor, the *Firebird* music also shows traces of the refined French harmonic and orchestral idiom.

It is interesting to observe the increasing mastery with which the composer assimilates Russian folk music in the three ballets under discussion. In *Firebird* the folk material is simply lifted out of anthologies edited and collected by Balakirev and Rimsky-Korsakov; a comparison of the original folk source (Ex. 9/1) and its transplantation into the last movement of the *Firebird Suite* (Ex. 9/1/a and Ex. 9/1/b) shows that the material was taken over virtually unchanged:

EX. 9/1 Folk Song from the *Balakirev Anthology* (1873)

EX. 9/1/a *Firebird Suite,*[4] fourth movement, mm. 9–12

EX. 9/1/b Fourth movement, study no. 19

As far as orchestral sound is concerned, *The Firebird* is shimmering, opulent, and sensuous. In accordance with romantic practice, the strings are used for their mellowness and the solo violin and solo cello set forth sustained melodies. In the next two ballets the emphasis shifts from the mellow strings toward the brass and percussion sections, resulting in a hardened sound.

The only movement in *The Firebird* that foreshadows the later style is the "Infernal Dance." This movement is marked by striking rhythmic force and could not have been written by any other composer but Stravinsky. Hard syncopations are hammered out by the brass and percussion instruments and the music is saturated with displaced accents, syncopations, and cross-rhythms. The strings, if employed, are used merely for their percussive effects.

The first Paris performance of *The Firebird* was a resounding success; Debussy, who was present among the many notables, predicted a brilliant future for the young composer.

PETROUCHKA

The next two ballets, *Petrouchka* and *The Rite of Spring,* according to the composer, were conceived of in dreamlike states. The idea of *The Rite of Spring* first occurred to Stravinsky at a time when he was still occupied with the last section of *The Firebird.* In a dream or vision he had seen "a solemn pagan rite; sage elders seated in a circle watched a young girl dance herself to death. They were sacrificing her to propitiate the god of spring." The work was intended as a symphony of spring, with its central idea based on the pagan rites which heralded the advent of spring in prehistoric Russia. As soon as Diaghilev saw

[4] Reprinted by permission of E. F. Kalmus.

**PLATE 7. IGOR STRAVINSKY WITH
WASLAW NIJINSKY as Petrouchka** (1911)
The Bettmann Archive, New York

the first sketches, he prevailed upon the composer to adapt the topic for the Ballet Russe and immediately secured the collaboration of Nicolai Roerich, a noted expert in Russian mythology.

The project seemed an arduous one and the young composer, still exhausted from the strenuous task of meeting the deadline for *The Firebird,* felt the need to "refresh" himself with a less demanding task. This time he planned a piano solo work (*Konzertstück*) with orchestra. The inception of the work is described in the *Autobiography* as follows:

> I had in my mind a distinct picture of a puppet, suddenly endowed with life, exasperating the patience of the orchestra with diabolic cascades of arpeggios. The orchestra in turn retaliates with menacing trumpet blasts. The outcome is a terrific noise which reaches its climax and ends in the sorrowful and querulous collapse of the poor puppet.[5]

When Diaghilev arrived in Switzerland to see what progress his friend had made on *The Rite of Spring,* he was surprised to find him engaged in a new project. Once again he persuaded Stravinsky to alter his plans and change the orchestral piece into a ballet, based on the theme of the puppet's suffering.

These two ballets became Stravinsky's most widely acclaimed works, and are considered by many critics as his best creative efforts. The fact that both works were prompted by visual images while the composer was in a dreamlike state suggests that Stravinsky's creativity was nourished at this period by the deepest layers of his consciousness. By the same token, the relative paleness and aridity of many later works may have been the result of the composer's feeling of estrangement.

In *Petrouchka* the magic splendor of *Firebird* is left behind. Instead of princes and princesses a carnival crowd of sailors, coachmen, nursemaids now occupies the stage. Life is portrayed in its reality with a mixture of the comic and tragic, the pathetic and the grotesque. Correspondingly, the music is less refined: plasticity and linear textures take precedence over the subtle harmonic shadings of *The Firebird.* The melodies are now more fragmented, propelled by jagged and twisted rhythms, infusing an extraordinary animation into the music. Clashing meters and harmonies are superimposed, while asymmetrical groupings of beats and phrases bring about tension and excitement. Like *Firebird, Petrouchka* has also become a favorite both in its ballet form and also as a purely orchestral composition. Since *Petrouchka* is Stravinsky's first truly original work and is representative of his early style, it will be examined in some detail.

The music consists of four scenes; Petrouchka's appearance is delayed until the second scene. The opening section deals with an Easter carnival in St. Petersburg. The first measures (Ex. 9/2) suggest people merrily bustling about in colorful attire:

---

[5] Stravinsky, *An Autobiography,* p. 31.

EX. 9/2 *Petrouchka,*[6] opening

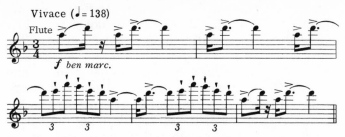

It should be noted in Example 9/2 that the melody is rhythmically designed so that the accented figure (A–D) appears on every one of the three beats in the measure. This rhythmic juggling with a motive became one of Stravinsky's favorite practices and was adopted by many of his followers. The recurring interval of the fourth suggests the Slavic folk idiom. The flute melody is accompanied by two French horns and two clarinets, and consists of alternating open fifths and minor thirds. In the clarinet line the alternation of the intervals occurs twice as often as in the horns; both accompanying instruments play *piano,* while the flute is marked *forte.* The total effect is completely novel, unlike anything written in the nineteenth century.

At study number 2,[7] while the excitement of the carnival is maintained by the persistent clarinet-French horn figure, which now gains support from other instruments, the flute melody disappears. Instead, the attention is drawn to the bass line, where for three measures an innocuous motive appears:

EX. 9/3 *Petrouchka,* mm. 14–16

The rhythmic disturbance, caused by the displaced accents of Example 9/3, is soon increased by clashing meters: in measures 30–31 while the piccolos and oboes play in $\frac{5}{8}$, the rest of the orchestra adheres to the $\frac{2}{4}$ meter. This is soon followed by clashing $\frac{7}{8}$ and $\frac{3}{4}$ meters.

The motive cited in Example 9/3 foreshadows events to come: some 20 measures later, at study number 5, it becomes the main figure pre-

---

[6]Copyright 1912 by Edition Russe de Musique. All rights assigned to Boosey & Hawkes, Inc.; revised edition copyright by Boosey & Hawkes, Inc., 1947. Reprinted by permission.

[7]The study numbers refer to the original version of the score.

sented by the whole orchestra, signifying the passing by of a group of drunken men. This compositional device, whereby the music portrays dramatic events and gestures while maintaining its motivic self-sufficiency, makes the music so successful both as a ballet and as an abstract piece of music.

Example 9/4 and its subsequent development furnishes an interesting example of how Stravinsky's imagination is fired by extramusical events. What is so brilliantly captured here is the feeling of anticipation conveyed by the motive of Example 9/3. The aim at this point was still to keep the noise of the fair in the foreground, merely suggesting the approach of the crowd by the displaced rhythmic accents. This ingenious anticipation becomes apparent to the listener only at study number 5, when the same melody appears in $\frac{2}{4}$ meter (Ex. 9/4) with no more displaced accents and is played by the full orchestra, heralding the arrival of the group.

EX. 9/4 *Petrouchka*, study no. 5

The melody appearing in Example 9/4 is based on a folk song, "Christ is Risen," contained in Rimsky-Korsakov's *Collection of 100 Russian Folk Songs* of 1876, where it appears as follows:

EX. 9/5 "Christ is Risen"

A comparison of the two versions shows that, while the melody is taken over almost unchanged, the harmonization is typically Stravinskyan. It is based on the superimposition of diatonic chords (discussed as pandiatonicism in Chapter 4), a device that appears throughout all his stylistic periods.

It is also apparent from the comparison that now the composer assimilates folk material in a more sophisticated way than was apparent in *The Firebird* (see Ex. 9/1, 9/1/a and b).

The following section (study no. 7) has a typically Stravinskyan imprint both in rhythm and in sonorities. After a heavy downbeat, reinforced by trombone, tuba, timpani, and basses, the violins and woodwinds carry out swift metric changes ($\frac{3}{8}, \frac{4}{8}, \frac{2}{8}, \frac{5}{8}$) in a *stringendo* passage; this section returns several times within the tableau, resulting in a sense of unity. The fair theme then cuts across the noise and gradually the tune of an approaching barrel organist emerges:

EX. 9/6 *Petrouchka,* 3 mm. after study no. 12

By a brilliant stroke of orchestration, the composer lets the listener know, through the piccolo and flute figurations, that the barrel organ is creaking and is in need of oil.

A French dance tune ("She had a Wooden Leg") is unexpectedly heard:

EX. 9/7 *Petrouchka,* study no. 13

Soon the French tune, now in $\frac{3}{4}$, is combined with a variant of Example 9/6 and later with the dotted rhythm of the opening motive, played now by the oboes.

In spite of all these disparate elements, unity is maintained by repeating earlier sections; the opening theme and the march of the crowd recur several times, interspersed with the section consisting of metric changes. Already, in this early work, the composer displays his unsurpassed skill in integrating heterogeneous elements. Despite its seeming incongruities, such as a vulgar, French street-song, Russian folk melody, the use of sophisticated rhythmic procedures, and a very advanced orchestral technique, the entire first scene leaves the listener with the impression of a unified work.

A climactic crescendo leads to a solo percussion section signifying that the curtain of the puppet theatre is about to rise. The director, a magician, appears in a setting reminiscent of *The Firebird*. He plays a cadenza on his flute and finishes with three descending couplets of notes:

EX. 9/8 *Petrouchka*, mm. 8–10, after study no. 32

He animates the three puppets, Petrouchka, the Ballerina, and the Moor, all of whom immediately burst into a Russian Dance, to the amazement of the onlooking crowd. The dance (Ex. 9/9), which is somewhat stiff and metallic, brings the first scene to an end.

EX. 9/9 *Petrouchka*, study no. 33

The key of C major and the superimposed antagonistic harmonies give a sense of crude naturalness to the music; the rhythmic pulsation is somewhat mechanical, perhaps reminding one that the dancers are puppets after all. A completely novel effect is created by the sonorities of the piano, two harps, celesta, and xylophone.

The central character of the second scene is Petrouchka, who cuts a pathetic figure. Although made of sawdust, he is the most human of the three puppets; he is the only one who knows the feeling of suffering. He is in love with the Ballerina but she is repelled by his grotesque ugliness. His motive (Ex. 9/10), moving on two tonal planes (C major and F sharp major), symbolizes the puppet's dual nature, and the duality of the harmonic scheme pervades the entire scene.

EX. 9/10 *Petrouchka,* study no. 49

The Ballerina, attracted to the Moor, passes by in front of Petrouchka's cell, causing him to misinterpret her appearance as a promising sign. When he realizes her total indifference, he bursts out in a fury, expressed in dissonant harmonic superimpositions (study no. 51), heightened by screaming trumpet and piston figures.

The third scene takes place in the luxurious setting of the Moor's cell. His dance is sensuous; its exotic accent is brought out by the intricate rhythmic pattern of the soft percussion instruments:

EX. 9/11 *Petrouchka,* study no. 65, partial score

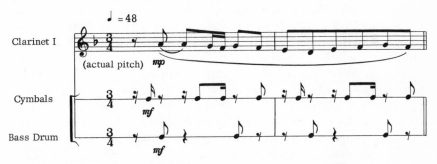

It is impossible to list all the ingenious, novel instrumental effects; however, one additional example is cited in the brief English horn solo at study no. 66. The solo, accompanied by a soft, dissonant *sul ponti-cello*[8] cello-bass figure, has an ominous ring that anticipates the Moor's future evil actions (Ex. 9/12).

[8] *Sul ponticello*—a sound effect achieved on a string instrument by playing with the bow very near to the bridge.

EX. 9/12 *Petrouchka,* study no. 66

The Moor's dance is interrupted by the appearance of the Ballerina; the trumpet solo with snare drum accompaniment (study no. 69) captures her light-footed, swift, yet slightly angular dance in a striking way. Suddenly the music unexpectedly changes to a waltz, based on a tune contained in an *Anthology of Styrian Dances.* The waltz is marked *sentimentalmente e cantabile* for a few measures, but soon a faster waltz theme, "Dorfschwaben in Oesterreich," is introduced, marked now *poco grotesco.* Once again, as in the first scene, the dividing line between serious and popular music all but disappears. When the Moor joins in the dance (9 measures after no. 72), in a different meter as he cannot keep up with the swift Ballerina, it becomes obvious that the entire scene is a sophisticated, immensely clever parody of the flirtation between the two puppets. At study no. 76 the triplet figure in the trumpet signals Petrouchka's appearance. Conveyed by some of the most dissonant harmonies of the entire work, he enters in a rage of jealousy, but is thrown out by the Moor.

Following the brief middle scenes, the last tableau is comparable to the opening one in size and weight. Themes from the first scene reappear, altered and combined with new melodies. The opening melody of the first scene appears in the form of a canon and combined with a new folk theme (study no. 92) entitled "The Dance of the Nursemaids":

EX. 9/13 *Petrouchka,* study no. 92, (partial score: piccolo, flute, violin)

The pitch of the merrymaking increases; the popular figures of Russian carnivals, the coachmen, the wealthy merchant who scatters banknotes among the crowd, the bear tamer, and a group of masqueraders appear in quick succession. Suddenly the attention centers on the puppet theatre from which Petrouchka emerges closely pursued by the Moor. The music takes an ominous turn; Petrouchka's motive is heard again in its bitonal setting. The Moor catches up with Petrouchka and strikes him down with his sword, Petrouchka's end is marked by a *fortissimo, sul ponticello glissando* in the strings. The same piping flute and piccolo sounds which signified the animation of the puppets in the opening scene are heard again, as Petrouchka's dual existence comes to an end. The magician appears on the scene; as he carries the body toward the theatre, Petrouchka's ghost is sneering at him menacingly. The music comes to an unresolved ending on an F sharp, preceded by a C, bringing into focus the two main harmonic poles of Petrouchka's dual nature. The last pages of the score convey the feeling of a coda, summarizing the composition by condensing its material; as before, the dramatic purpose and the purely musical plane are marvelously combined. It is not surprising that fifty years later Stravinsky is still "more proud of these last pages than of anything else in the score."

THE RITE OF SPRING

Although the Russian period extends beyond *The Rite of Spring,* this epoch-making work represents a terminal point in the composer's early stylistic development.

The comparison between *The Firebird* and *Petrouchka* indicated the direction in which the composer was headed; in *The Rite of Spring* he reaches the end of this road. This cataclysmic work all but destroyed the foundations of Western music as it had been known in the last four or five centuries.

The Rite of Spring leaves behind the refined sonorities of *The Firebird* and the grotesque, pathetic world of *Petrouchka's* puppets. Its subject matter turns to a mystical, pagan vision, rooted in the collective racial past. It deals with the advent of spring, whose elemental forces are the symbols of life, and also of primitive man's untamed, instinctual drives. In order to pacify those forces, the life of a young girl is offered as a sacrifice in a mystical ceremony.

The music has a visionary grandeur and its pounding rhythms and harsh dissonances caused the first night's audience to release its anxiety in a tumultuous riot. A year later, however, the same music in a concert version was received with great enthusiasm. Never again did Stravinsky write music in which the control over the material was so threatened by the unleashing of deep, unconscious forces. Only the reverberations of *The Rite of Spring* are heard, in some later works sounding like distant rumblings from the bottom of an inactive volcano.

The work, subtitled "Pictures from Pagan Russia," falls into two parts: I. The Fertility of the Earth; II. The Sacrifice. In the original production the choreography was carefully worked out in accordance with a sequence of eleven numbers.

When the ballet was revived in 1921, the choreography was stripped of its pictorial and story suggestions, resulting in purely formal movements which pleased the composer, who found "moments of great beauty in the group movements when the plastic expression was in perfect accord with the music." In the *Autobiography* he denies that the work had any pictorial implications and is reluctant to discuss the "feelings" by which he was prompted to write the music.

This distortion of the past was probably necessary as the result of the composer's newly formulated antiromantic and antiexpressive esthetic credo, which will be discussed in more detail in the next section.

The outer structure of the work does not show any clear-cut pattern of unfolding, except that the orchestral introductions to both parts are soft and relatively melodic, while the closing sections in both parts are frenzied and climactic. The form of the single movements does not follow any sectional or symmetrical design either; short motives appear and reappear in ever new rhythmic settings and with harmonic alterations. Stravinsky states: "I was guided by no system whatever in *Le Sacre*. . . . Very little immediate tradition lies behind it. I had only my ear to help me. I heard and I wrote what I heard."[9]

The work has a strong Russian, or rather, Asiatic flavor. Despite this folk music quality, with the exception of the opening melody which is based on a Lithuanian folk song, the melodies are not derived from specific folk sources. It seems that now the composer's melodic invention coincides with the racial idiom of his native country.

What rules supreme in the work is rhythm with its unprecedented drive. Never in the history of Western music has rhythm occupied such a dominant position. According to a French author, Siohan, *Le Sacre* conveys the chill of a blizzard blowing from the Russian steppe and penetrating to the bone.

The rhythmic devices in the work include changing meters on a scale never attempted before, while displaced accents are frequently hammered out by eight French horns and a large percussion section. Cross-rhythms and metric superimpositions also appear with much greater frequency than in *Petrouchka*. Rhythmic ostinatos are often introduced, binding together extended sections of the work.

The melodies are even shorter and more fragmented than in *Petrouchka*, with even less legato articulation. The orchestral sound is also harder than in the earlier ballets; the hammering and pounding often bring to mind the drumbeats of primitive music. The size of the orchestra surpasses anything the composer ever attempted.

The harmonies, too, reach a new peak of boldness. Although no "system" is apparent, the famous bitonal superimposition of the opening chords of the "Dance of the Youths and Maidens" (Ex. 9/14) has a germinating influence on the total harmonic conception of the work. It is particularly the diminished octave that is often derived from the F flat—E flat superimposition.

[9] Stravinsky-Craft, *Expositions and Developments,* p. 169.

EX. 9/14 *The Rite of Spring,* "Dance of the Youths and Maidens,"[10] opening

The rhythmic and harmonic superimpositions result in the strained quality of the music which often approaches the breaking point. The impact of the work had a profound influence upon composers on both sides of the Atlantic.

The Rite of Spring is pure Stravinsky; it stands apart from all subsequent works in which one always finds that the master's style appears in an amalgam with various stylistic components from the past. Perhaps the only work that matches this "purity" of style is *The Wedding.*

Although the Russian style extends beyond *Le Sacre,* this work represented a turning point. Stravinsky did not allow the breakthrough of almost uncontrollable inner forces to happen again. Many years later his explanation for the change was formulated in the *Poetics of Music:*

> What is important for the lucid ordering of the work—for its crystallization—is that all the Dionysian elements which set the imagination of the artist in motion must be properly subjugated before they intoxicate us, and must finally be made to submit to the law: Apollo demands it.[11]

OTHER COMPOSITIONS FROM

THE RUSSIAN PERIOD

After the production of *Le Sacre,* a few short vocal compositions followed in addition to the *Three Pieces for String Quartet.* Disregarding his *Renard* (1915–1916), a "Burlesque in Song and Dance" built on Russian folk tales, two major compositions—both hampered by long interruptions—occupied the composer during these years. These were *The Nightingale* and *The Wedding,* the latter often referred to by its French title, *Les Noces.*

The Nightingale, an opera based on a story by Hans Christian Andersen, was started in 1908 and interrupted the next year by the com-

[10]Copyright 1921 by Edition Russe de Musique. Copyright assigned to Boosey & Hawkes, Inc., 1947. Reprinted by permission.
[11]Stravinsky, *Poetics of Music,* p. 83.

mission for *The Firebird.* Work was resumed five years later and, as a result, it suffers from stylistic inconsistencies. When it was finally produced by the Diaghilev company in 1914, it received only two performances.

Les Noces, a cantata, also demanded long and difficult labor. Its composition took almost four years (1914–1918), and the instrumentation was completed only five years later, in 1923. The arduous labor of composition indicates the crisis the composer lived through during these years. His brother died on the Rumanian front and a very old and beloved friend of his childhood passed away. Because of the Revolution he was cut off from his income. During this crucial period vacillation also marked his creative work: at first he planned a 150-piece orchestra for *Les Noces,* but after years of indecision, during which time he turned to chamber music style in *L'Histoire du Soldat,* he decided on a completely novel orchestration, consisting of four pianos and a large group of percussion instruments.

The Wedding is "Russian" in the same sense that *The Rite of Spring* is Russian. The essentials of Russian folk music are captured without recourse to actual folk songs, with the exception of the factory song used in the last scene.

The Wedding shows a similarity in its rawness and in its prosody to Mussorgsky's settings of Russian texts. Otherwise, it lacks Mussorgsky's human compassion or his dramatic portrayal of the tortures of the human soul. The characters in *Les Noces* have a puppetlike quality and are surrounded by an air of objectivity.

The Russian folk influence strongly diminished by the end of World War I, with *L'Histoire du Soldat* (1918) forming a dividing line. As an extension of the Russian period, *Mavra,* a one-act *opera buffa,* should be mentioned; composed in 1921, it was dedicated to the memory of Pushkin, Glinka, and Tchaikovsky. The work met with little success.

ATTITUDE TOWARD RUSSIA

An analysis of Stravinsky's Russian period would remain incomplete without an examination of the composer's attitude toward his native country. The chronology of his works clearly indicates that the Russian revolution roughly coincided with the composer's abandonment of the Russian style. Whether or not this was a conscious decision is difficult to determine, as there is a lack of specific information in the biographical data.

The *Autobiography* does not communicate Stravinsky's feelings concerning his exile. Although the day-to-day events, travels of this period, are treated in detail, the composer devotes only a single sentence to world events, stating that the news of the war aroused patriotic feelings and a "sense of sadness" for being so far from his native country. Otherwise, there is no hint of the extent to which he allowed such feelings as homesickness or nostalgia to enter his consciousness.

The *Poetics of Music* contains a bitter denunciation of the moral and cultural values of Soviet Russian society. As a result, Stravinsky was considered a traitor by his compatriots and performances of his works were banned until quite recently. If there was a deep, smoldering love for his fatherland, this was not apparent even to his closest friends.

It is only in the Craft volumes that we get any insight into the depth of Stravinsky's attachment to his native land. The vividness of childhood memories is evident from the fond description of the early Russian milieu. His unswerving affection for his native country is apparent from the fourth volume of the Craft series which contains an account of the composer's visit to Russia after an absence of almost fifty years. It is evident that he never got over the break and was profoundly moved by the warmth of his reception. Craft records with amazement how quickly the composer shed the cloak of the world citizen and transformed into a Russian. Western journalists recorded with astonishment a statement made by the composer at a reception of the Soviet Minister of Education:

> A man has one birthplace, one fatherland, one country—he *can* have only one country—and the place of his birth is the most important factor in his life. I regret that circumstances separated me from my fatherland, that I did not bring my works to birth there, and, above all, that I was not there to help the new Soviet Union create its new music. But I did not leave Russia only by my own will, even though I admit that I disliked much in my Russia and in Russia generally, but the right to criticize Russia is mine, because Russia is mine and because I love it. I do not give any foreigner that right.[12]

The gratitude with which he accepted the restored love of his native country and his deep regret for his self-imposed exile suggest that his abandonment of the Russian style was caused by the pain of the separation. Furthermore, it is likely that he avoided this topic in the *Autobiography* because, at the time, these issues may have been too painful and had to be repressed along with other saddening childhood experiences. The inner control necessary for this repression may have also contributed to his renunciation of the free reign of the Dionysian creativity.

---

[12] Stravinsky-Craft, *Dialogues and a Diary,* p. 246.

L'HISTOIRE DU SOLDAT TO
OEDIPUS REX (1918–1927)

During the decade that passed from L'Histoire to Oedipus Rex, Stravinsky gave up his Swiss residence and settled in France.

The first novel source of interest was jazz, made available to him by his friend, the Swiss conductor, Ernest Ansermet, who returned from a visit to the United States in 1918 with various jazz manuscripts. The Russian composer at first "felt a passion" for the new idiom. Incorporation of the idiom may be seen in the "Ragtime" of L'Histoire, in Ragtime for Eleven Instruments, and in the Piano Rag Music, all composed in 1918–1919. Actually, several features of jazz were anticipated in his earlier style, namely the intricate syncopations and some of the timbres peculiar to jazz, such as the special use of the trumpet, trombone, and percussion instruments.

Turning away from the Russian style, Stravinsky evinced a new interest in chamber music. None of the works written in the period under discussion employs a large orchestra. With the trend toward chamber music, a greater interest in contrapuntal devices is also noted, together with an increased plasticity of texture. This plasticity is aided by the unique mastery of Stravinsky's instrumentation. Instead of blending the sounds of his instruments, his scoring brings out the independent timbre value of each voice, setting off the sonorous values into sharp relief. In contrast to the nineteenth-century concept of orchestration, where the instruments were used to create blended sonorities, the novel use of instrumentation is placed at the service of the plasticity of the musical ideas. The resultant sound has a typically clear ring, mixed often with a modicum of dry acidity. This palette lends itself excellently to mock sentimentality, grotesque characterizations, and the portrayal of a mood in which irony is mixed with wistfulness. Although Stravinsky adheres to this principle of plasticity of sound in all of his subsequent periods, these expressive values are particularly pronounced in the works from this period. It is only natural that wistfulness and nostalgia should be his dominant moods at a time when exile was still a fresh experience for him.

L'Histoire du Soldat (1918), the first work in the post-Russian period, exemplifies the mentioned tendencies. It is of a unique genre, a work to be read, played, and danced. It was written for a small group of dancers to allow performances on the small stages of Swiss villages and for a small group of players, because orchestras were in a state of disorganization at the end of the war.

The story of the work, based on a tale of Afanasief adapted by Ramuz, is Faustian: a deserting soldier makes a deal with the Devil and after a temporary rise in his fortunes, in the course of which he marries a princess, is finally destroyed by the Devil. The narrator communicates not only with the audience, but also interferes with the action—a device borrowed from Pirandello.

Once again, heterogeneous musical elements, such as jazz, an Argentinian tango, a Viennese waltz, and the like are welded into a unified whole. The waltz (Ex. 9/15) illustrates the parodizing nostalgia mentioned earlier. The feeling evoked is not unlike the one conveyed by the waltz in *Petrouchka,* namely, a bitter realization that this lighthearted dance is lost for modern man.

EX. 9/15 *L'Histoire du Soldat,*[13] study no. 12

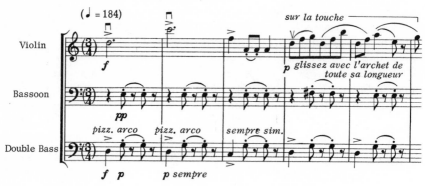

Throughout the waltz this split feeling is reflected in harmonic clashes: the music is anchored on C and D, respectively in the bass, and particularly over the D bass there are numerous F sharp–F clashes. The simultaneous sound of major and minor thirds remained one of the composer's fondest harmonic devices.

The instrumental setting of *L'Histoire* is of great importance: the composer relates in *Expositions and Developments* that the "shoe-string economics" of the production kept him to a handful of instruments. He employed six instruments: violin, double bass, clarinet, bassoon, trumpet, trombone, and percussion. We learn from the Craft dialogues that the composer modeled his group after a jazz band, substituting the bassoon for the saxophone.

L'Histoire was followed by *Pulcinella* (1919), a work conceived originally by Diaghilev. It undoubtedly marks an amazing turning point in the composer's career. One can think of no greater stylistic discontinuity than that which exists between *Pulcinella* and the preceding works. For the first time, though not of his own volition, he turned to a composer of the past, Pergolesi (1710-1736), as a source of inspiration.

[13] Reprinted by permission of E. F. Kalmus.

The potency of the musical heritage, and particularly that of the eighteenth century, remained one of the main components in the composer's art for the next thirty years. His adoption of certain musical practices of the eighteenth century resulted in the *neoclassic* label given his music, even by himself. The term is vulnerable to criticism because the composer tapped sources other than classicism, as for instance Rossini, Weber, and Tchaikovsky from the nineteenth century and Bach from the Baroque era.

Disregarding for the moment the appropriateness of the term and the validity of resuscitating an earlier composer's style in a modern setting, *Pulcinella* is an important milestone in the composer's output. He himself admits its significance, forty years after its composition:

> *Pulcinella* was my discovery of the past, the epiphany through which the whole of my late work became possible. It was a backward look, of course—the first of many love affairs in that direction—but it was a look in the mirror too.[14]

For the next thirty years Stravinsky followed the method of reinterpreting the musical past through his own personal style. While *Pulcinella* was the first work in the new style, the work itself is not typical of most of the subsequent, so-called neoclassic compositions because he was rarely to rely so closely on the thematic material of a specific composer. His usual method was to recapture and reinterpret certain compositional practices of earlier centuries, but without actual quotations or near-quotations of thematic material. Two examples will illustrate how closely related the thematic material of *Pulcinella* is to its original source. In Example 9/16/a the opening motive of *Pulcinella* is quoted, while following that, in Example 9/16/b, the original source (Pergolesi's First Trio Sonata, first movement) is given:

EX. 9/16/a *Pulcinella,*[15] opening (partial score)

[14] Stravinsky-Craft, *Expositions and Developments,* pp. 128–129.
[15] Copyright 1924 by Edition Russe de Musique; renewed 1952. Revised versions © 1949 by Boosey & Hawkes, Inc. Reprinted by permission of Boosey & Hawkes, Inc.

EX. 9/16/b PERGOLESI, *First Trio Sonata,* opening

Except for their rhythmic shape, the identity of the two melodies is obvious. Stravinsky also incorporated Pergolesi's bass; the changes occur mostly in the middle voices, and of course in the instrumentation.

In the next example from the same movement, the melodic line is taken again unchanged, but now a second independent voice is added by Stravinsky:

EX. 9/17 *Pulcinella,* first movement, mm. 1–8

As one listens to the successive movements of *Pulcinella,* one is left with the feeling that Stravinsky increasingly asserts himself, and that while the music of the first movement sounds more like Pergolesi, the Russian composer's imprint becomes more apparent in the later movements.

NEOCLASSICISM

While *Pulcinella* was almost the result of an "accident," since its idea was not conceived by the composer, its stylistic climate coincided with the composer's new orientation. The need for order and control were already in evidence in *L'Histoire.* A more precise reconstruction of how the composer arrived at his new outlook is not an easy task because his esthetic theories were published so much later.

Beginning with the most recent account, in the *Conversations* Stravinsky emphasizes the consciousness with which he turned to eighteenth-century musical practices:

> Dotted rhythms are characteristic eighteenth-century rhythms. My uses of them in works of that period, such as the introduction to my Piano Concerto, are conscious stylistic references. I attempted to build a new music on eighteenth-century classicism, using the constructive principles of that classicism and even evoking it stylistically by such means as dotted rhythms.[16]

This conscious turn to eighteenth-century music may have been the result of several factors. First, the composer may have turned to the Western heritage *in general* because the Russian past lost its meaning for him. It is also possible that the ballet as a musical form at least temporarily lost its attractiveness, and that he was finding his way to purely abstract instrumental forms. As control and order were his guideposts, one can see why the eighteenth century *specifically* seemed the most suitable model. Eighteenth-century music had an additional advantage: it was abstract, and nonsuggestive of extramusical meanings which may have seemed "safe" at a time when he felt impelled to deny the story content of *The Rite of Spring*. It is entirely possible that the composer still felt a lingering anxiety as the aftermath of *The Rite of Spring*. Perhaps this is the key to the often quoted controversial statement in the *Autobiography* denying the expressiveness of music:

> For I consider that music is, by its very nature, essentially powerless to *express* anything at all, whether a feeling, an attitude of mind, a psychological mood, a phenomenon of nature, etc. *Expression* has never been an inherent property of music. . . . If, as is nearly always the case, music appears to express something, this is only an illusion and not a reality . . . . The phenomenon of music is given to us with the sole purpose of establishing an order in things, including, and particularly, the coordination between *man* and *time*.[17]

In *Expositions and Developments*, Robert Craft obviously wished to give the composer an opportunity to rectify this extreme statement when he posed the following question: "What did you mean by that much quoted statement that music is powerless to express anything at all?" The composer answered as follows:

> That overpublicized bit about expression (or nonexpression) was simply a way of saying that music is suprapersonal and superreal and as such beyond verbal meanings and verbal descriptions. It was aimed against the notion that a piece of music is in reality a transcendental idea "expressed in terms of" music . . . . It was off-hand and annoyingly incomplete, but even the stupider critics could have seen that it did not

---

[16] Stravinsky-Craft, *Conversations,* p. 18.
[17] Stravinsky, *An Autobiography,* pp. 53–54.

deny musical expressivity, but only the validity of a type of verbal statement about musical expressivity. I stand by the remark, incidentally,
though today I would put it the other way around: music expresses
itself.[18]

Whatever the merit of this clarification may be, his other writings
show that he yearned for order and control and only felt "safe" if he
imposed limitations on himself. He writes in the *Poetics of Music:*

> I experience a sort of terror when, at the moment of setting to work
> and finding myself before the infinitude of possibilities that present them-
> selves. I have the feeling that everything is permissible to me .... Will I
> then have to lose myself in this abyss of freedom? To what shall I cling in
> order to escape the dizziness that seizes me before the virtuality of
> this infinitude? However, ... I shall overcome my terror. ...[19]

One can understand in the light of this statement why the form-
conscious, well-ordered, emotionally restrained, that is, Apollonian,
music of the eighteenth century was a desirable model.

The neoclassic orientation after *Pulcinella* can be seen in several
purely instrumental compositions, such as the *Octet for Wind Instruments* (1923) and the *Piano Concerto* (1924).

The new style was received with incredulity and disappointment.
Aaron Copland, who was present at the premiere of the *Octet,* gives the
following account:

> One can attest to the general feeling of mystification that followed
> the initial hearing. Here was Stravinsky having created a neoprimitive
> style all his own, based on native Russian sources . . . now suddenly,
> without any seeming explanation, making an about-face and presenting
> a piece to the public that bore no conceivable resemblance to the in-
> dividual style with which he had hitherto been identified. Everyone was
> asking why Stravinsky should have exchanged his Russian heritage for
> what looked very much like a mess of eighteenth-century mannerisms.
> The whole thing seemed like a bad joke . . . and gained Stravinsky the
> unanimous disapproval of the press. No one could possibly have fore-
> seen, first, that Stravinsky was to persist in this new manner of his or,
> second, that the *Octet* was destined to influence composers all over
> the world in bringing the latent objectivity of modern music to full
> consciousness by frankly adopting the ideals, forms, and textures of
> the preromantic era.[20]

Copland, although an enthusiast of Stravinsky's music, also expresses
disappointment about the new turn and discerns a "reactionary tendency." He acknowledges that these new works constitute a new phenomenon in music, an "art grafted on art," which will secure a place
for Stravinsky in the history of music irrespective of their esthetic
merit.

---

[18] Stravinsky-Craft, *Expositions and Developments,* pp. 114–115.
[19] Stravinsky, *Poetics of Music,* p. 66.
[20] Aaron Copland, *Our New Music* (New York: Whittlesey House, 1941), pp. 101–102.

Even stronger criticism is voiced by Hodeir, who, labeling the neo-classic orientation as "The Decline and Fall of Stravinsky," writes:

> Most of Stravinsky's neoclassic works were attempts to create a new musical synthesis by absorbing the most heterogeneous elements in Western musical tradition . . . . A composer who copies the development of a piece of music from a borrowed pattern—even borrowed from a masterpiece—is simply confessing his inability to renew a form of composition. Similarly, a composer who grafts dissonant harmonies onto a conventional melody has merely found an easy way to elude the problems of musical language. Considering the insignificance of the works on which Stravinsky squandered his talents trying to work out his retrogressive, contradictory synthesis, it is sad to think back upon that mighty artist who, at the turn of the century, devised a revolutionary approach to the problems of rhythm in music.[21]

Constant Lambert is also strongly critical of Stravinsky's "time-traveling" and synthetic approach; neoclassicism, according to him, attempts to produce a "creature of flesh and blood out of fossil fragments."

The most vehement criticism comes, of course, from Soviet Russian sources. Soviet critics find Stravinsky's music "anemic and decadent," placing a fallacious emphasis on constructivism. It suffers, according to them, from unbearable dryness and its mood is described as that of artificial cheerfulness with an occasional tear.

A more objective biographer, Eric White, sees the positive, integrative aspect of the neoclassic style:

> The truth is that he (Stravinsky) was steadily developing an acute historical perception of the presence of the past, and at the same time successfully extracting the objective content of such historical material as interested him and using it for his own creative purposes.[22]

Edward T. Cone also sees the significance of the eighteenth-century sources as secondary. He holds that Stravinsky approaches these models from without and radically reinterprets and transforms them to fit his own needs, and thereby they remain only superficially related to the original source. He summarizes:

> What Stravinsky has demonstrated convincingly is the feasibility of putting manneristic elements to good use in the service of a powerful style.[23]

From the critics' formulations it appears as if the validity of Stravinsky's neoclassic style merely hinges on semantics: his opponents claim that he is using *mannerisms* of earlier historical periods, while

---

[21] André Hodeir, *Since Debussy: A View of Contemporary Music* (New York: Grove Press, Inc., 1961, translated by Noel Burch), pp. 33–34.

[22] Eric White, "Stravinsky," *European Music in the Twentieth Century*, edited by Howard Hartog (New York: Frederick A. Praeger, Inc., 1957), p. 53.

[23] Edward T. Cone, "The Uses of Convention: Stravinsky and his Models," *Musical Quarterly*, **48**, No. 3 (1962), pp. 287–299.

his supporters hold that the composer founded a *manner* all his own, based on the traditions of the past. According to the composer himself, "The musical heritage appears as an heirloom that one receives on condition of making it bear fruit before passing it on to one's descendants."

Both sides would agree, however, that whatever problem Stravinsky set for himself, he always came up with a solution that exemplified his own style. In other words, regardless of how many diverse stylistic reinterpretations there may be, there is always the unmistakable signature of his own on all his works from *The Firebird* to the serial works.

The question that presents itself bears more on the quality of the creative act than on the validity of certain compositional manners or mannerisms. All that is known about artistic creation is that it is based on a subtle interplay of conscious and unconscious forces. Undoubtedly, in the composer's works after 1920 conscious forces gained the upper hand. Lucidity, order, and control were embraced and the ordered cosmos won out over the passions, visions, and dreams that inhabit the deeper layers of man's mind. The criticism that may be leveled at the neoclassic works (and this also holds true for the serial period) is *not* that they are derived from the musical heritage, but that the treatment is too conscious—sometimes even self-conscious—too cerebral.

All these works are marvelously tooled, but they lack the strength of *Petrouchka* or *Le Sacre* or the depth that touched audiences. In Lang's words, Stravinsky lacks *introspection* and that even when he is lyrical—which is rare—"he sings with a certain planned precision."

While such reservations cannot be verified scientifically, one can point to the fact that the motivations which led to the inception of many of the neoclassic works had their source in conscious, practical reality rather than in deep, inner stirrings. Thus, the Piano Concerto (1924) was written to provide a vehicle for the composer as soloist. When he admittedly became tired of this work, he composed the *Capriccio* for piano and orchestra to add a new piece to his repertory. The *Serenade in La* for piano was the result of his fascination with composing a piece in which the playing time of each movement was determined by the time limit of one side of a 78 "rpm" record, that is, four and a half minutes. Later, the *Concerto for Two Pianos* was written for joint performance with his son.

In summary, the shortcomings of the neoclassic works do not lie in their reliance on past musical styles. Other great composers also turned to the past and reinterpreted their musical heritage. This is true of Bach as well as of Mozart, Beethoven, Brahms, and others. The difference is, however, that these masters, instead of analytically observing how past styles would work for them, welded the past and present together in the heat of their inspiration—a word that is anathema to Stravinsky— guided by both conscious and unconscious forces. In their compositions the influence of the past is more fully absorbed and, perhaps because the welding occurred at a higher emotional voltage, the single stylistic ingredients of the past are more submerged than in Stravinsky's music, where the *consciousness* with which he reached out for stylistic features of the past is often too apparent.

The *Octet for Wind Instruments* (1923)—received in Cocteau's words with a "scandal du silence"—bears no stylistic reference to earlier composers. The first movement is entitled "Sinfonia," an allusion to eighteenth-century overturelike movements; the second movement is in variation form, Stravinsky's first essay in this form. The last movement was composed with the Two-Part Inventions of Bach "in the remote back of his mind." The premier of the *Octet* was conducted by the composer, who, in the preceding years, had made a reputation for himself as the interpreter of his own music.

Next, as a performer, he turned to the piano. The *Concerto for Piano and Wind Instruments,* (1924) is the first in a series of piano works. The three movements bring forth frequent associations with Bach; the dotted rhythms of the introduction are akin to the "G minor Prelude" (*Well-Tempered Clavier,* Book II), while the main motive of the opening of the fast movement resembles the opening of the *Third Brandenburg Concerto,* as well as the first movement of the *Gamba Sonata* in G minor. The opening of the slow movement is not unlike the slow movement of Bach's *Italian Concerto* in atmosphere.

The harmonic scheme of Stravinsky's *Concerto* abounds in frictions of major and minor thirds as seen in Ex. 9/18:

EX. 9/18 *Concerto for Piano and Wind Instruments*[24] (two-piano version), 1 m. after study no. 5

The Sonata for Piano (1924), also in three movements, was preceded by a re-examination of Beethoven's Piano Sonatas, even though the sound and the contrapuntal texture point rather to Bach.

OEDIPUS REX

In view of Stravinsky's allegiance to the Apollonian ideal it was natural that his interest turned to Hellenic subjects. *Oedipus Rex* (1926–1927), an opera-oratorio, is perhaps the best known and most successful among these works, which include *Apollon Musagetes* (1927–1928), an allegorical ballet; *Perséphone* (1933), a melodrama based on Gide's text; and *Orpheus* (1947).

The idea of choosing Sophocles' timeless tragedy emerged gradually. First, the composer searched for a universally familiar subject upon which he could base an opera or an oratorio. He also felt that Latin should be the language for the projected work. As stated by the composer, "The choice had the great advantage of giving me a medium not dead, but turned to stone and so monumentalized as to have become immune from all risk of vulgarization."[25]

Finally, with Cocteau's collaboration the Oedipus myth, based on Sophocles' drama, was chosen as the subject. The work was retranslated into Latin from French. The enthusiasm with which the composer plunged into the work is evident from the *Autobiography:*

> What a joy it is to compose music to a language of convention, almost of ritual, the very nature of which imposes a lofty dignity! One no longer feels dominated by the phrase, the literal meaning of the words. Cast in an immutable mold which adequately expresses their value, they do not require any further commentary. The text thus becomes purely phonetic material for the composer. He can dissect it at will and concentrate all his attention on its primary constituent element, that is to say, on the syllable. Was not this method of treating the text that of the old masters of austere style? This, too, has for centuries been the Church's attitude toward music, and has prevented it from falling into sentimentalism, and consequently into individualism.[26]

Indeed, there is a ritualistic quality in *Oedipus;* it is static and statuesque and points to the *Symphony of Psalms* and other religious works to follow. The mood is severe and dark; in all but one scene only male voices are heard.

The work, described by the author as an opera-oratorio, is divided into two acts, and each act into three scenes. Each scene is preceded by the narrator's comments. Nearly all action is frozen; the main characters are immobile on stage in their costumes and masks, only their heads and arms moving.

[25] Stravinsky, *An Autobiography*, p. 125.
[26] Stravinsky, *An Autobiography*, p. 128.

Rhythm is the main source of dramatic tension; the composer's intention was to freeze the drama in the music largely by rhythmic means: "The rhythms in *Oedipus* are more static and regular than in any other composition of mine to that date and the tension created by them. . . is greater than any tension that irregular, upset rhythms could produce."[27]

As can be seen from his statement, the composer still juggles with time, but counteracting it now more, as compared to the forward-moving, dynamic rhythmic motion of earlier works.

The work is another example of the composer's uncanny art in which he achieves unity despite the diverse stylistic elements on which he draws. His magic wand once more unifies the baroque oratorio idiom, Russian ("Gloria Jocasta") influence, and Verdi's style (Act II, Scene I). The over-all purpose was to capture the Greek fate-tragedies, with the chorus commenting on events governed by the implacable forces of destiny.

In addition to solo voices and chorus, a large orchestra is used once again in *Oedipus* after a decade of smaller instrumental works. However, orchestral *tuttis* are rare. Structurally, the work is divided into set numbers (solo aria, duet, chorus, and so on) in line with the classical operatic tradition.

The opening chords in *Oedipus Rex* give a foretaste of the monumentality of the work. Interrupted by pounding B flat minor chords, the Thebans (chorus) implore Oedipus to liberate them from the plague. The basso ostinato figure (Ex. 9/19) should be noted, as it is employed as a motto in the work and recurs in the final scene in which the fate of Oedipus is sealed. The giant arch suggests the trap set by the gods from which there is no escape.

EX. 9/19 *Oedipus Rex*,[28] Act I, Scene 1, mm. 23–25

The opening chorus exemplifies the composer's intention to "dissect the text" and his free manipulation of the syllables. He dwells mostly on three-syllable words (Oe-di-pus, li-be-ra, mo-ri-tur) since these are best fitted to the ternary pulsation of the ostinato figure.[29] The chorus has a percussive sound (see Ex. 2/22 in Chapter 2) and the lines become

[27] Stravinsky-Craft, *Dialogues and a Diary*, p. 12.

[28] Copyright 1927 by Russischer Musikverlag; renewed 1955. Copyright and renewal assigned to Boosey & Hawkes, Inc. Reprinted by permission.

[29] Since in both the orchestral and piano-voc⸱ score only the Latin text is printed, the English translation appears in Appendix B.

increasingly contrapuntal as the scene proceeds. The last lines of the
chorus are accompanied by a clarinet figure that will become the accompaniment to Oedipus' forthcoming aria.

Oedipus' answer is couched in sweet flourishes of the tenor range;
both his line and that of the accompanying clarinet are marked *dolce*
—an instruction rare in Stravinsky's scores. The King reassures the
Thebans in an impassioned tone of supreme self-confidence ("Ego
clarissimus Oedipus – I the most famed Oedipus") that he will free the
city from the plague. The chorus, supported by the insistent B flat
minor basso ostinato, asks Oedipus what should be done to achieve
their liberation. He tells them the oracles have been consulted by
Creon, the brother of his wife, and that he will return soon with the
answer. The chorus' anticipation of the answer is expressed by strong
dominant preparation leading to Creon's firm C major melody (Ex. 9/20)
that sounds reassuring and effective:

EX. 9/20 Act I, Scene 2, mm. 1–2

The straightforward feeling implied by the key of C major suggests
that Creon is essentially uninvolved in the tragedy. Later, Creon's message takes an ominous turn, and the key changes to F minor when he
announces that the plague is a punishment for the murder of King
Laius and that the murderer hides in Thebes ("Thebis peremptor latet").
Toward the end of the aria, as Creon relays Apollo's message that the
murderer has to be found, clashing A's and A flats result in harmonic
ambiguities. The aria finally ends in C major, which then turns to the
minor mode as Oedipus promises to find the murderer. The key soon
veers to E flat major, a key in which a variant of the King's florid aria
from the first scene is heard.

The third scene opens with the earlier basso ostinato figure, raised
now by a half step to B minor, over which the chorus sings a somewhat
strained invocation. Tiresias, the blind seer, the fountain of truth, appears. At first he refuses to talk, but when Oedipus accuses him of
being the murderer, Tiresias refutes the charge over a pathetic sounding A minor chord ("Miserando dico"), suggesting that he foresees
Oedipus' fate.

The key words of the ensuing aria are "Regis est rex peremptor (The
murderer of the king is a king)." The final D of Tiresias' aria is taken over
by Oedipus, perhaps symbolizing some kind of humility and acceptance.
In his response, the earlier conceit is replaced by a somewhat plaintive
and querulous tone, as if he felt his authority challenged. Act I ends

with the chorus hailing the arrival of Queen Jocasta, the wife of Oedipus and the widow of the murdered king.

The opening scene of Act II represents the dramatic climax of the work. The Queen's voice rings out over the contrapuntal lines of the clarinets, accompanied by the harp. The texture suddenly lightens and the tempo becomes much faster: the metronome signature changes from ♪ = 84 to ♩ = 84. Over brilliant woodwind figures the Queen insists that the oracles are liars ("Oracula quae semper mentiantur"). As proof, she cites that the prophecy according to which the king was to be slain by their son was not fulfilled, for he was killed by a thief at a crossroad ("trivium"). A powerful B flat major chord in its second inversion pulsates through the orchestra now, over which the chorus repeats four times the word *trivium*. Jocasta's story of the murder and the word *trivium* precipitate a fearful chain of associations in the King's mind. In great contrast to his earlier conceit, he is gripped by fear ("pavesco subite maximum – I'm suddenly terribly afraid"). A concrete memory is then recalled in a recitative over the ominous rumbling of the timpani: "I killed an old man at the crossroads."

An operatic duet ensues (the only one in the work); Jocasta still insists that the oracles lie, while Oedipus seeks to learn the truth. In the next scene the story is pieced together from the accounts of a messenger and a shepherd. They tell how Oedipus was found as an infant on the mountainside, placed there by his father in an attempt to elude the oracle's prediction that he would be slain by his son. The infant was brought to King Polybus who raised the child as his own. Now the King's death is announced and also the fact that he was merely an adoptive father to Oedipus. The awful truth is now apparent to Oedipus: he is the son of Laius and Jocasta, the slayer of his father, and the husband of his mother. His acceptance of the horrible truth is the most moving moment in the opera:

EX. 9/21 Act II, Scene 2, study no. 169

The descending B minor chord finds repose on a D ending; the simple harmonic device has the quality of a revelation.

Oedipus cannot bear to see the truth and blinds himself. Then, three times the messenger announces Jocasta's suicide (Ex. 9/22), while the orchestra restates the rushing scale passages of the opening measures:

EX. 9/22 Act II, Scene 3, study no. 172

As Oedipus leaves for exile, the chorus bids him farewell; although they realize the magnitude of his sins, their voices are gentle as they understand that fate is stronger than man's will. The final scene ends with the triplet ostinato figure softly intoned by the cello, bass, and timpani.

Oedipus is one of Stravinsky's most frequently performed works of the neoclassic period, and its stark austerity and dramatic force also make it one of his most impressive works.

**PLATE 8. STRAVINSKY
IN THE 1930s**

Music Collection,
Library and Museum of
the Performing Arts
at Lincoln Center,
New York

AFTER OEDIPUS REX TO
THE RAKE'S PROGRESS (1928–1950)

In this period a large amount of Stravinsky's time was devoted to concert tours and guest conducting. As a result, there was a decrease in his output, particularly in the 1930s.

The first outstanding work of the period is the *Symphony of Psalms* (1930), dedicated to the fiftieth anniversary of the Boston Symphony, and to the glory of God. The work, divided into three parts, is written for male chorus, boy choir, and an orchestra without violins, violas, or clarinets. It bears a resemblance to *Oedipus* in several respects. Its mood is dark due to the absence of female voices or high strings. Again the text is Latin, this time based on the verses of the Vulgate. The syllabic treatment of the text and the percussive use of the human voice are also related to the style of *Oedipus*.

The choice of religious subject matter astonished many of Stravinsky's followers; apart from an earlier minor work, this was his first major, nonsecular composition. The sincerity of the composer's religious sentiments was questioned, as it seemed unlikely that the composer of the Ballet Russe, the cosmopolitan world citizen, could be serious about religion. However, in the light of all biographical material and in view of the numerous religious works which followed, particularly in the serial period, there is no doubt that to the composer his relation to God was of genuine concern. While his church music never conveys a transcendental feeling or personal involvement, it often establishes the ritualistic qualities of the liturgy. Even if Stravinsky lacked, as expressed by Lang, "the final inwardness of life," this, in itself, is not enough evidence to doubt the genuineness of the composer's religious feelings.

The opening of the *Symphony of Psalms* shows a specific resemblance to *Oedipus:* the E minor chords have a punctuating quality as the B-flat minor chords had in the earlier work. The minor third has again motivic significance, reappearing also in the fugue subject of the second movement. As in the earlier work, ostinato techniques are used. Stylistically, *Symphony of Psalms* is more homogeneous than *Oedipus* and most of the works of this period. Despite its austerity, *Symphony of Psalms* has considerable intensity and is felt by many to be one of the composer's finest works.

The ballet works of the period, *Apollo Musagetes* (1927–1928) and *The Fairy Kiss* (1928), preceded the *Symphony of Psalms*. The first work, commissioned by Mrs. Elisabeth Sprague Coolidge for the American

Contemporary Music Festival, came on the heels of *Oedipus*. Nevertheless, the amalgamation of Greek mythology and eighteenth-century musical practices is completely different in this work. In *Apollo Musagetes*, the approach is purely "classical"; serenity and calm reign. The work is scored for strings only, and there is *blended* sound instead of the distinctive, sharply etched timbres one generally expects from the composer. Most of the music is in a major key, and the tempi are on the slow side. The music is almost free from tension, most harmonies are diatonic, and there are only a few contrasts. It is perhaps for these reasons that the work never established itself in the concert repertory.

Melodic emphasis and blended sound also characterize *The Fairy's Kiss*. The work is dedicated to Tchaikovsky's memory and, as in *Pulcinella*, the composer once again uses specific thematic material of an earlier composer. This fundamental similarity, however, does not result in the application of similar musical procedures; whereas Pergolesi's music was treated with humor and a slightly parodizing attitude, Tchaikovsky's themes (altogether some fourteen piano and voice-piano sources) are treated seriously. It seems as if Stravinsky turned to his childhood idol's music for purely sentimental reasons, as their musical styles have little in common. This ambivalent attitude may also explain the almost didactic approach with which Stravinsky transforms his source material. According to Lawrence Morton, "Tchaikovsky's faults—his banalities and routine procedures—are composed *out* of the music and Stravinsky's virtues are composed *into* it."[30]

The next ballet, *A Card Game*, composed in 1936, was commissioned by the American Ballet Company. Its subject matter is a poker game, in which three deals are worked into three choreographic scenes. The musical merrymaking, which brings to mind bits of Beethoven, Rossini, Delibes, and others, often seems forced, and it is easy to see why the work is gradually disappearing from the repertory.

Two abstract ballets, *Danses Concertantes* (1941–1942) and *Scènes de Ballets* (1944) followed, both composed in the United States, where the composer found a new home in 1939. They are abstract in design. Both works are fairly uninspired, supporting the theory that the composer was not at his best when restricted to purely abstract musical thought without story, images, or text to spur his imagination.

Orpheus (1947), a ballet based again on a subject of Greek mythology, is one of the composer's outstanding works of this period. It has a subdued, frozen beauty similar to *Oedipus* and *Symphony of Psalms*. The opening scene, in which Orpheus weeps over Eurydice's death, es-

---

[30]Lawrence Morton, "The Fairy Kiss," *Musical Quarterly,* **48,** No. 3 (1962), pp. 313–326.

tablishes an archaic mood. The linear harp melody over modal string harmonies creates a lovely effect and later four solo celli intone an *expressivo* figure suggesting Orpheus' sobbing. The soft-pedaled agitation and threats of the Furies bring to mind sublimated echoes of the composer's early style. The highpoint in the work is Orpheus' aria, in which he attempts to pacify the Furies; the melancholy oboe figure in F minor, accompanied by the harp, has the flavor of a Bach Trio Sonata, and a lyric beauty seldom attained by the composer:

EX. 9/23 *Orpheus,*[31] study no. 80

The piano compositions of the period include the *Capriccio* (1928), the *Concerto for Two Solo Pianos* (1935), and the *Sonata for Two Pianos* (1943–1944).

The violin works, the Violin Concerto (1931) and the *Duo Concertante* for violin and piano (1932) owe their existence to a sympathetic violinist, Samuel Dushkin, who showed keen interest in the master's music. In both works Stravinsky received valuable advice from the violinist to whom the Concerto is dedicated. The *Duo Concertant,* which contains allusions to the pastoral poets of antiquity, is the more successful work. The difficult problem of balance between the two instruments is well solved by writing in a linear, lean style for the piano.

A number of commercial ventures, among them a *Circus Polka* (1942), written for Ringling Brothers, and *Four Norwegian Moods* (1942),

---

[31] Copyright 1948 by Boosey & Hawkes, Inc. Reprinted by permission.

originally composed as film music, are counterbalanced by the austere *Mass* (1944–1947). Planning and composing the latter work occupied the composer for a long time. It is one of the few more recent works that was not commissioned.

A number of commentators saw the fulfillment of neoclassicism in Stravinsky's return to the symphonic form in the 1940s. His only essay, Symphony, Op. 1, in this form dates from 1905. Perhaps one should not read too much significance into his return to this form since both symphonies were commissioned, the *Symphony in C* (1939–1940) by the Chicago Symphony Orchestra and the *Symphony in Three Movements* (1942–1945) by the New York Philharmonic Orchestra.

The different character of the two symphonies is indicated by their scoring; whereas the *Symphony in C* is written for an eighteenth-century orchestra, the latter work includes a bass clarinet, a contrabassoon, a harp, and a large percussion section that includes the piano. Accordingly, the earlier symphony has a light, transparent texture reminiscent of Haydn or Mozart, whereas the *Symphony in Three Movements* is rich in dramatic contrasts and rhythmic punctuations recalling the composer's primitivistic style.

Structurally, also, the two symphonies show marked differences. The first movement of the *Symphony in C* is in sonata form—a form very rarely used by Stravinsky—and the other movements have simple, symmetrical designs, while the later work has a much more complex architecture. The problematic nature of Stravinsky's musical procedures is shown by the fact that the first movement has been analyzed in diametrically opposite ways by two commentators, Ingolf Dahl and Tansman, both composers and members of Stravinsky's inner circle. According to Tansman's view:

> The construction of this allegro follows the sonata form rather strictly, but is more closely related this time to the Beethovenian conception, particularly to the first allegro of the Fifth Symphony.[32]

The opposite view expressed by Dahl holds that:

> We have to take notice that in his new symphony Stravinsky has moved on to the exact opposite of traditional symphonic form. In this new work there is *no sonata form* [my italics] to be expounded, there is no "development" of closely defined themes, which would be stated, restated, interlocked, combined and metamorphosized as symphonic themes are wont to be. Here, on the contrary, we have another example of that additive construction, for the invention of which Stravinsky is justly famous and which has proved so influential on the younger composer.[33]

[32] Alexandre Tansman, *Stravinsky* (New York: G. P. Putnam's Sons, 1949), p. 267.
[33] Ingolf Dahl, *Comments* on Columbia record jacket, ML 4129.

The present writer is in agreement with Dahl's view; the movement has rather a mosaiclike architecture than an organically evolving one. Tensions are created by juxtaposing blocks on different sonorous planes, with friction being added by major-minor superimpositions. A motto motive, identical, incidentally, in intervallic structure with that of

Brahms' *Third Symphony*, unifies the movement:

The last work of this period is *The Rake's Progress* (1948–1951), a three-act opera in English based on a libretto written by W. A. Auden and Chester Kallman. In developing their story the librettists loosely followed the main episodes of a series of drawings by Hogarth. The main characters are archetypal representations; several commentators agree that Tom Rakewell is a mixture of Faust, Don Juan, and Peer Gynt; Nick Shadow is the symbol of the Devil, and Anne, the embodiment of pure love. The aura of the eighteenth-century morality play prompted the composer to turn to the conventional style of the classical opera. The work consists of set numbers, such as solo arias and duets, and makes use of such devices as da capo arias, secco recitatives with harpsichord accompaniment, and the like. The music itself invokes stylistic features of Mozart, Verdi, Gluck, and others. These elements are combined with the Stravinskyan imprint. Most critics, with the exception of Joseph Kerman, who claims that the work, along with *Wozzeck,* is the greatest opera of the twentieth century, agree that the synthesis on the whole is unconvincing. According to the French critic, Siohan, the diverse elements resulted in a "baroque potpourri." Whatever the final judgment will be concerning this work, it is the last and the most extreme link in a long series of works in which seventeenth- or eighteenth-century musical procedures served as sources of inspiration.

SERIAL WORKS (1951–   )

Until midcentury Stravinsky and Schoenberg were believed to represent opposite and irreconcilable poles in contemporary musical thought. This view was borne out by the differences in their styles and also by the personal antagonism between the two great composers. Although their homes in California were within a short distance of each other, they avoided personal contact.

In the summer of 1951 Schoenberg died, and one is tempted to speculate that the passing of the originator of the twelve-tone method may have been a contributing factor in Stravinsky's turn to serialism. He felt perhaps that with Schoenberg's death the domain of serial music had become *past* musical heritage and that he could turn to this

PLATE 9. STRAVINSKY CONDUCTING HIS MUSIC
Columbia Records Photo, New York

legacy and use the reinterpretative approach he had used for the music of the seventeenth and eighteenth centuries. Thus, while in certain ways his works from the serial period may sound different from the works based on the neoclassic approach, it is incorrect to assume that the incorporation of certain serial techniques represents a major "conversion" or revolution in Stravinsky's style. The "serial" Stravinsky remains his own self, and the process of "giving" and "taking" also remained the same, only the source from which he now draws is the twentieth-century idiom of the Viennese atonal school. The significant change now is that he subscribes to certain premises and self-limitations that form the basis of the musical style of serial composers. If one recalls statements from the *Poetics of Music*, for instance, "The more art is controlled, limited, worked over, the more it is free," it seems rather surprising that the composer waited so long to try his hand at the method. Also, his fondness for the use of intervals and chords as germinating cells for an entire composition and, in general, his methodical approach to certain precompositional processes, such as the choice of specific instruments or voices (or the avoidance of certain timbres) made this shift almost predictable. The composer himself acknowledges that working with the new technique suits his temperament, when he states in the *Conversations:* "The serial technique I use impels me to greater discipline than ever before."

Whatever inner obstacles had prevented the composer from exploring the method earlier, his friendship with Robert Craft helped him to overcome them.

Craft, who became Stravinsky's musical assistant in the late 1940s, is an enthusiastic propagator of the music of the Viennese atonal school, and is a frequent interpreter of Webern's music in particular. It is also Webern for whom Stravinsky expresses wholehearted admiration. He calls Webern: "the discoverer of a new distance between the musical object and ourselves, and, therefore, of a new measure of musical time; as such he is supremely important."[34] In another instance he expresses even greater enthusiasm:

> Of the music of this century I am still most attracted by two periods of Webern; the later instrumental works, and the songs he wrote after the first twelve opus numbers and before the Trio . . . . People who do not share my feeling for this music still wonder at my attitude. So I explain: Webern is for me the *juste de la musique,* and I do not hesitate to shelter myself by the beneficent protection of his not yet canonized art.[35]

Stravinsky approached serialism gradually, slowly feeling his way. In the *Cantata* for soprano, tenor, female chorus and instruments (1951–1952), based on fifteenth- and sixteenth-century semisacred English poetry, certain canonic devices are used which flourished in the time of the great Flemish composers. For instance, in the *Cantus Cancrizan,* a series of pitches, presented first in their original form, appear later in their inversion and in crab form. Thus, Stravinsky turned to the same phase of the musical past into which Schoenberg had delved at the time he formulated the method of twelve-tone composition.

The first tone row Stravinsky employed appears in the ensuing work, the *Septet* (1952–1953) for piano, violin, viola, cello, clarinet, bassoon, and French horn. Example 9/24/a contains the tone row of the first movement of this work.

EX. 9/24/a Tone row of *Septet*

Tone row: Septet

[34] Stravinsky-Craft, *Memories and Commentaries,* p. 97.
[35] Stravinsky-Craft, *Conversations,* p. 146.

EX. 9/24/b Tone row of *In Memoriam Dylan Thomas*

EX. 9/24/c Tone row of *Canticum Sacrum*

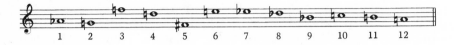

From Example 9/24/a it can be seen that the first tone row the composer employed was strictly tonal, consisting of six tones.

The row in Example 9/24/b is the one upon which *In Memoriam Dylan Thomas* (1954), a work for tenor, string quartet, and four trombones, is based. The tone row here consists of only five notes with an undefined tonality.

Example 9/24/c contains the first twelve-tone row Stravinsky employed in the middle movements of *Canticum Sacrum ad honorem Sancti Marci Nominis* (1955), a work dedicated to the City of Venice in praise of its Patron Saint, the blessed Apostle Mark. We will now examine briefly the *Canticum Sacrum,* postponing Stravinsky's further explorations into serialism for later.

CANTICUM SACRUM

Canticum Sacrum is scored for solo tenor and baritone, chorus, flute, two oboes, English horn, two bassoons and contrabassoon, three trumpets and bass trumpet, three trombones and contrabass trombone, harp, organ, violas, and double basses. It is obvious from the scoring that instruments with low and dark sonorities are strongly represented. The Latin text is taken from both the Old and New Testaments; the work itself is laid out in five movements, suggesting the five domes of St. Mark's Cathedral.

After a brief dedication sung by the two soloists, the first section opens with a powerful *tutti* of chorus and orchestra. The forceful tone expresses the Apostolic message: "Euntes in mundum universum, predicate evangelium omni creaturae – Go ye into all the world, and preach the Gospel to every creature." The strong punctuation of chords once again recalls the opening of *Oedipus,* and the friction of the augmented octave (B flat–B) brings to mind many earlier Stravinsky works. Actually, the clashing intervals point to clashing tonalities, namely to B flat major and B minor. The movement is organized into five subdivisions, in an A–B–A$_1$–B–A$_2$ design, in which each recurring A section

is shortened by one measure. The B sections contain quiet organ interludes, whose bass lines are reinforced by the bassoons. It should
be noted here that the final movement of the work, which contains
the fulfillment of the Apostolic message, consists of a cancrizan (retrograde) form of the first movement.

In contrast to the massive harmonic style of the first and last movements, the middle movements employing the twelve-tone method,
contain intricate contrapuntal lines, often using canonic devices based
on varied set operations.

The second section ("Surge aquila") of the *Canticum Sacrum* is
the most nearly secular section. The lyric fervor of the tenor solo resembles Oedipus' first aria. It is preceded by three chords made up of
the retrograde version of the set (Ex. 9/25) intoned by three solo double
basses and the harp:

EX. 9/25 *Canticum Sacrum,*[36] m. 46

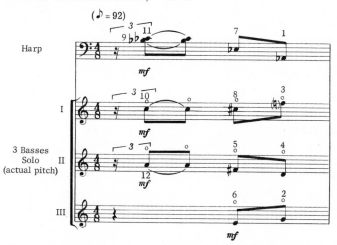

Stravinsky's use of double bass harmonics and of the low register of
the harp is typical of his late style and can be found in many other
works.

The first line of the tenor solo encompasses the twelve tones of the
set (Ex. 9/26). This kind of thematic use of the set, which was also ob-

EX. 9/26 Mm. 47–49

served in one stylistic period of Schoenberg, is characteristic of Stravinsky at this time.

The shape of the set is often transformed by rhythmic manipulations, as can be observed in Example 9/27 in which asymmetrical meters are introduced:

EX. 9/27 Mm. 74–79

The last appearance of the set (Ex. 9/28) at the end of the movement brings out the latent tonal feeling suggested by the last three notes of the set:

EX. 9/28 Mm. 89–93

The third movement is an exposition of the Saint's three virtues: "Caritas" (charity), "Spes" (hope), and "Fides" (faith).

In the opening section of "Caritas" the organ establishes continuity in sonority and presents the set of the previous movement in a reorganized way:

EX. 9/29 Prime set of "Caritas"

Later in the movement a canon of the chorus is followed by a delayed canon in augmentations by the bass trumpet. "Spes" opens with the organ presenting the set transposed a minor third up. Unique sonorities are achieved by juxtaposing the male solo voices with their trumpet and trombone support to the female voices of the chorus, which are joined by the oboes and tenor trombone.

In the "Fides" section antiphonal scoring achieves intensification. The inverted set in the altos is followed in equalized, longer note values by the contrabass trombone with a *sforzato* accent on each note:

EX. 9/30 Mm. 219–224 (partial score)

In the fourth section, "Brevis Motus Cantilenae," the set is segmented, divided among baritone solo, chorus, and a few solo instruments. At *piu agitato* a four-part *a cappella* section starts; closer inspection of the score reveals Stravinsky's mastery of the row technique, as he combines the original, the retrograde, the inverted, and the retrograde-inverted forms of the set. The most impressive moment of the work is reached with the baritone's outcry, marked quasi *rubato discreto*, "cum lacrimis aiebat Credo Domine (said with tears, Lord, I believe)," from which point on a double bass pizzicato D ostinato persists until the end of the movement.

The work is undoubtedly impressive, and once again many elements are woven together into a convincing whole: twelve-tone technique is bent to the demands of the composer's harmonic style, maintaining tonal poles of attraction. The sonorities attest to the fact that in this realm, too, new refinements have taken place. Final evaluation of the work will have to wait until more performances allow closer examination. Roman Vlad, Stravinsky's most recent biographer, has unqualified praise for the work:

> To my mind, *Canticum* is the most comprehensive and essential synthesis of elements it is possible to imagine at this particular stage in the evolution of European music. The multitude of ingredients which go into this "summa" is staggering; but because of the homogeneity achieved by the fusion of elements and the very size of the work . . . very few of its qualities can be appreciated at first sight or at first hearing; they need to be heard again and again before they yield up their secrets.[37]

WORKS AFTER THE *CANTICUM*

After the *Canticum* Stravinsky returned once more to the ballet form in *Agon,* a work begun in 1953 before the *Canticum,* but finished in 1957. It is perhaps due to this interruption that the style of the work is not quite consistent. The opening numbers are more diatonic and, generally, simpler in style, whereas the later sections following the "Sarabande" have a rarefied atmosphere, leaner textures, and more jagged melodic lines. The work does not follow any plot; instead, the sequence is established by a number of French, seventeenth-century dances. In this work Stravinsky returns to a large orchestra which includes a harp, a piano, a mandolin, and a large percussion section. Almost throughout the entire work row technique is used; three different twelve-tone sets are employed with a great deal of segmentation.

The orchestration reflects the discontinuity in style; the first incongruity occurs in the coda to the "Gailliarde," whose refined sonorities stand in sharp contrast to the style of earlier sections. The effects of the mandolin, muted trumpet, harp and cello glissandi are fascinating and definitely suggest Webern's instrumental style. Additional magical effects are contained later in the coda, where *sul ponticello* string glissandi, single notes of the piano, bass trombone and harp sonorities are combined. The "Gailliarde," with its harp and mandolin lines supported by double bass pizzicati, is a marvel of tonal imagination. An extraordinary passage occurs later in the "Bransle Gay" where an exotic flute line is accompanied by a *col legno* castagnet.

The entire "Pas-de-Deux" section and the adjoining coda (mm. 411–

---

[37] Roman Vlad, *Stravinsky* (New York: Oxford University Press, 1960, translated by Frederick and Ann Fuller), p. 185.

519) illustrate a most remarkable adaptation of the principle of *Klangfar-benmelodie.* Example 9/31 furnishes one instance of the amazing sonorities produced by the violin-cello-mandolin-harp combination:

EX. 9/31 *Agon,*[38] mm. 504–507

From abstract ballet the composer returned to sacred music, producing the most extended work of his late period, *Threni: id est lamentationes Jeremiae Prophetae* (Threnodies: Being the Lamentations of the Prophet Jeremiah). The text is taken from the Vulgate and selected from the first, third, and fifth elegies. The work, composed in 1958, uses larger vocal forces than those used in the *Canticum,* with the orchestra playing a comparatively subordinate role. The work is scored for six solo voices, mixed chorus, and a standard orchestra, to which is added a contralto bugle and a sarrusophone, a double reed instrument of the oboe family made of metal.

The entire work is based on a single twelve-tone set (Ex. 9/32) and its permutations, consisting of intervals which lend themselves to the formation of triadic harmonies:

EX. 9/32 Prime set of *Threni*

Although complex segmentations and permutations are widely employed, the set is also used thematically. One such appearance is shown in Example 9/33 where the first tenors sing the original set, while the second tenor line represents the retrograde inversion:

EX. 9/33 *Threni,* "Diphona I"[39]

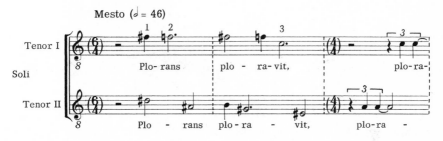

The descending half step from F sharp to F in Example 9/34 assumes motivic significance throughout the work. This interval appears, highlighted by repetitions in the "Elegia Tertia" in the second bass solo voice (Ex. 9/34/a), in the "Sensus Spei" section in the soprano and alto line (Ex. 9/34/b), and later in the soprano line (Ex. 9/34/c):

EX. 9/34/a Mm. 172–173

EX. 9/34/b Mm. 231-232

EX. 9/34/c Mm. 310-311

Whenever the repeated half step appears, it reflects some elegiac meaning in the text. Contrariwise, through octave displacement, the same interval yields an augmented octave that is repeatedly employed for the expression of anger and wrath.

Threni is more clearly liturgical than *Canticum* and its style more homogeneous. The structure of the work has a unique delineation of the verses by the choral setting of the Hebrew alphabet. The letters serve not only as devices of paragraphing, but also represent textural contrasts, as they stand out with their block harmonies in the generally contrapuntal texture. Another unifying device, used for the first time by the composer, is the speaking chorus.

While the work shows that Stravinsky is now completely at home in all the intricacies of serialism, it lacks the spontaneity of the *Canticum*. Its sustained austerity seems unrelieved. One critic found a kind of "archaic aloofness" in the work and cited the "contrived sophistication" with which Stravinsky employs serialism.

As *Canticum* and *Threni* are related in several respects, the same is true of the two subsequent works, namely the *Movements for Piano and Orchestra* (1959) and *A Sermon, a Narrative, and a Prayer* (1960-1961).

In both works the composer breaks new ground. He states in the *Diary and Conversations* that he has now become not less, but more of a serial composer. He considers the *Movements* the most advanced music he has ever written from the viewpoint of construction. He sees himself approaching what he calls "antitonality."

The *Movements* is perhaps the only work in Stravinsky's oeuvre that is not immediately recognizable as the master's own. One reason for this is the lack of any tonal feeling. Another reason is the non-thematic character of the music that seems more closely related to Webern's style than to any previous works. The opening of the first section of the *Movements* shows the composer's new approach to the row:

EX. 9/35 *Movements for Piano and Orchestra*,[40] opening

The *Movements* has five divisions and is scored for solo piano and orchestra without percussion instruments. Each movement ends with a short orchestral epilogue that establishes a connection with the next movement.

While the *Movements* is one of Stravinsky's most puzzling pieces, *A Sermon, A Narrative and A Prayer*, perhaps due to the suggestions of the text, is more accessible to the listener. It is scored for alto and tenor soloists, speaker, chorus, and orchestra. As suggested by the title, the work is divided into three parts. A "Sermon" is based on excerpts of the letters of St. Paul. The theme of the English text is hope and faith. The prime set (Ex. 9/36) immediately appears in the opening

EX. 9/36 STRAVINSKY, *A Sermon, a Narrative, and a Prayer*,[41]

in a fragmented shape. The writing verges on Webern's athematic style as may be seen in Ex. 9/37:

---

[40] Copyright 1960 by Hawkes & Son (London) Ltd. Reprinted by permission of Boosey & Hawkes, Inc.

[41] Copyright 1961 by Boosey and Company Ltd. Reprinted by permission of Boosey & Hawkes, Inc.

EX. 9/37 STRAVINSKY, *A Sermon, a Narrative, and a Prayer*, mm. 90–91

The intervals in the set described by 3, 4, 5, 6 are repeated by 9, 10, 11, and 12.

The first movement has an archlike design, with alternating orchestral and choral sections. Again the device of speaking chorus is used, accompanied by *tremolo* and *sul ponticello* strings. Double bass harmonics are used effectively both here and in the *Movements*.

The "Narrative" concerns the story of St. Stephen, as related in chapters VI and VII of The Acts and centers on the Council's false accusations brought against the saint. The increasing density of the texture suggests the accumulation of charges and a dramatic climax is reached in measure 165. The wide leaps, the glissandi, and the condensed writing are strongly suggestive of the further assimilation of Webern's style.

The "Prayer" is based on the setting of a text by the English playwright, Thomas Dekker (1570–1641), and dedicated to the memory of Reverend James McLane, an Episcopalian minister and friend of the composer.

The music has a calm, ritualistic quality enhanced by the quaint sound of three tam-tams, the dynamics never rising above a *mezzoforte*.

Both works are too novel and complex to allow a judicious appraisal. Nonetheless, they stand as amazing examples of the work of an octogenarian. The fact that he succeeds in achieving such dramatic power, unprecedented in his earlier serial works, as in the "Narrative," and with his bold renunciation of tonal harmonies—a practice he followed for more than half a century—furnishes proof that old age has not diminished the composer's astonishing creative powers or lessened the inquisitiveness and curiosity of his musical mind.

Among the most recent works, *The Flood* (1962), a Stravinsky-Balanchine-Craft television production, and *Abraham and Isaac* (1963) should be mentioned. The latter, a sacred ballad, is composed for baritone and small orchestra, and based on the Hebrew text of Genesis, Chapter XXII.

Also of recent vintage are the *Variations for Orchestra* (1964) and the *Requiem Canticles* (1966), the latter commissioned by and first performed at Princeton University.

SUMMARY

The works of Stravinsky from *The Firebird* to the serial compositions contain certain stylistic features that remained constant even when used for different expressive purposes. The same unifying force with which the composer welded together disparate elements into a cohesive whole in a single work unites his total oeuvre.

Generally rhythm has remained the dominant force throughout the different stylistic phases, even though devices, such as ostinati, changing meters, and the like, are used differently in the earlier works in comparison to the later compositions. The most striking feature of Stravinsky's music is, undoubtedly, his rhythmic imagination, rooted in the asymmetrical metric groupings found in the folk music of his native country. This aspect of his art has had a most profound influence on two generations of composers both in Europe and in the United States.

Stravinsky's melodic ideas are terse and usually confined to a narrow ambitus. Their construction allows the free reign of rhythmic forces.

Harmonically, Stravinsky remained essentially tonal with a preference for the diatonic. Superimposition of such harmonies frequently appears (pandiatonicism) with bitonal suggestions. Superimposition of major and minor thirds is another hallmark of his harmonic style.

The textures, from *L'Histoire* on, are predominantly contrapuntal; the lines are always clearly delineated by sharply etched sonorities. The typical Stravinskyan sound is unmistakable however different the scoring. In his late music the sound becomes more attenuated as a result of the influence of Webern.

Structurally, Stravinsky's works show an amazing variety of solutions.

In his purely instrumental works, more often than not, he uses the "additive" method, building by blocks, in a somewhat baroque manner. This aspect of his music, along with dotted rhythmic patterns, earned him the neoclassic label. Among the classical forms, he uses the variation most frequently, but rarely the formal delineations of sonata or rondo forms.

In an over-all sense, only the three early ballets form a stylistically contiguous group in their openly Russian character and in their exciting pulsation. From *L'Histoire* to the most recent works, one finds an amazing variety of adaptations of the heritage of Western music, from pre-Baroque practices to serialism, always viewed and reinterpreted by the composer's unique perception and suited to his expressive aims.

STRAVINSKY'S MAJOR WORKS[42]

Works inspired by story, gesture or text		*Abstract instrumental works*	

I. RUSSIAN PERIOD

The Firebird (ballet)	1909	Three Pieces for string quartet	1914
Petrouchka (ballet)	1910–1911		
The Rite of Spring (ballet)	1911–1913		
The Nightingale (opera)	1908–1914		
Pribaoutki (Songs)	1914		
The Wedding (cantata)	1914–1923		
Renard (burlesque)	1915–1916		

II. THE NEOCLASSIC PERIOD

L'Histoire du Soldat (ballet)	1918	Ragtime for eleven instruments	1918
Pulcinella (ballet)	1919	Symphonies of Wind Instruments	1920
Mavra (opera)	1921–1922	Octet for Wind Instruments	1922–1923
		Piano Concerto	1924
		Concerto for Piano and Wind Instruments	1924
Oedipus Rex (opera-oratorio)	1926–1927	Sonata for piano	1924
Apollon Musagetes (ballet)	1927		
		Sérénade en La	1925

[42] A complete list of Stravinsky's works may be found in Eric Walter White, *Stravinsky* (Berkeley and Los Angeles: University of California Press, 1966).

The Fairy's Kiss (ballet)	1928	*Capriccio* for piano and	
Symphony of Psalms	1930	orchestra	1928-1929
Perséphone (melodrama)	1933-1934	Violin Concerto	1931
		Duo Concertant	1932
The Card Game (ballet)	1936	Concerto for two pianos	
			1935
Danses Concertantes (ballet)		*Symphony in C*	
	1941-1942		1939-1940
Scènes de Ballet	1944	Sonata for two pianos	
			1943-1944
Orfeo (ballet)	1947	*Symphony in Three*	
Mass	1944-1947	*Movements*	1942-1945
The Rake's Progress (opera)	1948-1951	*Ebony Concerto*	1945
Cantata	1951-1952		

III. THE SERIAL PERIOD

Canticum Sacrum	1955	Septet	1952-1953
Agon (ballet)	1954-1957		
Threni (sacred text)	1958	*Movements* for Piano and	
		Orchestra	1959
A Sermon, a Narrative, and a Prayer			
	1960-1961		
The Flood (television play)	1962	Variations for Orchestra	
Abraham and Isaac	1963		1964
Requiem Canticles	1966		

BÉLA BARTÓK (1881–1945)

It is peasant music which holds our roots.
BARTÓK

In contrast to the puzzling ambiguities encountered in the assessment of Stravinsky's personality and musical style, Bartók's art and ideas have a clear-cut and consistent quality. The motivating forces that led to Bartók's musical destination are clearly revealed in the biographical data, partially contained in Halsey Stevens' volume,[1] and partially in the composer's collected letters[2] (published so far in Hungarian only), and other writings. These sources also enable one to draw a profile of Bartók, the man, and the uncompromising nature of his character and his deep concern for the major issues of the world.

[1] Halsey Stevens, *The Life and Music of Béla Bartók* (New York: Oxford University Press, 1953; rev. ed., 1964).
[2] János Demény (Ed.), *Bartók Béla Levelei* (Letters of Béla Bartók). (Budapest: Magyar Müvészeti Tanács, 1948, Vol. I; Magyar Nép Könyvkiadó, 1951, Vol. II).

EARLY YEARS

Bartók was born in 1881, in Nagyszentmiklós, a town situated in an area where four nationalities (Hungarian, German, Serb, and Rumanian) live in close proximity. At an early age this geographical reality must have made Bartók aware of the heterogeneous minorities that were thrown together in the framework of the Austro-Hungarian monarchy. Doubtless he soon became cognizant of the tensions caused by the various national and cultural aspirations of these groups.

This geographical awareness probably led Bartók in his first composition, *The Stream of the Danube,* written at the age of eleven, to seek out the countries on the map through which the Danube traverses and utilize their folk music. Thus, in the opening of the piece, austere German melodies are combined with light Austrian tunes, and later Hungarian, Rumanian, and Bulgarian folk songs are introduced. The composition foreshadows Bartók's later scholarly interest in folk music, and is also an early manifestation of his lifelong interest in the sights and sounds of nature. Many later works exemplify the fascinating ways in which nature is filtered through his art. A few instances of his unique musical characterizations are seen in the mysterious forest of the *Wooden Prince,* or in the musical portrayal of the cool well in the *Cantata Profana.*

Bartók was born into a middle-class family; his father, an amateur musician, was the director of an agricultural school and his mother was a music teacher, from whom he received his first piano instruction. The young child's preschool years were marred by a serious and highly contagious skin affliction, on account of which he had to be isolated from the outside world. At the age of seven he lost his father, and the task of bringing up young Béla and his sister, Elsi, four years his junior, fell to the widow.

Soon the family moved to Nagyszöllös, where his mother secured a more renumerative teaching position. Here, Bartók's piano teacher foresaw a brilliant future for the young boy. With the next move to Pozsony (now Bratislava), Bartók was able to receive instruction in music theory from a competent teacher. Also, an academically strict middle school provided him with a broad educational background. After his graduation in 1899, Bartók decided to continue his studies at the Royal Academy of Music in Budapest. His mother stayed in the provinces, and the separation gave rise to an intense correspondence between mother and son. It is through these letters that one learns about young Bartók's political convictions and musical affinities.

PLATE 11. BÉLA BARTÓK,
THE STUDENT, 1899
G. D. Mackett, New York

CHAUVINISM

One of the main themes of these letters was the young boy's fierce nationalism and his bitter denunciation of the Habsburg regime. In 1903 he wrote:

> The present conditions resemble dangerously the situation that existed before 1848. The Hungarians have awakened from their inertia and are demanding their rights. The Croatians, too, are revolting and the wisest Secretary of War issues the most stupid decrees, stirring up the situation even more. And the good Hungarian King! The constitutional King. He dares to state that it is his privilege to decide what should be the language of command in the Hungarian Army. A Habsburg as a constitutional King is as absurd as "an iron ring made out of wood."[3]

When drawing up a mailing list of persons to be invited to his concert a few months later, he wrote to his mother:

> In case you should meet Rigele, tell him not to invite the Archduke; I am not going to play for such bribing, criminal murderers.

[3] *Bartók Béla Levelei*, Vol. II, p. 43.

224

This patriotic zeal prompted Bartók to write his first symphonic work, the *Kossuth Symphony,* in 1902–1903. Although called a symphony, the work is a tone poem following the Straussian models. The composition, based on a ten-part story written by Bartók himself, starts with a musical characterization of Kossuth (leader of the Hungarian independence movement in 1848), who sounds a warning about the danger threatening the country. The warning is followed by a call to arms. A sinister theme, played by the bass clarinet, symbolizes the tyranny of the Habsburgs. Later a distorted version of the Austrian National Anthem signals the death struggle resulting in national catastrophe. The country mourns, but even mourning is banned.

Bartók's complete dedication to his country is summed up in a letter (September 8, 1903) to his mother:

> It is imperative that every youth, when he reaches maturity, should decide for what ideal he wants to struggle . . . . As far I am concerned, I shall serve but one purpose in my whole life with all means at my disposal: that which is in the best interest of the Hungarian nation.[4]

At this time Bartók realized that the music played by gypsy bands, the same music that inspired Brahms and Liszt to write their "Hungarian" Dances and Rhapsodies, was different from the old Hungarian peasant music. An ardent lover of his country, Bartók soon dedicated himself to the recovery of this almost forgotten racial heritage. The only way to find this treasure was to travel to those remote parts of the country where it still lived. With this purpose in mind, Bartók, accompanied by Kodály, his friend and fellow composer, set out on countless trips covering various sections of Hungary. Later, when Bartók became interested in the music of the neighboring countries, trips followed to Rumania, Slovakia, Bulgaria and later extended as far as Turkey and North Africa.

The results of these journeys were published in a monograph[5] characterized by painstaking scholarship, followed by many articles and studies. The last volume, written in collaboration with Albert B. Lord, published after his death, is a study of Serbo-Croatian folk songs.[6]

In 1907 Bartók received an appointment as professor of piano at the Academy, a post he held for some thirty years. He declined to teach composition as he felt it would interfere with his creative work.

---

[4] *Bartók Béla Levelei,* Vol. I, p. 43.
[5] Béla Bartók, *Hungarian Folk Music* (London: Oxford University Press, 1931).
[6] Béla Bartók and Albert B. Lord, *Serbo-Croatian Folk Songs* (New York: Columbia University Press, 1951).

HUMANISM

The period during which Bartók extended his trips beyond the boundaries of Hungary marked an important phase in his maturation. As his vision broadened, Bartók discovered the narrowness of his earlier chauvinism. Meeting the people in foreign countries made him realize that the common man generally feels friendly toward other nationalities, and that hostile attitudes are usually fostered by the ruling circles. He also discovered that the texts of folk songs never expressed hatred or bias toward other nations. As a result of these experiences the composer's early, ultranationalistic feelings gave way to a deeply humanistic outlook. Bartók strove for the highest ethical principles; he was reluctant to join any political party, for he sensed that politics always implied compromises and partial solutions. Despite Bartók's strong craving for identification with a larger group, his wish remained unrealized throughout his life. In his personal life, too, he felt predestined for loneliness. His letters reflect the kind of isolation and loneliness also found in the letters of Beethoven. The two composers had a further kinship in their deep concern for humanity.

The outbreak of World War I was a hard blow for this man, who always hoped for understanding among all peoples. There are few letters left from 1914–1918, but the words uttered by Beethoven in 1809, "What disturbing wild life around me, nothing but drums, cannons, men, misery of all sorts," could have been written by Bartók about a hundred years later.

After the war, Bartók resumed research in folk music. It was to be expected that his travels would be looked upon with suspicion by the Hungarian authorities, because in the semifeudal social setting anyone who showed interest in the activities of peasants was viewed as a "radical" or "subversive." In the years following the war, Bartók was also accused of being unpatriotic since he devoted himself to the study of the folk music of Rumania, a country with which relations at the time were greatly strained.

In the meantime his fame as a concert pianist spread; in the next two decades he toured Western Europe, Soviet Russia, and, in 1928, the United States. He often performed his own works which seemed to have won greater acclaim abroad than in his native country. The bitterness Bartók felt about the lack of recognition of his music by his fellow countrymen is expressed in a letter to his mother:

> With the Hungarian fools—I refer to the concert audiences—I shall not struggle anymore. Let them drown in their "Merry Widows" and other operettas. It seems to me that every serious cultural production has to be taken abroad.[7]

[7] *Bartók Béla Levelei*, Vol. I, p. 82.

When fascism spread, Bartók became one of its most outspoken critics. He refused to go to Italy even for a vacation and banned the performance of his works there and in Germany. When the anti-Semitic laws were introduced in Hungary, and the admission of Jewish students at the Academy restricted, Bartók resigned his position. The occupation of Austria by Hitler in 1938 convinced the composer that his position in Hungary would soon become untenable.

A letter, written in October 1938 to a former American student, shows the keen perception with which Bartók followed world events. He gives an astute analysis of the Chamberlain-Hitler meeting and of the resulting appeasement in Munich. He adds:

> Thus the influence of this system (Nazi) of lies will spread more in Europe. One has to go somewhere, but where? I live even more withdrawn, if that is possible. I don't feel like seeing people; everyone who lives is a potential Nazi . . . . It is a painful situation . . . . I would like to finish my work before the imminent world catastrophe.[8]

Finally the day came (October 12, 1940) when Bartók, in his sixtieth year, left his beloved native country and went into voluntary exile in the United States. An excerpt from his will, made out a few days before he left Hungary, includes the following passage:

> My burial should be as simple as possible. In case after my death they should want to name a street after me, I have the following wish: As long as the former Oktogon Square and the former Körönd[9] bear the names of *those individuals*,[10] or as long as any public street, square or building carries their names, no public street, square or building should bear my name.[11]

At the end of October 1940, Bartók arrived in New York. Adjustment in the new country was difficult; in the first place, mass production and the automatization of American culture made him nostalgic. His sentiments are expressed in an article written soon after his arrival:

> Here in America people cannot even imagine that in Europe there are still areas where practically every article used, from clothing to tools, is made at home; where one cannot see stereotyped, factory-made trash, where the shape and style of objects vary from region to region, often even from village to village.[12]

Bartók was also discontent with his work. His temporary appointment at Columbia University in the department of ethnomusicology

---

[8]*Bartók Béla Levelei,* Vol. II, p. 140.

[9]Oktogon and Körönd were the names of two squares in Budapest, renamed Mussolini and Hitler Squares, respectively, during the war.

[10]"Those individuals" refers of course, to Mussolini and Hitler.

[11]*Bartók Béla Levelei,* Vol. II, p. 153.

[12]Béla Bartók, "Diversity of Material Yielded up in Profusion in European Melting Pot," *Musical America* (1943), p. 27.

expired. From then on, his only source of income was from a few lecture-recitals and a few joint appearances with his wife, Ditta Pásztory, also a concert pianist. He writes to Mrs. Creel, a former student, in March, 1942:

> Our situation becomes worse from day to day. All I can say is that never in my life, since I have earned my living, have I found myself in such a horrible situation as seems to lie before me in the very near future . . . . I have lost my trust in people, in countries, in everything.[13]

Finally, his health became affected. Recurrent attacks of fever were diagnosed as leukemia. Despite his gradually worsening condition, a letter dated August 1944 indicates that he was still concerned about the fate of the world:

> I am glad about the good news[14] but everything comes too late. Too late for me, and surely too late for those who are being murdered by the Nazis.[15]

During the last years of his illness, ASCAP (the American Society of Composers, Authors, and Publishers) insured him a modest financial security. In 1945 Bartók died and the voluntary exile came to an end.

MUSICAL INFLUENCES

In a brief autobiographical note[16] written in 1921, Bartók acknowledges the influence of three composers: Richard Strauss, Liszt, and Debussy. Strauss had a strong initial impact on the young composer. In 1902 Bartók stated: "I was roused as by a lightning stroke at the first Budapest performance of *Thus Spake Zarathustra*. The work filled me with the greatest enthusiasm." Despite its intensity, the Straussian spell did not last long and its effects can be seen in only a few of the early works, in the *Kossuth Symphony* (1903) and in the *First Orchestral Suite* (1905).

We also learn from the same source, that Bartók studied Liszt's works very closely. Liszt's music was frequently performed at that time in Hungary and he himself, some twenty years after his death, remained a legendary figure. The Music Academy where Bartók studied was

---

[13] *Bartók Béla Levelei,* Vol. II, pp. 169–170.
[14] Reference is made to the Allied landing at Normandy.
[15] *Bartók Béla Levelei,* Vol. II, p. 188.
[16] "Autobiographical Note"; *Béla Bartók, A Memorial Review* (articles reprinted from *Tempo,* 1949–1950), published by Boosey & Hawkes, New York, 1950, pp. 7–10.

founded by Liszt, and Bartók's piano teacher, Thoman, was a former pupil of Liszt. Under these circumstances Bartók's interest and idolization of Liszt's music is understandable. "A really thorough study of Liszt's oeuvre, especially of his lesser known works . . . revealed to me the essence of composition," comments Bartók, adding that, "for the future development of music his compositions seem to me of far greater importance than those of Strauss or even Wagner."

One would assume from this statement that Bartók's music would reveal strong Lisztian influences. The fact is, however, that with the exception of the Lisztian transformation of themes in his *Two Portraits* (1907), there is relatively little evidence of his influence. Bartók's admiration for Liszt is expressed in an article[17] describing the multitude of marvelous ideas that occur in the *Faust Symphony,* and emphasizing that this is the first musical portrayal of diabolic irony.

Bartók discovered Debussy in 1907, two years after he had set out on his research trips. It is likely that some elements found in the Hungarian folk style (as for instance the usage of the pentatonic scale, and a certain improvisatory character) made Bartók particulary receptive to the French master's art. Of the three influences, Debussy's was the most lasting; the luminosity of the impressionistic color scheme can be observed even in some of Bartók's later works.

Bartók's style became increasingly individualistic as it matured, and the influence of a single composer can seldom be detected.

He gradually assimilated the dominant twentieth-century tendencies; thus, in the two violin sonatas a trace of Schoenberg's expressionism is felt, beyond which Bartók did not follow the path of the Viennese composer. Atonality and the method of twelve-tone composition were foreign and unacceptable to Bartók's mode of thinking. It is difficult to determine the extent of Stravinsky's influence on Bartók's works; the listener may ascribe some of Bartók's highly rhythmic compositions to the impact of Stravinsky's primitivistic style. The resemblance, however, may be a reflection of their common East European and Asiatic ancestry.

Since in commentaries on Bartók's works affinities to Beethoven's music are so frequently encountered, this point needs elaboration. While undoubtedly a deepseated kinship exists between the music of the two composers, this kinship cannot be described as an "influence" in the usual sense of the term. It would be misleading to state that Bartók took over certain stylistic features found in the music of Beethoven. Rather, the similarity lies in the essence of their musical geniuses; both masters controlled explosive instinctual forces by virtue of

---

[17] Béla Bartók, "Liszt zenéje és a mai közönség" (Liszt's Music and Today's Audiences), *Népművelés,* **14** (1911), pp. 359-362.

the constructive formation of their thematic logic. This struggle for control gives forcefulness and inner tension to their music. Further, both masters showed an increased interest in counterpoint as their styles matured, and both found their supreme attainment in the field of string quartet writing.

THE INFLUENCE OF FOLK MUSIC

It has been mentioned earlier that Bartók was led by patriotism in his search for the old Hungarian peasant music. It is impossible to determine whether in his search for folk material, the composer also aimed at establishing his own musical style. Undoubtedly, he felt at the time, as did other composers, that music had reached a turning point and that a break with the nineteenth-century idiom was necessary. In any case, the influence of folk music was strongly felt in Bartók's compositions. In his brief autobiographical sketch he offers an account of how deeply he was influenced by the material he had collected:

> The outcome of these studies was of decisive influence upon my work because it freed me from the tyrannical rule of the major and minor keys. The greater part of the collected treasure, and the more valuable part, was in old ecclesiastical or old Greek modes, or based on more primitive (pentatonic) scales, and the melodies were full of the freest and most varied rhythmic phrases and changes of tempi . . . . It became clear to me that the old modes, which had been forgotten in our music, had lost nothing of their vigor. Their new employment made new rhythmic combinations possible.[18]

In another essay, Bartók assails the view, held by many, that it is an easy task to base one's style on folk material. He writes:

> To handle folk tunes is one of the most difficult tasks, as difficult if not more so than to write a major, original composition. If we keep in mind that borrowing a tune means being bound by its individual peculiarities, we shall understand one part of the difficulty. Another is created by the special character of the folk tune. We must penetrate it, feel it, and bring it out in sharp contours by the appropriate setting.[19]

In his writing Bartók emphasizes that one should not attribute too much significance to the invention of the "theme" of a composition. He cites the example of Shakespeare, who also borrowed the plots of his plays from various sources. It is not the invention of a theme or a

---

[18] "Autobiographical Note," p. 8.
[19] Béla Bartók, "On the Significance of Folk-music," *Béla Bartók, A Memorial Review*, p. 74.

story that is the essence of a work of art, but the creator's ability to find the right mold and treatment that will shed light on the true significance of the material.

A listing of all the folkloristic features—Hungarian, Rumanian, Slovak, Bulgarian, and others—that left an imprint on Bartók's style would go far beyond the scope of this study. It would be an even more complex task—not yet attempted by any of the Bartók scholars—to trace the process of assimilation and integration through which the Hungarian composer absorbed these various influences into his personal style. Therefore, only a few of the typical melodic, harmonic, and rhythmic folk characteristics which had a particularly strong effect on Bartók's style will be mentioned.

MELODIC ASPECTS

Undoubtedly, the most characteristic interval in Hungarian (as in other East European) folk songs is the perfect fourth. Example 10/1 furnishes a typical example of a Hungarian folk song that employs both the rising and the falling fourth.

EX. 10/1 *Hungarian Folk Song* (the interval of the fourth is in brackets)

Examples 10/2 and 10/3 illustrate the importance of this interval in Bartók's melodic thinking:

EX. 10/2 *Third Quartet*,[20] first movement, mm. 87–91.

[20] Copyright 1929 by Universal Edition; renewed 1956. Copyright and renewal assigned to Boosey & Hawkes, Inc. for the U.S.A. Reprinted by permission.

EX. 10/3 *Concerto for Orchestra,*[21] introduction

Andante non troppo (♩ = ca. 73-64)
Cellos & Basses
p legato

Another interval that influenced the composer's melodic style is the augmented fourth (tritone). His employment of this interval is derived partly from folk songs in the Lydian mode (frequently encountered in Slovak songs and illustrated in Example 10/4) and partly from works of the late romantics, such as Richard Strauss, Mussorgsky, and others.

EX. 10/4 *Slovak Folk Song*

From the countless examples of the tritone in the music of Bartók, two are quoted below:

EX. 10/5 *Second Quartet,*[22] second movement, opening

Allegro molto capriccioso (♩ = 132)
Violins I & II

EX. 10/6 *Sixth Quartet,*[23] first movement, cello line from m. 36

Vivace (♩ = ca. 140)
Cello
p

Perhaps stronger than the employment of single intervals is the influence of the scales and modes to which many folk songs owe their particular flavor. The influence of the pentatonic scale is very strong in Bartók's melodic thinking; he often follows a practice, also derived from folk sources, whereby he uses essentially the five notes of the pentatonic scale, while the two additional notes, which would complete the heptatonic (seven-note) scale appear only in embellishments or on weak beats. Of the modal melodic influences the Dorian is the strongest, although Lydian, Mixolydian, and Phrygian melodies can also be found in Bartók's compositions.

Arabic Melodic Influence   The absorption of Arabic elements in Bartók's music is not sufficiently recognized in the Bartók literature.

An examination of the composer's collection of Arabic folk songs reveals that the melodic idiom of the Second Quartet was strongly influenced by the peculiarities of the Arabic scale system. This connection is made even more plausible by the fact that the composer's trip to Biskra in North Africa preceded the composition of the quartet by only a few years.

The characteristic feature of the Arabic melodies is that they are derived from scales consisting of three or four notes. A comparison of one of these scales with the melodic idiom of the Second Quartet shows marked similarity. Thus, the melody appearing in Example 10/7 from the Second Quartet can be reduced to a scale pattern almost identical to the one quoted by Bartók in his Biskra essay (Ex. 10/8):

EX. 10/7 *Second Quartet,* second movement, 6 mm. before
study no. 2.

EX. 10/8 Biskra Scale Pattern

Likewise, it is more correct to associate the opening theme of the second movement of the Second Quartet (Ex. 10/9) with the Biskra scale pattern than to see it as an interplay of major and minor thirds.

Another derivation from the Biskra scale pattern is the frequent melodic use of minor seconds, occasionally interspersed with minor thirds. This became one of the trademarks of the Bartókian melodic

EX. 10/9 *Second Quartet,* second movement, study no. 1

style both in the Second Quartet and in later works. Examples 10/10, 10/11, and 10/12 show the adaptation of this melodic pattern in three different works:

EX. 10/10 *Second Quartet,* second movement, mm. 3–4 after
study no. 43

EX. 10/11 *Miraculous Mandarin* (1918),[24] study no. 66

EX. 10/12 *Music for Strings, Percussion, and Celesta* (1936),[25]
first movement, mm. 5–6

Melodic Embellishments The melodic embellishments of East European folk music are amazingly varied. In most of these folk songs there is one principal note per syllable; all additional pitches attached to the same syllable are considered ornamental and are usually sung with a lighter delivery than the principal notes. As a rule, these lighter ornamental notes lead from one principal note to the following one, or they embellish it by circling around it in the form of a mordent or inverted mordent. In certain areas, however, particularly in Croatia, Bartók found "heavy" ornaments; these heavy ornamentations, which often include glissandi, form a highly expressive pattern and lend a luxurious quality to the ornamented melody. Example 10/13/a presents such an ornamented melody; the original melody appears in Example 10/13/b:

EX. 10/13/a *Serbo-Croatian Folk Collection,*[26] No. 28, mm. 1–2

EX. 10/13/b Original Version

From the countless examples that could be cited from Bartók's music, Example 10/14 illustrates light ornamentation:

EX. 10/14 Rhapsody,[27] second movement, mm. 52–55
　　　　　No. 1 for violin and piano

Example 10/15 contains a sample of the more expressive heavy ornamentation:

EX. 10/15 *Fourth Quartet,*[28] third movement, mm. 6–9

---

[26] Used by permission of The Béla Bartók Archives, New York.

[27] Copyright 1930 by Universal Edition; renewed 1957. Copyright and renewal assigned to Boosey & Hawkes, Inc. Reprinted by permission.

[28] Copyright 1929 by Universal Edition; renewed 1956. Copyright and renewal assigned to Boosey & Hawkes, Inc. for the U.S.A. Reprinted by permission.

Glissandi appear frequently in Bartók's music, particularly in his string quartets; one ingenious employment is shown in Example 10/16:

EX. 10/16 *Fourth Quartet,* second movement mm. 137–139

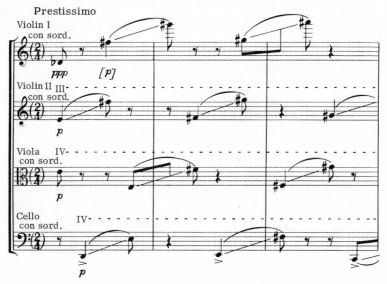

HARMONIC IMPLICATIONS OF
FOLK INFLUENCES

The most direct harmonic implications of folk influences appear when the typical melodic intervals (the fourth and the tritone) are used in harmonizations. In Example 10/17 both the melody and the harmony are constructed in fourths.

EX. 10/17 *Duke Bluebeard's Castle,*[29] piano-vocal score, p. 57

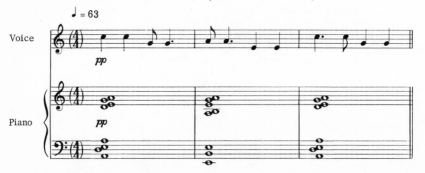

[29]Copyright 1921 by Universal Edition; renewed 1948. Copyright and renewal assigned to Boosey & Hawkes, Inc. for the U.S.A. Reprinted by permission.

In Example 10/18 a pentatonic theme, harmonized in parallel moving tritones, is cited:

EX. 10/18 *The Miraculous Mandarin,* 3 measures after study no. 34

The tritone relationship assumed much greater significance in Bartók's late music than a means of harmonization. In the Sixth Quartet, for instance, the D–G sharp, and the F–B pairs of tritones form the harmonic pillars of the entire composition.

Another feature of Bartók's harmonic style, derived from the harmonic implications of the pentatonic scale, is the consonant use of the seventh. For example, in the F sharp–A–B–C sharp–E pentatonic scale, Bartók considers the F sharp–E interval as consonant, and he treats the F sharp–A–C sharp–E chord as a consonant chord, one of repose which may conclude a composition.

Bartók realized the latent harmonic implications of folk music when he started to arrange folk songs. He soon came to see that the usual harmonizations built on the triads of the tonic, subdominant, and dominant would not be applicable to the modal and pentatonic songs. In general, the trend in his harmonizations was one toward increasing harmonic complexity; one can observe this trend by comparing the setting of an early song such as "Esős az Ég Felettem (Skies Above Are Heavy with Rain)" from the *Twenty Hungarian Folksongs* (1907) quoted in Example 10/19, with one from a collection published some twenty years later, "A Tömlöcben (In Prison)" (Ex. 10/20).

Finding a musically valid harmonization for the folk songs challenged the composer. In the course of experimentation Bartók arrived at the surprising conclusion that the simpler the melody, the more complex and unorthodox the harmonization could be. The *Improvisations on Hungarian Peasant Songs* for piano (1920) illustrates interesting harmonic solutions. Improvisation No. 1 furnishes an object lesson in the accomplished treatment of three different harmonic settings (Ex. 10/21) of a simple modal peasant melody.

Each of the different harmonizations in Example 10/21 has a distinctive character. The first setting, employing the major second, has a dissonant, tenuous quality, while the second setting creates constant

EX. 10/19 *Twenty Hungarian Folksongs* (1907).[30] "Esös az Ég Felettem," mm. 1–6

EX. 10/20 *Twenty Hungarian Folksongs* (1929)[31] "A Tömlöcben," mm. 23–25

[30] Rózsavölgyi és Társa, Budapest, publisher.

[31] Copyright 1932 by Universal Edition; renewed 1959. Copyright and renewal assigned to Boosey & Hawkes, Inc. for the U.S.A. Reprinted by permission.

EX. 10/21 *Improvisations on Hungarian Peasant Songs[32] for piano,*
Op. 20, No. 1 (1920)

surprise in the unpredictable alternation of major and minor thirds. The last setting blossoms out with the large embellished chords, many of which are built in fourths. A lovely color is derived from the parallel fifths in the left hand in the brief epilogue.

Improvisation No. 2 illustrates how a simple melody may receive an extremely complex harmonization. The feeling conveyed is that of a modern composer viewing his racial past.

RHYTHMIC FOLK INFLUENCES

In considering the rhythmic characteristics of East European folk songs, a distinction is made between their *over-all* rhythmic style and the specific peculiarities of metric groupings and accentuations.

The over-all rhythmic style of the old Hungarian peasant songs has two modalities: 1) the so-called *parlando-rubato* style, that is, the free declamatory style that follows the inflection of the spoken word and which cannot be fitted into either an unchanging tempo or symmetrical, regular metric groupings; and 2) the *tempo giusto* style, which employs a more consistent tempo, inspired by dance patterns.

Both rhythmic styles had an impact on Bartók's approach to rhythm. The *parlando-rubato* manner is clearly recognizable, for instance, in the middle section of the first movement and in the last movement of the First Quartet; in the First Violin Rhapsody (opening movement); and in the introduction to the *Concerto for Orchestra.* The *tempo giusto* style is applied to many first movements written in sonata form and to numerous fast, rondo-type last movements.

Among the more specific rhythmic characteristics of East European folk songs the asymmetrical groupings of beats (5, 7, and so on) and the changing meters are prominent. These rhythmic features, introduced by Bartók and Stravinsky almost simultaneously, found both the performer and the listener unprepared, since in the music of the eighteenth and nineteenth centuries only duple or triple meters (or their multiples) were employed and one meter, as a rule, governed an entire movement.

Asymmetrical groupings and changing meters are shown as they appear in Hungarian, Rumanian, and Bulgarian folk songs in the following examples:

EX. 10/22 Hungarian Folk Song

EX. 10/23 Rumanian Folk Song

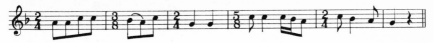

EX. 10/24 Bulgarian Folk Song

As can be seen from the examples, the Bulgarian rhythm shows the greatest complexity. Another rhythmic peculiarity of Bulgarian folk songs is that although they employ an otherwise conventional meter, the beats appear in unusual subdivisions. Thus a Bulgarian folk song in $\frac{9}{8}$ meter may have a $\dfrac{3 + 2 + 2 + 2}{8}$ grouping, that is, $\frac{9}{8}$ ♩♩♩ ♩♩ ♩♩ | instead of the usual Western ternary subdivision:

$\frac{9}{8}$ ♩♩♩ ♩♩♩ ♩♩♩ |

Bartók's music contains frequent references to Bulgarian rhythms; examples can be observed in the last six pieces of the *Mikrokosmos*, and in the Scherzo movement of the Fifth Quartet, which has a $\frac{10}{8}$ meter signature with a $\dfrac{3 + 2 + 2 + 3}{8}$ beat pattern.

Two rhythmic characteristics of the Hungarian folk songs should be ascribed to the accentuations of the Hungarian language which, almost without exception, fall on the *first* syllable of words. It is very likely due to this peculiarity of the language that Hungarian folk songs start *on the beat,* without an upbeat. An examination of some 300 folk songs in Bartók's *Hungarian Folk Music* shows that there are not more than five or six songs beginning with an upbeat, and in these the upbeat is due to a word of exclamation, such as "Hej (Hey)," which precedes the text proper. This rhythmic tendency manifests itself in Bartók's music too; his melodies are less upbeat oriented than those of German composers.

The inflection of the Hungarian language is also responsible for the second rhythmic characteristic, a short accentuated note followed by a longer unaccented one. This pattern, known as the "Magyar (Hungarian)" rhythm, appears frequently both in Hungarian folk songs and in the composer's music, an example of which is found in the slow movement of the *Divertimento* and in the slow movement of the Fourth Quartet.

In the foregoing discussion a number of typical melodic, harmonic, and rhythmic characteristics of Bartók's style were linked to their folk origin. The process of assimilation occurred in various ways; in some instances the listener is reminded of the folk origin of a certain stylistic trait, while in others the folk influence has become sublimated. An example of the latter process can be found in the changing meters of the first movement of the *Music for String, Percussion, and Celesta*, in which the changing meters are merely a faint reminder of the metric changes found in folk music.

STYLE DEVELOPMENT

Bartók's growth as a composer falls into three clearly delineated phases, to which the brief American "exile" period may be added as an epilogue.

In the first period (1905–1920), the composer's main concern was a new reconciliation of melody and harmony; hence, this phase is aptly called the *melodic-harmonic* period.

In the works of the second period (1920–1930), the rhythmic component is strongly emphasized and a new interest in contrapuntal processes is shown. Harsh dissonances and percussive sonorities make the works of this *rhythmic-polyphonic* period less accessible than those of the first or third period.

In the decade from 1930–1940 (the *synthesis* period) the composer attained the peak of his achievements. During the last five years of the composer's life (1940–1945), often referred to as the exile-period, a decline in his creative powers is in evidence.

THE MELODIC-HARMONIC PERIOD
(1905-1920)

This period is marked by the absorption of folk elements and, as mentioned, a new reconciliation of melody and harmony.

As a pianist, it is only natural that the composer turned to his own instrument for experimentation. The piano parts receive considerable attention in the harmonizations of folk songs; in the process of this activity Bartók probably became aware of the need for new harmonic solutions.

In comparing this early period with subsequent phases of the composer's development, it can be said that Bartók began with short compositions; his interest, and perhaps ability, in writing large-scale works developed later. The first and second quartets and the three stage works, of course, are exceptions to this generalization.

PIANO WORKS

Throughout this period the dominant influence of folk music can be seen from the titles of a large number of piano pieces, such as *Fifteen Hungarian Peasant Songs, Two Rumanian Dances, Rumanian Folk Dances, Seven Folk Sketches,* and *Evening in Transylvania.*

Remarkable originality and boldness are revealed in the *Fourteen Bagatelles* (1908). Pentatonic melodies that do not yield to Western harmonizations are provided with dissonant accompaniments, frequently utilizing the interval of the fourth, second, seventh, and even consecutive augmented triads. Bitonal superimpositions are also used frequently.

For Children (1908–1909) and *Ten Easy Piano Pieces* (1908) are invaluable contributions to the materials of piano pedagogy, anticipating the more systematic *Mikrokosmos* (1926–1937).

The most prophetic piano work of the period is the *Allegro Barbaro* (1911) which, with its driving rhythm and steely martellato style, foreshadows the piano works of the second period.

In the *Improvisations on Hungarian Peasant Songs* (1920), Bartók fully establishes an independent style in which folk elements are successfully integrated with twentieth-century Western European stylistic features. The work also shows that the composer found a satisfactory solution to the integration of melody and harmony, and that he was now ready to turn to new tasks.

FIRST AND SECOND QUARTETS

The First Quartet (1908) is the least homogeneous of the six quartets, which, incidentally, occupy a central position in Bartók's oeuvre. Composed at a time when Bartók's folk music research had just begun, the quartet does not yet show the assimilation of folk material which will ultimately characterize his style. Harmonically, Debussy's style and Wagnerian chromaticism cast a shadow upon the work. The tightness of organization, the hallmark of the five later quartets, is also missing.

Despite these shortcomings, the slow fugal opening has a transcendental quality. The unconventional sequence of the three movements (*Lento-Allegretto-Allegro vivace*) does not represent isolated mood sequences, but points toward a unified, continuous thought process, as found in middle and late Beethoven quartets. At times Bartók's continuity between movements is based on an intangible musical thread, while in other instances one detects a subtle growth or transformation of a motive. Thus, the accompanying motive of the second movement (Ex. 10/25) becomes, with slight modifications, the main theme of the last movement (Ex. 10/26):

EX. 10/25 *First Quartet,*[33] second movement, mm. 18-21

EX. 10/26 *First Quartet,* third movement, mm. 5-6

While this relationship between the two movements is pointed out in every analysis of the work, it is less obvious that both motives owe their derivation to the descending sixth of the opening fugue motive (Ex. 10/27), which can be considered as a germinating cell for the entire composition.

EX. 10/27 *First Quartet,* first movement, opening

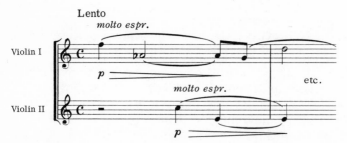

The Second Quartet (1917–1918) in three movements (*Moderato–Allegro molto capriccioso–Lento*) almost reverses the tempo cycle of the earlier quartet. Unlike its predecessor, this quartet is the product of Bartók's complete mastery over the medium and the highly successful integration of folk elements.

The first movement follows the outline of sonata form. Although many sources refer to it as being in A minor, it should be kept in mind that Bartók does not build his music on the major-minor key system, and A is merely the focal point that clearly dominates at the end of the movement. The bimodal arrangement of the coda (quoted in Ex. 4/14) with the clashing C and C sharp is additional evidence that the composer's thinking went beyond clear-cut major or minor modalities. The first movement shows an amazing economy of motivic development; the way in which a three-note motive dominates the whole movement again brings Beethoven to mind. The growth of thematic material can also be noted as the motive of the main theme of the first movement reappears, transformed, in the last movement. The savage rhythms of the second movement point to Bartók's next period. Mention was made earlier of the Arabic influences in this movement. Throughout the entire work the part writing shows perfect equalization, particularly in the second movement where fascinating tonal effects are evident.

STAGE WORKS

Bartók wrote three stage works in his early period. Whether he refrained from returning later to the composition of stage works because they met with such resistance or simply because his taste changed remains a matter of speculation.

Duke Bluebeard's Castle (1911), a one-act opera first produced only in 1918, was soon banned because the librettist, Béla Balázs, became a bitter opponent of the new Horthy regime established in 1919. The work was revived only after Bartók's death, in 1948. *The Wooden Prince* (1914–1916), a ballet in one act, based on a story by Balázs, also disappeared from the repertory. *The Miraculous Mandarin* (1918–1919), a pantomime based on a libretto by Menyhért Lengyel, encountered different obstacles. Because of the unusually daring story, the police repeatedly refused to give permission for its performance. Although the work was widely performed in other European cities, it was not premiered in Budapest until 1946.

Bartók found himself breaking new ground during the composition of *Duke Bluebeard's Castle*. There was no model to look back to; all earlier Hungarian operas were purely derivative, following German or

Italian styles. Therefore, this work has special significance in that it established a genuine Hungarian operatic idiom based on a novel *parlando-recitative* style.

The work shows some obvious characteristics of Debussy's *Pelléas et Mélisande;* in both operas the vocal lines are recitative, while the main melody is usually assigned to the orchestra. Yet, the similarity of the recitative style is superficial only, because the Hungarian prosody demands an entirely different treatment from the French. Thus, while the examples shown from the two works (Ex. 10/28/a and 10/28/b) may seem similar to the eye, the vocal inflections are very different.

EX. 10/28/a DEBUSSY, *Pelléas et Mélisande,*[34] piano-vocal score, p. 7

EX. 10/28/b BARTÓK, *Duke Bluebeard's Castle,* piano-vocal score, pp. 12–13

The *Bluebeard* legend has seen many literary and musical adaptations. Bartók captures the mysticism of the eternal conflict between man and woman. The mood is introspective, searching, and serious. The style is unified and magical effects are reached through an imaginative orchestration and a luxurious harmonic palette.

The *Wooden Prince* is a less successful work. Bartók may have used Stravinsky's *Petrouchka* as a model in which many disparate elements were so deftly unified. In any case, the Hungarian composer failed to solidify the romantic, folkloristic, parodizing, and symbolic elements, even though there are many lovely sections in the work.

The *Miraculous Mandarin* owes some of its primitivism to Stravinsky. The musical delineation of the characters is extremely successful. Ostinato technique is used frequently and the driving rhythms, bold harmonic scheme, and brilliant orchestration make it one of Bartók's most successful, though not sufficiently known, works.

---

[34] Permission for reprint granted by Durand et Cie., Paris, France, copyright owners; Elkan-Vogel Co., Inc., Philadelphia, Pa., agents.

THE RHYTHMIC-POLYPHONIC PERIOD
(1920-1930)

Whereas at the end of the first period Bartók succeeded in the assimilation of the folk idiom, he turned to its sublimation during the second period. This means that the materials of folk origin were used in large instrumental works and in undergoing the process of thematic elaboration the folkloristic element became tenuous. Works during this period were created in curious pairs: two violin sonatas, two quartets, two violin rhapsodies, and two piano concertos. To this list one might add the Piano Sonata, the *Out of Doors* suite, and the *Cantata Profana*. Folk song arrangements were limited to the *Twenty Hungarian Folksongs*.

The instrumental works of this period are characterized by a certain hard and uncompromising quality, in contrast to the earlier, more colorful melodic-harmonic style.

As suggested before, the folk influence diminished. Bartók's turning away from folkloristic sources is also evident in his increasing interest in contrapuntal processes. Denser textures are particularly noticeable in the third and fourth quartets, which show highly developed fugatos and canonic devices. Tension is created not only by the increased den-

PLATE 12. PROFESSOR
BARTÓK, 1926

sity of the lines, but also by the harsh dissonances and frequent complex rhythmic superimpositions. In most of the works of the period tonality is tenuous; Bartók never came closer to the boundaries of atonality than in this second period.

VIOLIN WORKS

The two sonatas for violin and piano, dated 1921 and 1922, respectively, are problematical for both performer and listener. The works are intensively expressive; the first betrays Schoenbergian influences with octave displacements (Ex. 10/29):

EX. 10/29 *Sonata No. 1 for Violin and Piano,*[35] first movement,
mm. 17–22

Neither of the sonatas follows the established path of "sonata" style for the two instruments involved. Although the violin is undoubtedly the lead instrument, the piano, without overshadowing or endangering the clarity of the texture, maintains an independent part. Although the intensity of the two lines rises and falls together, there is actually little motivic interplay between them.

The two violin rhapsodies (1928) exist in several versions (violin-piano, violin-orchestra, cello-piano); Bartók made several revisions even after the works were published. Both works are virtuoso pieces and show more folk influence than any other compositions of this period. Their rich ornamentation and dazzling style make them easily the most accessible middle works.

PIANO MUSIC

Within one year (1926) Bartók composed three major piano works: a Sonata, the First Concerto, and the *Out of Doors Suite*.

The Piano Sonata, in three movements, is an austere work. The *martellato* style prevails and even the slow movement fails to achieve any lyricism or singing expression. The forms used are the classical ones. Thus, the first movement is in sonata form, and the slow movement in ternary song form, leading to a rondo-type finale. The rhythmic-polyphonic label of the period certainly fits this work; hard sonorities with biting dissonances and intricate contrapuntal devices make the Sonata sound unyielding. The compelling quality of the music and its inner logic emerge only after many hearings.

The *Out of Doors* suite is a fascinating composition, considerably more accessible than the Sonata. Perhaps the suggestions of the titles of the five movements ("With Drums and Pipes," "Barcarolla," "Musettes," "Night's Music," and "Chase") help to orient the listener. The most imaginative movement is, undoubtedly, "Night's Music," the atmosphere of which will recur in many later works. It is misleading to label these sounds as twittering and chirping, as described by Stevens, because Bartók does not intend to portray the sounds of night. His sounds do not exist in nature, but rather in the composer's inner world.

Of the two piano concertos, the second one, written in 1930, is the more interesting and aptly summarizes the gains of the rhythmic-polyphonic period. In the first movement the strings are tacet (silent); the piano-wind combinations bring Stravinsky's neoclassic period to mind. The second movement, however, is deeply Bartókian, another instance of "night" music. The last movement in rondo form presents material from the first movement in new rhythmic guises.

THIRD AND FOURTH QUARTETS

The two middle quartets, dated 1927 and 1928, respectively, represent the transition from the second to the third period. While the Third Quartet belongs decidedly to the second period, the architecture and the sound conception of the Fourth Quartet points to the changes that will characterize the composer's next phase. The comparison of the first movements of the two quartets shows important differences; whereas the first movement of the earlier quartet has a modicum of the expressionism of the violin sonatas, the first movement of the latter work is devoid of this quality. Harmonically, the Third Quartet is highly tenuous, whereas the Fourth (see Chapter 6) more strongly suggests gravitation to a harmonic center.

Structurally, the growth of the arch pattern is evident. The three movements of the Third Quartet are architecturally less developed than the wide arches that support the five movements of the later work. In the Third Quartet, two related movements flank the fast, dancelike middle movement. The *Ricapitulazione della prima parte* (Recapitulation of the first part) is highly condensed, capturing the atmosphere rather than the actual motivic content of the first part. The ensuing coda places enormous demands on the performers; in *allegro molto* tempo, a canon rushes by, *sul ponticello,* separated in the four parts by one eighth note.

In the Fourth Quartet the arch idea is further developed. Of the five movements, the third one occupies a central position. It is surrounded by two arches: one, formed by the first and fifth movements which share motivic material; the other by the related, scherzolike second and fourth movements.

There are several reasons why the Fourth Quartet is more accessible than its predecessor. First, its sheer virtuosity dazzles even the unsympathetic listener. Second, the slow movement has a lovely, lyrical quality which is missing in the Third Quartet. The lyrical, improvisatory melody is sustained by the cello, supported by alternating vibrato and nonvibrato chords. The all-pizzicato fourth movement is a veritable tour de force, leading to a rondo-type finale that has decidedly more folklike flavor than the earlier work. While the Third Quartet is performed relatively infrequently, the Fourth Quartet has established itself in the repertory. The Fourth Quartet, according to Halsey Stevens "comes close to being, if it actually does not represent, Bartók's greatest and most profound achievement."

The last work of this period is the *Cantata Profana* (1929–1930), perhaps Bartók's most important vocal work. It is scored for tenor and baritone soloists, double mixed chorus, and large orchestra. Based on a Rumanian folk legend rich in symbolic meaning, the work has an immediate appeal. Its intricate contrapuntal lines and clashing dissonances bear the marks of the composer's middle period, but the masterful solution of problems of architecture and the mature synthesis of folkloristic and nonfolkloristic elements point toward the period of consummate mastery.

THE SYNTHESIS PERIOD (1930–1940)

Bartók achieved a masterful synthesis of his art during the third period. The folkloristic explorations of the first period and the bold experimentations of the 1920s ripened into a wonderfully integrated art. The most significant works of the period are the Fifth Quartet (1934), the Sixth Quartet (1939), *Music for Strings, Percussion, and Celesta* (1936), the Violin Concerto (1937), *Sonata for Two Pianos and Percussion* (1937), and the *Divertimento for String Orchestra* (1939).

As in the second period, the majority of the works are instrumental, in three or four movements, and employ the forms of the classical tradition. Whereas the formal aspects may be based on tradition, the tonal effects open up a new world of sound. For novelty of sound, the *Sonata for Two Pianos and Percussion* is the most remarkable; the combination of percussion instruments (xylophone, timpani, suspended and fixed cymbals, side drums, bass drum) with two pianos produces the most extraordinary sound effects.

In order to demonstrate the integration of diverse elements in Bartók's period of synthesis, the *Music for Strings, Percussion, and Celesta,* considered by many as Bartók's greatest work, will be examined in detail.

MUSIC FOR STRINGS, PERCUSSION, AND CELESTA

This composition in four movements is written for two string orchestras, harp, celesta, timpani, side drums, tam-tam, bass drum, xylophone, and celesta.

First Movement–Andante tranquillo   The opening movement, a fugue, is a most remarkable composition. The music, conveying the feeling of some tortuous inertia, is so deeply expressive that the listener hardly realizes how carefully the movement is planned and how consciously the material has been developed.

The subject of the fugue, first sounded by the muted violas, was partially quoted in Example 10/12 and mention was made of the almost exclusive use of half steps and minor thirds in the construction of the theme, suggesting Arabic influence. Since the subject serves as a germinating motive for the entire composition, it is necessary to quote it in full:

EX. 10/30 *Music for Strings, Percussion, and Celesta,* first movement, opening

The asymmetrical metric organization of the theme should be noted; it is probably because of the changing meters that the movement is surrounded by an aura of restlessness.

The second fugue entrance (answer) is regular, but at this point the experienced ear will notice something unusual. In almost all fugues, when the second voice enters, an independent contrapuntal part, a countersubject, based on *new* melodic material, appears in the opening voice. However, in this fugue—and this holds true for subsequent entrances—*all* the material is derived from the opening subject. As a result, the whole movement is highly unified and concentrated. The middle section of the fugue begins after eight entrances. At this point (m. 34) the timpani enter for the first time with a long ominous trill and the strings play *senza sordino* (without mute), as if to prepare themselves for the events to come. But there are other signs of mounting tension. In measure 38 the tempo is slightly accelerated (the metronome signature changes from the earlier ♪ = 116-122 to ♪ = 120-126) and the word *expressivo* urges the player to rise to a higher level of expressiveness, while the dynamic level reaches a *mezzo-piano* in contrast to the opening *pianissimo*. The stage is set now for the real buildup. In measure 40 a *crescendo* brings the dynamic level first to a *forte* (m. 45) and then at measure 52, to a *fortissimo*. Finally in measure 56, the climax is reached with a *triple forte*. This dynamic climax coincides with a climax in harmonic tension, as the movement reaches its greatest dissonance with a clash of E flat with E.

Another interesting aspect of the climax is that it is reached on E flat, the exact "geographical" midpoint (setting up the tritone relationship from A to E flat, and E flat to A) of the opening and closing notes of the movement. The continuity after the climax sounds organic and natural even to the nonanalytical ear. The trained musician, however, will observe that it is the opening subject that is played, now inverted (Ex. 10/31).

EX. 10/31 First movement, mm. 69-70

The material is now considerably condensed and the dynamic level gradually subsides; when *pianissimo* is reached, the strings are muted, at which point (m. 78) the celesta enters for the first time. This is a most exquisite moment. The celesta color is in the background and the fourth violins play the opening motive, while the first violins sound the inversion of the motive three octaves higher. The remarkable sound of this texture is enriched by a dissonant, quivering violin tremolo.

The impressionistic mist suddenly evaporates and once more a segment of the opening subject appears simultaneously in its original and inverted version (m. 82); then a smaller part and finally a half step and a minor third are sounded, ascending and descending (m. 85). The voices finally arrive at their final destination in contrary motion, both converging on A, the key center of the movement.

A graphic outline of the movement appears thus:

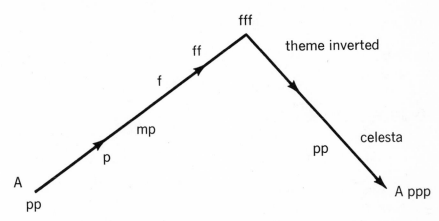

Second Movement–Allegro   The tonal center of this movement is C, (a minor third above the key center of the first movement) and its two opening notes (A–C) represent the tonal centers of the first and second movements. The movement is in sonata form; a bold and assertive mood replaces the oppressive atmosphere of the first movement. The music is highly rhythmic, shifting back and forth from a jovial *scherzando* to aggressive, metallic sounding sections.

On the surface, the opening motive (Ex. 10/32) is only loosely related to the germ motive of the first movement.

EX. 10/32 Second movement, mm. 5–7

As the material is tossed about latent motivic relations emerge. At measure 100, a rising half step and minor third (opening of the fugue subject) motive is treated in a sequential manner:

EX. 10/33 Second movement, mm. 100–103

The development is reached at measure 167; soon a savage rhythmic section is introduced. The string players are instructed to pluck the string in such a way that it rebounds on the fingerboard. The piano, harp, and xylophone join in, and the effect is a remarkable, metallic-percussive texture. Unexpectedly, at measure 207, the motive (Ex. 10/34) appears, but in a new rhythmic guise:

EX. 10/34 Second movement, m. 207

Later, another rhythmic transformation is played by the xylophone:

EX. 10/35 Second movement, mm. 223–235

In the second half of the development a fugue appears, based on the opening motive of the movement. After a climax, the recapitulation is reached (m. 373) with the main theme in a new metric configuration:

EX. 10/36 Second movement, mm. 373–375

After a stormy coda, containing antiphonal effects, the movement ends with a strong emphasis on C, the central tone of the movement.

Third Movement – Adagio   This movement on F sharp is another that can be described as night music. The introduction begins with an eerie xylophone-timpani duet, which will reappear in the concluding measures of the movement. Thus, the Bartókian arch form is at work again; also, the opening viola melody (A) recurs toward the end of the movement, at the far end of the arch. The layout of the movement follows an Introduction–A–B–C–D–[C B]–A–Epilogue outline (C and B appear in brackets, signifying that the two sections appear in simultaneous combination). The fugue subject of the first movement is employed melodically, with some modifications, and also as the material of connecting links. An example of the latter function can be seen in measure 19, where, after the viola melody of A comes to an end, the following notes of the fugue subject establish the link to the next section.

The opening measures of B contain some extraordinary sonorities: the divided, dissonant violin trills suggest nocturnal sounds of nature, known, however, only to the composer's uniquely sensitive perception. In this same section a melody is announced (mm. 25–26) that is an obvious variant of the fugue subject, accompanied by *secco* chords on the piano and dense violin trills.

The next section (C at m. 35) delights the ear with new sound combinations: celesta, harp, and piano join forces in arpeggiated and glissando cascades of notes, under which a tremolo string figure, in canon, suggests the fugue subject.

The beginning of D is marked by a change of meter to $\frac{5}{4}$ in measure 45. The main thought of this section (Ex. 10/37) appears in diminutions and also in retrograde forms.

EX. 10/37 Third movement, m. 46

The motives of B and C appear combined, leading to an abbreviated version of the opening viola melody (A), assigned now to the violins. As mentioned previously, the mysterious sounds of the xylophone and timpani bring the movement to an end.

Fourth Movement – Allegro molto   This movement is a spirited rondo in A major in which the Hungarian flavor is more in evidence than in the preceding movements. The highly syncopated opening melody is dancelike. The mounting tension and the dynamic climax once again coincide with the harmonic high point, the latter consisting of a sequence of parallel major sevenths and minor seconds in measure 170. The tempo is also accelerated from the original ♩ = 130 to ♩ = 176 (*vivacissimo*) at first, and then to ♩ = 210 at *presto strepitoso*. The outcome of this frenzied section is most unexpected. With a sudden tempo change (*molto moderato*), the opening fugue subject of the first movement reappears, but instead of the original, highly chromatic, narrow arrangement of the notes, the intervals now are spacious and diatonic (Ex. 10/38). The music now sounds choral-like, as if a solution to an inner crisis had been reached.

The entire composition conveys the synthesis of opposing forces; the strictest forms (fugues) are reconciled with the improvisational and visionary, the folkloristic with the cosmopolitan, the chromatic with the diatonic, and the lyric with the dramatic.

EX. 10/38 Fourth movement, m. 210

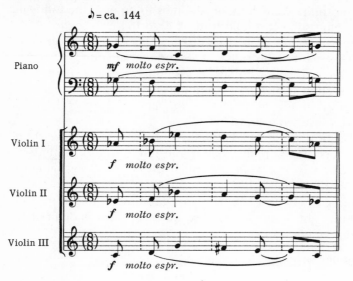

OTHER WORKS FROM THE PERIOD

Although each work from the period under discussion is a master-piece, limitations of space allow merely fleeting comments.

The Violin Concerto (1937), in three movements, is rapidly establishing itself in the standard repertory. The main theme of the first movement, built on melodic fourths, has a distinct Hungarian flavor. The slow movement, with its subtle orchestral colors, is one of the composer's rather infrequent essays in variation form. The last movement contains rhythmic transformations of the motivic material of the first.

The Fifth Quartet (1934), adapting the arch pattern of the Fourth Quartet, is also divided into five movements: *Allegro, Adagio molto, Scherzo alla Bulgarese, Andante,* and *Allegro vivace.* It is now the Scherzo movement that is surrounded by double arches.

The first and last movements are in highly organized sonata forms, employing a greater variety of material than the corresponding movements of the middle quartets. The recapitulations bring back the material in their inverted form, a device noted in the restatement of the first movement of the *Music for Strings, Percussion, and Celesta.* The texture, although contrapuntal, is less dense than that of the middle quartets. Both slow movements are in ternary form, and both have sections that suggest the night music atmosphere.

In the Sixth Quartet (1939) the unifying principle is a motto theme that precedes each of the four movements in different settings. This quartet, incidentally, is the only one that has the traditional four movements and, harmonically, it is the most clearly tonal.

As the Fourth Quartet represented a more accessible style in comparison to its predecessor, the same is true of the Sixth Quartet. Two of the movements ("Marcia" and "Burletta") are made approachable by their titles. The "Marcia" shows kinship to the "Verbunkos" movement of the Contrasts (1938), scored for violin, clarinet, and piano, commissioned by Benny Goodman. The "Burletta" has a grotesque, almost macabre, character; it abounds in ornamentations and glissandi.

Rounding out the list of the works of the synthesis period is the Divertimento for string orchestra (1939), one of Bartók's most light-hearted works. The humor and joviality of the first and third movements are contrasted with the searching slow movement. The accessibility of the work is also due to its clearly defined tonalities.

Mikrokosmos (1926–1937)   The Mikrokosmos, a collection of 153 short piano pieces arranged progressively in six volumes, is the product of both the second and third periods. The first two volumes were written for and dedicated to Bartók's son, Peter, and were designed for his musical education. According to the composer's original intentions, no other material but the first two volumes of the Mikrokosmos should be used in the first two years of piano study.

The greatest value of the Mikrokosmos lies in its concentration on problems of twentieth-century music. The beginning pianist is introduced very early in his studies to modal, bimodal, and bitonal melodies; to chord clusters, irregular and changing meters, and to various contrapuntal devices.

A careful study of the Mikrokosmos will not only help the student to master problems of modern music, but will also give him a glimpse of Bartók's private universe. Some of the melodies are based on Hungarian and Rumanian folk songs; in other pieces Bulgarian rhythms are employed. Some pieces have suggestive titles ("Wrestling," "Diary of a Fly"), while others merely point to the particular technical problem represented by the piece, such as "Diminished Fifth," "Ostinato," "Overtones," and the like. The latter pieces are just as imaginative as the pieces with suggestive titles. For example, under the unpromising title "Major seconds, simultaneously and broken" hides one of the most expressive pieces of the whole collection.

That Bartók saw greater musical value in this collection than merely its pedagogical objective is obvious from the fact that he performed these pieces frequently at his recitals. Several of them were arranged for orchestra and for string quartet by Bartók's friend and student, Tibor Serly.

PLATE 13.
BARTÓK IN
EXILE, 1940

WORKS FROM EXILE (1940-1945)

Of the four major works written in the United States, the *Concerto for Orchestra* (1943) and the Third Piano Concerto (1945) achieved the greatest popularity. The Solo Violin Sonata (1944), although among the finest of the master's works, made little headway in recognition, while the Viola Concerto (1945), completed from Bartók's sketches by Tibor Serly, is the least convincing work of the period.

At first, the crisis of the emigration silenced the composer in his new environment. The first American work, the *Concerto for Orchestra,* commissioned by Koussevitzky for the Boston Symphony Orchestra, was written at a time when the composer's health was steadily declining. The unusual title of the work indicates that virtuoso treatment is accorded to each orchestral part. The five movements of the work do not follow an arch design and there is little carry-over of thematic material from movement to movement.

For the novice the *Concerto* serves perhaps as the best introduction to Bartók's large-scale works. The melodies are appealing and firmly rooted in clear-cut tonalities; the presentation of the musical ideas and their treatment are straightforward and easy to follow. Stevens, who considers the work one of the greatest of the century, feels that it represents the total integration of Bartók's life experience. He finds that all of the elements encountered by the composer—the folk elements and various influences of Liszt, Strauss, Debussy, Stravinsky, Schoenberg, and even Bach—gain a "superlative integration."

In the view of other critics, the *Concerto* does not surpass in quality any of the works of the synthesis period; while undoubtedly an attractive and well-tooled work, they claim that it lacks the inner tension, the uncompromising strength, and the vitality of the earlier works.

The same opinion is held of the Third Piano Concerto. Although there are lovely sections in the first movement, the night music part of the slow movement is pale compared to similar movements of previous works, and the last movement lacks the drive and bite of many earlier finales.

Among the last works, the Sonata for Solo Violin, commissioned by Yehudi Menuhin, ranks in quality with the composer's best works. Its technical challenge is not unlike Bach's *Partitas* for solo violin; the Bartók work demands not only highly accomplished instrumental technique, but also fluency in the idiom of twentieth-century music.

The first movement (*tempo di chaconna*) is actually in sonata form. Anchored on G, it mirrors strong traces of Hungarian folk influence. Both the motivic development and the sonorities are marvels of the composer's resourcefulness despite the difficulty of the medium. The ensuing *Fuga* movement is a brilliant example of how an essentially melodic instrument can be employed to cope with intricate contrapuntal lines. After the intense, songlike third movement (*Melodia*) the work ends with a technically demanding rondo-type movement.

SUMMARY

Bartók's recognition as one of the leading composers of the twentieth century is rather recent; handbooks on contemporary music published in the 1940s still considered Bartók a minor figure.

Bartók's art represents a unique synthesis of East European folk sources and contemporary Western musical thought. This synthesis has been the result of a life-long growth process.

At first, motivated by ardent nationalism, the composer explored only the folk music of his native country. Soon, however, he expanded his travels to tap the rich reservoir of East European (Rumanian, Bulgarian, Slovak) and Arabic folk music. As his musical horizon widened, his narrow nationalism gave way to a broader humanistic viewpoint.

Once the rich melodic inspiration of the folk material and its potential for new harmonic solutions became absorbed, the composer turned to experiment. Complex rhythmic and contrapuntal devices govern the works of his second period (1920–1930), also marked by a tenuous use of tonality.

From 1930 on, a tendency toward economy and equilibrium is evident; the masterpieces from this period of "synthesis" restored the folk element in a more sublimated form and in a clearly tonal harmonic style.

The significance of East European folk elements in the music of Bartók makes a comparison with Stravinsky's style inevitable.

The most common traits of the music of the two composers are the vital role of rhythmic forces and a fondness for asymmetrical rhythmic groupings and ostinati. Undoubtedly, Stravinsky's "Russian" style made a strong impression on the Hungarian composer.

While their harmonic thinking differs in many details, both remain essentially within the boundaries of tonality. Their style development, however, followed different paths; while Bartók maintained his essentially folk-oriented approach, Stravinsky abandoned his national style and turned to a unique stylistic reinterpretation of the musical heritage on his own terms.

The two composers also differ radically in their treatment of form; Bartók adhered to the principles of classical structures, whereas Stravinsky created new musical designs for almost every new composition.

Bartók exerted a smaller influence on subsequent generations of composers than Stravinsky; yet, the depth of his music, its intensity and spontaneity held together with the strictest musical logic, make him one of the most distinctive figures of the twentieth century.

CHRONOLOGICAL LIST OF BARTÓK'S PRINCIPAL WORKS

I. MELODIC-HARMONIC PERIOD   1905-1920

Twenty Hungarian Folksongs for voice and piano   1905
Two Portraits for orchestra   1907
Fourteen Bagatelles for piano   1908
Ten Easy Pieces for piano   1908
String Quartet No. 1   1908
For Children for piano   1908-1909
Duke Bluebeard's Castle, a one-act opera   1911
Allegro Barbaro for piano   1911
The Wooden Prince, ballet   1914-1916
Suite for Piano   1916
Five Songs for voice and piano   1916
String Quartet No. 2   1917
The Miraculous Mandarin, pantomime   1918-1919
Eight Improvisations on Hungarian Peasant Songs for piano   1920

II. RHYTHMIC-POLYPHONIC PERIOD   1920-1930

Sonata No. 1 for violin and piano   1921
Sonata No. 2 for violin and piano   1922
Dance Suite for orchestra   1923
Sonata for piano   1926
Out of Doors Suite for piano   1926
Concerto No. 1 for piano and orchestra   1926
String Quartet No. 3   1927
Rhapsody No. 1 and Rhapsody No. 2 for violin and piano   1928
String Quartet No. 4   1928
Twenty Hungarian Folksongs   1929
Concerto No. 2 for piano and orchestra   1929-1930
Cantata Profana   1930

III. SYNTHESIS PERIOD   1930-1940

String Quartet No. 5   1934
Music for Strings, Percussion, and Celesta   1936   Arch forms
Sonata for two pianos and percussion   1937
Mikrokosmos, 153 pieces for piano   1926-1937
Contrasts for violin, clarinet, and piano   1938

Concerto for violin and orchestra   1938
Divertimento for string orchestra   1939
String Quartet No. 6   1939   ✳

IV. EXILE   1940–1945

Concerto for Orchestra   1943 ✳
Sonata for solo violin   1944   ✳
Concerto No. 3 for piano and orchestra   1945
Concerto for viola and orchestra (unfinished)   1945

ARNOLD SCHOENBERG (1874-1951)

Music conveys a prophetic message revealing a higher form of life toward which mankind evolves.

SCHOENBERG

Schoenberg is one of the most controversial composers of the twentieth century. It is ironical that his music, deeply steeped in the Austro-German musical tradition, was consistently rejected, while the works of Bartók and Stravinsky, based on hitherto unknown East European and Asiatic idioms, met with less resistance.

Schoenberg took the rejection of his music philosophically, as he was convinced of his genius and of the validity of his musical procedures. In his writings he repeatedly predicted that his music would not be accepted in his lifetime, for he understood that "the laws of the nature of genius are the laws of the future humanity."[1] When his *Songs,* Op. 1, were premiered in

[1] Arnold Schoenberg, *Harmonielehre* (Vienna: Universal Verlag, 1911; enlarged ed., 1923), p. 496.

Vienna, the audience booed and hissed: ". . . from now on the scandal will never come to an end," Schoenberg commented to a friend.

The attacks upon Schoenberg were not always confined to his music, but often extended to his person. His Collected Letters[2] contain several angry polemical exchanges with Thomas Mann, Kandinsky, and Olin Downes. The letters also reveal his uncompromising attitude regardless of whether ethical or musical principles were at stake.

Schoenberg's creative activities covered a wide range; his keen and analytical mind loved to seek out theoretical problems. His systematized outlook on theory was published in *Harmonielehre* and later translated into English in an abridged edition.[3] Another theoretical volume, *Structural Functions of Harmony*,[4] was published in the United States. He is also the author of many articles and a volume of essays.[5] Schoenberg was active as a poet, writing some of the texts for his operas, and early in his career he established fame for himself as a painter, presenting a one-man exhibition in Vienna. His personal history, based in part on Stuckenschmidt's biography,[6] will demonstrate the intensity and friction with which Schoenberg experienced life.

LIFE

Arnold Schoenberg, son of a businessman of modest means, was born in Vienna in 1874. He lost his father at an early age and, as in Bartók's case, his mother eked out a difficult living by giving piano lessons.

At the age of eight the young boy began to play the violin and later the cello. Without formal instruction Schoenberg acquired reasonable proficiency on both instruments and soon began to compose for small string ensembles.

Music was hardly considered a professional goal when Schoenberg was graduated from high school. Consequently, he accepted a position as a bank clerk to augment the family income.

In his spare time he played in an amateur orchestra and became a friend of the conductor, Alexander Zemlinsky. Zemlinsky, although his senior by only two years, became his mentor and his teacher for a short period of time. These lessons constituted Schoenberg's only formal mu-

---

[2] *Arnold Schoenberg Letters,* selected and edited by Erwin Stein, translated by Eithne Wilkins and Ernst Kaiser (New York: St. Martin's Press, Inc., 1965).

[3] Arnold Schoenberg. *Theory of Harmony* (New York: Philosophical Library, Inc., 1948).

[4] Arnold Schoenberg, *Structural Functions of Harmony* (New York: W. W. Norton & Company, Inc., 1954).

[5] Arnold Schoenberg, *Style and Idea* (New York: Philosophical Library, Inc., 1950).

[6] H. H. Stuckenschmidt, *Arnold Schoenberg,* translated by Edith Temple Roberts and Humphrey Searle (New York: Grove Press, Inc., 1953).

sical education. Zemlinsky recognized his student's outstanding talent; his encouragement and persuasion eventually led Schoenberg to decide upon a career in music. This decision may have been influenced by the fact that the banking house for which Schoenberg worked went into bankruptcy and he lost his position.

The friendship between Schoenberg and Zemlinsky was further deepened when Schoenberg married Zemlinsky's sister in 1901. At the time Schoenberg's earnings were limited to the small salary he received as conductor of a workers' chorus. To supplement this meager income he undertook orchestrations of popular music and operettas. According to one of Schoenberg's biographers, he orchestrated more than 6,000 pages of popular music. Under these circumstances he gratefully accepted an invitation to become the musical director of the *Buntes Theater* in Berlin, where recommended by Richard Strauss, he also obtained a teaching position at the Stern Conservatory. Strauss was greatly impressed by Schoenberg's *Gurrelieder,* a choral-orchestral work whose orchestration occupied Schoenberg from 1901 to 1911. Strauss, however, soon changed his opinion of Schoenberg's music. He wrote to Mrs. Mahler: "The only person who can help poor Schoenberg now is a psychiatrist . . . . I think he'd do better to shovel snow instead of scribbling on music-paper." [7]

Schoenberg's first stay in Berlin lasted only twenty months. In 1903 the composer returned to Vienna where composition classes were arranged for him at the well-known Schwarzwald School. At this point he had established himself as a teacher, and during this period Alban Berg and Anton Webern began their studies with him. His friendship with Mahler, who was at that time director of the Vienna Opera, also dates from this period. When Schoenberg organized a new group, "Vereinigung schaffender Tonkünstler" (Association of Creative Artists) with the aim of promoting new music, Mahler became honorary president. As a result of hostile criticism and indifferent audience reaction, the group soon discontinued its activities. Yet, Mahler's backing must have lent a great deal of prestige to the relatively unknown group; in turn, Schoenberg became a champion of Mahler's music and many years later came to the defense of the older composer in an impassioned essay. [8]

Gradually, Schoenberg's name became known in Vienna as a composer too, although largely through the scandals that occurred regularly at performances of his works. Despite these reactions, there were a number of outstanding musicians in Vienna in addition to Mahler who identified themselves with the new music, among them the members of the noted Rosé String Quartet. Their excellent rendering of Schoenberg's

[7] *Arnold Schoenberg Letters,* p. 50.
[8] *Style and Idea,* pp. 7–35.

PLATE 14. ARNOLD SCHOENBERG:
The Victor, 1919
Gondolat Könyvkiadó,
Budapest, Hungary

First and Second Quartets was a great service to the composer, even though both works were received with hostility.

Schoenberg's abandonment of tonality in 1908 alienated his audiences even further. However, he proceeded on the new path unperturbed. The strength of his inner conviction is apparent from the program note he wrote for the premiere of the *Book of the Hanging Gardens,* his first large-scale atonal work:

> Now that I finally entered the new path, I am conscious of breaking through the boundaries of earlier esthetics. As I strive toward this new goal with assuredness, I am aware of the resistance I shall have to overcome. I sense the emotional intensity with which my work will be rejected . . . and I suspect that even those who believed in me up to now, will not realize the need for the new development [my translation].

During these years of feverish activity, Schoenberg took an increased interest in painting; his works included color fantasies, portraits, and nature studies. Both his music and painting of this period are marked by burning intensity and a visionary quality recognized as the hallmarks of *expressionism.* (See Plate 2 on p. 8 and Plate 14 above.)

As Schoenberg's financial situation failed to improve, he seriously considered earning money as a painter. He asked a friend, the director of the Universal Publishing Company, to find wealthy people who would commission him to paint their portraits:

> Only you must not tell people that they *will* like my pictures. You must make them realize that they cannot but like my pictures, because they have been praised by authorities on painting; and above all that it is much more interesting to have one's portrait done by or to own a painting by a musician of my reputation than to be painted by some mere practitioner of painting whose name will be forgotten in 20 years, whereas even now my name belongs to the history of music.[9]

In 1911 Schoenberg moved to Berlin again. It was in Berlin that he composed *Pierrot Lunaire,* a song cycle of epochal significance. After the Berlin premiere, the work was performed in many cities in Germany and Austria.

As the composer approached his fortieth year, he experienced his first Viennese success. The occasion was the first full performance of *Gurrelieder.* Embittered by the numerous earlier rejections, the composer

---

[9] *Arnold Schoenberg Letters,* pp. 25–26.

did not acknowledge the audience's ovation and bowed only to the conductor and to the members of the chorus and orchestra. The acceptance of the composer's early style, however, did not mean that the Viennese audiences were ready to take the later works in stride. Only a month after the great success of *Gurrelieder,* a free-for-all fight broke out in the concert hall at a performance of the Chamber Symphony, in the course of which a number of demonstrators were arrested. At the ensuing court hearing a witness, a physician, testified that "the effect of the music was so unnerving and damaging to the nervous system that many who attended showed symptoms of a serious mental depression."

Despite such setbacks, Schoenberg's name spread all over Europe in the years immediately preceding World War I. He appeared as conductor of his works in London and Amsterdam; audience reactions there suggested that his music was more readily accepted outside of the Austro-German orbit than in his native Vienna.

Travels abroad were discontinued after the outbreak of the war when communication between the musical centers was disrupted. Schoenberg deeply resented the banning of German music in France and that disparaging remarks were made about German music by leading French musicians such as Lalo, Saint-Saëns, and others.

The war years coincided with Schoenberg's self-imposed silence as a composer; he searched for a solution to the crisis brought about by his renunciation of tonality. Soon the war intruded into his private life, as he was called to serve two tours of duty in the Austrian Army.

Discharged in 1917, he again dedicated himself to teaching. His zeal as a teacher was not merely confined to his students. He felt that the audiences should be educated too. With this goal in mind, in 1918 he organized the "Verein für musikalische Privataufführungen" (Society for Private Musical Performances). Members had to carry identification cards bearing their photographs and pledge to refrain from any expression of approval or disapproval at the performances. Music critics were not admitted to the concerts. New works were studied in the most painstaking way; it was not unusual to devote thirty to forty rehearsals to the study of a single work. Novelties were performed twice or even three times at the same concert to enable the listeners to form a more valid opinion of a work than a single hearing would afford.

In 1923 the first twelve-tone composition appeared that led to new theoretical polemics (see Chapter 7). Despite vociferous criticism Schoenberg had now achieved an international reputation; his fame had reached the United States, too. In October 1922, Edgar Varèse, then director of the International Composers' Guild, invited Schoenberg to attend a performance of *Pierrot Lunaire* in New York. Schoenberg's answer reflects both his chauvinism as a German and his supersensitivity concerning the performance of his music. He writes:

> I hope you received my telegram saying that I do not know your objectives. But that is not the only reason why for the present I cannot join. There are also several others:
>
> I. Above all: from your manifesto and the programmes of the three concerts I gather that you have hitherto attached no importance to German music. No single German among 27 composers performed! So then you have been international to the exclusion of the Germans!
>
> II. What offends me equally, however, is that without asking me whether you *can and may* do so you simply set a definitive date for my *Pierrot Lunaire*. But do you even know whether you can manage it? Have you already got a suitable speaker (*Sprecherin*); a violinist, a pianist, a conductor . . . etc.? How many rehearsals do you mean to hold, etc. . . .etc.? In Vienna, with everyone starving and shivering, something like 100 rehearsals were held and an impeccable ensemble achieved with my collaboration. But you people simply fix a date and think that's all there is to it! Have you any inkling of the difficulties, of the style; of the declamation; of the *tempi*; of the dynamics and all that? And you expect me to associate myself with it? [10]

[10] *Arnold Schoenberg Letters*, pp. 78–79.

Schoenberg's fiftieth birthday in 1924 brought him many accolades and in the next year he accepted the chair of composition at the Prussian Academy of Fine Arts in Berlin. At that time, Berlin had taken the cultural leadership from Vienna and Schoenberg enjoyed the stimulating environment until 1933 when his tenure was abruptly discontinued. This blow was not entirely unexpected. During the previous summer while vacationing in Spain, the composer had given serious thought to not returning to Germany for political reasons. However, currency regulations made it impossible for him to obtain money from Berlin. From Barcelona he wrote to a friend:

> I am surely the only composer of my standing there has been for at least a hundred years who could not live on what he made from his creative work without having to eke out his income by teaching. And when I think how many things rich people find money for, I simply can't understand that there still isn't some rich Jew, or even several, who together or single-handed would give me an annuity so that at long last I needn't do anything but create! [11]

The letter of dismissal from the Prussian Academy of Arts gave him ten days' notice, even though his contract was to expire two years later. The Academy's action was a serious blow to Schoenberg in more ways than one. It brought home to him the fact that his strong identification with German culture and tradition had no reality. His dismissal made it evident that he was not accepted as a *German* and that despite his earlier conversion to Catholicism, he was still considered a Jew. Even prior to his dismissal from the Academy he wrote to Kandinsky stating:

> For I have at last learnt the lesson that has been forced upon me during this year, and I shall not ever forget it. It is that I am not a German, not a European, indeed perhaps scarcely even a human being (at least, the Europeans prefer the worst of their race to me) but I am a Jew. [12]

Upon his dismissal he went to Paris where his first action was to rejoin Judaism. As Paris seemed unpromising professionally, the only choice left to him was emigration to the United States. In a letter written to Alban Berg before his departure Schoenberg reveals the misgivings and anxiety he felt about the New World:

> There's no knowing how disregarded, slighted and without influence I may be there. [13]

Schoenberg arrived in New York on October 31, 1933, seven years before Bartók.

---

[11] *Arnold Schoenberg Letters*, p. 163.
[12] *Arnold Schoenberg Letters*, p. 88.
[13] *Arnold Schoenberg Letters*, p. 184.

Schoenberg first settled in Boston. As the climate of the East Coast did not agree with his health, he had to give up his first position in Boston and, after declining an offer from the Juilliard School of Music, he settled in Los Angeles. He held teaching positions at the University of Southern California and later at the University of California, Los Angeles (UCLA), until his retirement in 1944.

A curious mixture of recognition and failure remained his fate for the rest of his life. Although he received a $1,000 prize for outstanding achievements in music from the American Academy of Arts and Letters in 1947, his application for a Guggenheim fellowship was turned down. As his short tenure at UCLA secured him a monthly pension of only thirty-eight dollars, he was compelled to give private instruction during the years in which his health was failing.

**PLATE 16.
SCHOENBERG
TEACHING AT THE
UNIVERSITY OF
CALIFORNIA**
The Bettmann
Archive, New York

Perhaps of all the honors bestowed on Schoenberg, the most cherished one was a letter of invitation from the Mayor of Vienna (May 5, 1946) asking him to return to help build up the musical life of his native city. In 1949 Schoenberg was made an honorary citizen of Vienna. Unfortunately the composer was not well enough to receive these honors in person. He died on July 13, 1951, without seeing his beloved Vienna again.

MUSICAL INFLUENCES

There is no composer of Schoenberg's rank in the history of music who achieved such mastery without the guiding hand of a teacher or without rigorous training at a conservatory.

Schoenberg's unprecedented achievement was made possible by his will power and inner drive, and because he recognized that the great masters are the ultimate source of learning. Thus, he assiduously studied the music of Bach, Haydn, Mozart, Beethoven, Schubert, Brahms, and Wagner, the masters of the Austro-German heritage. He was and remained a traditionalist at heart, despite the musical revolution he brought about. In his teaching, too, he drew his examples from the works of the named composers, seldom venturing beyond Brahms. His students all testify to his amazing knowledge of the literature and his ability to shed new light on a Bach fugue or Beethoven string quartet.

Although his music clearly stems from the Austro-German ancestry, as pointed out by Dika Newlin in her fine study,[14] it has none of the folk flavor of the region that is so apparent in the works of Haydn, Schubert, and Mahler. Newlin also emphasizes the exclusive influence of the Austro-German heritage; Schoenberg's music remained almost untouched by any foreign (French, Russian, or Italian) idiom. This fact clearly distinguishes Schoenberg's style from that of Bartók and Stravinsky, both of whom felt the need to infuse novel elements into the Central European tradition. Therefore, the music of Schoenberg and of his school should be looked upon as the last link in a long line of musical evolution. It represents the crystallization and distillation of a long historical process, and it speaks with the sophistication and differentiation of the accumulated knowledge of many generations. It is probably for this reason that this music, despite its familiar roots, places heavier demands on the listener than the music of Bartók or Stravinsky, both of whom partly at least resorted to the vigorous energies of hitherto untapped musical cultures.

[14] Dika Newlin, *Bruckner, Mahler, Schoenberg* (New York: Columbia University Press, 1947).

With regard to the specific composers who played the greatest role in Schoenberg's musical growth, we may refer to the composer's own words in his essay, "My Evolution."[15] Here the composer relates that he was a Brahmsian when he first met Zemlinsky. Zemlinsky's influence caused him to embrace Wagner and become "an equally confirmed addict" of both Brahms and Wagner. In another source, Schoenberg points out that it was Strauss and Mahler who clarified for him that Wagner and Brahms did not have to be considered antagonistic and opposite poles. Schoenberg came to see not only the harmonic fluidity of Wagner's music but also its "organizational order, if not pedantry." Schoenberg also realized that Brahms, in addition to his traditionalist leanings, had "daring, courage, and even bizarre fantasy."

Undoubtedly, Brahms and Wagner are the most strongly felt influences in Schoenberg's early style. Even in later works Wagner's harmonic freedom and Brahms' contrapuntal thinking hover in the background.

Strauss' influence was short-lived compared to that of Mahler. Although Schoenberg repeatedly emphasizes his indebtedness to Mahler, he fails to specify the exact manner in which he was influenced by the Moravian composer. The common element in their thinking seems to be their approach to sound. Instruments and tonal effects were always chosen with extreme care; sound is never externalized, but is an essential part of the musical architecture. Often Mahler's delicate colors are at the root of Schoenberg's inspiration; even the employment of some instruments, such as the mandolin, guitar, and a certain use of the harp, are incorporated into the composer's style. Beyond specific technical devices, the parodizing, mocking, and often bitter quality of Mahler's moods is recognizable in Schoenberg's music.

"My Evolution" does not cite any other influence; from about 1908 on, the composer strikes out on a path entirely his own. In his new style the functional harmonic framework is abandoned and strict contrapuntal techniques are used as a means of organization. The composer employs devices such as inversions, mirror canons, and cancrizans, harking back to the practices of the great Netherland contrapuntalists.

Schoenberg's stylistic development can be divided into three phases: the first period (1896–1908) characterized by highly chromatic contrapuntal writing that eventually led to the dissolution of tonality; the second period (1908–1912) of free atonality; and after almost twelve years of silence, the period of twelve-tone style (1923–1951), although not every work from this period follows the new method of composition.

[15] Arnold Schoenberg, "My Evolution," *Musical Quarterly,* **38**, No. 4 (1952).

THE FIRST PERIOD (1896-1908)

Two salient trends characterize the works Schoenberg composed during this stage. One is the increasing harmonic complexity that led to
the abandonment of tonality in the last work of the period; the other
is the shift from works based on literary inspiration (tone poems and
songs) to abstract instrumental forms.

A glance at Schoenberg's works reveals the composer's predilection
for the human voice; among the eleven works of the period, eight
employ the voice. The same preference is also noticeable in the second
period.

The early songs (Op. 1, 2, 3, and 6) suggest the stylistic evolution
that will take place later in the larger works. Thus, while the two songs
of Op. 1 remind one of Brahms with their firmly delineated bass lines,
their scale or triadlike melodic contours suggest earlier models; the four
songs of Op. 2 show considerable advancement. The first song of this
group, a setting of Dehmel's "Erwartung" (not to be confused with
Erwartung, a monodrama of the second period), is based on a germinating chord built in fourths (Ex. 11/1), which unifies the entire song:

EX. 11/1 SCHOENBERG, "Erwartung," Op. 2,[16] opening

The chord of Example 11/1 is always resolved stepwise throughout
the entire song. The vocal line is doubled in the harmonies, except in
a few instances where the voice is used to carry out harmonic resolutions. In contrast to Op. 1, the vocal line is highly chromatic; its articulation often verges on declamation. In the later songs an added feature
is the employment of large skips. (Ex. 11/2).

The first three groups of songs were followed by *Verklärte Nacht*
(Transfigured Night), a tone poem for string sextet composed in 1899
and based on a poem by Richard Dehmel. As such, it is perhaps the
first tone poem in the field of chamber music. The work, which is cast
in a single movement, is highly expressive; its mood ranging from

[16]Quoted by permission of Mrs. Gertrud Schoenberg and Universal Edition, publisher of the first edition.

EX. 11/2 "Traumleben,"[17] Op. 6, no. 1, mm. 5–9

tender lyricism to dramatic passion. The chromatic richness owes much to Wagner, and more specifically to *Tristan*. The influence of Brahms is less obvious, and Schoenberg draws attention to it in "My Evolution." He points out that the thematic construction of the work is partially based on Brahms' "developing variation" technique, and he also ascribes the usage of asymmetrical phrase structure (Ex. 11/3) to Brahms' influence.

EX. 11/3 *Verklärte Nacht*[18] mm. 320–327 (partial score)

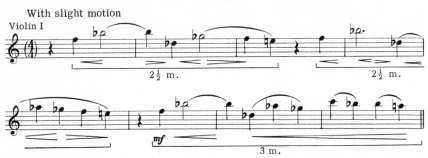

Next, the composer embarked on his gigantic *Gurrelieder* (1900), the orchestration of which occupied him intermittently for ten years, during which time his energies were often taken up by projects necessary to earn a living. The *Gurrelieder*—bearing no opus number—is a cantata, based on the poems of Jens Peter Jacobsen. The themes of the passionate story, taken from Scandinavian mythology, are love, death, and resurrection. The size of the orchestra extends beyond anything previously attempted, even by Richard Strauss. Commensurate with the mammoth orchestra are the vocal forces, consisting of five solo voices, one speaking voice, three male choruses, and an eight-part mixed chorus. Here, for the first time, the composer used a device, the spoken word linked to pitches (*Sprechstimme*), that assumed great significance in later works. (See Chapter 2.)

---

[17] Quoted by permission of Mrs. Gertrud Schoenberg and Universal Edition, publisher of the first edition.

[18] Quoted by permission of Mrs. Gertrud Schoenberg and Universal Edition, publisher of the first edition.

Beyond the obvious Wagnerian influence, the *Gurrelieder* also points to Mahler's large musical canvases. It is erroneous, however, to link this work to Mahler's Eighth Symphony, as do several commentators, since the symphony was premiered in 1910, by which time Schoenberg had all but finished his *Gurrelieder.*

The next work, *Pelleas und Melisande,* (1902-1903), a tone poem in one movement, is also based on a program, namely Maeterlinck's drama. While Schoenberg worked on his tone poem, Debussy—contemporaneously and independently—put the finishing touches on his *Pelléas.*

Schoenberg's *Pelleas* shows a Straussian influence more distinctly than any other of his works. It was Strauss, in fact, who had originally suggested the subject matter to Schoenberg. The tone poem quite clearly follows the sequence of the drama. The harmonic idiom is more dissonant and the tonality more tenuous than in the *Gurrelieder,* but the orchestral style is massive and rich in novel effects, the most striking of which are the trombone glissandi, supported by *sul ponticello,* and tremolo cello figurations (see study number 30, m. 5).

After *Pelleas,* Schoenberg's interest turned from the programmatic, orchestral style to abstract chamber music. Among the three chamber works of this period (the two quartets and the Chamber Symphony), the First Quartet, Op. 7, in D minor (1904-1905), is of the greatest breadth. The motivic work is extremely elaborate; there is hardly a line in the four instrumental parts without thematic significance. For this reason, Alban Berg, in an article entitled, "Why is Schoenberg's Music So Hard to Understand?"[19] uses the opening of the first movement as illustrative material. Berg's interesting analysis demonstrates the complexity of the phrase structure, the condensation of the musical thought, and the rhythmic intricacies. Berg emphasizes that the listener will only be able to cope with the perceptual demands of the work after a number of concentrated hearings.

The outer structure of the four movements is as follows:

I.   Main theme group, transition, second theme group, first development;
II.   Scherzo, development, recapitulation of main theme group;
III. Adagio, recapitulation of second theme group, transition;
IV.   Rondo finale, recapitulation of earlier motives, closing section.

There are no separations between the four movements, which flow from one to another like the movements of some of the late Beethoven

---

[19] Alban Berg, "Why Is Schoenberg's Music So Hard to Understand?" *Contemporary Composers on Contemporary Music,* edited by Elliott Schwartz and Barney Childs (New York: Holt, Rinehart and Winston, Inc., 1967).

quartets. Beethoven is brought to mind also in the first major development section which is deliberately modeled after the development
section of the "Eroica" Symphony. The details of the parallel organization are traced in Dika Newlin's study.

The Chamber Symphony (Kammersymphonie) Op. 9, for fifteen solo
instruments (1906), has a light quality and shows greater economy in
writing than the First Quartet. The four movements are again interlocked; the over-all scheme follows a large sonata form outline in
which the development section is flanked by a scherzo and slow movement, respectively, resulting in the following arrangement:

exposition-scherzo-development-slow movement-recapitulation.

The harmonic idiom shows new advances, as the entire work is
pervaded by the usage of the interval of the fourth; successive fourths
accumulate in the melodic line, and the harmonies, too, are frequently
built in fourths (Ex. 11/4).

EX. 11/4 *Chamber Symphony,* Op. 9,[20] m. 2

Five successive fourths appear briefly in the melody played by the
French horn (Ex. 11/5):

EX. 11/5 M. 5

In Example 11/6 both the melody and harmony appear in fourths,
and in Example 11/7 the descending fourths are used.

The derivation of both melodic and harmonic material from the same
source anticipates the composer's later conception of "two-dimen-

---

[20] Quoted by permission of Mrs. Gertrud Schoenberg and G. Schirmer, Inc.

EX. 11/6 study no. 78

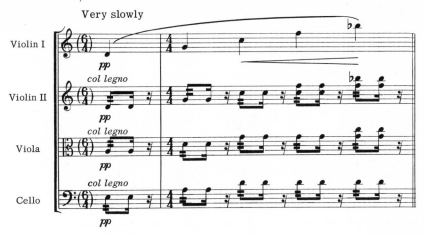

EX. 11/7 2 mm. before study no. 114 (partial score)

Violin II (in unison with Clarinet and Bass Clarinet)

sional musical space" (see Chapter 7), a concept that became the fundamental principle of Schoenberg's method of composing with twelve tones.

Schoenberg's employment of the fourths in his chords was an attempt to replace triadic harmonies; also chords built in fourths help to break up the tonal feeling (see Ex. 11/5). Schoenberg's motivation in using the fourth was entirely different from that of Bartók. The Hungarian composer, who also used this interval frequently, seldom used it in multiple succession, as the dissolution of tonality was not his aim.

The Second Quartet (1908) is the last work of the first period. This composition shows the consolidation of Schoenberg's earlier attainments, and the last movement ushers in his atonal period. Because this work occupies a pivotal position it will be examined in detail.

SECOND QUARTET

Of the four movements of the Second Quartet the first two are purely instrumental, while in the last two movements a soprano voice is added. The mixture of instruments with the voice is seen by several commentators as a Mahlerian influence.

First Movement The first movement of the quartet, in F sharp minor, follows the outline of sonata form rather clearly. The main theme (Ex. 11/8) is lyrical, slightly capricious, and not unlike some of Schumann's melodies:

EX. 11/8 *Second Quartet,*[21] first movement, opening measure
(partial score)

Using a swift harmonic change, the theme reappears immediately in A minor, reaching a brief *fortissimo* that leads to the *Hauptzeitmass* (main tempo) of the movement. The viola now suggests a descending chromatic line, which is imitated in a simpler manner by the cello. This viola melody represents the skeleton of the second theme which reaches fruition later. First, the main theme reappears and the second theme enters at measure 43:

EX. 11/9 first movement, mm. 43–46 (partial score)

Soon a new motive, marked *animato,* is introduced (Ex. 11/10), the second measure of which points to the second measure of the second theme:

EX. 11/10 first movement, mm. 58–59 (partial score)

[21] Quoted by permission of Mrs. Gertrud Schoenberg and Universal Edition, publisher of the first edition.

With great suddenness the motive of Example 11/10 is worked out
in canon among the four instruments with several voices representing
the inversion of the motive:

EX. 11/11 first movement, mm. 62-64

Example 11/11 suggests the rapidly increasing complexity of the
texture.

After a brief dynamic climax abounding in dissonant harmonies, the
tension recedes and the exposition ends with a motive suggesting the
main theme without the dotted rhythm, with the rising line reaching
a fourth instead of the fifth of the opening theme. Both changes (Ex.
11/12) convey a feeling of weariness.

EX. 11/12 first movement, mm. 86-89

The development is rather brief (mm. 90-160), assumedly because
several ideas in the exposition will receive a delayed developmental treatment in the third movement. The development commences with the
main theme, which is played *sul ponticello.* Soon the motive of the
closing section and the second theme enter into combination, both
at times inverted. At study number 120, a canon develops between the
cello and the first violin (Ex. 11/13), suggesting Brahms' style.

EX. 11/13 first movement, mm. 120–121

The pace becomes calmer again (*wieder ruhiger*), and after study number 130 a tender canon develops on the motive of the second theme. The motive of the closing section follows amidst rising harmonic tension. The development concludes with the viola playing the main theme in A minor, after which a descending violin figure and a rising

EX. 11/14 first movement, mm. 186–190

viola-cello line converge to establish the key of F sharp minor at measure 159; this point may be considered the beginning of the irregular
recapitulation section.

The recapitulation begins with the second theme in canonic imitation.
Soon the main theme appears in a tense canon between the second
violin, viola, and cello, while the first violin adds a counterpoint, suggesting a diminution of the same motive (Ex. 11/14).

In the last example (Ex. 11/14) one can see how intervallic expansion
occurs with the rising harmonic and dynamic tension. The rising fifth
is expanded first into a sixth and later into a seventh and an octave.

From measure 202 on the music has the character of a coda. This
section begins with a reaffirmation of F sharp minor with contrary
motion of the violins throughout. The cello firmly holds on to an F
sharp pedal point. With irregular chromaticism, the cello then rises
to the F sharp, an octave higher, after which it falls back again to the
low F sharp. The closing theme is heard in each of the four instruments
once more. Then, only the violin repeats the theme *pianissimo,* this
time without the dotted rhythm which suggests ebbing energy. The
movement ends on F sharp minor chords.

Second Movement   The scherzolike second movement in D minor, marked *sehr rasch* (very fast), follows a ternary design. The following analysis of the movement suggests a different outline from the one
printed in the preface to the score.

A	a mm.	5–13
	b	14–19
	a_1	20–34
	b_1	35–64
	c	65–78
	transition	79–84
	a_2	85–97

B (Trio)	d	98–164
	e	165–192
	transition	193–194

A_1	a_3 mm.	195–202
	b_2	203–218
	c_1	219–237
	a_4	238–258 (including transition)

Coda	259–275

The main motive (a), consisting of short, staccato notes, appears first
in the second violin, with a countermelody stated in the viola.

EX. 11/15 second movement, mm. 5–6 (partial score)

When the viola takes up "a," the first violin expands the earlier viola counter-melody into octave steps (Ex. 11/16), which will become the main idea of "c."

Ex. 11/16 second movement, mm. 7–8 (partial score)

The next short section (b) seems to be a preview; its melodic material (Ex. 11/17) will be elaborated upon in "b_1" and later in the third movement of the composition.

EX. 11/17 second movement, mm. 14–16 (partial score)

A variant of "a" follows now (a_1) with rhythmic changes in the counterpoint.

The next section (b_1) is the longest. It contains a detailed elaboration of "b"; the major third seen in Example 11/17 now appears in its inversion and the eighth note figure in diminution.

Section "c" features the octave figure from "a" (see Ex. 11/16) with a pizzicato accompaniment. The same figure will appear in the trio section of the movement as the countermelody to the famous Vienna street song "O du lieber Augustin." The bizarre mood of that section is anticipated here. A brief variant of "a" (a_2) terminates the A section.

The trio (B) of the Scherzo in D major opens with a brilliant section (d) in which the descending violin line, consisting of alternating triplets and sixteenths, is combined with a legato melody in contrary motion.

In the second part (e), the street song appears, most unexpectedly, with a harmonization that has an absentminded quality.

Symmetry is fulfilled when the A section returns, the "a" is still in D major, later changing to D minor, the rest of the material is stated considerably altered and condensed. A brilliant coda, marked *presto,* and in unison almost throughout, brings the movement to an end.

Third Movement The third movement, marked *langsam* (Adagio), in E flat minor, although cast in theme and variation form, could be considered the development section of the first two movements. Here the soprano joins the instruments in a setting of Stefan George's "Litanei."[22]

The outer structure of the movement consists of the theme, five variations, and a codalike finale. The construction of the theme is an astonishing feat of compositional virtuosity, as it consists of four motivic strands derived from the first two movements.

EX. 11/18 third movement, mm. 1–8

---

[22] The German text of the two poems and an English translation appear in Appendix C.

Motive "a" is a derivative of the main theme of the first movement (Ex. 11/8), transposed, and with changed note values, while motive "b" is the transformation of the second theme of the first movement (Ex. 11/9). Motive "c" is taken from the Scherzo (Ex. 11/17), and "d" is an augmentation of the closing theme (Ex. 11/10) of the first movement. It is amazing that despite so much conscious manipulation, the theme sounds fresh and spontaneous.

The theme stated by the strings consists of eight measures, as do all of the variations. Each of the five ensuing variations is based on a clearly delineated four-line stanza. In the codalike finale, three stanzas are welded together without a pause.

The theme stated by the strings consists of eight measures, as do atmosphere. It sets the mood both for the first line of the text "Tief ist die Trauer (Deep is the mourning)" appearing in the first variation, as well as for the entire movement.

In the first variation (mm. 9–17) motive "a" of the theme appears an octave higher in the second violin; the dynamics are raised from the *pianissimo* opening to *piano*. In the second half of this variation the voice enters almost imperceptibly, supported by the violins in octaves. This employment of the voice as a participant rather than as a soloist is maintained throughout the movement.

In the second variation (mm. 17–25) the main material is assigned to the strings; motive "a" is again intoned by the second violin, this time starting *fortepiano*. Simultaneously, motive "c" appears in augmentation in the form of an inverted canon between the cello and the viola, with a strettolike intensification that leads to the first climax of the movement. The line of the voice is based on the relatively insignificant "b" motive, but when it reaches the high A, the voice soars above the instruments.

In the third variation (mm. 25–33) the soprano dominates with several large ascending skips, with a counterpoint by the viola, and accompanied by muted, *sul ponticello,* violin figures.

In the next variation (mm. 33–41) the voice calmly descends in semitones, accompanied by intricate syncopated rhythmic lines in the strings.

The last variation (mm. 41–49) commences *pianissimo* again, with a tremolo, *sul ponticello,* in the strings. The variation gradually rises to a *fortissimo* climax in the last measure. The ascent to the climax is accomplished by intervallic expansion of "a," with some skips rising a half step beyond the octave.

In the coda (mm. 50–77) the levels of intensity are similar to those of the last variation. The rise to the climax starts from a triple *piano* level in the voice, and ascends through all the dynamic gradations. A triple *forte* climax is reached on a high C on the word *Liebe,* achieving almost simultaneously the most dissonant harmonies of the movement.

EX. 11/19 third movement, mm. 64–66

An instrumental postlude concludes the movement with a strong reaffirmation of E flat minor, a key that pervades the entire movement.

Fourth Movement The last movement, marked *sehr langsam* (very slow), is based on Stefan George's "Entrückung." Together with the previous movement an unusual sequence of two slow movements is formed. The tempo indication is not specified by metronome signatures which are frequently used in the first two movements.

The last movement features the first instance of Schoenberg's atonal writing. Schoenberg entered into a new musical sphere as reflected by the first line of the poem: "I breathe air from another planet." Equal significance could be attached to the first line of the fourth stanza: "Ich löse mich in Tönen, kreisend, webend (I liberate myself in the web of whirling, circling sounds)." Despite the implications of the text, Schoenberg did not attempt to write a "setting" of the poem. He did not express the meaning of each subsequent stanza musically; rather he captured the outer-space feeling conveyed by the first line, and, in general, the rapturous, passionate feelings, although viewed from a distance. At times climaxes that are not particularly motivated by the text appear in the music. The greatest climax, set to the last line of the poem: "Ich bin ein Dröhnen nur der heiligen Stimme (I'm but a reverberation of the holy voice)," is somewhat unmotivated.

Nevertheless, the *general* correspondence between the text and the music is obvious. It is also easy to see why Schoenberg chose this particular poem for his first atonal venture. The thoughts of the poem unfold along a chain of free associations rather than through a logical sequence. This is the type of poetry that inspired Schoenberg throughout his free atonal period.

Structurally, the last movement is in free fantasy form rather than sonata form, as suggested by the analysis printed in the score. It is divided into four main sections in which motivic material is freely interchanged, followed by an altered restatement of the opening section. Thus, the outer structure of the movement is an A–B–C–D–A$_1$ design, preceded by an introduction and followed by a postlude.

The introduction (mm. 1–21), employing muted, whispering, ascending figurations (Ex. 11/20) used motivically throughout the entire movement, establishes a unique mood.

EX. 11/20 fourth movement, opening

At measure 10, the strange viola-cello motive should be noted, as it will reappear later in a modified form. Also, the violin motive at measure 13, with a major third and minor third figure (Ex. 11/21), recurs in the course of the movement.

EX. 11/21 fourth movement, m. 13

Section A begins at measure 21 with the entrance of the voice. Although these opening measures were quoted earlier in Example 4/9, the opening phrase of the soprano is restated:

EX. 11/22 fourth movement, mm. 21-25

Ich füh - le luft von an -de-rem pla - ne - ten. ____

Soon a passage appears in the cello, built on the four notes of the vocal melody just quoted (Ex. 11/23/a), and is followed by a transposition of the same passage in the viola (Ex. 11/23/b).

EX. 11/23/a fourth movement, m. 29

EX. 11/23/b fourth movement, m. 36

At measure 39 the opening notes of the introductory motive (Ex. 11/20) appear in the second violin assuming an entirely new meaning (Ex. 11/24). The passage is immediately taken up in tremolo, first by the viola and then by the first violin, the latter starting a half step higher.

EX. 11/24 fourth movement, mm. 39-40 (partial score)

The texture now becomes increasingly dense; rising passages based on Ex. 11/21 (rising thirds), in combination with various other motives, including the opening motive of the introduction, lead to the climactic end of the section. At this point the first six notes of the introductory motive appear four times, in a sequential pattern.

The main motive of section B (starting at m. 51) is announced by the soprano and first violin in unison.

EX. 11/25 fourth movement, mm. 51-55 (partial score)

Soon the motive appears in the form of a canon between the cello and viola, while the second violin plays the motive of Example 11/19 from the introduction. The entire passage (mm. 65-74), in the course of which the canon unfolds in diminution, is stated in Example 11/26 as documentation of Schoenberg's contrapuntal mastery.

EX. 11/26 fourth movement, mm. 65-74

EX. 11/26 (cont.)

The soprano enters at measure 74 continuing the canon in double-diminution; here, the cello-viola line derived from the introductory duet should be noted. Soon this motive gains prominence in rising sequences.

Section C begins at measure 83 with a variant of the earlier cello-viola duet played by the violins. The motive is switched to the second violin and viola, while the voice enters with a descending chromatic line, suggesting an inversion of the opening motive of B. Suddenly the main motive of A appears in the soprano in a new rhythmic guise, while the first violin adds rapid figurations (Ex. 11/27).

Section D begins at measure 92; the soprano sings over an airy texture consisting of harmonics and *ppp* pizzicato. The plucked, pulsating notes and the quivering second violin line suggest the text: "Der Boden schüttert weiss und weich (The earth rumbles white and soft)." A double-dotted *legato* figure emerges as the main material of this section which concludes with the second violin repeating the first six notes of the opening introductory motive twelve times.

EX. 11/27 fourth movement, m. 88 (partial score)

At measure 100 (A₁) the main motive of A, lowered by a half step, is resumed and combined with the tremolo version of the main theme of B in the violins.

EX. 11/28 fourth movement, mm. 100–102 (partial score)

After a gradual rise, the climax of the movement is reached on the words "heiliger Stimme (holy voice)"; each syllable is sustained for the length of a whole note, rising to the highest pitches (A and B flat) of the movement.

At measure 120 the coda begins; a motive with quarter-triplets assumes prominence, suggesting measures 59–61 of the B section. At measure 135, the second violin announces the opening motive of A. Soon the movement is concluded by a new melodic version of the introductory motive, played *sehr zart* (very tenderly) by the cello and continued by the second violin (Ex. 11/29).

The movement unexpectedly ends on an F sharp chord which is felt more as a harmonic *déjà-vu* than a tonic arrival.

No greater tribute can be paid to the effect of this movement than that of Zillig (a former Schoenberg student): "It seems as if Schoenberg's music had existed first, and George's poem is a comment on the music."[23]

[23]Winfried Zillig, *Variationen uber neue Musik* (Munchen: Nymphenburger Verlagshandlung, 1959), p. 74.

EX. 11/29 fourth movement, mm. 152–156

The last movement of the Second Quartet is the dividing line between Schoenberg's first and second creative periods. As a transition piece the movement deserves special attention, since works at stylistic crossroads yield the best understanding of the process of change. It will be fruitful, therefore, to compare the third and fourth movements, that is, the tonal versus atonal settings of the two poems.

From the texts it is obvious that the symbology and imagery of "Litanei" is simpler and less exalted than "Entrückung." Also, the central theme of "Litanei" is clearly defined. It is the prayer of a tortured soul to the Lord for spiritual peace. "Entrückung," on the other hand, makes a much greater demand on the reader. Written in the form of an interior monologue, the content is generated by free association, often employing a bizarre imagery. The poem expresses a highly subjective inner experience, a yearning to fuse with a mysterious, cosmic universe. This type of poetry, reflecting highly personal and intense inner psychic processes, attracted Schoenberg throughout his free atonal period.

The musical settings of the two poems show many stylistic differences; "Litanei" is tonal and "Entrückung" atonal. The first phrase of "Litanei," in the key of E flat minor, ushers in a certain atmosphere; the minor key, in itself, for reasons which are not fully understood, conveys sad connotations, particularly in a slow tempo. In addition, the key of E flat minor carries a dark sombre tone. The mood of "Litanei" is set before the voice enters. By comparison, the capricious figurations of the opening measures of "Entrückung," which lack any harmonic destination, achieve an effect difficult to define. Instead of establishing a mood, rather a state of consciousness is created. This somewhat amorphous experience, which the listener may not be ready to verbally characterize may cause him to say that he does not know what the "music is about."

Turning now to more specific musical characteristics, "Litanei" is cast in strict form with a symmetrical phrase structure, while the atonal "Entrückung" is in the form of a fantasy with a freer type of articulation. The melodic line of "Entrückung" is also freer and often declamatory, compared to the more singable "Litanei." Rhythmically, the atonal movement is much more complex, employing great diversity in the length of the note values. Also, greater differentiation occurs in the intricate contrapuntal lines; devices such as augmentation, diminution, and canon are frequently used. The sonorities of "Entrückung" are differently conceived and more individualistic than those of the tonal movement. At times unusual and novel sonorities are achieved by the independent horizontal movement of the four parts; the wide spacing of the chords also creates unusual tonal effects (mm. 21–25 and 140–152). On the whole, melody, rhythm, harmony, and texture are used differently in the atonal setting, as if each of these elements were mobilized to achieve a new order of structural differentiation instead of the older order based on tonality.

THE FREE ATONAL PERIOD (1908–1912)

In this four-year period—coinciding with the four years during which Stravinsky wrote his three famous ballets—Schoenberg was engaged in the most feverish activity of his entire career. He wrote ten major works in which he established a new style, known for its inward intensity as *expressionism.*

To consolidate the new ground gained by "Entrückung," Schoenberg returned to Stefan George's poetry, selecting fifteen poems from *Das Buch der hängenden Garten* (The Book of the Hanging Gardens) as the text for his song cycle, Op. 15. The repeated choice of George's poetry —also used in one song of Op. 14—suggests the special attraction that the German poet's verse held for the composer. Stefan George (1868–1933) was a soul mate indeed. Surrounded, like Schoenberg, by a little band of admiring disciples, he also addressed himself to a small, exclusive audience. His art, too, erupted from an almost uncontrollable impulse, which he also felt needed strong discipline (*Zucht*). Living in Paris as a young man, he came under the influence of the French symbolist poets (such as Mallarmé and Verlaine), absorbing their style, their vagueness and ambiguities. The central theme of his poetry also became *l'état d'âme* (the state of the soul). Schoenberg also drew upon literary sources of the French orbit during this period; *Herzgewächse*, Op. 20 (1912) for voice, harmonium, harp, and celesta was based on Maeterlinck's poem, and *Pierrot Lunaire* on Giraud's text. In both cases German translations of the French texts were used.

It is paradoxical that Schoenberg, heir to the German musical tradition, found the spirit of French poetry more congenial to him as a song writer during this period than that of the great poets (Goethe, Schiller, and Heine) of his own German heritage.

George's *Book of the Hanging Gardens* refers neither to the famous gardens of Babylon nor to any specific gardens. Rather the image is suggestive of the unreal and subtle terrains of the human soul. The poems relate a love story—a love forbidden and not quite fulfilled—in a luxurious, exotic setting. The sequence of events unfolds with somewhat blurred outlines; strange stirrings of passions come to the fore among frequent allusions to the sights and sounds of nature.

The songs, all without a key signature, show a great variety of forms with a minimum of repetition. The voice recites rather than sings, while the piano part maintains a curious independence. In fact, the organizing principle of the song, whether an interval, a chord, or a figure, is usually found in the piano part. Although functional harmonies and keys do not play any role in the scheme, half steps are often used as "as if" leading notes, whereby swift harmonic changes occur "as if by force of suction," in Stuckenschmidt's words. Despite this harmonic freedom, there is no feeling of arbitrariness or lawlessness, harmonically or otherwise. On the contrary, an inexorable logic seems to order relationships, weigh balances and intensities. In the free, declamatory vocal line the only consistent principle in evidence seems to be the rhythm of breathing, a natural pattern of tension and relaxation. Cadences are usually not established by harmonic delineations but rather by the phrase structure of the melodic line.

As Schoenberg himself considered this song cycle a decisive work, "coming near for the first time to an ideal of expression and form I had in mind," one of the songs (No. XIII) will be examined.

The English translation of the text reads as follows:

> You lean against a silvery willow
> On the shore, with the fan's stiff points
> Surrounding your head as with a crown of lightning;
> And sway, while fingering your jewels.
> I'm in the boat, protecting the vault of leaves,
> To which, in vain, I tried to lure you . . .
> I see the willows bending deeper
> And scattered flowers floating down the stream.[24]

[24] Translated by Peter Fritsch from Stefan George's *Das Buch der hängenden Garten*, Lyrichord Record LL42. By permission of Peter Fritsch, Lyrichord Records, and Helmut Küpper, publisher, Dusseldörf.

EX. 11/30 *The Book of the Hanging Gardens,*[25] *No. XIII*

[25] Quoted by permission of Belmont Music Company and Universal Edition, publisher of the first edition.

wie mit Blit - zen und rollst __ als ob du

sempre pp senza cresc.

spiel- test dein Ge-schmei-de. Ich bin im Boot,___ das

Laub - ge-wöl - be wah - ren, in das ich dich ver -

Most of the words create an atmosphere rather than depict an event; the most salient feeling is that of resignation, as the girl refuses the boy's invitation to step into his boat. The music is calm and brooding; the soft recitativelike vocal line is intoned *pianissimo* or at its loudest, *piano*. A touch of tone painting is achieved in the piano part; first in measures 3–4 the staccato notes suggest the *starren Spitzen* (stiff points), and in measure 5 the lightning is suggested by the slight disturbance caused by the thirty-second notes. The only repetition in the melodic line occurs in measure 10, where, at the mention of *Weide* (willow), the same descending line employed in measures 1–2 occurs, where the same word appeared in the text.

Structural unity is achieved by the opening A flat–C–G–B chord, made up of two major thirds, to which almost immediately a high F is attached. The same chord terminates the song; it appears here an octave lower and is preceded by the high F. Immediately preceding the final cadence, an interval (C sharp–A) repeated five times draws attention. Had this interval been sounded together, it would have resulted in a chain of parallel thirds (Ex. 11/31) leading directly to the closing chord:

EX. 11/31 *Book of the Hanging Gardens, No. XIII,* parallel thirds implied in the last measures

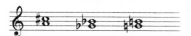

This very same harmonic progression takes place in reverse at measures 6–7, and again (underlining its significance) in measures 7–8, with the major thirds moving in contrary motion. The chord from which the harmonic movement begins is the opening A flat–C–G–B chord two octaves lower, with the added F three octaves lower than in the opening. The point of the novel spacing and registration is, of course, the avoidance of exact repetition. Hence, the song exemplifies a novel type of organization; the opening and closing harmonic progressions give the frame of unity and the same harmonic process is brought into focus at midpoint (mm. 6–8). The principle of organization is subtle and indicative of the heavy demands the song places on the listener's sensibilities.

Next, Schoenberg explored new media in the atonal style; piano compositions were followed by orchestral and stage works.

The *Three Piano Pieces,* Op. 11, were composed contemporaneously with the song cycle. Of the three pieces, the first two occasionally suggest some tonal feeling. They are both sectionally conceived with some motivic elaboration and repetition. In the third piece, however, the style approaches athematic writing. The same trend is pursued, but in an even more compressed form, in the *Six Little Piano Pieces,* Op. 19 (1911). Each of the pieces is epigrammatic; the composer succeeds in creating an intense atmosphere through the barest economy of means —an approach embraced by Webern. The music mirrors oscillations of the psychic life, which are experienced as highly charged but abstract currents. Verbalization concerning the "content" of the music is almost impossible.

Perhaps Schoenberg's awareness of the listener's difficulties in responding to his music caused him to provide titles for his *Five Orchestral Pieces,* Op. 16 (1909): "Premonitions," "Yesteryears," "Summer Morning by a Lake," "Peripetia,"[26] and the "Obligatory Recitative." Brevity, concentration of musical thought, and mainly athematic writing characterize the five pieces. The most striking one is the third, which employs the device of *Klangfarbenmelodie*[27] for the first time. The music does not consist of lines, but of a single chord set in five parts whose individual tones appear in ever-changing instrumentation and with different dynamics. The effect is similar to the one created by pointillism in painting, a technique that uses single dots instead of lines.

The orchestral pieces were followed by two stage works: *Erwartung* (Expectation), Op. 17 (1909), a monodrama for one female voice based on Marie Pappenheimer's text, and *Die glückliche Hand* (The Lucky Hand), Op. 18 (1910–1913), based on a text by Schoenberg.

If expressionism is defined as a style that deals with subjectivity in its extreme form, where high-pitched occurrences of the inner life touch upon unconscious symbolism and dreams, then these stage works represent the purest manifestation of this style.

In *Erwartung* the action consists of a woman's search for her lover in a forest, in the course of which she goes through anguish, hysteria, and terror. When she finds her lover dead, she is overwhelmed by ambivalent feelings, a mixture of love, accusations, guilt, and jealousy. The vocal line, a dramatic recitative often employing extremely large skips, is accompanied by a very large orchestra. The music, atonal throughout, is highly fragmentized with little repetition of any material. The effect of the work is stunning; it is a masterpiece and a milestone in the history of opera. Without it, Berg's *Wozzeck* would have been inconceivable. There are many striking resemblances between the two works; for instance, the rising parallel eleventh chords in the last measures of *Erwartung* are very closely recaptured in the music that accompanies Wozzeck's drowning. Unfortunately, *Erwartung* has seen very few productions, and remains relatively unknown. Mitchell[28] ad-

---

[26] Peripetia—a sudden crisis or reversal in Greek drama.

[27] *Klangfarbenmelodie*—a device whereby each note of a melody is assigned to a different instrument (see Chapter 2).

[28] Donald Mitchell, *The Language of Modern Music* (London: Faber & Faber, Ltd., 1963).

vances an interesting theory concerning audience reaction to *Erwartung* and *Wozzeck*. He feels that *Erwartung* failed to find an audience because there is no person in the cast with whom one could identify and the story, however gruesome, leaves the listener emotionally uninvolved. *Wozzeck,* on the other hand, is a moving story about human beings whose fate arouses compassion and a personal reaction in the audience. Hence its success. Perhaps one could expand upon Mitchell's observation and generalize that Schoenberg's creative imagination was extremely abstract on the whole, seldom allowing externalization of experience. This may be one of the reasons why his music, in general, is less accessible than that of Berg.

Die glückliche Hand is a less successful work. The story is built around three characters, two of whom act in pantomime. A speaking chorus comments upon events which again concern the eternal strife between man and woman. In this work Schoenberg experimented with color effects; orchestral crescendos are accompanied by rising intensities of colors projected on to the stage. The combination of sound and color fails either to clarify or intensify the drama; perhaps Schoenberg the painter intruded here upon Schoenberg the composer. In an interesting study of Schoenberg's stage works, Wörner[29] suggests that his experiment with colors was due to the influence of Kandinsky, for whom sound and color represented an inseparable, fused experience.

At the end of the period stands *Pierrot Lunaire,* Op. 21 (1912), a work scored for speaking voice and five instrumentalists. Three of the players have to double on other instruments—the flutist on the piccolo, the clarinetist on the bass clarinet, and the violinist on the viola—while the pianist and the cellist have single roles. The eight instruments appear in ever-changing combinations with the speaking voice; no instrumental combination appears twice, another application of the principle of perpetual variation.

The work, consisting of twenty-one short monodramas, has become one of Schoenberg's best-known compositions. The poetry of Giraud, a minor literary figure even in his native Belgium, has definitely faded but perhaps what attracted the composer was the bizarre content with its arbitrary, free-association type of discourse which used metaphors verging on the fantastic, a suitable vehicle for the atonal idiom. Also, the rigid structure of the stanzas (in each stanza the first two lines are repeated as lines seven and eight, and line one is repeated again in the closing thirteenth line) may have appeared conducive to the strict contrapuntal discipline with which the composer held together the free-floating harmonies. The text shows a distant relationship to *Erwartung* in the frequent personification of the moon. The following lines from

[29]H. Karl Wörner, "Arnold Schoenberg and the Theatre," *Musical Quarterly,* **48**, No. 4 (1962).

the monodrama reveal a similarity to the "Sick Moon" of *Pierrot:* "The moon is vicious . . . because it is empty of blood. Does it paint with red blood?"

Whatever the merit of Giraud's poetry, Schoenberg's setting is a masterpiece, whose originality remains fresh even in this age of electronic music.

The *Sprechstimme* used in the *Gurrelieder* is now brought to fulfillment. In the preface to the score, the composer precisely defines its mode of delivery; the indicated pitches should be sounded but not held by the singer; instead, he should immediately proceed with a rise or fall to the next pitch. If these instructions are carried out, the vocal line becomes immensely effective, especially in the context of the highly imaginative instrumental sonorities. There are few instances in contemporary music as fascinating as the flute-narrator duet in "The Sick Moon" or the dark-hued sound combinations of bass clarinet and cello in "The Night," in which "somber, shadowy, giant moth-wings killed the splendid shine of sun."

Pierrot influenced a large number of composers—Puccini, Debussy, Ravel, and Stravinsky—a list representing a wide spectrum of styles.

Pierrot Lunaire is the last important work of the atonal period, a period that was uniquely productive and that includes some of the composer's boldest and most original works. The greatness of the music is not realized yet either by concert audiences or professional musicians. For instance, a well-trained student of contemporary music, Reti,[30] maintains that the works from the free atonal period are among the weakest in the composer's oeuvre.

THE TWELVE-TONE PERIOD (1923-1951)

Schoenberg's twelve-tone period was preceded by a silence of nearly twelve years. It was during this time that the first experiments with the method took place. According to the composer, the first steps were taken in 1914 in the sketches of *Die Jacobsleiter,* an oratorio he never completed.

The historical and theoretical implications of the method were examined in Chapter 7. It was also mentioned that the composer's attitude with regard to the method underwent a change; while in the early twelve-tone works the method was used dogmatically, in the later

---

[30]Rudolph Reti, *Tonality, Atonality, Pantonality* (New York: Crowell-Collier and Macmillan Company, Inc., 1958).

works the composer was less concerned with the "rules." Actually, some late works, such as the *Organ Variations,* Op. 40 (1943), and the *Variations for Wind Orchestra,* Op. 43 (1943), are downright tonal and nonserial. When Schoenberg was asked for an explanation for this deviation from his earlier position, he answered:

> Trying to return to the older style was always vigorous in me; and from time to time I had to yield to that urge. This is how and why I sometimes write tonal music.[31]

The first two works from this period, *Five Piano Pieces,* Op. 23 (1923), and the *Serenade* for seven instruments and bass voice, Op. 24 (1923), show the method in its experimental stage (see Chapter 7).

The first full-fledged twelve-tone works were the Piano Suite, Op. 25 (1924), and the Woodwind Quintet, Op. 26 (1924). The application of the tone row in the Piano Suite has already been demonstrated (Ex. 7/8). Both works display a certain self-consciousness and academicism, as if the theoretician had hampered the creator.

The Third Quartet, Op. 30 (1926), has less freedom than was achieved in the Fourth Quartet, Op. 37 (1937), which is more limpid and less jagged than its predecessor. The Fourth Quartet employs combinatoriality (see Chapter 7), which provides novel harmonic and contrapuntal resources. Also, transpositions are used differently in the later quartet; whereas in the Third Quartet various transpositions occurred with great frequency, in the later quartet one area of transposition is stabilized for a considerable stretch. This approach to transposition characterized many later works, too, along with a simplification of texture and increased clarity in expression.

The Third Quartet was followed by the *Variations for Orchestra,* Op. 31 (1931), one of the composer's most successful and most accessible twelve-tone works. For this reason the work will be closely examined. Although set operations will be considered in order to illustrate the method, the analysis will center upon the purely musical values. Thus, in accordance with Schoenberg's wish, the work will be considered as twelve-tone *music,* and not as *twelve-tone* music.

VARIATIONS FOR ORCHESTRA, OP. 31

The work is scored for large orchestra, including mandolin, celesta, and a full percussion section. Built on a single row, the composition is divided into an introduction, theme, nine variations, and an extended finale. First we will examine the theme:

[31]*Style and Idea,* p. 213.

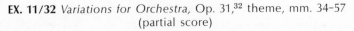

EX. 11/32 *Variations for Orchestra*, Op. 31,[32] theme, mm. 34–57
(partial score)

The rhythmic shape of the theme is characterized by an upbeat or afterbeat arrangement, and by frequent use of dotted patterns. Melodically, the tritone and the major sixth are the preferred intervals. Prominent also is the descending half step that appears at the end of the theme and at the end of the variations conveying a cadential feeling without the suggestion of any key centeredness.

The theme has the following tripartite division:

$$
\begin{array}{ll}
a & \begin{cases} \text{antecedent (mm. 1–5)} \\ \text{consequent (mm. 6–12)} \end{cases} \\
b & \text{contrasting section (mm. 13–17)} \\
a_1 & \text{condensation of "a" (mm. 18–24)}
\end{array}
$$

This ternary division is applied to the majority of the variations.

The over-all texture of the theme is light, with the dynamic level subdued to *piano* or *pianissimo*. The melody is assigned predominantly to the cellos and taken over in "a_1" by the violins. The instruction in the score indicates that the melody should be played *zart* (tenderly). The $\frac{3}{4}$ meter, the leisurely tempo, and the frequent dynamic swells add up to a light swaying feeling giving an almost imperceptible suggestion of a waltz.

Turning now to the row, the basic four forms are presented in Example 11/33.

---

[32] Quoted by permission of Mrs. Gertrud Schoenberg and Universal Edition, publisher of the first edition.

EX. 11/33 Basic forms of the tone row

The intervallic structure of the prime set shows two tritone formations and four dyads of half steps, both intervals prominent in the theme.

A comparison between the theme and the prime set points to the thematic use of the row; the twelve pitches of the prime set are employed in the antecedent. The pitches of the consequent (mm. 6–12), however, are not derived from the four forms of the prime set, but their source is in the RI_9 transposition. This transposition, in its inversion (I_9), establishes combinatoriality with the prime set. The four transposed forms are shown in Example 11/34.

EX. 11/34 P_9 Transposition, four forms of the tone row

Section "b" employs the R form of the prime set and "a_1" utilizes I_9. Expressed in nonserial terminology, the theme is constructed in such a way that section "b" utilizes the notes of the first five measures of the theme backwards, and in measures 6–12 one recognizes the pitches of "a_1," also backwards.

In accordance with Schoenberg's concept of two-dimensional musical space, the harmonies, too, are derived from the set and its transposition. The harmonies are derived from four sets, in the following order: I_9, R, RI_9, and P. With the help of the score these set operations can be easily traced.

Knowledge of both the theme and the row allows one to assess the function of the introduction. The composer evolves his material in this section gradually; first, single notes of the prime set are followed by the highlighting of an interval, the tritone, representing the first two pitches of the prime set. Soon a stronger intimation of the prime set appears in measure 10, where the first six notes of the prime set are announced in quarter notes by the flutes, harp, and first violins, marked as *Hauptstimme* (H⁻), that is, main voice. This motive is actually preceded by the employment of a segment of the I_9 transposition of the set. The complete set does not appear in the introduction; on the contrary, the composer seems to share with the listener the process of giving birth both to the basic set and to the theme. The amorphous feeling of some "prenatal" condition is enhanced by the fluidity of the changing meters ($\frac{6}{4}$, $\frac{7}{4}$, $\frac{12}{8}$). Gradually brief motives emerge and finally, at measure 24, the B–A–C–H motive[33] is intoned softly by the trombone.

EX. 11/35 M. 24

The B–A–C–H motive remains one of the main threads of the work, although these four pitches do not appear in this order in any of the sets.

At measure 34 the theme begins, followed by variation I at measure 58. This variation affords a good example of how a set operation may be placed in the service of expressiveness. It is obvious from the *cantabile* instruction in the score that the composer wanted to create an atmosphere of relaxation. In order to achieve this, he employs P_3 and I_3 (Ex. 11/36) along with P and I, resulting in consonant intervals such as thirds, sixths, and tenths (Ex. 11/37).

[33] The four notes making up Bach's name (the H being the German equivalent of our B natural) had been used repeatedly by earlier composers.

EX. 11/36

EX. 11/37 *Variation I,*[34] mm. 58–59 (partial score)

This is essentially a rhythmic variation in which the figure of the theme | 𝄽 𝅘𝅥𝅮. 𝅘𝅥𝅯 | 𝅗𝅥. | is changed into | 𝅘𝅥 𝅘𝅥𝅯𝅘𝅥𝅯𝅘𝅥𝅯 𝄽 | in the bass clarinets, bassoons, and contrabassoons. This new motive and its variants form the main material of the entire variation. Due to the movement of sixteenth notes and to the louder dynamics, the variation is experienced on a higher level of intensity than the theme.

Variation II, in slow $\frac{9}{8}$, is soft and subdued, employing mainly solo strings and woodwinds. In the opening the solo violin and the first oboe introduce the inverted theme in canonic imitation. Emphasis is placed on the rising tritone. The accompanying instruments are also paired in canonic imitations. The variation, marked *dolce* throughout,

---

[34] Quoted by permission of Mrs. Gertrud Schoenberg and Universal Edition, publisher of the first edition.

gains in expressiveness because of the slight dynamic swells. Toward the end (m. 99), the B–A–C–H motive is heard.

Variation III is powerful, *forte* or louder throughout. The repeated sixteenth notes, preserved from the preceding variation, form the background to the rhythmically dotted rising and falling tritones of the theme. Note should be taken of the opening measures of the French horn where the countermelody consists of the prime set.

EX. 11/38 *Variation III,*[35] mm. 106–107

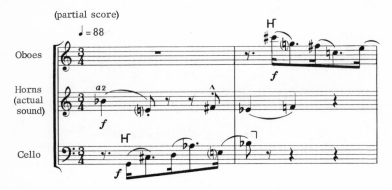

Variation IV, forty-seven measures in length, is a double variation (most of the other variations contain twenty-three measures). Marked *Walzertempo,* it has a tender mood, which is enhanced by exquisite sonorities. The notes of the prime set appear as an accompanying figure, each note repeated four times by harp and mandolin and supported by the celesta.

---

[35] Quoted by permission of Mrs. Gertrud Schoenberg and Universal Edition, publisher of the first edition.

EX. 11/39 *Variation IV,*[36] mm. 130–132 (partial score)

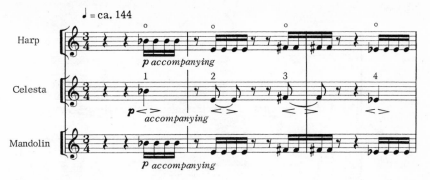

Accompanied by the lovely sonorities of Example 11/39, the flute sustains a new melody, which is later transferred to the violins, and then back again to the woodwinds.

Variation V, in contrast to the preceding variation, is violent and strongly accentuated. The skip of the major seventh, underlined by *crescendo–sforzato* accentuations persists throughout the variation. Jagged rhythms (sometimes reminiscent of the dotted rhythms of Variation III) give way to a calmer middle section at measure 190, which is followed again by the tense opening mood.

In Variation VI a duple meter $\frac{4}{8}$ is introduced and will be maintained in the next three variations. This is another instance where the tone row appears merely as an accompanying line (in the solo cellos) while the clarinet carries the main melody.

Variation VII, marked *langsam* (slow), stands out for the loveliness of its sonorities. While the bassoon introduces a new rhythmic shape (Ex. 11/40) that will be taken over by other instruments, the basic set appears as an accompanying figure with shimmering sonorities played by the piccolo and glockenspiel, and adorned in unison by the celesta and solo violin.

Variations VIII and IX are played as a unit. At the outset of the eighth variation the oboes play the theme, composed of the first six notes of I_9, and are answered by the bassoons whose motive consists of the last six notes of P (Ex. 11/41).

The fast tempo carries a strong pulsation, maintained by the *molto staccato* ostinato figure of the cellos. A *poco ritardando* leads into the ninth variation, which opens in a lyrical mood. Some of the shapes of

[36] Quoted by permission of Mrs. Gertrud Schoenberg and Universal Edition, publisher of the first edition.

EX. 11/40 *Variation VII,*[37] m. 238 (partial score)

* as softly as possible

EX. 11/41 *Variation VIII,*[38] mm. 262–263 (partial score)

the earlier variations return while three *poco sostenuto* interruptions suggest that the end of the section is near.

The Finale is an extended section of 211 measures. In a radio lecture[39] Schoenberg suggested that this section follows such models as the varia-

---

[37] Quoted by permission of Mrs. Gertrud Schoenberg and Universal Edition, publisher of the first edition.

[38] Quoted by permission of Mrs. Gertrud Schoenberg and Universal Edition, publisher of the first edition.

[39] Arnold Schoenberg, "Orchestral Variations, Op. 31," a lecture given in 1931 over the Frankfurt Radio. Reprinted in July, 1960.

tion movement of the "Eroica" Symphony and the finale of the Brahms *Variations on a Theme of Haydn.* Both Beethoven and Brahms wrote crowning endings to their movements, and the same is true of Schoenberg's Finale. Perhaps the B–A–C–H theme that pervades the entire Finale is a symbolic gesture to tradition. The motto-theme can be heard in measures 446–456 in the following shapes:

EX. 11/42/a Finale,[40] mm. 446–449

EX. 11/42/b

EX. 11/42/c

Finally, it appears *fortissimo* (mm. 497–500) in the trumpets:

EX. 11/43 Finale, mm. 497–500

OTHER INSTRUMENTAL WORKS

Although the composer's mastery of the orchestra is demonstrated in his *Variations,* this work was to be his last purely orchestral essay. His accomplished treatment of the orchestra, however, can be seen in the Violin Concerto, Op. 36 (1936), and in the Piano Concerto, Op. 42 (1942).

[40] Quoted by permission of Mrs. Gertrud Schoenberg and Universal Edition, publisher of the first edition.

In the three traditional movements of the Violin Concerto—although similar in texture to chamber music—a larger orchestra is employed than in the Piano Concerto. In the latter work, divided into four continuous movements, the solo piano is surrounded by rich orchestral sonorities, somewhat reminiscent of the textures of Brahms' piano concertos. While both solo parts demand a virtuoso performer, the difficulties of the Violin Concerto are almost prohibitive. In both works the row is used thematically and the musical discourse follows fairly traditional lines. The Piano Concerto is easier to grasp; the mood of the first movement has a romantic, melancholy quality. Striking orchestral effects abound in both compositions; in the first movement of the Violin Concerto (mm. 73–75) there is a particularly imaginative section, where the solo violin is accompanied by the glittering sounds of flute, xylophone, and plucked notes of the violins. An unusual effect is reached in the last section of the violin cadenza in the last movement, where a military drum accompanies the solo instrument. In the Piano Concerto the scoring of the opening of the Adagio movement is particularly striking.

Among the purely instrumental works that followed are the String Trio, Op. 45 (1946), and the *Violin Fantasy,* Op. 47 (1949). Their musical language is different from the two earlier works, as the composer's style is becoming increasingly athematic. The Trio is an emotionally intense work, whose musical shapes are jagged in a highly contrapuntal setting. The total impression is kaleidoscopic, created in part by swiftly changing instrumental effects such as pizzicato, glissando, *sul ponticello,* and *col legno.* The pace lessens in the "Tristanesque" First Episode, and in the highly expressive Coda (mm. 282–293).

The *Fantasy* represents a new point of departure in serial technique. In a detailed analysis Rufer[41] shows how the phrases are now interlocked. Each new phrase starts with the last note of the previous group causing an overlap both of the motives and the sets. He also points to passages that are made up of composite sets, employing notes alternatingly from different forms of the prime set. The violin carries the main line throughout the entire work, while the piano provides a percussive, rhythmic accompaniment. The *Fantasy* is even more problematical and less accessible than the Trio.

WORKS BASED ON TEXTS

Among the instrumental-vocal works of the period the following five will be examined: *Von Heute auf Morgen,* Op. 32 (1929), a one-act

[41] Josef Rufer, *Composition with Twelve Notes Related only to One Another* (London: Rockliff, 1954).

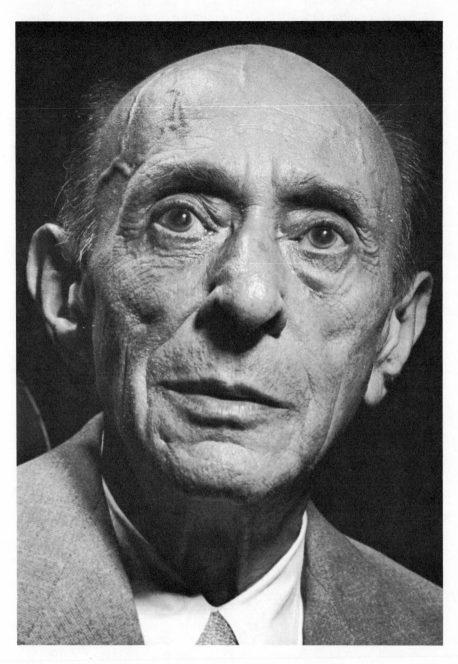

PLATE 17. SCHOENBERG IN THE LATER YEARS
Graphic House, New York

opera; *Kol Nidre,* Op. 39 (1938), for speaker, chorus, and orchestra; *Ode to Napoleon,* Op. 41 (1942), for narrator, string quartet, and piano; *A Survivor from Warsaw,* Op. 46 (1947), for narrator, chorus, and orchestra; and the unfinished opera, *Moses und Aron* (1930–1932). All five works bear on the philosophical, political, or religious aspects of the composer's *Weltanschauung.*

Von Heute auf Morgen, called by the composer a *heitere* (comic) opera, is based on a libretto by Max Blonda, a pseudonym for Schoenberg's wife by his second marriage. The work is a social satire pointing up, in the composer's words, how modern man lives "from unsure hand to greedy mouth, in marriage no less than in art, politics, and in his views of life." The cast, as in his expressionistic operas, consists of abstract characters, such as Man, Woman, and Female Friend. Although the work is highly inventive and has appealing vocal lines, supported by unusual and refined sonorities—the orchestra includes two saxophones, guitar, and mandolin—it failed to secure a place in the repertory.

Kol Nidre commissioned by Rabbi Jacob Sonderling, Los Angeles, California, is strongly tonal, representing one of the rare instances in which the composer elaborates on folkloristic material. The themes of the deeply felt work are repentance and reconciliation.

The *Ode to Napoleon,* set to a poem by Byron, was politically inspired. At a time when Hitler had reached the zenith of his power, Schoenberg felt that Byron's denunciation of Napoleon and of dictators in general had become timely. The narrator's *Sprechstimme,* not too different in style from that of *Pierrot,* ironically points to the futility of the conquests of dictators, thus predicting their downfall. The set operations in this work are handled with great freedom. The construction of the prime set (Ex. 11/44) is very different from earlier sets; successive groups of dyads, such as 1–2, 3–4, and 5–6, all form intervals of half steps. In the past such regularity in interval structures was avoided by the composer. Due to this construction of the row, references to tonal centers are frequent; in fact, the work ends on an E flat major chord.

EX. 11/44 *Ode to Napoleon,* prime set

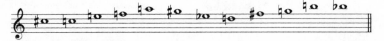

In *A Survivor from Warsaw,* the composer expressed his compassion with the sufferings of Hitler's victims. He wrote the text himself, based on a letter fragment smuggled out of the Warsaw ghetto during the uprising of the Jews. The terror of the captured Jews is described by the narrator; then the brutality of the Sergeant is related. When the hour of death arrives, the prisoners join in singing their holy song, the *Shema Ysroel.* The work, scored for large orchestra, is highly dramatic in its compressed, six-minute duration. The percussion section is handled with more prominence than in any of the earlier works; at times the narrator's words are accompanied only by percussion instruments. For example, at measures 38–40 the speaker is accompanied by military drum, bass drum, cymbals, tam-tam, and xylophone.

The final work to be discussed, *Moses und Aron,* is the composer's most significant work both musically and philosophically. The first two acts were written from 1930–1932; the second act was finished in Barcelona during a crisis in the composer's life. Emigration interrupted his major work on the opera, and although the composer made several attempts to write music for the third act, completion of the work was never realized. As late as 1949 the composer still grappled with the task. A letter from this year reports that he sketched out the music for the last act and needed but a few months to finish the work. Finally in 1951, a few months before his death, he wrote: "Agreed that it is possible for the third act simply to be spoken, in case I cannot complete the composition." Although the opera remained unfinished, the first two acts form a satisfying dramatic unit, both in scope and in size. They were first presented in a concert version in Hamburg in 1954; the first stage performance was given in Zurich in 1957, more than twenty-five years after the work was written. The opera has been performed only in Boston in the United States. But even in its recorded version the work makes a powerful impact. Perhaps its revelatory power lies in the crucial significance it had for the composer. When Schoenberg began the work he was faced with a dilemma: whether to stay in Nazi Germany or to seek refuge somewhere else. In addition to the events of reality, his identification with Germany and his conflict with Judaism were involved. Thus, his choice of Moses, who also searched for his God, as his main protagonist had deep personal implications. Another aspect of his identification with Moses may have been Moses' role as a leader who, although not understood by his people, followed the path of his uncompromising convictions. For both Moses and Schoenberg the problem was communication; neither of them was heard, yet they were both unwilling to change their ideals or lower their moral (musical) standards, even though such a lowering would have facilitated communication. Moses was aware of his difficulty in communication; his desperate outcry: "O word, thou word which fails me" may also have been uttered by the composer.

The text of the opera was written by Schoenberg and based on the second book of the Bible, Exodus. The story centers on the confrontation of the two brothers, Moses and Aron. In a sense they represent a dual union, as Mephistopheles is a part of Faust or Leporello of Don Giovanni. Moses stands for the abstract, invisible, unimaginable God, while Aron, who is presented as Moses' spokesman, offers a more tangible, concrete image of God to the people in the symbol of the Golden Calf. On another level Moses is the embodiment of spirit and Aron of the flesh. The latter is exemplified by the climactic "Dance around the Golden Calf" in the orgies of drunkenness and self-annihilation.

The work is scored for large orchestral and vocal forces. In addition to the solo singers on stage, the vocalists include six solo singers placed in the orchestra, the voices from the burning bush, a chorus of basses of the seventy elders, twelve tenors and basses of tribal leaders, a vocal quartet of virgins, a chorus of beggars, and a fully constituted chorus. Both the solo voices and the choruses use *Sprechstimme* and pitchless recitation, in addition to straight singing. The huge orchestra contains an unusually large percussion section and includes harp, piano, celesta, and two mandolins. This work, originating in the early 1930s, represents a summation of Schoenberg's music. Based on a single set, it demonstrates an effortless mastery of row technique. The sets and their transformations, plus the motivic material derived from the sets, are often employed as modernized versions of Wagner's leitmotif technique. The row pervades both the dramatic and musical events. Length and complexity notwithstanding, this work affords a view of the composer's art not found in his other works. Many of his musical devices which in a purely abstract musical setting may puzzle the listener become significant here through the dramatic purpose.

In the second scene of Act I, for example, the *Sprechstimme* gains new meaning as it highlights Moses' abstract form of communication, his solemnity and austerity. In contrast, Aron's part is written for lyric tenor, a symbolic expression of his seductive sensuality that captures the pleasures of the moment. The duet in this scene (Ex. 11/45), in which the *Sprechstimme* and singing voice appear simultaneously, is highly effective both musically and dramatically. This vocal setting also aids comprehension as the combination of the spoken and the sung words results in a clearer projection of the text than two singing voices could attain.

Also, the glissando and *col legno* passages gain meaning through the drama; for instance the orgy of annihilation—suicide by leaping from high rocks—is accompanied by trombone glissandi encompassing a two-octave range.

Just as early in the century Strauss' dissonances were understood by the listener because of the programmatic suggestions, Schoenberg's new musical language is made palpable by the drama. Thus, melodies jagged and smooth, sung or declaimed, the combination of vocal and

EX. 11/45 *Moses und Aron,*[42] Act I, Scene 2, mm. 125–127

instrumental sonorities, and the choice of instruments are actuated by dramatic necessities. As the musical devices—and this includes atonality too—become comprehensible in the light of the dramatic meanings, the listener will understand this musical language when it appears unaided by story or text. Not only the web of intricate musical relations brought about by the set operations merits study, but also the phonic value of the words, since the sound value of the words also plays a role in the total organization of the material.[43]

The opera made a deep impact on the audience, as reported by Karl Wörner who attended the Zurich premiere. In his opinion *Moses und Aron* is one of the most outstanding works of the first half of the twentieth century, and he considers the opera Schoenberg's chief work.

SUMMARY

The two crucial steps Schoenberg took in his career, the renunciation of tonality and the employment of the method of twelve-tone composition, changed the entire course of twentieth-century music.

[42] Quoted by permission of Mrs. Gertrud Schoenberg and Schott's Söhne.
[43] The booklet accompanying the Columbia recording of the work contains highly informative articles by Allen Forte and Milton Babbitt.

Paradoxically, the man whose innovations threatened to demolish the entire edifice of Western music was a traditionalist at heart. The abandonment of tonality seemed a gradual and logical step to Schoenberg, historically determined, even though the free atonal works sounded drastically different from any previous music. Works from the composer's atonal period are among his most daring. The aphoristic style of the *Six Little Piano Pieces* and the *Klangfarbenmelodie* of the third of the *Five Orchestral Pieces* profoundly influenced many composers, among them Webern and through him today's avant-garde.

With these works Schoenberg reached his most advanced position, from which he was eventually to retreat, as Stravinsky and, to a lesser extent, Bartók retreated from their advanced positions. Correctly viewed, the twelve-tone method of composition was a process of consolidation, inasmuch as its purpose was the harnessing of the free forces of atonality. Another sign of consolidation in the twelve-tone works is the composer's return to traditional forms.

Schoenberg's over-all style shows some consistent features despite changes in direction. Thus, frequent large melodic leaps of the twelve-tone works—a result of the principle of octave equivalence—can be observed in his earlier works. On the whole, Schoenberg's music is essentially oriented toward melody whose subjective expressiveness lends a romantic flavor to his music.

Throughout his creative phases, Schoenberg placed a strong emphasis on contrapuntal devices; the various set operations in the twelve-tone works furnish new possibilities for contrapuntal intricacies.

Rhythmic forces have a less dominant role when compared to the works of Stravinsky or Bartók. German music was never rhythmically conceived, and Schoenberg's music does not deviate from this tradition.

Schoenberg's imagination for sound is a fascinating aspect of his art; *Pierrot Lunaire* represents a peak in chamber music sonorities and *Moses und Aron* in the realm of massive sound. Characteristic instruments are the xylophone and the celesta, and among the string effects, harmonics, glissando, and *sul ponticello* are often employed. His use of *Sprechstimme* represents an entirely new approach to the use of the human voice.

The principle of perpetual variation is the most important structural device in Schoenberg's music. Adherence to this principle caused his music to be in a constant state of flux, even though the outer structure often conforms to traditional forms. This conservative treatment of form in the twelve-tone works, and an occasional suggestion of tonality, gave rise to criticism from avant-garde circles.

The concentrated thought processes of Schoenberg's music place heavy demands on the listener. Today only the early works are programmed with some degree of frequency. On the whole, his music is found much less accessible by concert audiences than that of Bartók or Stravinsky. Whatever the final judgment of his music may be, his belief in his mission, his uncompromising courage, and his writings and teaching make him one of the most compelling figures of the twentieth century. As a teacher he produced two outstanding students: Alban Berg and Anton Webern, whose music will be the subject of the next two chapters.

CHRONOLOGICAL LIST OF SCHOENBERG'S PRINCIPAL WORKS[44]

Verklärte Nacht (Transfigured Night), Op. 4   1899
Gurrelieder for soloists, chorus, and orchestra   1900–1911
Pelleas und Melisande, Op. 5   1902–1903
First String Quartet, in D minor, Op. 7   1904–1905
Chamber Symphony No.1., Op. 9   1906
Second String Quartet, in F sharp minor, Op. 10   1908
Three Piano Pieces, Op. 11   1908
Das Buch der hängenden Gärten (The Book of the Hanging Gardens) for voice and piano, based on poems by Stefan George, Op. 15   1908
Five Pieces for orchestra, Op. 16   1909
Erwartung (Expectation), one-act opera, Op. 17   1909
Die glückliche Hand (The Lucky Hand), one-act opera, Op. 18   1909–1913
Six Little Piano Pieces, Op. 19   1911
Pierrot Lunaire, Op. 21   1912
Five Piano Pieces, Op. 23   1923
Serenade for seven instruments and bass voice, Op. 24   1923
Suite for piano, Op. 25   1924
Wind Quintet, Op. 26   1924
Third String Quartet, Op. 30   1926
Variations for orchestra, Op. 31   1927–1928
Von Heute auf Morgen, one-act opera, Op. 32   1929
Two Piano Pieces, Op. 33   1932
Violin Concerto, Op. 36   1936
Fourth String Quartet, Op. 37   1937
Second Chamber Symphony, Op. 38   1940

[44] For a complete list of Schoenberg's works see Josef Rufer's *Das Werk Arnold Schoenberg's*, Bärenreiter, Kassel, 1959; English translation by Dika Newlin, *The Works of Arnold Schoenberg*, New York, 1963.

Kol Nidre for speaker, chorus, and orchestra, Op. 39   1938
Ode to Napoleon for speaker, string quartet, and piano, Op. 41   1942
Piano Concerto, Op. 42   1942
String Trio, Op. 45   1946
A Survivor from Warsaw for speaker, chorus, and orchestra, Op. 46   1947
Fantasy for violin, Op. 47   1949

Unfinished Works

Die Jakobsleiter, oratorio   1913–
Moses und Aron, opera   1931–

DODECAPHONY (12-TONE)

Serial technique

1. Basis of comp.: tone row (series)
2. tones used: successively (melodically)
   : vertically (harmony or counterpoint)

in any octave w/ any rhythm

1. no repetition of tones w/in row
2. inverted, retrograde, inverted retrograde
3. transposition

ALBAN BERG (1885–1935)

Berg was the enchanter of twelve-tone music.
ADORNO

Alban Berg and Anton Webern were fortunate not only in having such an inspiring teacher as Schoenberg, but also in having a new trail blazed for them by their master. Thus they could immerse themselves totally in their creative work, without being hampered by periods of crises, as was Schoenberg from 1912 to 1923, when theoretical speculations silenced him as a composer.

Berg and Webern, both descendants of the same Austro-German musical tradition, developed along entirely different lines, even though both of them followed Schoenberg along the road of atonality and serial writing. To Berg fell the role of establishing a link between the new style and the romantic past; a fact that made his music the most accessible among the Viennese atonal composers. Webern, on the other hand, broke new ground, and this forward-looking aspect of his art prompted a new generation of composers—the so-called post-Webernites—to embrace him as their spiritual leader. Both composers despite their different orientation greatly enriched the literature of the twentieth century.

LIFE

Alban Berg, son of a well-to-do business man, was born in Vienna. His father was a descendant of a distinguished Bavarian Catholic family, proud of its ancestry of high-ranking army officers and public servants.

According to Redlich's informative biography,[1] the boy's early interest centered on poetry rather than on music; this literary bent was put to use later in his life when Berg became a librettist for his own operas.

In early childhood, Berg's health was frail and it was further weakened at age fifteen—the year his father died—by a severe form of asthma that persisted throughout his entire lifetime. The physical vulnerability of his organism was coupled with an overwrought sensibility; a suicide attempt at the age of eighteen, following a school failure, indicates the extent of his pathology.

Perhaps it was due to this weak constitution that Berg never considered a career as a performer; almost from the beginning his musical interest centered on composition. Although he did not have Webern's rigorous musical training, Schoenberg saw enough promise in his early compositions to accept him as a student in 1904. The teacher-student relationship, which lasted for six years, was followed by a lifelong friendship. Berg's utmost devotion to his teacher was expressed in the dedication of several of his works to Schoenberg. An additional act of reverence was paid in Act II, Scene 3, of Wozzeck, where the stage orchestra is composed of the same fifteen instruments Schoenberg used in his First Chamber Symphony, a fact noted in the score of the opera.

In turn, Schoenberg included Berg's new works in a concert series that programmed his own compositions. Although Berg's music was written in a style distinctly different from his master's, the audiences responded to both with the same hostility. The premiere in 1913 of Berg's "Altenberg" Songs, Op. 4, precipitated the most violent rioting ever to occur in a Viennese concert hall.

In 1915, Berg was drafted into the Austrian army for limited service

[1] Hans F. Redlich, *Alban Berg* (London: John Calder, 1957).

in the War Ministry. At this time he saw a performance of Büchner's *Wozzeck,* and almost immediately decided to adapt the play for a music drama. The preparation of the libretto took until 1917 and by 1921 the opera was completed. The premiere, preceded by more than a hundred rehearsals, took place at the Berlin State Opera in 1925 under the direction of Erich Kleiber. From the first performance *Wozzeck* was a triumphant success. It was staged eleven times in Berlin during the same season and was presented in opera houses throughout the world. Thus, Berg's opera became the best-known and most celebrated work of the Viennese atonal school.

Success came at a crucial time in the composer's life, for the devaluation of the Austrian currency caused him to lose his family income. Financial rewards were soon followed by official recognition: in 1930

Berg was made a member of the Prussian Academy of Arts. Although pleased by this honor, it caused him to make bitter comments about the apathetic attitude shown by his native country. He wrote to Webern:

> Thanks for your congratulations to the "Academician." How it came about I don't myself know . . . . No actual appointment is involved. Nevertheless, it pleased me very much, especially on account of Vienna, *i.e.,* of Austria, which, as is well known, has virtually overloaded us for years with honors and appointments . . . .[2]

Three years later his music, together with that of Schoenberg and Webern, was banned in Germany and branded as products of *Kulturbolschevismus.*[3] While Berg was not subject to anti-Semitic laws, Schoenberg's exile affected him deeply. His reaction is expressed in a letter to Webern:

> What a fate! Now at the age of nearly sixty, expelled from the country where he could speak his mother tongue, homeless and uncertain *where* and on *what* to live, in a hotel room . . .[4]

Depressed by world events and weakened by repeated attacks of asthma, the only solace Berg found in his last years was in his newly acquired country home in Carinthia. During his last seven years he was occupied with *Lulu,* an opera based on two dramas by Wedekind, that was never completed. Berg died as a result of blood poisoning brought about by an insect bite.

EARLY MUSIC

Among the early works of Berg, his songs occupy a central position. Redlich's list[5] of unpublished works contains some seventy songs, all written before the "Seven Early Songs" (1905–1908)—bearing no opus number—which were the first fruits of his studies with Schoenberg. In these songs, particularly in "Sommertage," it is easy to detect the influence of his teacher, and also that of Wagner and Debussy. The latter's influence will be traced in subsequent works as it represents a special flavor in Berg's music that is totally absent from Schoenberg's style.

[2] Letter to Webern, dated February 10, 1930, *Alban Berg,* p. 238.

[3] *Kulturbolschevismus* — a generic term that ascribes a Communist origin to all advanced styles in art.

[4] Letter to Webern, dated July 6, 1933, *Alban Berg,* p. 240.

[5] *Alban Berg,* pp. 287–288.

The Piano Sonata, Op. 1 (1907–1908), in one movement cast in sonata form, occupies a position in Berg's oeuvre similar to that of Schoenberg's *Verklärte Nacht*. Both works show the strong influence of *Tristan's* harmonic world, although Berg's Sonata is structurally and harmonically more traditional than the early Schoenberg work.

The "Songs," Op. 2 (1909), testify to Berg's fast progress; the last song in the group with its rising fourths brings Schoenberg's Chamber Symphony to mind and also represents Berg's break with tonality.

The String Quartet, Op. 3 (1910), in two movements, is a remarkably mature work; it clearly indicates that the days of apprenticeship are over. The technical sureness and the highly developed quartet style are impressive, yet, despite the technical fluency, Schoenberg's imprint is still strong. It is seen in such structural devices as the quasi development function of the second movement and in the motivic elaboration of the material. The expressiveness and lyricism that will become the hallmarks of Berg's mature style, however, are still lacking. Debussy's influence is also strongly felt, particularly at measures 45–46 in the first movement (Ex. 12/1) and at measures 54–55 in the second (Ex. 12/2).

EX. 12/1 BERG, *String Quartet*, Op. 3,[6] first movement, mm. 45–46

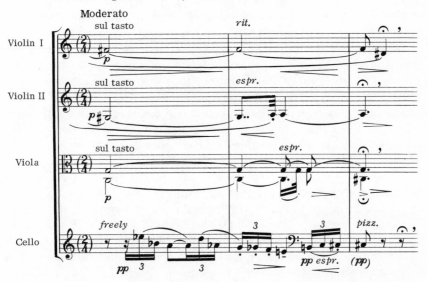

It is only in the "Orchestral Songs," Op. 4 (1912), written for voice and large orchestra, that Berg's originality fully emerges. The five songs of this opus are often referred to as the "Altenberg" Songs, as they are

[6]Copyright by Universal Edition, Vienna. Used by permission.

EX. 12/2 second movement, mm. 54–55

set to the picture postcard texts of the eccentric Viennese poet, Peter Altenberg. Both in this work and in the ensuing *Three Orchestral Pieces*, Op. 6 (1914), unexpected dramatic force is shown, foreshadowing the composer's imminent turn to music drama.

In addition to their dramatic impact, the "Altenberg" Songs are also rich in the tender, poignant moments so characteristic of Berg's later works. A highly sensitive mood is set in the first song where the voice enters on a B and vocalizes without any syllables attached. The voice enters *triple piano* within which a swell has to be negotiated with lightly closed lips. In the next measure the vocal line ascends to the C with the swell starting on a *double piano,* to be executed with half-open mouth according to the composer's instructions. In both instances, the attack and release should be executed *wie ein Hauch* (like a breath). After this infinitely subtle start the words of the poem begin: "Oh, soul, how much more beautiful and deeper are you after a snow storm. . . ."

While Berg's association with the past has been emphasized, the third and fifth songs point to his adventurousness. The harmonic plan of the third song is unusually bold, opening with a chord that contains all twelve tones of the chromatic scale. Gradually the texture thins out, until only a C sharp is left, held by the solo cello; then, the density of the texture again increases, and as the opening melody returns, the same aggregate of twelve tones is gradually reached in the last chord but with different spacing than in the opening.

The last song, "Hier ist Friede," actually anticipates twelve-tone procedures more strongly than anything written by Schoenberg up to that point. The song opens with a passacaglia theme in the bass, over which a countermelody appears (Ex. 12/3) using the twelve half steps of the chromatic scale, without repeating any one of its steps.

EX. 12/3 *"Hier ist Friede,"* Op. 4, no. 5,[7] opening (partial score)

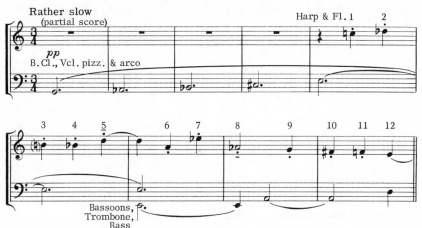

The twelve-tone motive is employed in row style; it is kept intact first as an inner voice (mm. 11–14), and later (one measure before study number 4 in the piano-vocal score) the first nine notes of the row appear in the voice, while 10, 11, and 12 are contained in the concluding chord of the piano.

Since Schoenberg was well acquainted with the song cycle, premiered at a time when he was in search of an organizing framework for atonality, it is not far-fetched to speculate that the last song of Op. 4 had some influence on his formulation of the twelve-tone method.

The *Three Pieces for Orchestra,* Op. 6 ("Prelude," "Round Dance," "March"), show more similarity to the styles of Mahler and Debussy than to Schoenberg. Mahler's idiom is strongly felt in the "Prelude," after study number 15; it is felt again in the sixteenth triplet brass figure of the last movement, and generally in the way rhythmic patterns assume motivic significance. Debussy's influence is apparent in the opening and closing sections of the middle movement.

The *Three Pieces for Orchestra* drew high praise from Stravinsky who was not otherwise attracted to Berg's idiom. The Russian composer states his views as follows:

> The perfect work . . . and I think the essential work, with *Wozzeck,* for the study of all of his music is the Three Pieces for Orchestra, Op. 6. Berg's personality is mature in these pieces, and they seem to me a richer and freer expression of his talent than the twelve-note serial pieces. When one considers their early date—1914; Berg was twenty-nine—they are something of a miracle.[8]

[7]Copyright by Universal Edition, Vienna. Used by permission.

[8]Igor Stravinsky and Robert Craft, *Conversations with Igor Stravinsky* (New York: Doubleday & Company, Inc., 1959), p. 80.

Having reached the height of his creative powers, Berg turned now to his first large scale work, *Wozzeck,* an outstanding example of how atonal music can be human, accessible, and emotionally compelling.

WOZZECK

If ever there was a literary prodigy, it was Georg Büchner (1813–1837), the author of *Wozzeck.* The offspring of an intellectual German family, he first studied medicine and later earned a doctorate in philosophy. Soon his political activities forced him to leave his native Hessen and find asylum in Switzerland. There, at the age of twenty, he lectured on brain anatomy at the University of Zurich.

His participation in politics was motivated by his deep compassion for the poor and oppressed. His political pamphlet, *The Hessian Courier,* bore the subtitle "Freedom for the Huts—War on the Palaces!" Büchner's careful study of the history of the French Revolution yielded the subject matter for his first play, *Danton's Death* (1835). The young playwright's thoughts were so much ahead of his time that, as late as 1891, a Berlin editor of a literary periodical was sentenced to four months' imprisonment for reprinting excerpts from *Danton's Death.* The play saw its first production only in 1902.

Büchner's intense feelings for the suffering of the underprivileged caused him to choose *Woyzeck* (the original spelling) as the subject of his next play. Büchner's penchant for realism probably led him to base his plays on real-life stories; Woyzeck was actually the name of a soldier in the Austrian army who, charged with murdering his lover, was executed in 1824 despite pleas for dismissal on the grounds of insanity.

The play has contemporary relevance on other counts too. Aside from Büchner's brilliance as a dramatist, it is one of the first dramatic presentations of the predicament of modern man. Also, the mode of presentation is novel and anticipates the naturalistic movement. Finally, the portrayal of psychopathology—frustration, guilt, and aggression—shows an uncanny preknowledge of the Freudian understanding of the unconscious. Dramatically, the haunted character of Woyzeck and his hallucinatory states have the aura of the Theater of the Absurd. Added to these elements is the social viewpoint, the outcry for the wretched life of the poor people, victims of forces much stronger than themselves. This social message was most important to Berg, as he made obvious in his postscript to *Wozzeck:*

What I do consider my particular accomplishment is this. No one in the audience, no matter how aware he may be of the musical forms contained in the framework of the opera, of the precision and logic with which it has been worked out, no one, from the moment the curtain parts until it closes for the last time, pays any attention to the various fugues, inventions, suites, sonata movements, variations, and passacaglias about which so much has been written. No one gives heed to anything but the vast social implications of the work which by far transcend the personal destiny of Wozzeck. This, I believe, is my achievement.[9]

The play was actually left unfinished by Büchner in the form of twenty-nine jumbled scenes. Berg telescoped them into fifteen scenes and grouped them into three acts.

The five scenes of Act I introduce the main characters, among whom only Wozzeck, the poor uneducated soldier, and his mistress, Marie, mother of their illegitimate child, are strongly delineated. In four of the five scenes Wozzeck is projected against his environment. In the opening scene, Wozzeck responds with puppetlike, mechanical answers to the Captain's vulgar reproaches about his moral sense. Wozzeck's defense is that poor people ("wir arme Leut") are not bound to morality. Later, he formulates his thoughts more articulately:

If I were a lord, sir, and wore a silk hat and had a watch and an eyeglass too, and could talk genteelly, then I would be virtuous too . . . I am a simple soul. Folk like us are always unfortunate.

In the following scene Wozzeck and a fellow soldier, Andres, collect firewood for the Captain. The blazing sunset induces a state of great anxiety in Wozzeck: "A fire there. It rises from earth into heaven, and with a tumult falling, just like trumpets . . . . How it rattles." Next, Marie views a military band from the window, headed by the handsome Drum Major. As she sings a lullaby to her child, Wozzeck appears quite distraught and incoherent. Then, in the study of the Army Doctor, Wozzeck submits himself to some physiological experiments in order to earn a few pennies. The Doctor's mad dream is to achieve world fame by proving his theories. In the last scene the Drum Major seduces Marie, easily overcoming her feeble resistance.

In Act II, Wozzeck's pathology becomes more apparent as he realizes the role the Drum Major plays in Marie's life. The pathological characters of the Captain and the Doctor also become increasingly evident; the Doctor's paranoia has a sadistic tinge, while the Captain suffers from an acute state of anxiety. Obviously, the implication is that with rank and status one can survive despite pathology, whereas the poor cannot get away with anything and must perish. Both the Captain and

---

[9] Alban Berg, "Postscript to Wozzeck," Musical Quarterly, **38**, No. 1 (1952), p. 21.

the Doctor torment Wozzeck by drawing his attention in a vulgar way to Marie's relation with the Drum Major. Soon Wozzeck obtains first-hand evidence of their association when he sees Marie dance with the Drum Major in the tavern scene. A fool—very much modeled after the fools in the plays of Shakespeare—whispers to Wozzeck an eerie pre-monition about blood. Later, in the barracks, the drunk Drum Major openly boasts of his conquest and challenges Wozzeck to a fight. Wozzeck is subdued and his last words in the act, "One defeat after the other . . ." suggest that he has reached the breaking point.

Act III opens with a scene in Marie's room; she reads from the Bible, a gesture of repentance. Then an ominous conversation takes place be-tween Wozzeck and Marie by a pond. The redness of Marie's lips and the redness of the moon trigger an irrational chain of associations in Wozzeck, who finally stabs Marie to death. He rushes to the tavern, but when the girl with whom he has started to dance questions him about the blood on his sleeve, he leaves in a panic and returns to the pond. Here, in a state of utter disintegration, he drowns himself. In the last scene a group of children is playing, among them the child of Marie and Wozzeck. When news of Marie's death arrives all the chil-dren rush to inspect the body, with the exception of her own child, who remains on stage riding his hobbyhorse. When he notices that all the children have left, he goes off after them as the curtain falls.

In Büchner's play the children's scene was the penultimate scene, the last scene taking place in the morgue with Wozzeck standing amidst policemen dumbly looking at Marie's body. It is easy to see why the morgue scene would not lend itself to a satisfactory musico-dramatic ending, and why Berg's solution is more successful. The implication is that life has to go on and that the deaths of Marie and Wozzeck have tragic consequences apart from their own pathetic fates. The child's presence on stage in the final scene humanizes the drama; it suggests that despite murder, pathology, and suicide, the next generation may yet entertain hope and begin anew. At the same time presenting the child as the innocent victim of circumstances underlines the social significance of the play. Against this interpretation stands Kerman's view,[10] according to which the last scene "smacks fatally of a trick ending."

To the history of *Wozzeck* belongs Schoenberg's disapproval of Berg's plan to use Büchner's play as a libretto for an opera. In a recollection Schoenberg writes:

> . . . I was greatly surprised when this soft-hearted, timid young man had the courage to engage in a venture which seemed to invite misfor-tune; to compose *Wozzeck,* a drama of such extraordinary tragic [sic],

---

[10] Joseph Kerman, *Opera as Drama* (New York: Alfred A. Knopf, 1959), p. 233.

that seemed forbidding to music. And even more: it contained scenes of everyday life which were contrary to the concept of opera which still lived on stylized costumes and conventionalized characters. He suc-ceeded. *Wozzeck* was one of the greatest successes of opera.[11]

These lines shed light on the creative character of both composers. On the one hand, they point to the abstract nature of Schoenberg's imag-ination to which the sordid, realistic story of the depraved soldier did not appeal. In fact, none of Schoenberg's stage works deal with rela-tionships among real people; his heroes in *Erwartung, Die glückliche Hand, Von Heute auf Morgen,* and *Moses und Aron* are all abstractions.

On the other hand, Berg was inspired by the gruesome story of Woy-zeck, so fraught with naturalism and symbolism. More specifically, his musical imagination was fired by a story in which lust and violence are mingled with moments of poignancy and tenderness. The fact that he proceeded with the project of *Wozzeck* despite objections from the revered master also shows the strength of his convictions and his faith-fulness to his ideals.

PROBLEMS OF MUSICAL ORGANIZATION

When Berg embarked upon this large scale atonal work, he faced the same problems in organization that finally led Schoenberg to invent the twelve-tone method of composition. Berg summed up the prob-lem of organization in atonal music as follows:

On deciding to compose a full-length opera I was confronted by a new problem, at least from the angle of harmony: how to achieve the same degree of cohesion and of structural unification without the use of the hitherto accepted medium of tonality and of its creative poten-tialities—cohesion, moreover, not only in the smaller forms of dramatic sections but also the more difficult unification in the bigger formal units of a whole act and in the structure of the whole opera.[12]

Schoenberg's answer to the problem of organization of atonal mu-sic was a method with vast ramifications. Berg's solution, however, was a specific one, a perfect one for *Wozzeck*, but inimitable otherwise.

The organization of the opera is planned on several levels; first, the outer structure has a symmetrical cast, achieved not only through the symmetry of the three acts, each containing five scenes, but also through the specific balancing of the acts. Equilibrium is brought about by flanking the weightiest and long second act with short first and third acts. Also, whereas the middle act has the fluidity of a continuous whole, the other two acts consist of tableaulike units.

[11] *Alban Berg,* pp. 245-246.
[12] *Alban Berg,* p. 262.

By employing well-known forms of abstract instrumental music in the vocal, operatic scenes, Berg achieved a completely novel inner organization of the material. Thus, the continuous Act II is laid out along the lines of an enlarged symphony in five movements: a first section in sonata form, followed by a fantasy and fugue, a largo, a scherzo, and a rondolike finale. The developmental nature of the musical processes accords with the dramatic exigencies of the act. The same is true of all forms used in the opera; their employment is always motivated by the dramatic demands. Thus, in Act I where the main characters of the drama are drawn, strongly delineated musical forms such as passacaglia, suite, and march are used. Likewise, sharply etched musical structures are also employed in Act III where the catastrophe and the epilogue are organized in the form of six inventions built on single elements, such as a theme, a tone, or a rhythm.

In a lecture on *Wozzeck*[13] Berg states that neither "antiquarian leanings" nor "atavistic back to . . . [sic]" movements prompted him to employ the old instrumental forms, but that he used them for their organizational and dramatic values.

Additional unifying structural devices used by the composer are the orchestral interludes which contribute, although not always with the same purpose, to the inevitable flow of both the music and the drama. While some orchestral interludes have the function of codas or epilogues to preceding scenes, others bridge those forthcoming. The longest and most effective interlude occurs after the fourth scene in Act III; cast in D minor, it achieves a powerful summation of the whole drama.

Despite the atonal style, unity is achieved to some degree by harmonic centeredness; thus, an obvious harmonic link is constituted by the G–D bass of the closing chords of Act I and Act III.

One of the most novel and expressive harmonic devices is the occasional use of tonality within a generally atonal context. Each time the music becomes tonal, there is a dramatic motivation; thus in the first scene of Act III, as Marie reads from the Bible, the music turns tonal, thus providing a source of relief. Also, in the orchestral interlude of Act III, tonality is introduced following the moment of greatest tension. This device has an almost cathartic effect, as if the tragedy were now viewed from the outside. The reconciliation of tonality with atonality, in addition to its value as an organizational device, has a powerful emotional impact. In the over-all context of pathology in the drama, tonality becomes a vehicle for normality.

Unification is also achieved by repetition or elaboration of thematic

---

[13] *Alban Berg,* p. 267.

material, but is done in a more subtle fashion than in the Wagnerian opera based on leitmotive technique. For instance, the musical
motive of the Drum Major's brutality—used in the theme of Marie's
seduction—appears later in the wrestling scene between the Drum Major and Wozzeck. Another subtle instance of repetition of motives occurs in the sleeping scene in the barracks in Act II; the fact that Wozzeck is unable to fall asleep because his memory lingers on what he
has seen in the tavern is suggested by the reappearance of the theme
of the tavern scene.

USE OF ORCHESTRAL AND VOCAL RESOURCES

Wozzeck is scored for a large orchestra that is employed largely *tutti*
in the interludes. Otherwise chamber music style is prevalent; often a
specific group of instruments is featured for a protracted time in order to lend consistency to a scene or mood.

The way the orchestra is used resembles Debussy's orchestral technique in *Pelléas;* in both operas specific instrumental combinations
establish a mood, which is then reinforced by orchestral interludes. In
Wozzeck, however, these summations are more succinct, and, on the
whole, action and music are welded together even more closely than in
Pelléas. The music never takes the attention away from the action because the orchestra is not only mirroring events, as occurs in *Pelléas,*
but actually becomes part of the action, as if both the music and action would turn into one unified perceptual experience. The listener is
simultaneously engulfed in the drama and in the music; in Kerman's
words, "the orchestra pit is brought out into the audience instead of
up onto the stage." [14] In the unfolding of the drama, the music seems
to bypass the perceptual control of the listener, touching upon the
deepest, unconscious layers. The unity of sound and drama causes
even the listener who is unaccustomed to the atonal style to fall under
the spell of the opera.

Vocally, Berg uses the whole gamut of possibilities offered by the
human voice; there are occasional *bel canto* lines, various types of
Schoenbergian *Sprechstimme,* and simple spoken lines accompanied by
music. Perhaps the most novel vocal device is the superimposition of
real singing and *Sprechstimme* in the dialogue of Wozzeck and Andres
(Act I, Scene 2, m. 55), a device adopted later by Schoenberg in *Moses
und Aron.*

---

[14] *Opera as Drama,* p. 224. The entire chapter on *Wozzeck* and *The Rake's Progress*
deserves reading (pp. 219–249).

THE MUSIC

Act I   The first scene, in which Wozzeck shaves the Captain, utilizes stylized baroque dances such as the pavane, gavotte, and gigue. The dances are preceded by a prelude that recurs in retrograde motion at the end of the scene. The composer uses this string of isolated dances in order to match the setting created by the loosely connected topics of the discussion between the Captain and Wozzeck. Two motives should be noted: the first in measure 4, associated with the Captain (Ex. 12/4), and the second, Wozzeck's motive (Ex. 12/5), set to the motto of "wir arme Leut."

EX. 12/4 *Wozzeck,*[15] Act I, Scene 1, m. 4

EX. 12/5 Act I, Scene 1, m. 136

Both motives yield a great deal of material; the latter is the most important motive of the entire opera.

In the second scene nature, in the form of an eerie sunset, infiltrates the action for the first time. The unifying principle is based on three chords.

EX. 12/6 Act I, Scene 2, opening, m. 201ff., three basic chords

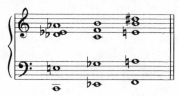

[15] Copyright by Universal Edition, Vienna. Used by permission.

These chords provide material for the entire scene; the notes appear in various rhythmic and instrumental guises, as seen at measure 225 and in measures 227–234.

Another important feature of this scene is Andres' folklike song (starting at m. 212), in which the interval of the fourth is emphasized.

Wozzeck's mounting anxiety at the end of the scene is musically depicted in the ascending and descending glissandos of the strings and trombones, and later in the *crescendo-accelerando* string passages, played tremolo and *sul ponticello.*

Band music heralds the next scene. A descending bugle call brings Mahler to mind, while the divided, muted strings have a Debussyan touch. Soon a military band emerges in full strength. Marie, after a brief but unpleasant argument with a neighbor, slams the window and sings a tender lullaby to her child. The melody (Ex. 12/7) is accompanied by sustained chords:

EX. 12/7 Act I, Scene 3, mm. 380–383

The open fifths appearing in measures 425–426 (Ex. 12/8) remain associated with Marie; according to the composer, these hollow chords express her purposeless and indefinable attitude of waiting which finds its final solution in death.

The fourth scene is cast in the form of a passacaglia; this "learned" form is probably a gesture to the Army Doctor, a theoretician himself, who dominates the scene. The passacaglia theme is made up of a series of twelve different pitches, a procedure also observed in one of the "Altenberg" songs. The development of the theme in twenty-one varia-

EX. 12/8 Act I, Scene 3, mm. 425–426

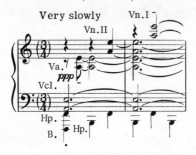

tions (mm. 496–642) anticipates Schoenberg's method which was formulated several years later. The passacaglia theme is presented by the clarinet in Example 12/9/a; Example 12/9/b is one of its variants in which the pitches are used vertically as well as horizontally and in which octave displacement occurs.

EX. 12/9/a Act I, Scene 5, mm. 486–487

EX. 12/9/b Act I, Scene 5, m. 537

In Variation 7 permutation (changing of the order of the pitches) occurs—a device not used by Schoenberg until later—with a retrograde version of the set.

The final scene opens, *andante affetuoso,* with a sustained melody that will recur in the Interlude of Act III (at m. 352). The motive of the seduction at measure 700 (Ex. 12/10), intoned by trumpets and horns, has future implications, too.

EX. 12/10 Act I, Scene 5, m. 700

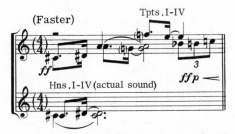

The climax of the scene (mm. 708-709) that culminates with Marie's yielding to the Drum Major ("Have your way then, it's all the same") has a truly Straussian ring.

Act II   The five scenes of this act are organized along the lines of a five-movement symphony. The first scene is cast in sonata form; three thematic groups can be identified in the exposition:

a) a tender Mahleresque melody in the strings, as Marie examines the jewelry received from the Drum Major (Ex. 12/11):

EX. 12/11 Act II, Scene 1, mm. 7-12

b) Marie's line at measures 43–46:

EX. 12/12 Act II, Scene 1, mm. 43–46

c) A closing group, signifying the fear of Marie's child:

EX. 12/13 Act II, Scene 1, mm. 55–56

Next the exposition is repeated (mm. 60–96), recomposed, and condensed: the closing theme is treated canonically by the trombones (mm. 93–96).

The development begins when Wozzeck suddenly appears and discovers Marie's jewelry. The ensuing dramatic confrontation with Marie is signified by the musical juxtaposition of the thematic material. The development reaches its climax with the motto theme of "Wir arme Leut," a modified version of Example 12/5.

EX. 12/14 Act II, Scene 1, mm. 113–114

Over a held C major chord Wozzeck gives money to Marie. According to the composer's explanation, the C major chord is best suited to express the "objectivity of money."[16] The use of tonality at this point corroborates the theory that "normality" in *Wozzeck* is associated with tonality.

After Wozzeck's exit, the recapitulation begins; there is a hint at the tenderness of the opening exposition and later the woodwinds, at measures 141–142, take up the violin figure (mm. 19–20) from the ex-

[16]Such "objectivity" was also associated with C major in Stravinsky's *Oedipus Rex* (see Ex. 9/20).

position. The closing theme appears in a *stretto* (starting at m. 162) in a much faster tempo.

The next scene, cast in the form of a fantasy and fugue, is built on three motives, all used in earlier scenes and distributed among Wozzeck and his tormenters, the Captain and the Doctor. Limitations of space rule out an analysis of this extremely complex, contrapuntal scene. Therefore, only the theme is quoted in its first appearance at measure 171. Later this theme (Ex. 12/15/a) becomes the subject of the figure and one of its rhythmic transformations (Ex. 12/15/b).

EX. 12/15/a Act II, Scene 2, mm. 171-172

EX. 12/15/b Act II, Scene 2, m. 326. (Note the octave displacement in the high A of the violin part.)

The following scene, *Largo*, corresponds to the slow movement of a symphony; it opens with a chamber ensemble (at this point Berg pays homage to his former teacher by using the same group of instruments as Schoenberg did in his Chamber Symphony) which is later joined by the rest of the orchestra. In this scene Wozzeck openly expresses his jealousy; the cellos and basses sound the motive of the child's fear (Ex. 12/13), marked *molto agitato,* as Wozzeck raises his hand threatening Marie. The fear motive fades away during her ominous words: "Better a knife blade in my heart than to lay a hand on me." Wozzeck's reply, "Man is an abyss; it's giddy looking into his inner depth," is accompanied by rising and falling orchestral glissandos and ascending and descending flute-viola passages, which suggest both the dizziness and the abyss.

The structure of the following extended scherzo section (mm. 406-735)—the music of the tavern scene—is nebulous even in the composer's analysis. Willi Reich,[17] who leans heavily on Berg's analysis,

[17]Willi Reich, "A Guide to *Wozzeck," Musical Quarterly,* **38**, No. 1 (1952).

sees the form as a scherzo with two trios (A-B-A-C-A) such as is often found in Schumann's symphonies. The music seems, however, to follow an A-B-C-D-A_1-B_1-C_1 organization as outlined below:

Outline of the Scherzo

A	Ländler	(mm. 402–441)	D (mm. 560–591)	A_1	Ländler (mm. 592–604)
B	Song	(mm. 442–480)	Hunting song	B_1	Song (mm. 605–660)
C	Waltz	(mm. 481–560)		C_1	Waltz (mm. 651–735)

The sections bearing the same letter names are considerably altered when they appear for the second time. Thus A is purely instrumental, whereas in A_1 the instruments accompany a dialogue between Wozzeck and Andres; B, the song of the two apprentices, is even more radically changed in B_1, where the basic harmonies of B are split and utilized in sustained notes for a chorale melody. This forms the basis for the section called "melodrame," a parody of a sermon. The waltz section (C) receives an extended symphonic treatment in C_1. The choral middle section (D) owes its coarse humor to the clash of voices. The six vocal soloists all start on C, but they all finish on different pitches, as a result of which C, D, E, F, G, and A are sounded together.

The harmonic scheme of this scene is different from any other in the opera; perhaps to suggest the folk character of the village tavern

EX. 12/16 Act II, Scene 4, mm. 561–562

tonal expectations are built up. These, however, remain unresolved or are unexpectedly turned into bitonal clusters. Along with the clashing tonalities the sonorities of the tavern band and the regular orchestra rub against each other. A touch of realism is added to the sound of the band by the fact that some of the violins are instructed to tune a quarter of a tone higher (from m. 654), resulting in an imitation of the out-of-tune playing of country fiddlers. The whole scene is marvelously animated, although not without an undertone of eeriness as Wozzeck watches impassively.

The dance music suddenly comes to a halt, and as the scene changes to the barracks, the chorus of snoring soldiers is heard through the lowered curtain. Soon the finale, the *rondo marciale,* is introduced; the Drum Major subdues Wozzeck after a fight as the seduction theme (Ex. 12/11) from the previous act is sounded.

Act III   In this act the form-generating principles are similar to those employed in Act I. While in the earlier act cohesion was achieved by a set of character pieces in each scene, here variational treatment of one musical element—be it a theme, a tone, or a chord—furnishes the framework for unity. Although in his analysis the composer merely refers to "variational treatment of musical elements," both Willi Reich and Redlich in their analyses employ the term invention instead.

The first scene, in which Marie reads from the Bible, is based on the invention of a theme (Ex. 12/17).

EX. 12/17 Act III, Scene 1, mm. 3–5

Seven short variations follow in which soft strings play a dominant part. The key of F minor, clearly established in Variation 5 (mm. 33–39), gives a poignant touch to the words: "And once there was a poor wee child and he had no father nor any mother." The variations are followed by a fugue built on two themes (Ex. 12/18/a and b), each consisting of seven tones:

EX. 12/18/a Act III, Scene 1, m. 54

EX. 12/18/b Act III, Scene 1, mm. 57–58

Hei - land! __ ich möch-te Dir die ...

As the curtain falls at the end of the scene, the two themes appear superimposed in the strings.

EX. 12/19 Act III, Scene 1, m. 63

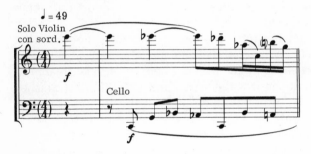

Later the superimposition occurs in an orchestral *tutti* which suddenly softens, ushering in Scene 2.

In the bass a low B, the subject of invention in this scene, appears. With the first appearance of the low B, a highly original sound combination, made up of harp-celesta figurations in contrary motion (m. 71), suggests the watery texture of the pond. While Wozzeck and Marie carry on their ominous conversation, the B is ubiquitous, appearing in different registers and colors. In Examples 12/20/a, b, and c three different "inventions" of the one tone can be observed.

EX. 12/20/a Act III, Scene 2, m. 83

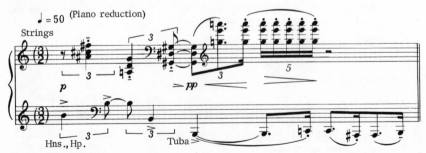

EX. 12/20/b m. 91

EX. 12/20/c m. 97

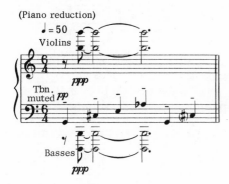

The whole scene is rich in tone painting; when Wozzeck, noticing Marie's uneasiness, asks her "Was zitterst," a quivering sound is heard from the orchestra, produced by the harp, celesta, and xylophone. In measure 97, the rise of the moon is depicted in an ascending figure played by four muted trombones, while the B is held in the strings spread in the range of five octaves.

Soon *pianissimo* drum beats are intoned on B, mounting to *fortissimo* as Wozzeck stabs Marie. As the curtain falls, the famous climax on B occurs; starting with a *pppp* of the muted horn, the instruments enter, one by one, rising to a *triple forte*. The single entrances cannot be perceived; all that is heard is a giant swell to a cataclysmic climax. Following this, the solo bass drum is heard at measure 114 providing the rhythmic pattern (Ex. 12/21) that will become the subject of the invention in the next scene.

EX. 12/21 Act III, Scene 2, mm. 114–115

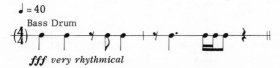

The third scene is set in a cheap tavern; a mistuned piano grinds out a polka tune (Ex. 12/22), insisting on the rhythm quoted in Example 12/21.

EX. 12/22 Act III, Scene 3, mm. 122–125

As the rhythmic pattern undergoes further changes, Margaret, the barmaid whom Wozzeck befriended, sings a ditty in folk style. Wozzeck is aroused, but Margaret's question about the blood on his sleeve, based on a new variant of the rhythmic pattern (Ex. 12/23), sobers him.

EX. 12/23 Act III, Scene 3, m. 185

When Wozzeck, under the pressure of questioning rushes out and heads for the pond, the rhythmic figure is used as a transition to Scene 4.

This scene is based on a six-tone chord (Ex. 12/24) that appears in measure 219.

EX. 12/24 Act III, Scene 4, m. 219

The entire scene is based on material derived from this chord. When Wozzeck is overcome by hallucinations, the chord appears in various registers, inversions, and segmentations. His drowning is also accompanied by the chord, held by six solo strings. This forms the bridge to an extended orchestral interlude in D minor. The meaning of the interlude is stated by the composer as follows:

> This [the interlude] should be understood from the dramatist's point of view as the Epilogue which follows Wozzeck's suicide; it should also be appreciated as the composer's confession, breaking through the framework of the dramatic plot and, likewise, even as an appeal to the audience, which is here meant to represent Humanity itself. From the musician's point of view this last orchestral interlude represents a thematic development section, utilizing all the important musical characters related to Wozzeck.[18]

The last scene is described by the composer as a *perpetuum mobile* (perpetual motion) because of the persistent triplet figure. The playing of the children is accompanied by the singing of a nursery rhyme. Their singing is casual, as suggested by the distortion of perfect fourths into diminished fourths. While the children are leaving, the curtain falls slowly; the flutes and the celesta maintain the triplets, as the strings gradually fade out on the G–D chord. The feeling generated is one of inconclusiveness, suggesting that life continues in spite of its tragedies.

WORKS AFTER *WOZZECK*

The chronology of Berg's works manifests the slow and painstaking pace of his creative productivity; only five major works appear on the list in the fourteen-year period following *Wozzeck*. Each of these works reflects the two seemingly contradictory traits of Berg's style: a firm tie to the expressiveness of the romantic past, and, at the same time, an original and bold application of Schoenberg's innovations. Thus, Berg in the process of reconciling the new style with the past also opened up unsuspected possibilities for the new idiom.

The Chamber Concerto for violin, piano, and thirteen wind instruments (1924–1925), dedicated to Schoenberg on his fiftieth birthday, is Berg's least accessible work. Written in the period when the composer was assimilating Schoenberg's serial technique, the work lacks the spontaneity and warmth otherwise so characteristic of Berg. Perhaps

---

[18] *Alban Berg*, p. 284.

the intellectual effort expended in gaining mastery over the new idiom cost the composer some loss in emotional freedom, an occurrence also observed in Schoenberg's first twelve-tone works. Neither did the application of musical anagrams, subjecting the names of Schoenberg, Berg, and Webern to musical motto themes, contribute to the spontaneity of the work.

The concerto opens with a motto epigraph in which the names of the three composers are welded together (Ex. 12/25); the three motives of the theme play an important part in the composition. The motto-theme, according to the instruction in the score, *must* be played, but *must* not be conducted.

EX. 12/25 *Chamber Concerto*[19] for violin, piano, and thirteen wind instruments, opening motto theme

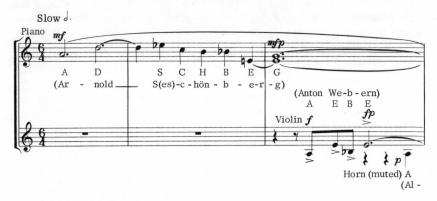

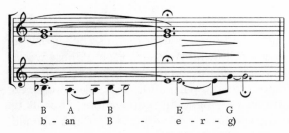

The number three is used recurrently by Berg in the design of the work. In a letter to Schoenberg, Berg refers in a somewhat mystical way to the establishment of a *Trinity of Events* in the motto theme, alluding to the proverb that "all good things come in threes." The composition is divided into three movements: I. *Thema scherzoso con variazioni;* II. *Adagio;* III. *Rondo ritmico.* Also, three types of instrumental

[19] Copyright by Universal Edition, Vienna. Used by permission.

sonorities (keyboard, string, and wind) are used. In the first movement the piano is featured as the solo instrument, in the second movement the violin, while in the last movement the two soloists and the winds join forces. The solo piano and violin, together with the thirteen wind instruments, make up a group of fifteen players, a number to which Berg refers as "sacred" because of the fifteen instruments Schoenberg employed in his First Chamber Symphony. There are additional allusions to the number three in the structural plan: thus, the variation theme is composed of thirty measures, divided into three sections; the slow movement is in three-part form and employs three combinations in its unification of the first two movements.

The thematic subjects, based on the letter association, can be considered "basic sets" without establishing full-fledged twelve-tone rows. Redlich, in his detailed analysis of the work, considers the notes which describe Schoenberg's name an eight-tone set.

EX. 12/26 Eight-tone set based on Schoenberg's name

The texture of the work is strongly contrapuntal and abounds in canonic imitations, inversions, and their retrogressions, all hallmarks of the twelve-tone style.

The slow movement stands out with its lovely sonorities, reminiscent of the world of postromantic composers.

In the last movement the motivic use of rhythm, anticipated in *Wozzeck,* is a novel feature. Such salient rhythmic patterns are marked *HR* (*Haupt-Ritmus,* meaning principal rhythm) in the score.

The Chamber Concerto was followed by a song, "Schliesse mir die Augen beide," based on Theodore Storm's verse. What lends particular interest to this song is the fact that twenty-five years earlier the composer wrote a setting to the same text. The occasion for which this poem was reset was the twenty-fifth anniversary of Universal Edition, a music publishing house in Vienna; both songs were dedicated to its director, Emil Hertzka. The whole incident points to Berg's historical sense and to his consciousness of both the old and the new.

The first setting is close to the nineteenth-century tradition of the Lied, whereas the later version is in twelve-tone style. The second setting of the song also establishes a link to Berg's next major work, *The Lyric Suite* (1925–1926) for string quartet, inasmuch as both works are based on the same tone row. The tone row and its application in the opening of both the song and the quartet are shown in Example 12/27a, b, and c.

EX. 12/27/a Prime set of *"Schliesse mir die Augen beide"* and the *Lyric Suite*

EX. 12/27/b *"Schliesse mir die Augen beide,"*[20] opening

EX. 12/27/c *Lyric Suite,*[21] first movement, mm. 2–4

The six movements of the quartet are the following:

I. Allegro Gioviale

II. Andante Amoroso

III. Allegro Misterioso

Trio Estatico

IV. Adagio Appassionato

V. Presto Delirando

Tenebroso

VI. Largo Desolato

The tempo indications take two directions: one consists of the obvious acceleration of the fast movements and the other of the decreasing speed of the slow movements. The qualifying adjectives of the tempo indications (*Gioviale–Amoroso–Misterioso–Estatico–Appassionato–Deli-*

---

rando–Desolato) suggest a program, a sequence of highly charged emotional experiences.

The *Lyric Suite* is one of the outstanding works of contemporary chamber music literature. With its well-defined moods it has a more direct appeal than the Chamber Concerto. The four parts of the quartet are perfectly equalized, producing the full gamut of twentieth-century quartet sonorities. Undoubtedly, Bartók, in his Fourth Quartet written a few years later, was affected by the sonorous world of Berg's *Lyric Suite;* the rushing, *pianissimo, sul ponticello* passages of the *Allegro misterioso* particularly seem to be echoed in the *prestissimo* movement of the Bartók work.

It should be noted that although Berg had complete mastery of the twelve-tone technique by this time, he applied the method only to some movements, composing others in free atonal style. In fact, the twelve-tone and the free atonal movements appear in the following carefully weighed balance: two movements (the first and sixth) are entirely serial, balanced by two (the second and fourth) free atonal movements. The third and fifth movements combine the two styles in a symmetrical manner; the twelve-tone A part of the tripartite third movement and the twelve-tone B part of the similarly tripartite fifth movement are counterbalanced by complementary nonserial sections. Thus, the work represents another feat of reconciliation: it shows that serial organization and free atonality can coexist in the same composition, even in the same movement. A link with the past is established in the quotation from the Prelude of Wagner's *Tristan* in measures 26–27 of the last movement.

Berg's next work, *Der Wein,* a concert aria for soprano and orchestra, shows even greater liberalization of the serial style. Set to Baudelaire's poetry as translated by Stefan George, the work has a strong tonal orientation, determined by a tone row (Ex. 12/28) whose first six notes represent a rising harmonic D minor scale.

EX. 12/28 Prime set of *Der Wein*

Another interesting feature of the work is the incorporation of the jazz idiom that occurs in the tango section where an alto saxophone accompanied by banjolike string pizzicatos assumes prominence. The jazz idiom also appears in Berg's unfinished opera, *Lulu.*

Berg's last completed work is the Violin Concerto (1935), one of his most moving compositions. Commissioned by the American violinist, Louis Krasner, it was dedicated to the "memory of an Angel," a reference to the sudden and untimely death of Manon Gropius, the beautiful eighteen-year-old daughter of Alma Mahler.

The work summarizes Berg's achievements. First among these was his ability to write deeply expressive lyrical music in serial style, thus contradicting those who consider the serial style as inherently "cerebral." The tone row of the work (Ex. 12/29) with its latent triads points to the composer's endeavor to write serial music with strong tonal implications.

Another contribution of Berg is the introduction of folk elements into the serial style; the Austrian folk flavor is felt in the Carinthian folk song, and in the *Wienerisch* (Viennese) and *rustico* sections.

**PLATE 19. BERG
IN THE LAST YEAR
OF HIS LIFE, 1935**
Bettmann Archive,
New York

EX. 12/29 Prime set of the *Violin Concerto*

Berg's fondness for musical quotations can be seen in the employment of Bach's chorale melody "Es ist genug" in the second movement. The chorale melody, ingeniously embedded in the basic set, underlines the requiemlike character of the work.

The solo part, although often set in the very high range of the instrument, presents less formidable difficulties for the soloist than the Schoenberg Violin Concerto. The orchestral accompaniment has a rich contrapuntal fabric, without endangering the clarity of the solo violin. For these reasons and for its poignant beauty, the concerto is assured a permanent place in the repertory.

Berg spent the last seven years of his life—apart from his work on the Violin Concerto—on *Lulu*, an opera based on two plays, *Earth Spirit* (1893) and *Pandora's Box* (1901), by the German dramatist, Wedekind (1864–1918). Although the opera is still relatively unknown—except for performances of orchestral excerpts entitled *Lulu Suite* and isolated stage performances (thus far performed only in Boston, New York, and Santa Fe, N.M., in the United States)—it is surrounded by a good deal of controversy.

One aspect of the controversy concerns the completion of the work. In 1936, one year after the composer's death, Universal Edition in Vienna published the first two acts of the opera in a vocal score arranged by Erwin Stein, a former student of Schoenberg. In the preface to this publication it was announced that Berg had completed the opera—save the scoring of the third act—and that the publication of the vocal score of that act was forthcoming. Political events, however, interrupted the engraving of the third act. On the basis of the surviving short score of the opera, both biographers of Berg—Willi Reich and Redlich—believed that the opera could be completed by a musician who was well acquainted with *Lulu* and with Berg's method of orchestration.

However, the task of completion was not attempted by anyone until 1939, when George Perle, the noted American composer and musicologist, took an interest in the matter. After an intensive study of a photostat of Berg's manuscript, he concluded that the work could be finished without great difficulty and offered to do so. He encountered curious resistance, however, and procrastination on the part of the publisher, who remained unaffected even by Stravinsky's intervention in behalf of the project.

The second aspect of the controversy centers on the music itself. Willi Reich's first analysis of the work,[22] authorized and approved by the composer, was accepted as an authoritative interpretation of *Lulu*. Every subsequent discussion of the opera with the exception of that of Redlich—quotes, paraphrases, or simply reiterates Reich's analysis. It was again Perle, who challenged the validity of the earlier source, claiming that 1) Reich's analysis was almost totally irrelevant to the actual music, and 2) that the analysis was based on the entirely unsound assumption that *one* single row explains the logic and unity of the work.

It would be entirely beyond the scope of this book to assemble the musical details of the opposing views. It seems, though, that Perle's analysis and criticism are borne out by the musical facts. If so, one would have to conclude that often the composer himself is not the best commentator on his own music. The question also arises whether Berg approved the theory of a single set governing the entire work in order not to challenge Schoenberg's tenets, which postulate *one* set for a composition.

Be that as it may, the serial organization of *Lulu* is unorthodox indeed. Not only are there three different basic rows used, but as Perle's analysis points out, the over-all harmonic textures are often not determined by set operations. Moreover, segmentations are used in which the pitch *content* is maintained but the *order* is altered, not unlike those found in Hauer's tropes.

A comparison with *Wozzeck* reveals more differences than similarities on both the dramatic and musical planes. While in *Wozzeck* Berg selected fifteen scenes from Büchner's fragmentary play, in *Lulu* he welded two of Wedekind's plays, both dealing with Lulu, into one; a total of seven acts were condensed into three. In the process of this telescoping, Berg cut out four-fifths of Wedekind's material, a more drastic literary operation than was carried out in the adaptation of *Wozzeck*. Perhaps because of this large scale revision and Büchner's superiority as a writer as compared to Wedekind, *Lulu* is less successful than *Wozzeck* in its dramatic impact.

Redlich considers *Lulu* an opera of social protest and compassion; the social criticism in *Lulu,* however, is of a less universal nature than in the earlier work and is aimed at one particular cultural group. Wedekind castigates the materialistic outlook, the sexual cynicism, and the debased values of the upperclass society in Central Europe at the turn of the century. By comparison, Wozzeck's theme, the misery of the poor, is more universal than *Lulu's,* the destructive, fateful woman. Redlich's comparison of Lulu's character to Goethe's Faust seems grossly exaggerated. Lulu's social climbing, her sexual drive, and her destructive

[22] Willi Reich, *Alban Berg* (New York: Harcourt, Brace & World, Inc., 1965), pp. 156–177.

nature re-enact the archetype of the "femme fatale," lacking, however, the basic human dilemma embodied in Faust's duality.

Dramatically *Lulu* is more limited than *Wozzeck,* yet its music surpasses that of the earlier work in originality, richness, and diversity. *Lulu* has a more distinctively vocal style than *Wozzeck;* this is apparent from the more singable vocal lines often written in coloratura style, and also from the titles given to some of the sections, such as Cavatina, Duettino, Aria. In a completely novel way Berg succeeded in integrating these vocal, quasi-set operatic numbers within a larger framework, based on organizational principles governing instrumental music. Thus, a sonata exposition, development, and recapitulation unify the second and third scenes of Act I, and a rondo binds together the first two scenes of Act II.

The harmonic style of *Lulu* is more varied than that of *Wozzeck.* Compared to the overwhelmingly atonal style of *Wozzeck, Lulu* has a variety of harmonic textures: tonal, based on triadic harmonies, atonal, bitonal, and twelve-tone with tonal suggestions.

Despite its larger scope, *Lulu* is scored for a smaller orchestra than *Wozzeck.* Two instruments, the saxophone and the vibraphone—neither of them used in the earlier opera—give a distinctive sonority to many sections of *Lulu.* Also the piano is used more extensively than in *Wozzeck.*

In *Lulu* the influence of Wagner and Mahler is no longer distinctly felt. Perhaps because of the cosmopolitan setting (scenes take place in Germany, Paris, and Rome) the Austrian folk element hardly makes itself felt; instead, the popular element is represented by a jazz band whose sonorities occasionally intermingle with those of the regular orchestra.

Interestingly enough, both Schoenberg's *Moses und Aron* and Berg's *Lulu,* the two most significant dramatic compositions of these composers, were left unfinished.

SUMMARY

Berg's role as a mediator between the Schoenberg innovations and the romantic outlook of the nineteenth century has been generally recognized. Frequently atonal music from the pen of Berg produces highly evocative moods, and twelve-tone music can sound lyrical and spontaneous, qualities rarely ascribed to the music of Schoenberg. The outstanding success of *Wozzeck* proves atonal music can be made palatable to the average listener.

Paradoxically, however, in his role as a mediator, Berg was an innovator himself. He was the first to see that tonal and atonal music were not irreconcilable. In *Wozzeck* tonal and atonal sections are juxtaposed, creating highly effective dramatic contrasts.

Berg also opened many new avenues of thinking in his employment of the twelve-tone method. He was not afraid to change the order of the row to suit his expressive purposes. Furthermore, he saw no reason why one stratum of a musical texture could not be derived from other sources than the row, as seen in some of the harmonies in *Lulu.* The most novel aspect of his row construction lies in his choice of intervals. By using the intervals of a scale or those of triads, he derived melodic and harmonic material that was closely linked to the past, yet governed by entirely new means of organization.

Another contribution attributed to Berg is the assimilation of folk elements into atonal and twelve-tone music, as in *Wozzeck, Lulu,* and the Violin Concerto. As a means of organization, Berg also applied abstract instrumental forms (sonata, rondo, and the like) to his operas.

Another novel feature Berg employed is the entirely new use of a rhythmic theme (HR), thus paving the way for those who later serialized rhythmic values.

The warmth and beauty of Berg's music is enhanced by his highly refined sense of instrumental color: his orchestral sound, often reminiscent of Debussy, is beautifully blended, another vestige of the romantic past.

Future assessment of the position Berg occupies in the history of music may well parallel that of Brahms, who in his time was merely considered a link with the past. Over half a century passed before his progressive role was realized, and perhaps the same discovery will be made about Berg in the future.

CHRONOLOGICAL LIST OF BERG'S WORKS

Sonata for Piano, Op. 1   1907–1908
Four Songs for voice and piano, Op. 2   1909–1910
String Quartet, Op. 3   1910
"Altenberg" Songs, Op. 4   1912
Four Pieces for clarinet and piano, Op. 5   1913
Three Pieces for Orchestra, Op. 6   1914
Wozzeck, opera in three acts, Op. 7   1917–1921
Chamber Concerto for piano, violin, and thirteen wind players   1923–1925
"Schliesse mir die Augen beide" (second setting of T. Storm's poem) for voice and piano   1925
Lyric Suite for string quartet   1926
Der Wein, a concert aria for voice and orchestra   1929
Lulu, opera in three acts (unfinished)   1928–1935
Violin Concerto   1935

ANTON WEBERN
(1883-1945)

All shapes in Nature resemble each other but not two are alike.

GOETHE

While Schoenberg achieved notoriety through scandalized audience reaction, and Berg gained fame through *Wozzeck,* Webern failed to evoke any kind of response. This complete void that more or less remained his share during his entire life is well captured in Eimert's words:

Like strange precious stones from unknown regions they [Webern's works] lay in the ground, not, as it were, ignored or neglected, but simply hidden from view.[1]

Even today, more than twenty years after the composer's death, his music has not reached large concert audiences.

[1] Herbert Eimert, "A Change of Focus," *Die Reihe,* No. **2** (1958), p. 30, edited by Herbert Eimert and Karlheinz Stockhausen. (Vienna: Universal Edition, 1955; Bryn Mawr, Pa.: Theodore Presser Co., 1958).

In sharp contrast to this general neglect, in the years following World War II, a small group of young composers, known as the Darmstadt School, adopted Webern as their spiritual leader. Their enthusiasm is shared by the octogenarian Stravinsky who recently expressed himself in glowing terms about Webern's art. The discrepancy between almost total neglect and the enthusiasm of a very small minority suggests an artist of the most unique disposition. Webern, indeed, was one of the most original figures in the history of music.

LIFE

At the time of this writing there is no biography of Webern available in English. Events of his life are pieced together from the following sources: a brief biographical sketch published in the "Webern Memorial Issue" of Die Reihe;[2] a brief outline of Webern's life, prefacing Kolneder's analytic study of the composer's music;[3] and Webern's letters, particularly his correspondence with an artist couple, Josef Humplik and Hildegard Jone.[4] An interesting source of Webern's esthetic outlook and of his views on the twelve-tone method is a volume entitled Der Weg zur Neuen Musik,[5] a series of lectures delivered by Webern to a lay audience.

Webern was born into a middle class Viennese family in 1883. His father was a mining engineer, who later became a department chief in the Ministry of Agriculture. The young boy received his primary and secondary education in Graz and Klagenfurt. Upon graduation, in 1902, he moved to Vienna to study musicology under Guido Adler, the famed music historian. Four years later Webern earned his doctorate with a dissertation on Henry Isaac's (1450–1517) Choralis Constantinus. Prior to that, he had begun to study composition with Schoenberg. The student-teacher relationship, as in Berg's case, changed into a lifelong friendship. Webern repeatedly expressed great enthusiasm about Schoenberg as a master-teacher and idolized him as a composer. This harmonious relationship is all the more interesting because Schoenberg did not

---

[2] Die Reihe, No. **2,** pp. 1–4.

[3] Walter Kolneder, Anton Webern; Einführung in Werk und Stil (Rodenkirchen/Rhein: Musikverlag P. J. Tonger, 1961).

[4] Anton Webern, correspondence with Hildegard Jone and Josef Humplik, edited by Josef Polnauer (Vienna: Universal Edition, 1959).

[5] Der Weg zur Neuen Musik, edited by Willi Reich (Vienna: Universal Edition, 1960); English translation: The Path to the New Music (Bryn Mawr, Pa.: Theodore Presser Co., 1963).

share Webern's scholarly interest in music; in fact he boasted of never having read a book on the history of music. Also, Webern's professional career followed a different path from that of Schoenberg and Berg; his main pursuit became conducting, whereas Berg never appeared as a conductor, and Schoenberg conducted only his own music.

From 1908 on, Webern held various positions as theater conductor, first in Vienna from 1908–1910, then in Danzig in 1911, followed by engagements in Stettin and Prague.

In the years following World War I Webern, who had served as a volunteer, took over the direction of the Vienna Workers' Symphony and later the Vienna Workers' Choral Union. With these essentially amateur groups he undertook staggering projects, such as the performance of Mahler's Eighth Symphony. In 1927 he was appointed regular conductor of the Austrian Radio and later its advisor on matters pertaining to contemporary music. In the 1930s he conducted abroad extensively.

After 1937 he withdrew from all public activities and his only source of income—barely adequate to support his family—came from private lessons. His music, infrequently performed in previous years, was now banned in Germany along with that of Schoenberg and Berg.

In these difficult years the composer found solace in mountaineering in the Alps. This was more than a hobby; his mystic union with nature was an essential part of his being, as is evident in a letter written to Berg:

> I have been to Hochschwab. It was glorious: because it is not sport to me, nor amusement, but something quite different; a search for the highest, for whatever in nature corresponds to those things on which I would wish to model myself, which I would have within me. And how fruitful my trip was! The deep valleys with their mountain pines and mysterious plants—the latter have the greatest appeal to me. But not because they are so "beautiful." It is not the beautiful landscape, the beautiful flowers in the usual romantic sense that move me. My object is the deep bottomless, inexhaustible meaning in all, and especially these manifestations of nature. I love all nature, but, most of all that which is found in the mountains.
>
> For a start I want to progress in the purely physical knowledge of all these phenomena. This is why I always carry my lexicon of Botany with me and always look for any writings that can help explain all that. This physical reality contains all the miracles. Experimenting, observing in physical nature is the highest metaphysics, theosophy for me. I got to know a plant called "wintergreen." A tiny plant, a little like a lily of the valley, homely, humble, and hardly noticeable. But a scent like balsam! What a scent. For me it contains all the tenderness, emotion, depth, purity.[6]

The letter reveals not only Webern's unusually differentiated perception of nature, but also the subdued, yet almost ecstatic, intense quality of his inner life. The same crystalline purity and quiet exaltation also pervade the composer's music.

To round out the events of Webern's life it should be added that he and his family left Vienna in 1945, as the battle line approached the city, and sought safety in Mittersill, Western Austria. Here, due to a tragic mistake, he was fatally shot by a member of the American occupation forces.[7]

---

[6] Letter to Alban Berg, dated August 1, 1919, *Die Reihe*, No. **2** (1958), p. 17.

[7] Hans Moldenhauer, *The Death of Anton Webern* (New York: Philosophical Library, Inc., 1962).

WEBERN'S MUSIC AND THE LISTENER

Webern's music presents a curious paradox: it has been analyzed in greater detail than that of any contemporary composer, yet to the majority of listeners it remains as inaccessible as ever. A glance at the customary analyses of Webern's music explains why these efforts remained unfruitful. It seems as if the brevity of the composer's works would cause his commentators to use a special method of approach that seeks to justify each and every note by showing to which set (inverted, transposed, etc.) it owes its place and existence. It goes without saying that such a mechanical approach, that has been likened to the counting of the "ands" and "buts" in the Bible—neither explains the musical thought process or the beauty of the music. Of little help also are the statistical tabulations and charts ascribing a serial plan to certain musical occurrences which were invented intuitively. The fact that even Webern's early music is received with bafflement more than half a century later suggests that his style demands a new perceptual approach or, in other words, the listener's reorientation.

At first, one of the most puzzling aspects of Webern's compositions seems to be their extreme brevity; the playing time of a movement often does not exceed one minute. It would be misleading, however, to stress the brevity of the music as causing the listener's puzzlement; the problem lies in the unprecedented *concentration of the musical thought.* Although we have no way of measuring the concentration of musical thought, it is obvious that it may move within a wide range. Incidental music, for instance, such as film music, will take a less concentrated form of expression than a self-contained composition, say, a symphony. Likewise, the musical thought is less concentrated in a Wagnerian opera than in a Beethoven string quartet, the purpose of the music being different in both cases. Obviously, a different kind of concentration will be demanded from the listener in the two examples. In thinking of the spectrum of concentration of musical thought, Webern's music falls at that end of the continuum that represents the highest degree of concentration. In his music *one tone* may assume the meaning of a musical period in another composer's work. The listener, of course, must mobilize his utmost concentration if he is to follow the musical discourse. Schoenberg, anticipating the listener's bewilderment about this particular point, wrote the following preface to Webern's *Bagatelles* for string quartet:

> Though the brevity of these pieces is a persuasive advocate for them, on the other hand, that very brevity itself requires an advocate.

Consider what moderation is required to express oneself so briefly. You can stretch every glance out into a poem, every sigh into a novel. But to express a novel in a single gesture, a joy in a breath—such concentration can only be present in proportion to the absence of self-pity.

These pieces will only be understood by those who share the faith that music can say things which can only be expressed by music . . .

Does the musician know how to play these pieces, does the listener know how to receive them? Can faithful musicians and listeners fail to surrender themselves to one another?

But what shall we do with the heathen? Fire and sword can keep them down; only believers need to be restrained. May this silence sound for them.[8]

Even though Schoenberg's language is somewhat effusive, the warning is clear: the listener must alert himself to a more concentrated form of musical speech than he encountered previously.

In terms of over-all expressiveness Webern's music is void of any nineteenth-century romanticism; we do not find Wagner's ghost hovering over his early works as was seen in the case of Schoenberg and Berg. Already in Webern's first published work, in the *Passacaglia* for orchestra, the unique qualities of his later music are felt. It is a universe of its own where calm and purity reign.

Webern's music cannot be readily sung or whistled; it has been called athematic—one commentator called it pulverized—because of its fragmentary nature. Although the music is devoid of melody or themes in the usual sense, it has a horizontal continuity achieved by the device of *Klangfarbenmelodie*. In terms of perceptual demands, in earlier music the listener had to correctly grasp the ordering of pitches and duration that conveyed the feeling of a whole that was more than the sum of its parts. In Webern's music the Gestalt quality of a phrase depends as much, or even more, on the recognition of timbre differences, as it depends on the recognition of pitch and durational differences. In this context the *single note* assumes a new meaning and the connection from note to note is more tenuous. For this reason, Webern's music demands an even more active participation on the listener's part than does the music of Schoenberg and Berg, whose rhetoric is closer to earlier musical tradition. The one composer in whose music the significance of the timbre of the fragmented phrase is anticipated is Debussy.

The French composer has another point in common with Webern in the importance attached to pauses. Reference has been made in Chapter 8 to Debussy's pauses, so fraught with expectation. In Webern's music the rests form an even more substantive part of the musical pattern. The function of the pause is not that of a *rest* as used in common

---

[8] Arnold Schoenberg, *Preface*, published in the score of Webern's *Bagatelles* for Quartet, Op. 9.

musical practice; the pause in Webern's music has a functional significance in the rhythmic scheme. There is in Webern's music a new relation between *sound* and *no sound*. Rhythm, in general, along with
dynamics, accentuations, and sonorities are not mere accessories to the
melodic-harmonic fabric, but structural ends in themselves. This novel
use of the elements of music represents the link between Webern and
those avant-garde composers who used rhythm, dynamics, and sonorities
as *parameters* for serial procedures (see Chapter 7).

The subtle use of timbre and rests will be lost on the listener who
approaches Webern's music through recordings. In such presentations
the *Klangfarbenmelodie* will be lost and, instead of the pauses, the
listener will become aware of the surface noise caused by the needle.

Although Webern was greatly concerned in his theoretical writings
with the problem of comprehensibility (*Fasslichkeit*), the architecture
of his music is not easy to grasp. His music seldom falls into clearly
delineated sections and literal repetitions are even more infrequent.
Instead, Webern pursues the principle of perpetual variation, that is, he
presents the same material, but always in a new way. Schoenberg also
adhered to this principle, but because his phrases had more discernible
melodic contours, the application of the principle is less difficult to
grasp. It is easier to perceive the music of Schoenberg and Berg through
the hierarchic relationship between the musical lines, suggested in the
score by such indications as *Hauptstimme* (main voice) and *Neben-
stimme* (secondary voice). The presence of main voice and secondary
voice, to which subordinate accompanying lines are added, definitely
points to a figure-background relationship which decidedly helps to order the listener's experience. Webern's music is not governed by such
principles; in the pulverized texture the single lines do not stand in any
hierarchic relationship.

Harmonically, too, Webern's style is more uncompromising than that
of Schoenberg or Berg; it does not give even those faint tonal suggestions that can be found in Schoenberg and much more so in the works
of Berg. The lack of tonal orientation, of course, is another item that
makes Webern's music difficult to approach.

To the perceptual difficulties of the composer's music, the intricacies of contrapuntal devices should be added. One of Webern's
favorite devices is the canon: unlike Schoenberg who often subjected
a theme to canonic treatment, Webern usually selects a nucleus of
two or three notes, often treating them in mirror or crab canons. Frequently, the crossing of the voices makes it impossible to follow the
canon clearly. Perhaps the canon is not meant to be followed; nevertheless, one should be conscious of how the small nucleus of notes
undergoes subtle changes, much like the multicolored crystals change

in a kaleidoscope. Whether or not the canon is perceived by the listener, it surely constitutes the most concentrated means of emphasizing coherence (*Zusammenhang*), a principle highly valued by Webern.

The beauty of Webern's music is hard to describe; it transcends the logic and perfection of its order. There is a tender and pure spirit that pervades the strictest organizational means. Perhaps an understanding of the man—ascetic yet passionate—and of his view of music as a manifestation of nature, will bring the listener closer to the essence of his work than an analysis of set operations.

WEBERN'S MUSIC

Webern's oeuvre contains thirty-one numbered works; for the purposes of examination they will be divided into two groups: the pre-twelve-tone works (Op. 1–Op. 16) and the twelve-tone works (Op. 17–Op. 31). With the exception of the *Passacaglia*, all works in the first group are short instrumental pieces or songs, while those in the second group based on twelve-tone organization are more extended.

WORKS FROM OPUS 1 TO OPUS 16

Like Berg, Webern adhered to tonal writing only in his first two compositions; these are the *Passacaglia* for orchestra, Op. 1 (1908), and "Entflieht auf leichten Kähnen," Op. 2 (1908), an a *cappella* choral work based on a poem by Stefan George.

These two works anticipate many features of Webern's later style. Thus, the *Passacaglia* foreshadows his generally polyphonic orientation and his adherence to the principle of perpetual variation. A passacaglia is after all—to use the composer words—"always the same and always different." Also, the preference for soft dynamics, found in both early works, will remain a permanent feature of the composer's style. The use of frequent rests in the *Passacaglia* points to one of the most unique characteristics of Webern's style, for which he was called the "master of silence." Furthermore, the *Passacaglia* theme (Ex. 13/1), composed of single notes rather than a continuous melody, can be looked upon as foreshadowing the composer's later turn to athematic writing. Inversion, another favorite device, can also be observed in the theme; the fourth, fifth, and the sixth notes constitute an inversion of the first three notes.

EX. 13/1 WEBERN, *Passacaglia*, Op. 1,[9] opening (partial score)

(Viola & Cello double in lower octave)

The use of canon is also found in the Op. 2 work, whose brevity
establishes once and for all the composer's condensation of musical
thought.

In the next two works, Songs, Op. 3 and 4 (1909), based on the
poetry of Stefan George, the composer abandons tonality. The influence of Schoenberg's Songs, Op. 15,[10] is felt; Webern's athematic
writing with the structural use of small cells gives these songs an even
bolder physiognomy than those of his teacher. The songs also show a
definite preference for the interval of the minor second and its spatially
expanded derivatives, the major seventh and the minor ninth. In Example 13/2 the transformations of the minor second are shown, as
well as how octave equivalence can bring about even larger constructions.

EX. 13/2 Interval class of the minor second

These intervals, which remain the most frequently used intervals in
the composer's music, are not employed with melodic or thematic
continuity but seem to form self-contained horizontal and vertical
entities. They play a significant role both in the architectural plan of a
single movement and in the subtle tension pattern, laid out with carefully planned gradations (for example, slight dynamic changes, changes
in articulation, and the like). Here the minor second is totally divested
of its tonal implications; it is used in an altogether different manner
from Schoenberg's "as if" (see p. 293) leading tones. As expressed by
Pousseur,[11] a specialist in Webern's music, "Webern breathes a new

[9] Copyright by Universal Edition, Vienna. Used by permission.
[10] See Chapter 11.
[11] *Die Reihe*, pp. 51–60.

spirit into chromaticism" purifying it of all Wagnerian and post-Wagnerian chromatic harmony, as if he had restored its "primal innocence." It is exactly this firm interval consciousness of Webern's earlier music that will make his transition to the twelve-tone idiom a smooth one. As will be seen, the interval of the minor second is used far more often in his tone rows than any other interval.

To demonstrate the significance of the interval class of the minor second [12] in the early songs, the last three measures of No. 3 of the Songs, Op. 3, are shown in Example 13/3:

EX. 13/3 *Song,* Op. 3, No. 3,[13] last three measures. (The brackets
indicate the interval class of the minor second.)

A unique expressive quality is gained by keeping these chords, fraught with tension potential, at a *pianissimo* level. Eimert[14] speaks of the "lyric geometry" of Webern's free floating, yet tightly braced system.

In the Op. 4 songs wide melodic leaps, another trait of Webern's music, appear (Ex. 13/4):

EX. 13/4 *Song,* Op. 4, No. 3,[15] mm. 9–10

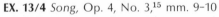

[12] The term *interval class of the minor second* will be used when referring to the mentioned intervals.
[13] Copyright by Universal Edition, Vienna. Used by permission.
[14] *Die Reihe,* p. 34.
[15] Copyright by Universal Edition, Vienna. Used by permission.

Triplet figures, another typical trait of Webern's later music, also establish themselves in these songs.

In the *Five Movements,* Op. 5 (1900), and the *Six Bagatelles,* Op. 9 (1913), both for string quartet, the sound value of the string instruments adds a new dimension to the subtle expressiveness of the songs. In these extremely short pieces (see Schoenberg's note on page 357) the chromatic relationships are enhanced by the imaginative use of *Klangfarbenmelodie*. Chromatic notes are linked in various registers by an ever-changing color chain created by the use of harmonics, pizzicato, *col legno, sul ponticello, sul tasto,* and other effects. Example 13/5 demonstrates an instance from the first movement of Op. 5 in which five-fold chromatic tensions appear simultaneously.

EX. 13/5 Op. 5, No. 1,[16] m. 5

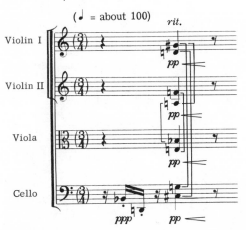

The use of *Klangfarbenmelodie* and the increasing attention given to the structural use of shifting rhythms is illustrated in Example 13/6 in the Op. 9, No. 5, *Bagatelle.*

Example 13/6 also illustrates Webern's athematic style. Frictions of the seconds (or their derivatives) are observable in every measure, except in the second bar where a single note is plucked by the first violin. These pieces sound bewildering to the unaccustomed ear even today, more than half a century after their inception.

Almost simultaneously with the string quartet works two groups of orchestral pieces were written: *Six Pieces* for large orchestra, Op. 6 (1910), and the *Five Pieces for Orchestra,* Op. 10 (1911–1913), followed by two sets of string pieces, *Four Pieces* for violin and piano, Op. 7 (1910), and *Three Small Pieces* for cello and piano, Op. 11 (1914).

---

[16]Copyright by Universal Edition, Vienna. Used by permission.

The earlier set of orchestral pieces—probably influenced by Schoenberg's *Five Orchestral Pieces*—is similar in conception to the Op. 5 quartet, but now the *Klangfarbenmelodie* is enriched by the multicolored palette of a large orchestra. The second orchestral work is for a smaller orchestra that includes guitar, mandolin, and harmonium. Tonal effects reach extreme attenuation; for instance, in the last measure of the first piece of the Op. 10 group, *Klangfarbenmelodie* is applied to *one* pitch. As seen in Example 13/7, an F is played in succession by flute, muted trumpet, and celesta.

EX. 13/7 *Five Pieces for Orchestra*, Op. 10, No. 1,[18] last measure

The application of *Klangfarbenmelodie* to one pitch indicates that in Webern's sound conception timbre is considered as important as pitch. In several of these pieces twelve-tone "fields" (a successive appearance of all twelve pitches of the chromatic scale without repeating any one of them) appear, foreshadowing the impending turn to twelve-tone writing.

Among the four violin pieces, Op. 7, the second piece should be noted for its extreme tempo fluctuations; sixteen different tempo indications appear in the course of its twenty-four measures. The tempo sequence shows a nearly serial plan: Fast–Rit–Broad–Fast–Rit–Broad–Slow–Rit–Fast–Rit–Slow–Acc.–Fast–Molto Rit ♩ = 48, Tempo I.

The violin pieces also contain frequent chromatic clashes both horizontally and vertically; Piece 4 contains an aggregate of six tones, among which are three clashing pairs of the interval class of the minor second (Ex. 13/8).

EX. 13/8 *Violin-Piano Piece*, Op. 7, No. 4,[19] m. 10

The cello pieces represent an extreme manifestation of Webern's aphoristic style; the second piece, with a duration of thirteen seconds, is probably the shortest piece in the music literature. The work is completely athematic, and the music is all but pulverized. Many years later the composer mentioned in a letter to Willi Reich that these pieces were experimental.

The Songs, Op. 12, ushered in a twelve-year period (1914–1926) during which time Webern composed songs exclusively. From Op. 13 on, the piano as the accompanying instrument is replaced by various combinations of instruments, among which the clarinet and the bass clarinet are the most frequently used. The texts are based on poems by Rainer Maria Rilke, Goethe, Georg Trakl, and others.

In the three groups of Op. 12 through Op. 15 (1914–1922) the thread of Webern's musical development is not easily traced because the opus numbers do not always reflect the chronology of composition. Nevertheless, certain generalizations can be made: on the whole, the songs of Op. 12 are similar to the early songs. The last song in the group, based on Goethe's "Gleich und Gleich" has a beguiling charm. The piano in this song opens with a twelve-tone field (Ex. 13/9), an occurrence becoming more and more frequent in Webern's music.

EX. 13/9 *"Gleich und Gleich,"* Op. 12,[20] opening measures

The songs of this group and of the following opuses are more extended than the earlier instrumental pieces. In the Op. 13 group, for instance, the duration of two songs is over five minutes each. In the last mentioned group the voice is accompanied by thirteen instruments, which include the celesta, harp, and glockenspiel. Undoubtedly, the influence of Schoenberg's *Pierrot Lunaire* is felt here, although Webern does not use *Sprechstimme*. One aspect of the vocal writing, however, often lends a declamatory character to the vocal part, namely, the frequent use of rests between short phrases. Commencing with the

[20]Copyright by Universal Edition, Vienna. Used by permission.

Op. 13 group the use of the interval class of the minor second becomes even more pronounced than before.

The last song of Op. 13, and all six songs of Op. 14, are based on Trakl's poetry. Webern's affinity to Trakl's poetry is borne out by the many similarities between the two men and their art. Trakl was also drawn to religious mysticism, and he won the distinction of being the most laconic among German expressionist poets. His penchant for color epithets, such as "golden coolness," "golden boat," and "golden war cry" form a chain of word pairs approximating a *Klangfarbenmelodie* of words. The comment of a German literary critic characterizing the Austrian poet's verse as a "series of microcosmic variations" could also be applied to Webern's music.

In the Op. 14 group the number of accompanying instruments is reduced to four: clarinet, bass clarinet, violin, and cello. Despite the smaller ensemble, the texture is more polyphonic (Ex. 13/10) than in the earlier songs.

EX. 13/10 *Six Songs,* Op. 14, No. 2,[21] mm. 15–16

The three layers of dynamics seen in Example 13/10 point to the infinite care the composer gives to matters of balance. The same example also shows the preponderance of the interval class of the minor second, both horizontally and vertically. The frequent use of minor ninths and major sevenths presents formidable difficulties for the vocalist.

The influence of Schoenberg's *Pierrot* can also be seen in the varied combination of instrumental resources; the four instruments appear in five different combinations in the six songs. Only in the last song are all four instruments used. The tender opening of the last song (Ex. 13/11) illustrates the subtle use of *Klangfarbenmelodie.*

EX. 13/11 Op. 14, No. 6,[22] opening

Webern's increasing interest in contrapuntal writing led to the employment of canonic devices—a hallmark of the composer's late style—in the last song of the *Five Sacred Songs,* Op. 15, and in the *Five Canons on Latin Text,* Op. 16 (1924).

The *Five Sacred Songs,* scored for voice, flute, clarinet (bass clarinet), trumpet, harp, violin (also viola), are considered by Craft,[23] a Webern specialist, the composer's incomparable masterpieces. The scoring is even more imaginative than that of the Trakl songs; again, each song has a different instrumental setting. The opening of the fourth song conveys the otherworldly quality of this music:

EX. 13/12 *Five Sacred Songs,* Op. 15, No. 4,[24] opening

[22] Copyright by Universal Edition, Vienna. Used by permission.
[23] Craft's booklet, accompanying the recordings of Webern's oeuvre contains valuable information.
[24] Copyright by Universal Edition, Vienna. Used by permission.

The opening of the last song, a double canon in contrary motion, is shown in Example 13/13.

EX. 13/13 Op. 15, No. 5,[25] opening

In the *Five Canons on Latin Text,* Op. 16, the voice is joined by clarinet and bass clarinet in the first, third, and fifth songs, while the second and fourth are duets between voice and clarinet, and voice and bass clarinet, respectively. Thus, Webern's concern for the principle of perpetual variation can be seen in his scoring; the writing is strictly instrumental for the vocalist, too (Ex. 13/14), placing an almost unbearable strain on the performer.

EX. 13/14 Op. 16, No. 1,[26] opening

The voice enters a whole step higher and one measure later than the clarinet, the bass clarinet entering a half measure after the clarinet, a minor third below, and in contrary motion. The strong accents in the instrumental parts should be noted, as well as the dominance of the interval class of the minor second. The latter becomes even more pronounced in the middle section where a strettolike intensification occurs.

EX. 13/15 Op. 16, No. 1, mm. 8–9

Such rigorous employment of intervallic relationships makes it èasy to understand why the adoption of the twelve-tone method was a natural step for Webern. Indeed, the next two groups of songs, based on the twelve-tone method, hardly differ in sound or character from the preceding works. Webern embraced the twelve-tone method not for dogmatic reasons or out of reverence for his former teacher, but because it was in line both with his expressive aims and with his passion for coherence. Once he used the method in the songs of Op. 17, he never abandoned it. Neither did he compromise with a partial application of the method nor with allusions to tonality.

TWELVE-TONE WORKS FROM OPUS 17–OPUS 31

In the first three twelve-tone works, Op. 17, 18, and 19, the adherence to the same interval class as in the earlier songs is evident. A glance at the tone rows of Op. 17, songs for voice, violin, viola, clarinet, and bass clarinet, shows that the composer designed his sets in such a way as to insure the dominance of the interval class of the minor second. The row of the first song of Op. 17 (Ex. 13/16) is built on seven dyads of half steps.

EX. 13/16 Tone row of Op. 17, No. 1

The tone row of the third song of Op. 17 also contains seven dyads of half steps, though arranged in a different order.

EX. 13/17 Tone row of Op. 17, No. 3

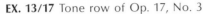
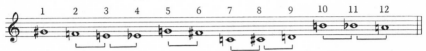

An examination of the vocal line of Op. 17, No. 3 (Ex. 13/18), shows that the outline of the song is undistinguishable from that of the earlier songs; again major sevenths and minor ninths dominate.

EX. 13/18 *Song, Op. 17, No. 3*[27]

In the instrumental parts of the Op. 17 songs, segments of the row appear in a rather free treatment; these segments often form a twelve-tone field with the notes of the vocal line they accompany. Thus, in the first phrase, as the pitches 1–3 appear in the voice, pitches 4–12 are divided among the accompanying instruments.

Turning to the songs of Op. 18, it seems at first glance as if the tone row (Ex. 13/19) of the second song would discard the preponderance of half steps:

EX. 13/19 Tone row of Op. 18, No. 2

A closer examination reveals, however, that the odd-numbered pitches (1–3–5–7–9–11), to which 12 can be added, form a descending chromatic line. Also, 2–4–6 and 8–10 form a series of half steps. This arrangement makes the dominance of the interval class of the minor second possible, at the same time allowing a wider range of harmonic possibilities.

In the songs of Op. 18, inversion and retrograde versions of the row are used by Webern for the first time. These devices, although recognizable to the eye, do not seem to make any difference in the actual sound of the music. Three forms of the row are used in the second song of this group in the three-sided conversation between Mary, Christ, and God. The prime set is used for Mary's lines, the I (inversion) for Christ (Ex. 13/20), and the R (retrograde) form for God.

EX. 13/20 Inverted tone row of Op. 18, No. 2

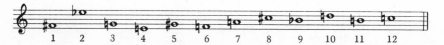

Example 13/21 shows that when Christ's opening words appear, the even-numbered members of the inverted set are used in the minor ninths and major sevenths of the vocal line.

The same example also shows that the inverted set appears in almost two complete successions within the boundary of a single measure. Whether or not the specific use of the rows has any metaphysical connotations is a matter of speculation.

The setting of the text in Webern's songs, in general, is highly unconventional, since there is no attempt made to underline the meaning of the words by special musical means. Thus, the words and the music do

EX. 13/21 Op. 18, No. 2[28] m. 7

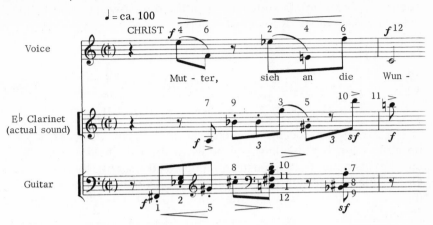

not enter into an emotional tie as is the case with the romantic Lied. Instead, the words are used as vehicles of the intervallic structure that pervades the over-all fabric of the music. Expressiveness is gained by subtle manipulation of rhythmic values, particularly striking in the songs of Op. 18 (Ex. 13/22) and by the device of *Klangfarbenmelodie*.

EX. 13/22 Op. 18, No. 3,[29] m. 18

The String Trio, Op. 20 (1927), is one of Webern's most difficult compositions both for the performer and the listener. The nearly total dominance of the interval class of the minor second is evident from Example 13/24/a and b, and a glance at the tone row (Ex. 13/23) shows that it consists of six dyads of half steps.

EX. 13/23 Prime set of the *String Trio,* Op. 20

The String Trio occupies a crucial position in Webern's oeuvre because it forms a dividing line between the earlier miniature pieces and the subsequent extended instrumental works, such as the Symphony, Op. 21, the Quartet Op. 22, the *Concerto for Nine Instruments,* Op. 24, the Piano Variations, Op. 27, the String Quartet, Op. 28, and the Orchestral Variations, Op. 30.

Now Webern's task was to solve the problem of musical architecture in the atonal, twelve-tone setting without the aid of a text. Unlike Schoenberg, Webern did not resort to the old forms of tonal music, with the exception of the variation form. Only in the String Trio does the composer attempt to adapt the rondo form and the sonata form to his purposes. Although the skeleton of these forms is recognizable because of the sectionalizations, the actual musical procedures are quite different from traditional practices. The outline of Webern's rondo therefore, is similar to the typical "formula" of the traditional rondo but, as seen in the outline, is actually organized according to the principle of perpetual variation. An analysis of the first movement shows that the return of the sections entails drastic recomposition of the elements, to such an extent that the ear would hardly experience these as recurrences.

The outline of the rondo of the first movement is as follows:

Introduction	Mm. 1–3
A	4–9
B	10–15
A_1	16–21
C	22–30
C_1	31–40
Introduction	41–43
A_2	44–50
B_1	51–56
A_3	57–62
Introduction	63–65

In Examples 13/24/a and b, sections B and B_1 appear to illustrate the drastic changes that mark the recurrence of a section.

EX. 13/24/a *String Trio,* Op. 20,[30] first movement, mm. 10–15

EX. 13/24/b *String Trio,* Op. 20, first movement, mm. 51–56

The Symphony, Op. 21 (1928), in two movements, has a purer sound than the String Trio. Scored for a small orchestra—clarinet, bass clarinet, two French horns, harp, and strings without double bass—the work is a model for Webern's condensed and simplified style. His aim of presenting musical ideas in the simplest, clearest, and most coherent way is achieved in the first movement by the device of canon. The canon, after all, is the barest and most economical contrapuntal expression because it is devoid of anything extraneous: "always the same, only at different times," as Webern expressed it. That Webern turned to the canon as an organizational device both in this and in later works is not surprising in view of his extensive research into the music of Heinrich Isaac, who used double canons, four part canons, and crab canons extensively.

The first movement of Webern's Symphony is a four-part double canon in contrary motion. This movement is Webern's most frequently analyzed work; every commentator accounts for the twelve tones of each of the four main forms of the set used simultaneously.

The tone row of the Symphony (Ex. 13/25), replete with half steps, is constructed in such a way that its second half mirrors the intervals of the first half:

EX. 13/25 Tone row of the *Symphony,* Op. 21

Example 13/25 illustrates that the descending minor third between 1 and 2 is mirrored between 12 and 11, and the rising half step between 2 and 3 is mirrored between 11 and 10. Such inner intervallic relationships, and even more complex symmetrical row constructions, will be found in several later works. It is easy to see how such a row easily lends itself to motivic relations and to canonic constructions. All canon formations in the Symphony are orchestrated with a highly refined *Klangfarbenmelodie.*

In a brief analysis of the second movement of the Symphony, Webern made the following reference to the row:

> It has the peculiarity that the second half is the crab of the first. This is a specially close interrelationship. It also means that there are only 24 set forms[31] because two are always identical. . . . The first variation is a transposition of the row; while the accompaniment is a double canon. More coherence is not possible. Even the Netherlanders could not have matched this.[32]

[31] Each set normally has forty-eight forms: the twelve appearances of P, R, I, and RI (see Chapter 7).

[32] *Der Weg zur Neuen Musik,* p. 60.

The same tonal imagination is apparent in a smaller setting, in the Quartet for violin, clarinet, tenor saxophone, and piano, Op. 22 (1930). The unusual choice of instruments and their fascinating sound combinations astounded even Alban Berg, who commented in a letter to Webern: "Yes, this quartet is a miraculous work. What astonishes me is its originality."

PLATE 21.
WEBERN IN HIS
MIDDLE YEARS
Bettmann
Archive,
New York

The *Concerto for Nine Instruments,* Op. 24 (1934), is another work that provoked several Webern specialists to write extended analyses, studded with charts and statistical tabulations. The composition is truly an intricate network of motivic relations based on Webern's increasing ingenuity in row construction. The prime set is constructed of four "microsets," which stand in motivic relation to one another:

EX. 13/26 Prime set of the *Concerto for Nine Instruments,* Op. 24

In Example 13/26 the motive "b" is the retrograde inversion of the intervals of motive "a," motive "c" the retrograde form of "a," and "d" the inversion of "a." From the viewpoint of intervallic construction each motive consists of a major third and a minor second. By now Webern applies the principle of perpetual variation within the tone row.

The opening of the first movement (Ex. 13/27) illustrates the employment of *Klangfarbenmelodie* and the four different rhythmic shapes in which the overlapping motives appear.

EX. 13/27 *Concerto for Nine Instruments,* Op. 24,[33] opening

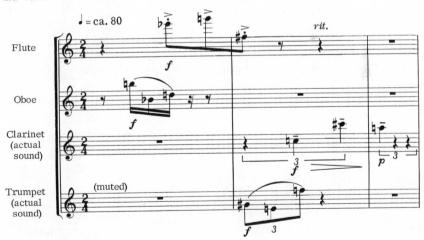

The String Quartet, Op. 28 (1938), is built on an even more intricate tone row.

[33] Copyright by Universal Edition, Vienna. Used by permission.

EX. 13/28 Prime set of the *String Quartet,* Op. 28

Again, the second half of the row is a retrograde inversion of the first half, but here the row has an additional inner motivic structure, inasmuch as groups of four notes are organized in such a way that 5, 6, 7, and 8 form the inversion of 1, 2, 3, and 4 (the B–A–C–H motive), and 9, 10, 11, and 12 form a transposition of 1, 2, 3, snd 4.

The String Quartet and the String Trio have a less intriguing sonorous appeal than other late works. One might be led to generalize that the larger variety of instruments results in a more subtle and varied organization of *Klangfarbenmelodie* than three of four string instruments. However, the case of the Piano Variations, Op. 27 (1936), proves the composer could elicit tonal effects of great beauty and variety from a single instrument.

The last instrumental work, the *Variations for Orchestra,* Op. 30 (1940), will be discussed in some detail as it sheds additional light on Webern's late style.

VARIATIONS FOR ORCHESTRA[34]

In his correspondence with Hildegard Jone, Webern commented several times on the *Variations.* In a letter dated August 8, 1940, he wrote: "It will be a purely instrumental work; quite a colorful one, but based on rigorous construction." In a later letter he mentions that he has almost finished the *Variations,* a very long and self-contained work.

The work consists of a theme and six variations. The theme (mm. 1–20) opens with a four-note motive in the double bass (a), followed by a four-note motive in the oboe (b), and a four-note motive in the trombone (c) (EX. 13/29).

Actually, the double bass and oboe motives are the germinating cells of the entire composition. Motive "c" is not really new material since it is a derivation of motive "a," specifically a crab version in diminution. Even the second half of the oboe phrase is formed by the same interval as the first half with retrogression in the rhythmic values.

The intricate motivic relations are, of course, derived from a row of complex construction (Ex. 13/30).

---

[34] The discussion in this section is partly based on Kolneder's analysis.

EX. 13/29 *Variations for Orchestra,*[35] opening measures

EX. 13/30 Prime set of the *Variations for Orchestra*

Once again, 7–12 form a retrograde inversion of the first hexachord. In addition, a segmentation of the row into groups shows new relationships: 9–12 ("c" in Ex. 13/30) are the retrograde inversions of 1–4 ("a" in Ex. 13/30), while 7 and 8 are the retrograde inversions of 5 and 6 (hence, the inner symmetry of motive "b"). The row consists of only two types of intervals: minor thirds and minor seconds. There are seven dyads of minor seconds.

Motive "a" remains dominant throughout the theme; one of its variants appears in the viola figure (Ex. 13/29), which is transposed a half step higher and appears in a new rhythmic shape. The rest of the theme demonstrates Webern's method of perpetual variation. In Example 13/31 four such variants can be seen; each one has a different *Klangfarbe,* a new rhythmic shape, and different accentuation and dynamic level:

EX. 13/31 *Variations for Orchestra,* first movement

a) mm. 7–9

b) mm. 10-11

c) mm. 13-14

d) mm. 15-16

Rhythmic variety is achieved not only through varying the shapes of motive cells, but also through a continuously changing meter, and by frequent tempo fluctuations. The theme ends on two four-tone chords, in sixteenth-note value, consisting of a pair of major sevenths which establish the link to the next variation.

In Variation I (mm. 21–55) these chords, now in quarter-note values, become the harmonic accompaniment to motive "a," which assumes a more melodic character in the solo violin than it had in the previous section. The feeling is as if this variation were the theme, and the previous section (namely the theme) had the function of an introduction. When the motive appears in the clarinet and bass clarinet, the chords that first appeared in the brass section move to divided violas and cellos. Later the motive is intoned by the muted trumpet, accompanied by the same chords sounded now by harp and celesta. In the remaining part of the variation, the motive and the harmony undergo further rhythmic manipulations (augmentations, diminutions, and changes in the pattern of rests) and alterations of timbre and register.

Variation II (mm. 56–73) is felt as a transition; it consists almost exclusively of vertical arrangements, almost invariably made up of major sevenths and minor ninths. Variety is achieved by different spacing, registration, and dynamic levels. Again a link is established with the following variation, this time in the shape of a rhythmic figure (mm. 72–73).

Variation III (mm. 74–109) opens with the rhythmic figure just mentioned. Soon a new pattern emerges, consisting of three sixteenth notes, which assumes various guises, five of which are quoted in the following example.

EX. 13/32 *Variations for Orchestra*

a) mm. 83–84

b) m. 85

c) m. 86

d–e) m. 95

All variants quoted in Example 13/32 are formed by two interval classes, the minor second and minor thirds, the intervals upon which the row (see Ex. 13/30) is built. In terms of thematic relations the variants are nothing but alterations of motive "a" and "b" of the theme. This variation is an excellent example of the view that it is the *interval*

and not the theme that occupies a central position in Webern's music. The variation is marked *bedächtig* (to be played thoughtfully); the frequent rests and fermatas lend it a tenuous quality.

Variation IV (mm. 110–134) is similar to Variation I, but is more contrapuntal. The climax arrives at measure 125 (Ex. 13/33) where a combination of "a" and "b" appears on four levels, a half step apart (I_6, I_7, I_8, and I_9 forms of the prime set are used simultaneously). The motive appears one beat apart, altered rhythmically each time.

EX. 13/33 *Variations for Orchestra, mm. 125–127*

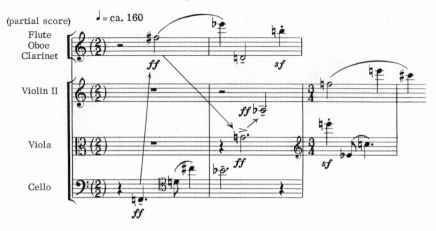

Variation V (mm. 135–145) is very brief and fluid. It presents a few modifications of motive "a."

Variation VI (mm. 146–179) has the character of a coda. Motive "a" appears in the strings and woodwinds, while the brass instruments hold chords in four parts. *Fortissimo* dyads of major sevenths and minor ninths bring the movement to a close.

Late Vocal Works   The five vocal works of Webern's late period, the Songs, Op. 23 and Op. 25, for voice and piano, *Das Augenlicht*, Op. 26 (1935), a cantata for chorus and orchestra, the First Cantata, Op. 29 (1938–1939), for soprano, chorus and orchestra, and the Second Cantata, Op. 31 (1941–1943) are based on texts by Hildegard Jone, a poet and painter. The published correspondence between the composer and Miss Jone indicates the significant part the poet played in Webern's life. It was undoubtedly the composer's intense feelings for Miss Jone that caused him to single out her poetry, whose literary value is much below that of other poets who inspired Webern earlier in his life. Their friendship, based on a mystic outlook on life, never reached fulfillment. The following passage from the first poem of the Op. 23 group can be read as the poet's veiled message to the composer, summing up also their relationship:

> The rivers of your soul,
> Thou man, loved by me,
> They flow into what is mine
> So that it will not wither.
> We do not belong to ourselves,
> Not I, not you, not anyone[36]

These songs are more serene than the earlier vocal works. The vocal line is less jagged and seldom resorts to wide leaps. The tone row of Op. 23 is constructed of intervals (such as the major and minor third and a perfect fourth) that allow a smoother approach to the human voice compared to the vocal line dominated by the interval class of the minor second. The piano part, too, furnishes a simplified accompaniment compared to the intricate tonal and rhythmic patterns of the Songs of Op. 13–Op. 19.

The three cantatas, unfortunately, can only be mentioned here, although each is a major work. *Das Augenlicht* stands out in tonal beauty and the First Cantata in dramatic power. In the last movement of the Second Cantata, Webern recaptures the rhythmic style of the early Netherland masters, insofar as each line maintains its independence in metric organization.

WEBERN'S INFLUENCE

After World War II the musical avant-garde accepted Webern's musical style as their point of departure. This musical movement, loosely called the Darmstadt School, advanced on two fronts: 1) The serialization of elements other than pitch, such as duration, timbre, densities, and dynamics, eventually led to *total organization,* that is, to the prearranged ordering of all the elements of music (see Chapter 7); 2) Motivated by total organization, the second and more far-reaching move was the production of sound through electronic means.

There is much disagreement among the members of the Darmstadt School about the link between the music of Webern and total organization. On the whole, there is little evidence to suggest that Webern

---

[36] Copyright 1939 by Universal Edition, Vienna. By permission of Theodore Presser Company, representative in the U.S., Canada, and Mexico.

aimed at the serialization of any *parameter* other than pitch. There is no hint of such an effort in his theoretical writings nor any evidence in his scores. There is only one source, of somewhat dubious value, mentioned in Kolneder's study, according to which Webern showed interest in the serialization of duration. This source consists of a recollection of Cesar Bresgen, Webern's friend, who spent much time with the composer during the last months of the war. According to Bresgen, Webern was engaged in a composition in which not only pitch but also duration was ordered serially. It is impossible to tell today whether or not the composer experimented in that direction. Based solely on the evidence of the scores, one can undoubtedly detect certain sequential appearances of rhythmic or dynamic values. There is no sign, however, that such an ordering of musical values was the result of a serial plan. It was merely the manifestation of the principle of perpetual variation: "to say the same but always in a different way." There is an order in Webern's music, but it is a functional order based on purely esthetic considerations and not on mechanical calculations. This order of Webern's music led Nono[37] to claim that in the *Variations for Orchestra* elements other than pitch also follow a serial plan. Zillig[38] also attributes to Webern a serial lawfulness applied to duration, dynamics, and the like.

Boulez, on the other hand, stated repeatedly that the expansion of serial technique to elements other than pitch was accomplished by himself and other composers of his group.

The link between Webern's art and electronic music is an even more clouded issue and is partly tied to the objectives of total organization. The advocates of this principle felt that the complex ordering of proportions of pitch, timbre, intensity, and duration can be achieved only through electronic production because human performance could never approximate the complex sound relationships which are to be achieved. The main tie between electronic music and Webern's art is seen in the use of *Klangfarbenmelodie*. This device, of course, entails manipulation of timbres, and the advocates of electronic music claim that a much wider use and greater variety of timbre could be produced if sound itself could be controlled scientifically, that is, electronically (see Chapter 7). The link between Webern's style and electronic music was formulated by Eimert as follows:

> Webern was the first composer to move on from the single level conception of the twelve-tone technique; namely that of a technique of organizing pitch levels . . . . Webern restricted his music to interval and

[37] Luigi Nono, "Die Entwickelung der Reihentechnik, *Darmstädter Beiträge,* **1** (1958).
[38] Winfried Zillig, *Variationen über Neue Musik* (München: Nymphenburger Verlagshandlung, 1959), p. 191.

single note, and composed structures which are not in the traditional sense developed in a continuum,[39] but which proceed by autonomous "leaps" (Sprünge), leaps which in the pre-electronic stage could achieve everything but that final step from the bounds of instrumentally tempered sound. Only in electronic music has the real sense of these developments been realized.[40]

Eimert's formulation unfortunately lacks lucidity, as, for instance, the concept of a "leap" is not explained.

The extent to which Webern is responsible for electronic music is merely that he accomplished previously unsuspected differentiations of nuances in timbre and dynamics. To Webern, who believed that music is one of nature's manifestations, nothing could be more alien than sound produced in a synthetic manner.

SUMMARY

It is astounding that Webern's small oeuvre, which amounts to less than four hours' playing time, should have had such an immense impact.

The two most salient features of his art are the high degree of concentration of musical thought and a passion for coherence. He also exhibited a refined instinct for sound and timbre that runs through his entire output. His music is devoid of romantic sentiment and effusiveness. His pulverized textures, understated dynamics, and intricate rhythmic scheme, in which the pause plays a significant role, suggest some kinship with Debussy.

The rigorous conception of intervallic relations allowed Webern to express himself so naturally in the twelve-tone idiom that the transition from atonal works to dodecaphony is hardly noticeable. In fact, had Schoenberg not invented the twelve-tone method, Webern might have arrived at it independently. His symmetrical sets with ingenious segmentation fulfilled his love for coherence and order, and he achieved further unity through the use of canonic devices.

Webern never returned to a more traditional outlook from his advanced position as did Schoenberg and Berg; there is no flirtation with tonality, and except for a few instances, no employment of the traditional forms.

The wide range of Webern's influence was seen in the previous section; it may be added that none of the numerous followers has succeeded in capturing the essence of their elusive idol.

[39] A rather misleading translation of the original German *kontinuierlich.*
[40] Herbert Eimert, "What Is Electronic Music," *Die Reihe,* No. 1 (1955), p. 8.

CHRONOLOGICAL LIST OF
WEBERN'S PRINCIPAL WORKS[41]

Passacaglia for orchestra, Op. 1   1908
Five Movements for string quartet, Op. 5   1909
Six Bagatelles for string quartet, Op. 9   1913
Songs, Op. 12–Op. 19   1914–1926
String Trio, Op. 20   1927
Symphony, Op. 21   1928
Quartet for violin, clarinet, tenor saxophone, and piano, Op. 22   1930
Concerto for Nine Instruments, Op. 24   1934
Das Augenlicht, for mixed chorus and orchestra, Op. 26   1935
Variations for Piano, Op. 27   1936
String Quartet, Op. 28   1938
First Cantata, Op. 29   1939
Variations for Orchestra, Op. 30   1940
Second Cantata, Op. 31   1941–1943

[41] For complete list of works and bibliography see *Anton Von Webern: Perspectives,* compiled by Hans Moldenhauer, edited by Demar Irvine (Seattle: University of Washington Press, 1966).

PAUL HINDEMITH
(1895–1963)

*. . . It seems wiser to gather knowledge, in
case our never-failing intuition should prove
nonexistent.*

HINDEMITH

Hindemith earned such a formidable reputation as composer,
performer, theorist, and teacher that during his life his position as one of the musical leaders of his time was seldom challenged. During the short period since his death, however, a re-
appraisal has taken place. A number of commentators expressed
the thought that Hindemith became an isolated figure in the
latter part of his life, "a semiretired elder statesman of music"
in Redlich's[1] words.

Despite this decline, Hindemith occupies an important position in the history of twentieth-century music; he was the un-
questioned leader of the new German music in the period following the end of World War I, and he held this position

---

[1] Hans F. Redlich, "Paul Hindemith; a Reassessment," *The Music Review,* **25,**
No. 3 (1964), pp. 241–257.

until forced into exile by the Third Reich. His vast contribution to the music literature in every branch of performance contains a handful of masterworks. Also, his theoretical writings and his views on music education made such an impact on the musical world that a detailed examination of the man and his music is warranted.

LIFE

Hindemith was born in 1895 in Hanau, near Frankfurt a/Main, in Germany. A descendant of a poor working-class family, he did not have the benefit of the middle-class education enjoyed by the other key figures of contemporary music. Instead, at an early age, he had to augment the family income by playing popular music in bars and taverns. His participation in jazz bands probably led him to experiment with the jazz idiom in his early style. According to Strobel[2]—Hindemith's only biographer thus far—the boy's playing at a nightclub drew the attention of a wealthy business man, who, recognizing young Hindemith's talent, then sponsored his musical education. Enrolled at the Conservatory in Frankfurt, Hindemith majored in violin, viola, and composition. His progress as a performer was so rapid that in 1915, at the age of twenty, he became the concertmaster of the Frankfurt Opera, a post he held for eight years. During this time he joined the Rebner Quartet (1915–1921) and later the noted Amar Quartet (1923–1929), a group that distinguished itself particularly in contemporary music.

Gradually, Hindemith's interest turned to composition and soon he fulfilled the ideal of earlier centuries when the composer and performer were one and the same person. He achieved his first great success in this dual role in 1921 when he participated as violist in the performance of his Second Quartet, Op. 16, at a festival of contemporary music at Donaueschingen, a small community in West Germany that remained the meeting place of the musical avant-garde for many years. The composer's fame spread quickly throughout Germany. Although considered an iconoclast and a controversial figure, he was appointed professor of composition at the Hochschule für Musik in Berlin in 1927.

In his new environment Hindemith realized the great gulf that separates the modern composer from his audiences. He became convinced that the music of the past had been too professional, too technical. As a result, he made an attempt to simplify his style. He also realized that many instruments such as the trumpet, trombone, and double bass

---

[2]Heinrich Strobel, *Paul Hindemith,* 3rd ed. (Mainz: B. Schott's Söhne, 1948).

PLATE 22. PAUL HINDEMITH, THE YOUNG VIOLIN PLAYER
Bettmann Archive, New York

lacked adequate solo literature. To remedy this situation he supplied works for all of these neglected instruments in the simplified new style.

Broader problems of music pedagogy, too, occupied his mind; he felt that in the layman's musical education there had been too much stress on listening and not enough on active participation. In order to encourage amateur performances, he wrote a vast amount of music, both vocal and instrumental, on various levels of difficulty.

The music in both categories, since it had been composed to be "used," received the name of *Gebrauchsmusik*. Attempts to translate this term into English, such as "workaday music" or "utilitarian music," did not result in popular usage. *Gebrauchsmusik*, whether written for neglected instruments or for the amateur, while perfectly fitting its purpose, was often not of high esthetic quality. It seems that in these works the composer did not even attempt to rise above the standards of good craftsmanship.

The same practical approach that Hindemith took as a composer also characterized his work as a teacher of composition. He felt that his advice to his students remained arbitrary, unless a system of the more recent harmonic practices were codified. With this thought in mind, he worked out a scientific system of harmony and melody (see Chapter 4), followed by additional didactic volumes on music theory.

Although by this time Hindemith assumed a traditionalist position, both in theory and practice, the Nazi regime could not forgive him for the adventurousness of his early works. His music was banned along with that of Schoenberg, Berg, and Webern, notwithstanding the fact that Hindemith himself was violently opposed to the school of the Viennese atonalists. Despite Furtwängler's intervention, Hindemith was forced to resign his post at the Hochschule. As his position became generally untenable, he soon left Germany. In the years preceding World War II he took up temporary residence in Switzerland, except for several visits to Turkey where, at the request of the Government, he worked out several proposals for the reorganization of music education.

In 1940 the composer arrived in the United States to accept a position at Yale University as professor of composition, a chair he held until 1953. Although no outstanding composer emerged from his classes, his work at Yale, and later at Tanglewood (Berkshire Music Center), greatly enriched the life of these musical communities. In addition to his classroom activities, he organized a *Collegium Musicum*, giving authentic renderings of works rarely performed. Hindemith's manifold activities in the United States and his rich contributions to American musical culture are well summarized in a comprehensive study by Howard Boatwright.[3] Several books resulted from the composer's teaching activities: the two books of *A Concentrated Course in Traditional Harmony, Harmony Exercises for Advanced Students,*[4] and *Elementary*

---

[3] Howard Boatwright, "Paul Hindemith as a Teacher," *Musical Quarterly*, **50**, No. 3 (1964), pp. 279–289.

[4] Paul Hindemith, *A Concentrated Course in Traditional Harmony,* Book I, and *Harmony Exercises for Advanced Students,* Book II (New York: Associated Music Publishers, Inc., 1943 and 1953, respectively).

Training for Musicians.[5] In 1949-1950 Hindemith gave the Charles Eliot Norton lectures at Harvard University; these have been published with some additional material in *A Composer's World.*[6]

[5] Paul Hindemith, *Elementary Training for Musicians,* 2d rev. ed. (New York: Associated Music Publishers, Inc., 1949).

[6] Paul Hindemith, *A Composer's World: Horizons and Limitations.* The Charles Eliot Norton Lectures presented at Harvard University in 1949-1950 (Cambridge, Mass.: Harvard University Press, 1952).

PLATE 23. HINDEMITH IN HIS LATER YEARS
Culver Pictures, New York

In 1949 the composer went back to Germany for a visit only to realize that he could not find a place in his former environment. Almost all leading German composers of the new generation were in the serial camp, whose basic tenets Hindemith had strongly repudiated.

In 1953 the composer gave up his American residence to accept a post at the University of Zurich, which remained his principal residence until his death. Many honors were bestowed on Hindemith, among them the Bach Award of the City of Hamburg and the Balzan Award, the Italian counterpart to the Nobel Prize. In the last years of his life Hindemith devoted himself almost entirely to conducting, ending his career as he had started it, as a performing artist. He died on December 28, 1963, during a concert tour in Frankfurt, the place of his great early successes.

HINDEMITH'S MUSIC

Hindemith's total output contains over 250 works written for almost every conceivable combination of instruments. To assess an output so vast, so diverse in character and purpose and so uneven in quality, is a difficult task. It is also difficult to distinguish a line of development or specific stylistic periods in this flood of music, although undoubtedly the early works sound different from the late ones. The compositions written during the last twenty-five years of the composer's life, however, do not show marked stylistic differences. Seeking out the peak achievements, such as *Das Marienleben,* the Third and Fourth String Quartets, and certain sections from *Mathis der Maler,* one finds that these works originate from a period that precedes the formulation of the composer's theoretical system, *Unterweisung im Tonsatz.* Several commentators have speculated that the conscious approach to the material of music, necessary for the formulation of a theoretical system, may have had a constricting effect on Hindemith's creative resources. The fact that the composer tried to justify his theories through his music is obvious, as he rewrote several earlier works, among them *Das Marienleben.* In the long preface to the revised edition (1948) Hindemith castigates himself for the misjudgments of the early version and explains the need for revision.

The profile of Hindemith's work will emerge most sharply by focusing on his string quartets, this form being the most serious manifestation of any composer's approach to his art. The six quartets also lend themselves to discussion because they cover a wide span (1919–1945) of the composer's creative life. The composer's music will be divided into two groups: the works composed before the publication of the *Unterweisung* and those written afterwards.

WORKS FROM 1919–1935

In approaching Hindemith's stylistic development it should be remembered that he belonged to a later generation than Schoenberg, Bartók, or Stravinsky. The latter composers made their impact on the musical world around 1910, whereas Hindemith's first works appeared about a decade later. In this light it is interesting to note that the early works of the youthful composer show hardly any effects of the innovations that shook the musical world ten years earlier.

The first works suggest a romantic orientation in the Brahmsian tradition. Brahms' influence is seen in Hindemith's leaning toward polyphony, which remained an integral part of his style. The other ingredient of his early style is his fondness for chromaticism. This tendency can be ascribed to the influence of Reger (1873–1916), a composer whose music was widely performed in the pre-World War I years in Germany. Reger also owed a great deal to Brahms, but his colossal fugues link him more closely to Bach. With these three composers Hindemith's musical ancestry is completed; Bach and the baroque art hovered over his music, and Brahms and Reger were the more immediate predecessors.

In the early works, such as the Op. 11 group of sonatas (outstanding among them is the Viola-Piano Sonata, Op. 11, No. 4) and the First String Quartet, Op. 10 (both works dated 1919), the romantic approach is more strongly pronounced. However, even in this early period the composer confined himself to abstract instrumental forms, shunning program music, the fashionable expression of the romantic temper. Melody with chordal accompaniment appears more often here than in later works, but already polyphonic textures embedded in rich chromaticism can be detected. Thus, for instance, the fugue that marks the beginning of the development section of the first movement of the First Quartet, Op. 10, marked *geheimnisvoll* (*misterioso*), furnishes a good example of the romantically inclined chromatic polyphony.

EX. 14/1 HINDEMITH, *First Quartet,*[7] *first movement,* mm. 72–74

[7]Quoted by permission of B. Schott's Söhne and Associated Music Publishers, Inc.

By the time the first violin enters with the subject, the texture is saturated with chromatic passages in the other three voices.

EX. 14/2 *First Quartet,* first movement, m. 84

Interest in polyphonic writing is also shown in the last movement of the solo Viola Sonata, Op. 11, No. 5, marked "in the tempo and form of a passacaglia."

On the heels of this solid and serious start came a brief period of adventurousness and experimentation. In turning to daringly erotic texts, such as Kokoschka's *Mörder, Hoffnung der Frauen,* Franz Blei's *Das Nusch-Nuschi,* and August Schramm's *Sancta Susanna*—all one-act operas written around 1920—Hindemith's style verges on expressionism. In the last work mentioned, the composer even pokes fun at Wagner's *Tristan* in a truly antiromantic gesture. Audiences were shocked both by the irreverent music and by the lurid texts; overnight Hindemith became the *enfant terrible* of German music.

To make matters worse, the composer employed the jazz idiom in the brilliant and original *Kleine Kammermusik,* Op. 24, No. 1 and 2. The last movement of No. 2 incorporated a contemporary foxtrot spiced with highly dissonant harmonies. German musical opinion was in an uproar; the serious Dr. Heuss wrote in the *Neue Zeitschrift für Musik* (February 1923):

> It has been done! The most modern German music succeeded in expressing the basest and most unseemly aspects of life. The composer who achieved this miracle is Paul Hindemith. In his *Kleine Kammermusik* Op. 24, No. 1, we are confronted with a piece such as no German com-

poser of any repute would have dared even to contemplate—let alone write . . . . This is music of such lasciviousness and frivolity that could be written only by a composer of a deranged mentality.

Hindemith, undisturbed by such criticism, went on to have more fun. In the "1922" Piano Suite, a jazz shimmy and ragtime are included with the following instruction to the performer:

> Don't pay any attention to what you learned in your piano lessons! Don't spend any time considering if you should play D sharp with the fourth or sixth finger.
> Play this piece very savagely, but always rigidly in rhythm like a machine. Consider the piano an interesting kind of percussion instrument and treat it accordingly.[8]

This reckless mood invades the otherwise serious solo Viola Sonata, Op. 25, No. 1. In the fourth movement of the sonata Hindemith prescribes a *rasendes Zeitmass* (madly racing tempo) with a metronome signature of $\quad$ = 600–640! The number of quarter notes varies in almost every measure in an asymmetrical *perpetuum mobile*. According to the instructions in the score, the manner of performance ought to be wild, and "the beauty of sound is secondary (Tonschönheit ist Nebensache)."

It is only in the realm of the string quartets that seriousness is maintained, although the composer's energy and vigor are apparent here too, but without resorting to extremes. Two quartets originate from this period: the Second Quartet, Op. 16 (1921), Hindemith's first great international success, and the surprisingly mature Third Quartet, Op. 22 (1922).

The first movement of the Second Quartet shows the composer's search for new solutions in form. The first section of this movement contains three groups of ideas, not unlike the usual exposition, but thereafter the rest of the movement is a free development. The climax is reached in a canon, in which the lower instruments follow the higher ones a half step lower, with one beat delays. The movement is *on* C, clearly declared in the opening and at the end of the movement. The slow movement has more expressiveness and intimacy than similar movements in the composer's late style. The finale deserves attention for its freedom and exuberance. Throughout the movement $\frac{2}{8}$ and $\frac{3}{8}$ meters are superimposed; according to the composer's instruction the duration of the measures has to be equalized. The resultant cross-rhythms are apparent in the following example:

---

[8]Quoted by permission of B. Schott's Söhne and Associated Music Publishers, Inc.

EX. 14/3 *Second Quartet,*[9] third movement, opening

In the quasi-cadenza section (starting at m. 458) the second violin plays the same dissonant, rapid figure "without regard for the rhythm and dynamics of the other players," for fifty-two measures. While the other three instruments reach a *fff* climax, ending in a passage marked *prestissimo herabstürzen* (to tumble down precipitously).

Compared to the Second Quartet, the Third Quartet in five movements, although written only a year later, shows a marked increase in control. The opening *fugato* indicates a return to tradition; the marking is *weich und ruhig* (softly and calmly), and later "warmly." Correspondingly, the sonorities have a sensuous appeal, a quality soon to disappear from Hindemith's music. In this movement the horizontal line assumes greater significance than the harmonic motivation, thus marking the start of a decisive stylistic change. This type of writing has been called linear or dissonant counterpoint.

The second, scherzolike movement has a restless vitality owing to the frequent metric changes between $\frac{5}{8}$ and $\frac{3}{4}$. Its ostinato figures and steady drive are reminiscent of Stravinsky's style.

The third movement, in A–B–A form with coda, is perhaps Hindemith's loveliest and most poignant inspiration up to this point. Its soft, muted harmonic frictions caused by an essentially bitonal plan create a haunting effect. The two main ideas, with pizzicato accompaniment, appear in the following two examples from the Third Quartet.

In the coda (study letter H) the two themes appear in close juxtaposition, quietly, and at a slower tempo, dying out with a whisper, *pppp*—a rare phenomenon in the composer's music.

[9]Quoted by permission of B. Schott's Söhne and Associated Music Publishers, Inc.

EX. 14/4 *Third Quartet,*[10] third movement, opening

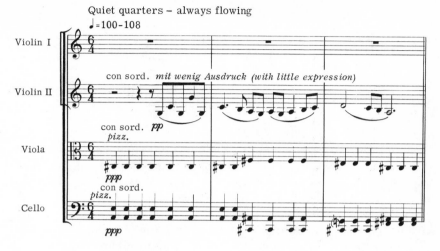

EX. 14/5 *Third Quartet,* third movement, mm. 37–39

The fourth movement is nearly a cello concerto; its virtuoso part is rivaled only by the tricky double stops of the viola. The brilliance of this movement almost transgresses the customary intimate atmosphere of chamber music.

The last movement, a rondo, establishes a calmer tone in its fluid course. The opening is quoted in Example 14/6; the rhythmic pattern, suggestive of baroque practices, remained a typical feature of Hindemith's music.

[10] Quoted by permission of B. Schott's Söhne and Associated Music Publishers, Inc.

EX. 14/6 *Third Quartet,* last movement, opening

In the year 1923 Hindemith produced two significant works: *Das Marienleben,* a song cycle of fifteen songs based on Rilke's poetry, dealing with the life of Christ's mother; and the Fourth Quartet, Op. 32. In 1924 these were followed by the First String Trio, Op. 34.

Das Marienleben is a work of great depth and inner concentration in which the vocal line is conceived as part of the polyphonic structure. In formal balance and spiritual expressiveness Hindemith never came closer to Bach's art than in this instance. In 1947 the composer revised the work thoroughly, and for this reason it will be examined in the context of the later works.

From this point on, polyphonic writing also became dominant in the composer's instrumental works. The independence of voice-leading and the emphasis on the horizontal line are masterfully achieved in the Fourth Quartet. Its two corner movements are cast in the favorite forms of the Baroque period: the fugue and the passacaglia.

The opening fugue subject (Ex. 14/7) is different, indeed, from the fugal opening (Ex. 14/8) of the Third Quartet. While the subject of the earlier quartet was expressive, sensuous, and had a songful, romantic quality, the subject of the later quartet is more objectified and formal, resembling in its shape baroque style. This style of writing, falling back on the practices of the early eighteenth century, was established by Stravinsky almost contemporaneously, and has been labeled, in lieu of a better term, *neoclassic.*

EX. 14/7 *Fourth Quartet,*[11] first movement, opening

[11] Quoted by permission of B. Schott's Söhne and Associated Music Publishers, Inc.

EX. 14/8 *Third Quartet,* first movement, opening

The first movement of the Fourth Quartet shows an interesting design integrating baroque fugal style with the classical sonata principle.
If one considers the fugal opening as the main theme, then the tender
theme at study number 6—to be played with "little expression" (wenig
Ausdruck)—would qualify as the second theme. The instruction suggesting "little expression" is of marked significance. It stands in strong contrast to the instructions (*weich, innig,* soft, expressive) given in the
opening of the Third Quartet. The change in expression indicates the
antiromantic turn, and the objective attitude of the neoclassic orientation.

The second theme is gradually intensified and leads to a climax, at
which point the two themes appear combined, suggesting the development section. At study number 16, the second climax of the movement,
the viola restates the opening fugue theme in an abbreviated form, indicating the recapitulation. Omitting the second theme, the movement
reaches its end rather abruptly.

The slow second movement opens with a canon between viola and
second violin a half step apart. After a quiet middle section in which
each instrument has a brief cadenza, the canon returns between the
first violin and cello a whole step apart, with considerable reworking
of the material.

The third movement, "a little march," opens with a staccato theme
combined with a double counterpoint. The tripartite design has an interesting dynamic curve: the movement starts *ppp* and after a steady
crescendo, sustained for fifty-five measures, reaches a *fff* peak, which
marks the end of the middle section. The return of the first section,
now considerably condensed, is again *ppp,* and ends with a virtuoso
viola flourish.

The last movement, a passacaglia, has a baroque severity; the seven-
measure theme (Ex. 14/9) is followed by twenty-seven variations, and
a *fugato* finale built on the material of the theme.

EX. 14/9 *Fourth Quartet,* fourth movement, opening

Example 14/10 contains one of the variations; it affords a view of the composer's consummate contrapuntal skill. The reader is urged to inspect the score of this movement in order to realize the tonal imagination and the rhythmic variety characteristic of this work at this particular stage of Hindemith's development.

EX. 14/10 *Fourth Quartet,* fourth movement, study no. 4

EX. 14/10 (cont.)

The First String Trio (1924) also employs baroque forms, such as a toccata (first movement) and fugue (last movement). Also the middle movements are strictly contrapuntal in the character of a Bach three-part invention.

Redlich, in an analysis of the composer's stylistic development, compares the First String Trio with the Second Trio, written ten years later in 1934. He concludes that the Second Trio already shows signs of "sterility and obsolescence." He also claims that Hindemith's music from the mid-1930s on fell into a fixed groove, and that his subsequent output is:

> . . . monotonous in the morose drabness of its shape, narrow in its acoustic compass, and extremely ugly in sound as a result of the angularities of its polyphony.[12]

Following the First String Trio, Hindemith turned his attention to the concerto form (the four concertos of Op. 36 and the *Concerto for Or-*

[12] Hans F. Redlich, "Paul Hindemith: A Reassessment," p. 247.

chestra, Op. 38) and wrote his first full-scale opera, Cardillac, the story of a pathological goldsmith, based on a tale by E. T. A. Hoffmann. The work, after an initial success in Germany, soon faded from the repertory; one reason may be that the overly dense orchestral writing weakened the dramatic impact. Much later, in 1952, Hindemith completely revised the opera, diminishing the participation of the orchestra and drawing more attention to the drama and action. It has never been performed or recorded in either version in the United States. Curiously, the first version of the opera was revived at the 1962 Holland Festival, and in Vienna and Amsterdam in 1964.

After the completion of Cardillac in 1926, Hindemith assumed his teaching post at the Hochschule in Berlin. His personal contact with students made him aware of the needs of the "consumers" of music. This new awareness resulted in the next years in a torrent of music for students and amateurs. Among these works first came Spielmusik (play music), Op. 43 (1927), a group of pieces to be sung and played. The next opus, entitled Schulwerk für Instrumental Zusammenspiel (School Music for Instrumental Ensembles), lists nine pieces in first position for two violins for slightly advanced students, eight pieces for string quartet in the first position for moderately advanced students, five pieces for string orchestra for advanced students. Op. 45 offered vocal music for amateurs, music for woodwinds and strings, and three-part choruses for boys. The aim in these compositions was not only to provide material for students and laymen, but also to expose them to the contemporary idiom. This was an entirely new thought and a section of the press reacted with hostility. "The experimentation with children," wrote the critic of the Zeitschrift für Musik, "is the more offensive because the content of the music does not justify the very strenuous efforts it demands. One can hardly imagine a more inept charlatanism than these children's choruses which are unsingable by children."

In 1930 Hindemith wrote music for a children's play, "Wir bauen eine Stadt" and, in 1932, a visit to a school in Plön produced the Plöner Musiktag. In this work the composer provided music for the daily life of a school; "Morning music for brass," "Dinner music (Tafelmusik)," and "Evening music." The day also included the performance of a cantata called "Admonition of youth to apply itself to music," based on a text by Martin Agricola, a music theorist and friend of Martin Luther. In addition, works were written for various instrumental combinations that were available in Plön; needs of very young children were served by recorder ensembles, and music was provided for those who were unfamiliar with musical notation.

This conviction that music should accompany all phases of life, including the varied expressions of modern living, manifested itself in the next stage work, *Neues vom Tage* (1929). Based on the text of a vaudeville writer, Marcellus Schiffer, Hindemith wrote a musical comment on the hectic, fun-seeking life of Berlin's fashionable society. The action centers on the handsome Hermann, who can be hired from an agency as a "divorce cause." The composer's lightened polyphonic style and jazzed-up orchestration are placed at the service of the situational humor of the play, which is packed with puns and quips. In the spirit of the new objectivity, romantic expressiveness is ridiculed in a parody of a love duet. The peak of hilarity is reached when the leading female character sings an aria in the bathtub. It was through this work that Hitler made his acquaintance with Hindemith's music and the Führer's outrage was so strong that, years later when he assumed power, he insisted that the composer be eliminated from Germany's musical life.

Another stage work, also a bitter comment on life, called *Lehrstück*, dates from the same year, and was based on a play by Bertold Brecht. The work is scored for two men's voices, narrator, mixed chorus, dancer, three clowns, and crowd. The orchestra can be made up of any combination of instruments; the three basic instrumental parts (high, medium, and low) can be played in the higher or lower octaves, and choral parts can be doubled by brass instruments. The intention behind this leeway in orchestration was to allow for local instrumental resources. In the preface to the score Hindemith wrote: "The course indicated in the score is rather a suggestion than a prescription. Omissions, additions, and rearrangements are possible." In allowing this kind of freedom, Hindemith anticipated certain procedures employed by the avant-garde of the midcentury, where the score is considered a point of departure rather than an unchangeable document of the composer's musical expression. Hindemith's belief that the listener should actively participate is expressed in several choral numbers in which audiences were asked to join. In order to facilitate audience participation, the music and the text of the choral numbers were projected on a screen.

Turning sharply from Brecht's realism, in his next work, the oratorio *Das Unaufhörliche* (The Perpetual, 1931), Hindemith chose a text from the work of Gottfried Benn, a poet noted for his mystic idealism.

The diversity of Hindemith's literary sources of this period suggests a personal quest for values on the composer's part, who at this time was approaching his fortieth year. Hindemith's biographer, Strobel, however, claims that the composer's interest in these widely varying literary sources was a purely musical one; every text was simply considered a new musical challenge. The musical setting of *Das Unaufhörliche* is inferior to the literary value of its text; in Copland's words "the musical language is sanctimonious and monotonous, entirely lacking the sense of elation of the literary source."

The assumption that the choice of texts was symptomatic of the composer's inner search is borne out by Hindemith's next major work: *Mathis der Maler* (1932–1934), an opera in seven scenes based on the composer's libretto, points to a personal crisis. The subject of the opera is the life of Grunewald, the master of the Isenheim altar pieces. His conflict—can the creative artist remain indifferent to the issues of the day—was of a profoundly personal concern to the composer. Mathis' outcry during the Peasants' War in the period following the Reformation —"I cannot paint anymore; the misery of the people paralyzes my arm and my spirit"—must have touched the composer deeply, as he witnessed the violence, book-burning, and destruction of the rising Nazi power.

Mathis is a deeply serious work, contemplative in character, drawing on the resources of German folklore. It is ironical that, at a time when the composer turned his attention to the German past, creating a work that is German *par excellence,* the national socialist regime vilified him and his art. Although the work had its stage premiere in Zurich in 1938, German audiences received a taste of the work earlier through the *Mathis Symphony,* an orchestral triptych (Angelic Concerto-Entombment-The Temptation of St. Anthony) drawn from the opera. This orchestral arrangement has become perhaps Hindemith's most widely performed work, and its middle movement is certainly one of his most inspired achievements. The opera, however, like *Cardillac,* did not gain popularity; its length, and the brooding, philosophical, undramatic mood are doubtless responsible for its lack of success.

Before a discussion of Hindemith's later period, the following works should be mentioned: *Concert Music for Piano, Brass, and Two Harps,* Op. 49 (1930); *Concert Music for String Orchestra and Brass Instruments,* Op. 50 (1930); the *Philharmonic Concerto* (1932), written for Wilhelm Furtwängler and the fiftieth anniversary of the Berlin Philharmonic; and *Der Schwanendreher* (1935), a concerto for viola based on traditional German folk songs.

The early 1930s represent the high watermark of the composer's standing, as summarized by Willi Reich in 1931:

> Paul Hindemith occupies a unique place among the living composers of Germany, inasmuch as today, at the age of thirty-six, after stormy beginnings, he must be regarded as the unrivaled leader of that section of the young generation which believes in carrying to its limits the idea that music should be adapted to the demands of its time.[13]

---

[13]Willi Reich, "Paul Hindemith," *Musical Quarterly,* **17** (1931), pp. 486–496.

WORKS AFTER 1935

Around 1935 the second phase of *Gebrauchsmusik* started to pour from Hindemith's pen. This time the works were written for the neglected instruments of the orchestra and intended for the professional performer. Sonatas were composed—always with the assistance of the piano—for flute, oboe, bassoon, clarinet, French horn, English horn, trombone, harp, and later, the double bass. From the same period (1935-1942) came three piano sonatas, a sonata for piano, four hands, and three organ sonatas.

Two ballet works from this period stand out: *Nobilissima Visione* (St. Francis, 1938)—the orchestral suite derived from the ballet is one of the most frequently performed later Hindemith works—and Theme and Variations: The "Four Temperaments" for piano and string orchestra (1940). Both works show freshness of inspiration and originality of musical thought.

A major work, also dated 1940, the Symphony in E flat, foreshadows the shortcomings of many later works. The symphony, more than half an hour long, fails to sustain interest. The sound lacks distinction and rhythmic monotony prevails. It also seems as if the composer had applied the rules expounded in the *Unterweisung* somewhat mechanically. The harmonic fluctuation achieves a predictable course; dissonances are resolved in obvious tonal cadences. In general, both melodic and harmonic movement is more sluggish than in earlier works.

A trend toward conservatism and a simplified style can be observed in comparing the Fifth Quartet (1942) to the earlier ones. Instead of the free and spontaneous harmonic style of the early quartets which often employ undefined tonal regions and bitonal frictions, the harmonic scheme of the Fifth Quartet is conceived in the framework of the *Unterweisung*.

THE FIFTH QUARTET

The Fifth Quartet, in four movements, is cyclic in form. The opening statements of each of the first three movements and the second theme of the second movement are integrated and developed in the last movement.

The first movement, marked "very quietly and with expression," is a fugue. Its subject (Ex. 14/11) shows a slight resemblance to the opening fugue of Beethoven's Quartet, Op. 131, in C sharp minor.

EX. 14/11 *Fifth Quartet,*[14] first movement, opening

The second movement, in sonata form, is anchored on E flat. Since the opening section is typical of many later works, it is shown in Example 14/12. In these eight measures a predictable progression of basic harmonic values (I–V–I) is separated by rather irrelevant chromatic episodes:

EX. 14/12 *Fifth Quartet,* second movement, opening

The second theme (Ex. 14/13) is typical of many melodies of the late period:

14 Quoted by permission of B. Schott's Söhne and Associated Music Publishers, Inc.

EX. 14/13 *Fifth Quartet,* second movement, mm. 27–36

The development section begins at letter M with a statement of the main theme on D flat played in unison, preceded by some canonic treatment in augmentation of the main theme. The recapitulation (letter R) leads to the coda (letter V); here the main theme is reiterated in unison, but now on G flat. The last eight measures of the movement follow very stilted harmonic procedures similar to those demonstrated in Example 14/12.

The third movement, in theme and variation form, centers on B. The first nine measures of the sixty-one measure theme is shown in Example 14/14:

EX. 14/14 *Fifth Quartet,* third movement, opening

The first variation (mm. 62–86) presents a new rhythmic version of the theme.

EX. 14/15 *Fifth Quartet,* third movement, mm. 74–75

In the second variation (mm. 86–139) the persistent dotted rhythm creates a monotonous effect, relieved somewhat in the third variation (mm. 139–173) by the sonority of the cello solo.

The fourth and last variation (mm. 173–244), despite its faster speed, sounds sterile and dry; the theme is hidden in the rapid eighth-note motion (Ex. 14/16) that pervades the entire variation.

EX. 14/16 *Fifth Quartet,* third movement, m. 173

The last movement, in sonata form and again on E flat, starts with an exposition featuring three different musical ideas: the opening theme, the second theme at letter C, and the closing section at letter E. At letter F the development begins and centers on the material of the closing section. First it is treated canonically and later it is combined with the themes of the earlier movements. After a *fff* climax (mm. 105–108), a lighthearted coda marked *Allegretto grazioso* brings the work to a close.

On the whole, the quartet lacks the spontaneity of the earlier quartets; in the new simplified style a strongly tonal foundation replaces the harmonic freedom of the earlier works.

THE REVISION OF *DAS MARIENLEBEN*

AND THE LATE WORKS

The composer's late conservative tendencies become apparent from a comparison of the revised edition of *Das Marienleben* (1948) with its original version (1923). The revised edition is prefaced by a lengthy essay in which the composer explains the need for the changes. Such a wordy comment in itself shows how much the composer's attitude altered from his youth. When he was asked to explain and analyze his music in 1922, he answered:

> I cannot give analyses of my works because I do not know how to explain a piece of music in a few words; I prefer to write a new piece in that time.

In sharp contrast to this attitude, in the preface to the revised edition of *Das Marienleben,* the reader is invited "to participate in the problems which are hidden beneath the surface."

In the revised edition two of the songs (Nos. 3 and 7) are entirely new, while Nos. 1, 2, 6, 8, 10, 13, 14, and 15 were thoroughly revised; one song (No. 12) remained unchanged.

The revision had three goals: 1) to make the vocal part more singable; 2) to eliminate badly balanced chromaticism by replacing harmonically ambiguous features with clearly defined tonalities; and 3) to unify the cycle by a carefully chosen sequence of keys. In the new version the songs are divided into four groups: 1-4, 5-9, 10-12, and 13-15. Carefully weighed dynamic and expressive climaxes are arranged so that the listener can grasp the cycle as a continuous and coherent whole, instead of as isolated songs in the earlier version.

Rudolph Stephan,[15] who made an exhaustive study of the two versions, shows how the expressive power of the first version has been sacrificed in the revised version to conform to the principles laid down in the composer's theoretical system.

Stephan cites the case of Song No. 4; in Examples 14/17/a and b one can see how the bitonality of the first version of *Das Marienleben* is replaced by a less imaginative setting in the second version.

EX. 14/17/a *Das Marienleben,*[16] Song No. 4, original version, opening

EX. 14/17/b Song No. 4, revised version, opening

[15] Rudolph Stephan, "Hindemith's *Marienleben:* An Assessment of Its Two Versions," *Music Review,* **15**, No. 4 (1954), pp. 275-287.

[16] Quoted by permission of B. Schott's Söhne and Associated Music Publishers, Inc.

The two versions of Song No. 10 (Ex. 14/18/a and b) show another instance of the composer's aim in the revision. Here the melodic line is smoothed out, as more conventional intervals (minor sevenths) replace the dissonant interval of the earlier version. Also, the tritone (C–G flat) of the third measure of the original version disappears in the revised edition. The rhythmic freedom of the original is also somewhat curtailed, as the *fermata* is deleted in the revision.

EX. 14/18/a Song No. 10,[17] original version, opening

EX. 14/18/b Song No. 10, revised version, opening

Concerning the revisions in general, Stephan's conclusions are the following:

> In place of spontaneity one is now faced with the concoctions of an unstable theory and with a handful of practical formulae which are used by Hindemith and his imitators within the confines of respectable academicism[18]

[17] Quoted by permission of B. Schott's Söhne and Associated Music Publishers, Inc. Text Maria Rainer Rilke's *Das Marienleben*, Frankfurt: Insel Verlag, 1921.

[18] Stephan, p. 187.

Despite the not too felicitous revisions, *Das Marienleben* remains one of the finest song cycles of the twentieth century.

Among the later works, an oratorio, "When Lilacs Last in the Door-yard Bloom'd" (Whitman), a requiem "For those we love" (1946) should be added to the list of the composer's genuine inspirations.

Other large-scale late works include: a) Stage works: *Die Harmonie der Welt* (The Harmony of the Universe, 1956–1957), an opera in five acts, and *The Long Christmas Dinner,* a one-act opera based on a text by Thornton Wilder (1960); b) For chorus, orchestra, and solo voices: *Ite, angeli veloces,* a cantata in three parts based on a text by Paul Claudel (1955); c) For orchestra: the frequently programmed *Symphonic Metamorphoses* of themes by Carl Maria von Weber (1943), the Sinfonietta in E (1950), and the *Pittsburgh Symphony* (1958), written for the bicentennial of the City of Pittsburgh; and d) Chamber works: Sixth String Quartet (1945), *Septet* for winds (1948), and *Octet* for winds and strings (1958).

In 1962 Hindemith wrote an Organ Concerto commissioned by the Lincoln Center for Performing Arts in New York for the inauguration of Lincoln Hall, and in the last year of his life, in 1963, a *Requiem* for a *cappella* chorus.

SUMMARY

The over-all course of Hindemith's stylistic development runs parallel to that of Stravinsky. Both composers, after starting in the late romantic style, soon shocked their audiences by composing avant-garde music. The impact of their work was so strong that both composers achieved leadership in their respective spheres of influence. They maintained this role, although they eventually receded from their advanced positions and turned to the past for inspiration.

Underneath these superficial similarities, however, the essential qualities of their music are entirely different; the primitivism and the shock value of *The Rite of Spring* have little in common with the irony and irreverence of Hindemith's Chamber Music, Op. 24, No. 1. Nevertheless, Hindemith's antiromantic outbursts and brush with expressionism caused a considerable uproar in the German musical world.

The irony and harshness, however, soon disappeared from the German composer's music. In 1923, *Das Marienleben* shows signs of consolidation, and soon the former iconoclast emerged as a preserver of the great German musical tradition. A link to the past can be seen in Hindemith's spiritual affinity to the music of Bach and in his use of baroque forms and textures. The German folk song was also a part of his style.

Hindemith became increasingly conscious of ethical and moral issues during his middle years. His sense of responsibility as a teacher of composition led him to lay the foundations of a new harmonic system. His concern for communication with his audiences resulted in a simplification of his style. His awareness of the musical and educational needs of the amateur and the young prompted him to write *Gebrauchsmusik.*

Since his death Hindemith's music seems to have declined in popularity; his repudiation of atonal and twelve-tone theories and his belief in the immutable laws of harmony are considered anachronistic by the younger generation of composers.

Despite his failure as a system builder, he contributed significantly to contemporary music theory. Musically, his very large output contains many routine works; however, his best compositions insure a place for him among the outstanding composers of the century.

A SELECTIVE LIST OF WORKS

First Quartet, Op. 10   1919

Sonatas No. 1 and 2 for violin-piano, No. 3 for cello-piano, No. 4 for viola-piano, No. 5 for unaccompanied viola, Op. 11   1918–1919

Second Quartet, Op. 16   1921

Chamber Music, Op. 24, No. 1 for solo instruments   1921

Third Quartet, Op. 22   1922

"Die junge Magd," songs for voice, flute, clarinet, and string quartet (George Trakl), Op. 23   1922

Little Chamber Music for woodwind quintet, Op. 24, No. 2   1922

Das Marienleben, a song cycle for voice and piano, based on Rilke's poetry, Op. 27, revised in 1948   1923

Fourth String Quartet, Op. 32   1923

First String Trio, Op. 34   1924

Concerto for Orchestra, Op. 38   1925

Cardillac, an opera in three acts, revised in 1952   1926

Neues vom Tage (News of the Day), a comic opera in three parts (Schiffer), revised in 1953   1928–1929

Lehrstück, a one-act opera (Brecht)   1929

Concert Music for piano, brass and two harps, Op. 49   1930

Concert Music for string orchestra and brass instruments, Op. 50   1930

Das Unaufhörliche (The Perpetual), an oratorio in three parts   1931

Philharmonic Concerto   1932

Plöner Musiktag (A Day of Music in Plön)   1932

Second String Trio   1933

Mathis der Maler (Matthias the Painter), an opera in seven scenes 1934-1935

Symphony "Mathis der Maler" (Angelic Concert–Entombment–Temptation of St. Anthony)   1934

Der Schwanendreher, concerto for viola and small orchestra   1935

Sonatas for the following instruments, with piano: oboe, English horn, clarinet, bassoon, French horn, trumpet, trombone, harp; and piano four hands, organ   1938-1942

Nobilissima Visione (St. Francis), a dance legend in three scenes   1938

The "Four Temperaments," a ballet for piano and string orchestra   1940

Symphony in E flat   1940

Ludus Tonalis for piano   1942

Symphonic Metamorphoses of themes by Carl Maria von Weber for orchestra   1943

Fifth String Quartet   1943

Sixth String Quartet   1945

"When Lilacs Last in the Dooryard Bloom'd," a requiem "For those we love" (Whitman), an oratorio in three parts   1946

Concerto for clarinet   1947

Septet for wind instruments   1948

Sonata for double-bass and piano   1949

Ite, angeli veloces, a cantata in three parts (Paul Claudel)   1955

Die Harmonie der Welt (The Harmony of the Universe), an opera in five acts   1956-1957

Pittsburgh Symphony   1958

Octet   1958

The Long Christmas Dinner, an opera in one act (Thornton Wilder)   1960

Organ Concerto   1962

Requiem for *a cappella* chorus   1963

PART III

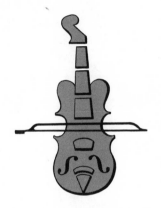

MUSICAL PANORAMA
OF EUROPE
AND THE UNITED STATES

THE EUROPEAN SCENE

The state of twentieth-century music in various European countries will be viewed in the present chapter. The position of the leading composers, and the trends they represent will be examined, without making an attempt to enumerate all the composers who have been active during the century. The order of examination will be the following: first the music of France, Germany, and Italy, the three countries that represent the most advanced musical thought in Europe today; next, two countries with conservative leanings, England and Soviet Russia; and finally, the smaller countries of Europe.

FRANCE

Debussy and Ravel, the two key figures in the musical renewal of France during the first quarter of the century (see Chapter 8), did not establish a school. Highly individualistic and introverted, they were unwilling or unable to organize a musical movement. They had followers and imitators, but it was apparent that neither Debussy's fluid and improvisational art, a closed universe in itself, nor Ravel's natural artificiality could be successfully imitated.

The void they left was filled by a group known as "Les Six." The members of the group, Milhaud, Honegger, Poulenc, Auric, Durey, and Tailleferre, were held together by bonds of friendship rather than by common musical goals. Their spokesman was Jean Cocteau, who also provided a liaison with the literary world. For a while they looked to Satie for musical leadership. Their rather nebulous aim, as formulated by Cocteau, was to create *French* music for France. Clarity was an additional goal in both literary and musical communication. Aside from these objectives, they were against everything that was associated with romanticism. They rejected chromaticism and its extension by Schoenberg; they also denounced the overt emotionalism and hypertrophy of form found in the works of the late romanticists. One positive aim was to re-establish diatonic harmonies in a firm tonal setting. Haydn and Rameau were used as models.

The ideals of *Les Six* were not unlike those of the neoclassic movement, initiated contemporaneously by Busoni, Stravinsky, Hindemith, and Prokofiev. The music of the French composers failed, however, to embody their program and had little to do with Haydn or Rameau, or with eighteenth-century musical practices. Nevertheless, they succeeded in breaking away from the esthetic outlook of the nineteenth century. They established a new image of the artist who "is a regular fellow and not the high priest of the art."[1] They wanted to write music to which one does not listen with one's head in one's hands, lost in reverie. This antiromantic thinking was behind their choice of subject matter too: for example, in Honegger's *Pacific 231* (1922), the musical portrayal of the sound of a locomotive, and in Milhaud's *Catalogue de Fleurs* (1920), the musical setting of the words taken from a seed catalog. For this same reason, the jazz rhythms of the music hall and night clubs found their way into the music of the group.[2]

[1] Aaron Copland, *Our New Music* (New York: McGraw-Hill, Inc., 1941), p. 79.
[2] Milhaud's essay, "My First Encounter with Jazz," *Contemporary Composers on Contemporary Music,* edited by Elliott Schwartz and Barney Childs (New York: Holt, Rinehart and Winston, Inc., 1967).

The group's existence was short-lived in spite of all the publicity and attention it received; Auric, Durey, and Tailleferre dropped out of sight, while Honegger, Poulenc, and Milhaud each followed a different path.

Arthur Honegger (1892–1955), of Swiss parentage, received his early musical education in Zurich. He had the least in common with the objectives of the group by training and inclination. The huge dramatic frescoes of his oratorios and the grandeur of his symphonies are strongly rooted in romanticism. Similarly, his harmonic style is rich in chromatic figurations. His textures recall baroque polyphony and his massive choruses are reminiscent of Bach. The only truly Gallic flavor in his music stems from the occasional use of French folk sources.

Honegger's most successful works are his dramatic oratorios: his first essay in this form, *King David* (1921), brought him world recognition. Outstanding among the oratorios that followed are: *Judith* (1926), *Jeanne d'Arc au Bûcher* (1938), and *Le Danse des Morts* (1940), with a text by Paul Claudel. Almost as prolific as Milhaud, Honegger wrote five symphonies, three string quartets, and a number of works for solo instruments with orchestra. His symphonies have sweep and drama, yet, along with his other works, they seem to have faded from the repertory. Twenty-five years ago Copland[3] felt that Honegger's music had not worn well because it "is conventional at its core."

In contrast to Honegger's strong romantic allegiance, Francis Poulenc (1899–1963) remained faithful to the principles of the group. A Parisian by birth, he studied with Charles Koechlin (1867–1951), a highly original and remote figure in the musical life of France. Poulenc's early compositions show a witty vein, clowning and jesting in the manner of Satie. A good deal of his piano music fits into the salon music category. Anyone familiar with just this side of Poulenc would not suspect his spiritual inclinations. His fine religious works include a Mass (1937), *Stabat Mater* (1950), and *Sept Répons de Ténèbres* (1961), written for Easter week.

Poulenc's strongest asset is his lyrical, melodic inventiveness; his 150 songs, many of them set to the verse of surrealist poets, rank high in twentieth-century vocal literature. His opera, *Dialogues des Carmélites* (1953–1955), based on the tragic play of a French Catholic poet, Georges Bernanos, won international recognition. Somewhat less well known is *La Voix Humaine* (1958), a one-act lyric tragedy based on Cocteau's play.

While Poulenc's music is still not familiar to the general public, it is safe to predict, on the basis of the warm reception accorded his works at various memorial concerts following his death, that it will have an ascendancy in the years to come.

[3]*Our New Music*, p. 81.

Undoubtedly, the most famous member of "Les Six" is Darius Milhaud (b. 1892), France's leading composer between the two wars, a period that lacked grandeur in French musical life, even though it produced a host of minor composers. Milhaud has often been compared to Hindemith. Both composers produced a torrent of music—Milhaud's output exceeds 300 works—of uneven quality. They contributed to almost every branch of musical literature with equal facility. Both composers experienced a spectacular success followed by a gradual disappearance of their works from the repertory. Milhaud's eighteen quartets or thirteen symphonies are rarely performed. Most commentators agree that stage works were his best medium; among the fifteen operas, thirteen ballets, and incidental music produced for more than fifty plays and films, the three operas—*Christophe Colomb* (1928), based on Claudel's libretto, *Les Malheurs d'Orphée* (1924), and *David* (1953), written for the 3,000th anniversary of the founding of the City of Jerusalem—are cited as his major achievements. However, even Milhaud's best works are surrounded by controversy. In the opinion of the Franco-Belgian commentator, Collaer,[4] *Christophe Colomb* is a "splendid work that should be considered the most representative, not only of its composer but of the first half of the twentieth century." Conversely, the highly regarded English critic, Drew, feels that the opera cannot maintain the listener's interest for long. He writes: "Reading this music, one is reminded by its disastrous heedlessness of a remark of Stravinsky: 'One should tremble at every chord.' If one trembles at *Christophe Colomb*, it is with rage and boredom."[5]

Milhaud's best compositions were of modest dimensions and, like Hindemith's, composed early in his career. The French composer also started out as the *enfant terrible* of the post-World War I years. His experimentations, first with polytonality and later with jazz, proved shocking. Satie's spirit hovers over the ballet, *Le Boeuf sur le toit* (1920), set in an American bar crowded with freakish people. *La Création du Monde* (1923), a jazz ballet, is one of the composer's most convincing works. Milhaud was also successful in integrating folk materials into his music. A strong flavor of Brazilian folk music permeates his music, as the result of his temporary residence in Brazil during World War I as a French cultural attaché. And, upon returing to France, he stopped briefly in New York, during which time he became fascinated with jazz in New York's Harlem section. (The composer moved to the United States in 1940, when he was forced to leave France in the face of the German occupation.) In addition to Brazilian folk music and American

[4] Paul Collaer, *A History of Modern Music,* translated from French by Sally Abeles (New York: Grosset & Dunlap, Inc., 1961).

[5] David Drew, "Modern French Music," *European Music in the Twentieth Century,* edited by Howard Hartog (London: Routledge & Kegan Ltd., 1957).

jazz sources, Milhaud also drew upon the folklore of his native country. Gallic influence is felt in the charming *Suite Provençale* for orchestra (1936) and the woodwind quintet, *La Cheminée du Roi René* (1939).

The attractive features of Milhaud's style are his melodic gift, lucidity in expression, and his ability to create lyric moods ranging from pastoral to nostalgic. His craftsmanship and sense of balance usually prevent him from being longwinded. The recognition of the solo role of percussion instruments, as seen in his *Concerto for Percussion and Small Orchestra* (1930), is a novel feature of his compositions.

According to critics, Milhaud lacks the deep creative urge, an inner commitment to principles or ideas. Compared to Schoenberg's search which produced atonality, Milhaud's polytonality is merely a stunt, as is the superimposition of his fourteenth and fifteenth quartets which resulted in an Octet. As expressed by Drew," . . . nothing—not a chord, not a counterpoint, not a modulation—nothing really matters."

Among the numerous composers who were active during the first half of the century, the figure of Albert Roussel (1869–1937) stands out. Chronologically, and on the basis of his early works, such as the ballet *The Spider's Feast* (1912), he belongs to Ravel's period. However, on the basis of his later achievements, such as the Third and Fourth Symphonies, (dated 1930 and 1935, respectively) and the *Sinfonietta* (1934), he belongs to a more recent phase in the history of French music. He actually fulfilled the aims of *Les Six* more successfully than did other members of the group. His incisive rhythms and elegant, abstract patterns, which were woven into a carefully wrought design, came closer to the spirit of Rameau than the six composers who officially aimed at re-establishing tradition. Roussel's counterpoint is light and has an elegant touch, next to which Honegger's textures sound overly dense. Roussel's art also featured an exotic flavor, the result of the composer's exposure to oriental music in the course of his many trips to the East. While his craftsmanship is, admittedly, not as fluid as that of Milhaud, this shortcoming is counterbalanced by a deep personal involvement and seriousness of purpose. He never tried to shock or dazzle the listener; instead, he created a personal style that was French without being overly romantic or coldly abstract. A number of younger composers based their point of departure on the style of Roussel, among them Henri Barraud (b. 1900), Henri Dutilleux (b. 1916), and André Jolivet (b. 1905).

Among the minor composers of some importance and contemporaneous with *Les Six*, Jacques Ibert (1890–1962), a musical caricaturist somewhat in the style of Satie, Henri Sauguet (b. 1901), and Jean Françaix (b. 1912) should be mentioned.

The inclination of French artists to form groups soon manifested itself in another movement, that of *La Jeune France*, instigated in 1936 by Olivier Messiaen (b. 1908), André Jolivet (b. 1905), Yves Baudrier (b. 1906), and Daniel Lesur (b. 1908). The objectives of the new group were not clearly formulated; their rejection of neoclassicism, however, distinguished them from *Les Six*. Nevertheless, the members of *La Jeune France* felt that the renewal of French music must be based on the great tradition of French masters of the past. A humanistic outlook, honesty, and integrity were their lofty, but nebulous aims. The real but undeclared objectives of the group were to counter the activities of *Le Triton,* another society specializing in contemporary music and known for its international associations. The aim of *La Jeune France* was to form a movement free of foreign influences.

The new group, however, like *Les Six,* soon disbanded and the members went their separate ways. Messiaen achieved international fame, while Jolivet earned a solid reputation; Baudrier devoted his abilities to writing music for films, and Lesur, a professor of the Schola Cantorum, was active in the academic world.

The commanding figure of Messiaen has been the center of many controversies. His music, without being revolutionary or avant-garde, has a striking originality. It is a curious blend of the old and the new, held together by a forceful personality for whom composition is an act of faith.

A descendant of an old Catholic family from the south of France, Messiaen studied at the Conservatoire in Paris, dividing his time between the organ and composition. After graduation he became organist at the Church of the Trinity, a post he continued to hold when he became an important and sought-after teacher of composition. Between 1945 and 1950 almost all of the leading European avant-garde composers attended his composition classes. Although admired by the avant-garde, Messiaen's music is deeply rooted in tradition. He adhered to tonality and believed in the supremacy of melody. Moreover, his conception of sound seems anachronistic at midcentury, as he believed in "an iridescent music, one which delights the auditory senses with delicate voluptuous pleasures." Undoubtedly, the sensuous quality of his music, often reminiscent of Debussy's textures, prompted several commentators to label Messiaen a neoromantic, a term of dubious value.

Messiaen revealed his originality in the field of rhythm. He employed the peculiarities of Hindu rhythms, a subject that fascinated him in his student days. It would be misleading, however, to think that the significance of Messiaen's contributions to rhythmic thinking consists merely of the borrowing of some rhythmic devices (see Chapter 3). In Messiaen's music rhythm is uniquely freed from melody and assumes an independent function. It is used like counterpoint, and accordingly, contrapuntal devices such as canon, crab canons, and the like, are applied to rhythmic patterns. The composer, who summarized his compositional approach in a treatise entitled *The Technique of My Musical Language,* is quoted in a concert program accompanying the American performance of *Mode de valeurs et d'intensités:*

> I tried to separate the study of duration from the study of sound. I tried to liberate rhythm not only from the measure but also from metric and symmetry. I tried to recover the secrets of ancient Hindu rhythmics, the most evolved in musical history, and to revive them. Finally, I utilized the permutations of duration; that is, a great number of possible directions in time.[6]

Messiaen's rhythmic approach colors the total picture of his music. It achieves a unique temporal quality of immobility, inflected by a sensation of a slight rubato. Time loses its meaning—some of his works last over two hours—conveying a quality of contemplation peculiar to Eastern mysticism.

Harmonically, too, Messiaen draws on the Hindu modes; his scales, known as "modes of limited transposition" are built on a non-Western arrangement of whole steps and half steps. His modes are used both melodically and harmonically, a procedure similar to Schoenberg's conception of the two-dimensional musical space.

The majority of Messiaen's earlier works are of a religious nature. The better known compositions are: *L'Ascension* (1933), a set of four symphonic meditations; *La Nativité du Seigneur* for organ (1935); *Les Chants de la Terre et du Ciel* (1938), based on his own poetry; *Les Corps Glorieux* (1939) for organ; *Quatuor pour la Fin du Temps,* a quartet for clarinet, violin, cello, and piano, written during World War II in a German prison camp; *Les Sept Visions d'Amen* for two pianos (1943); *Les Vingt Regards sur L'Enfant Jésus* for piano (1944); and *Les Trois Petites Liturgies de la Présence Divine* for chorus, piano, ondes martenot (an electronic instrument), and orchestra (1944). One of Messiaen's major works is the *Turangalila Symphony* (1946–1948), commissioned by the Koussevitsky Foundation and first performed in Boston. The Hindu influence is strongly felt in this work, whose title indicates a Hindu love song. Around 1950, Messiaen's style took a temporary turn toward a more abstract approach; works from this period comprise: *Mode de Valeurs et d'Intensités* (1949), and *Le Livre d'Orgue* (1951).

Thereafter, the composer's religious outlook evolved into a nature mysticism. After many years of collecting bird songs, he used birdcalls as the essential part of his melodic invention. Examples are *Le Merle Noir* for flute and piano (1952); *Le Réveil des Oiseaux* for piano and orchestra (1953); *Oiseaux Exotiques* for piano and winds (1955–1956); *Premier Catalogue d'Oiseaux* for piano (1958), and *Chronochromie*

---

[6]Olivier Messiaen, *Technique de mon langage musical* (Paris: Leduc, 1944); English transl. *The Technique of My Musical Language,* Paris, 1950).

(1960), based on bird songs collected in Mexico, France, Sweden, and Japan. The later works were less favorably received than the earlier compositions; a recurring criticism of Messiaen's music is the weakness of its structure.

The most striking figure in the field of French music today is, undoubtedly, Pierre Boulez (b. 1925). After studying with Messiaen and Leibowitz, Boulez emerged as the most promising composer of the avant-garde, its brilliant and most lucid spokesman, and as a conductor of first rank. Early in his career he took a strong position against Schoenberg's stylistic inconsistencies (see Chapter 7) and named Webern as the model. Boulez extended the serial principle to elements other than pitch, and soon wrote totally organized music in which rhythm, intensity, and timbre were also serialized. Total organization marked his serial works, such as his Second Sonata (1948) and the first set of his *Structures* for two pianos (1952). At this time, Boulez rewrote two of his earlier works: *Visage Nuptial* and *Le Soleil des Eaux,* both for voice and instruments and based on the poetry of René Char, his favorite poet.

Also from this self-conscious period originates *Polyphonie X* for eighteen solo instruments (1951), which the composer withdrew after its disastrous reception at the Donaueschingen Festival. The work is the result of the most relentless serial organization; "the organization is not only total, but totalitarian" in the composer's words. The "X" in the title of the work is a graphic symbol indicating the intersection of certain structures.

These cerebral works were followed by the composer's masterpiece, *Le Marteau sans Maître* (1953), perhaps the most widely known work in avant-garde literature. The work is based on three short poems by René Char and is scored for alto voice, flute, viola, guitar, vibraphone, xylorimba (an instrument whose tone combines the metallic sound of the xylophone and the softer sound of the marimba), and percussion. It marks a new freedom in the composer's style; technique is placed in the service of expressiveness. The short poems reflect upon the dilemma of modern man, how to break out of the confining shackles of materialistic existence that is doomed—the "hammer without a master." The work is divided into nine sections, among which only four employ the voice. The purely instrumental sections reflect upon the words or serve as introductions to the next lines. In each section the instruments appear in new combinations, a device borrowed from Schoenberg's *Pierrot Lunaire,* whose sonorities also may have left a trace on the extremely beautiful and imaginative scoring of the work. The fragile sonorities and fragmented melodies suggest Debussy and the exoticism of Far Eastern music, while the exploration of rhythmic cells points to Webern's middle period. The *Le Marteau sans Maître* represented a turning point in Boulez's style. He now admitted the futility of total organization:

. . . Now rhythm, tone color, and dynamics are organized, and all serve as fodder for the monstrous polyorganization from which one must break free if one is not to condemn oneself to deafness.[7]

In 1953, Boulez wrote *Deux Improvisations sur Mallarmé* for voice and instruments, a work of great tonal beauty. Next came the Third Piano Sonata, a "work-in-progress" discussed in an interesting essay by the composer.[8] At its premiere, the work consisted of five "formants" or movements, among which only three reached their final form. In this composition, Boulez applied the principles of limited indeterminacy, leaving certain choices to the performer. For instance, the performer can choose between a simple or a complex version; also, he has a choice of omitting ornamentations or variants. The freedom allowed by the composer is more limited than the leeway Stockhausen affords in his *Klavierstück XI* (see Chapter 7). The problem of indeterminacy, that is to say, the element of chance in composition, occupied Boulez theoretically, too. He summed up his views on the matter in an essay, entitled *Alea*.[9]

The latest works of Boulez, *Doubles* for orchestra (1958), *Poésie pour Pouvoir* (1958), *Pli selon pli* (1958) (the latter two for voice and orchestra), and *Eclat* for diverse instruments (1965), are unpublished, and not recorded, in the United States. The *Structures II* (1961) for two pianos was warmly received at its Los Angeles premiere; according to the correspondent of the *Musical Quarterly,* the work "produced an accumulative effect of powerful dramatic and expressive vitality." It is safe to predict that Boulez will play a major role in the music of the next decades.

Finally, mention should be made of a young French composer, Jean Barraqué (b. 1928), who, until a few years ago, seemed like a legendary figure, hailed in Hodeir's book[10] as France's greatest composer. The New York premiere of his *Séquences,* a work based on a text by Nietzsche for voice and instruments, did not fulfill Hodeir's exaggerated promise.

In addition to Barraqué, several young French composers, Jean-Louis Martinet, Serge Nigg, Michel Philippot, and Maurice Le Roux, are drawing increasing attention in their native country. So far they have remained merely names to American audiences, but even so they point to the rich contribution France is making to contemporary music.

---

[7] Pierre Boulez, *Penser la Musique aujourd' hui* (Paris: Gonthier, 1964).

[8] Pierre Boulez, "Sonata, que me veux-tu?" *Perspectives of New Music,* **1**, No. 2 (1963).

[9] Pierre Boulez, "Alea," *Perspectives of New Music,* **3**, No. 1 (1964).

[10] André Hodeir, *Since Debussy: A View of Contemporary Music* (New York: Grove Press, Inc., 1961).

GERMANY

In the years prior to World War I, Richard Strauss (see Chapter 8) dominated the German musical scene. Next, two late romanticists, Max Reger—mentioned as Hindemith's forerunner—and Hans Pfitzner (1869–1949), won considerable acclaim. Reger and Pfitzner were caught in the crisis precipitated by the dissolution of tonality and, subsequently, of form. Reger's solution was the application of contrapuntal devices to hold together the loose architecture of his music, while Pfitzner tried in vain to grapple with the same problem.

A prophetic voice, that of the German-Italian Ferruccio Busoni (1866–1924), warned in a provocative essay[11] that the renewal of music can be accomplished only in terms of a *new classicism,* by which he meant a consolidation of the attainments of earlier experimentation in "beautiful and firm forms." Clarity of architecture, lucidity in expression, and controlled emotions were his ideals. He felt he represented a "beginning" in the stream of European musical thought. It took a while, however, for his ideas to take root; in his lifetime, he was celebrated as a great piano virtuoso and pedagogue, while his esthetic views and compositions were equally ignored. Soon, however, his music became a potent force and a number of composers, among them the Italians Dallapiccola and Petrassi, benefited from his ideas. Now the music of Busoni is in the process of being re-evaluated; the New York premiere of his opera, *Doctor Faustus,* in 1964 won a good deal of recognition for the composer forty years after his death.

The vacuum that arose in German music after World War I was filled by Hindemith, who remained the unrivaled musical leader in Germany until his ouster in the 1930s (see Chapter 14). His music was banned along with that of Bartók, Stravinsky, and the Viennese atonalists, thereby paralyzing creative efforts in Germany. The generation that reached maturity during the Nazi regime failed to yield a composer of any rank. Only the composers born around the turn of the century remained active. Among these, Orff, Egk, Hartmann, and Blacher are prominent.

The best known among them is Carl Orff (b. 1895). His reputation rests on nine stage works, all composed after his fortieth birthday. Following the success of his first stage work, *Carmina Burana,* in 1935, he withdrew all of his earlier works. Orff's style, as exemplified in his stage works, is the result of a slow development in which his professional experience played a significant role. In his first post as the music di-

---

[11] Ferruccio Busoni, *Toward a New Esthetic of Music* (New York: G. Schirmer, Inc., 1911).

rector of the *Münchner Kammerspiele* theater—a company that excelled in the classics—he gained an intimate knowledge of the art of stage-craft. Next, as the head of the department of *Tänzerische Musikerziehung* (music education through movement and dance) at a Munich school, he realized the supreme significance of rhythm and gesture, and made these two elements the main ingredients of his art. Orff applied his ideas to music education too, and composed a great amount of *Gebrauchsmusik,* emphasizing the significance of ensemble work for children. Perhaps influenced by Hindemith, he felt impelled to write highly accessible music.

Orff's best-known work is his trilogy, *I Trionfi,* consisting of *Carmina Burana* (1935), *Catulli Carmina* (1943), and *Trionfo di Afrodite* (1951). All three works can be performed in concert form, although they are more effective in the theater. As stage works they are hard to categorize; they have been called scenic cantatas, in which speech, gesture, and music form a synthesis. The musical style is direct, and its appeal is more physiological than intellectual or emotional. Orff's music has been called primitivistic, because of its elemental rhythmic drive in which primary rhythmic patterns are repeated in endless and unvaried *ostinatos.* Whether the effect is found hypnotic or monotonous depends upon the listener's temperament and musical sophistication. On the positive side, the deft treatment of the text and the effective choral writing are noteworthy. The orchestration leans heavily on the percussion section in order to underline the rhythmic component. *Catulli Carmina,* for example, is scored for four pianos, four timpani, and ten to twelve percussionists.

The texts of the trilogy are derived from various sources: *Carmina Burana* is based on student songs in Latin, German, and French found in a thirteenth-century manuscript; *Catulli Carmina*—the most intense among Orff's works—is set to Latin poetry by Catullus; and *Trionfo di Afrodite* employs Latin and Greek texts by Catullus, Sappho, and Euripides.

Other stage plays include *Der Mond* (1938); *Die Kluge* (1942), one of Orff's most frequently staged works; *Die Bernauerin* (1945) and *Astutuli* (1946–1953), both Bavarian folk plays; and *Antigone* (1948), based on Hölderlin's German version of Sophocles' tragedy.

Orff's musico-dramatic approach resembles that of the earliest Italian operatic composers of the seventeenth century, whose consciousness focused on the drama, modeled after Greek tragedy. According to this conception, music is only one of the ingredients subordinate to the drama; in Orff's plays, music is reduced in significance to such an extent that it hardly has any self-sufficiency when performed without the text and stage.

Werner Egk (b. 1901), like Orff, was also drawn to the stage. More sensuous and atmospheric than Orff's, Egk's gift for tone painting brings Richard Strauss to mind. His operas include *Die Zaubergeige* (1935), a German folk opera; *Peer Gynt* (1938); *Columbus* (1942); *Circe* (1948), based on Calderon's play; *Irish Legend,* after a play by Yeats (1955); and *Der Revisor* (1957), based on Gogol's famous comedy, *The Inspector General.*

While Orff and Egk remained in the limelight during the years of Nazism, Karl Amadeus Hartmann (1905–1963) lived in complete seclusion. After the war Hartmann won considerable recognition as a symphonist in his native country. Although he studied with Webern in Vienna early in his career, Hartmann adhered to a romantic conception of the symphony. His style is rather individualistic; rhapsodic moods and passionate expressiveness are communicated, especially in the surging slow movements, suggesting an essentially nineteenth-century ideology. At the same time, there is a good deal of awareness of the idiom of the twentieth century. Hartmann's music made little impact outside of Germany; his last symphony, the Eighth, received a lukewarm reception at the ISCM Festival in Amsterdam in 1963.

Another important figure of the older generation is Boris Blacher (b. 1903), the present director of the famed Hochschule für Musik in West Berlin whose master classes in composition have a large international following. The son of German-Baltic parents, Blacher was born in China and settled in Germany in 1922. Strongly influenced by Stravinsky, Blacher's music is definitely antiromantic. Economy of style, objectivity, and a preoccupation with novel rhythmic groupings are the main features of his music. His "variable meter technique" (see Chapter 3) is related to rhythmic rows. His works include *The Grand Inquisitor* (1948) a dramatic oratorio; *Ornaments* for Piano (1952); Piano Concerto (1952); *Romeo und Julia,* a scenic oratorio premiered at the Salzburg Music Festival in 1950; and *Chiarina* (1950), a light satirical ballet.

The most progressive composer of the older generation is Wolfgang Fortner (b. 1907), whose music is highly regarded and frequently performed in Germany. His earlier music shows influences of Hindemith and Stravinsky, but he later incorporated serial technique into his style. His most frequently performed works include a Violin Concerto (1949), a Cello Sonata, three string quartets, and a *Fantasy* for two pianos and orchestra (1950). In some works, as in the "Serenade" for winds, he was drawn to sixteenth-century German folk songs. His ballet, *Die Weisse Rose* (The White Rose) (1950), based on a tale by Oscar Wilde, and *Bloodwedding* (1957), an opera based on Lorca's play, are his best achievements. Like Blacher, Fortner is also highly regarded as a pedagogue.

His outstanding student, Hans Werner Henze (b. 1926) is perhaps the most gifted composer of the German postwar generation. A restless, undisciplined artist, Henze expresses himself in a variety of styles. His first works, the First Symphony and the Concerto for flute, piano, and strings, show him as a follower of Stravinsky and Hindemith. After studying with Leibowitz, Henze aligned himself with the serialists, although maintaining his stylistic freedom even in his twelve-tone works. The *Apollo und Hyacinthus* (1949) for alto voice, harpsichord, and eight solo instruments, is a remarkably mature work for a twenty-three-year-old composer. Next, in the opera *Boulevard Solitude* (1951), Henze proved his dramatic gifts. In the following year, his String Quartet created a sensation at the Baden-Baden Music Festival.

Gradually, Henze broke with the advanced serial idiom, as he found the musical atmosphere of the Darmstadt School too cerebral. He expressed his disillusionment in the *Darmstädter Beiträge* as follows: "The freedom offered by dodecaphony in earlier days is no longer felt as a fresh impulse; it has become a vogue and a bore."[12]

Soon Henze, as so many German artists of the past, was drawn to the South, and he settled in Italy. The change of environment, coupled with his admiration for Bellini and Verdi, eventually made itself felt in his music. In his setting of Hölderlin's "In lieblicher Blaue" for tenor, guitar, and eight solo instruments, southern sensuousness and a *joie de vivre* are felt. His complete break with the serialists is evident from a comment he made about the Neapolitan canzona that appears in the second act of his opera, *König Hirsch* (*King Stag*) (1952–1955):

> It simply places the necessary expression in the melody and rhythm, while the guitar is the only possible accompaniment. No orchestral colors, no serial structure, no sinus tone. Just a melody with simple accompaniment.[13]

Henze is one of the most prodigious composers of the twentieth century; the list of his compositions includes four operas, five symphonies, ten ballets, in addition to numerous chamber music works. His style also includes a preoccupation with music of the "third stream" (a fusion of serious music with jazz), as seen in the ballet *Maratona di Danza* (1956), in which a Cuban rhythm band and a jazz combo are combined with the sounds of a regular symphonic orchestra. Among his later works the ballet, *Undine* (1959), and his operas, *Prinz von Homburg* (1960) and *Elegy for Young Lovers* (1961), have been most successful. In his most recent opera, *Der junge Lord* (1965) he uses the conventional methods of the *opera buffa*.

[12] Hans Werner Henze, "Wo stehen wir heute?" *Darmstädter Beiträge zur Neuen Musik* (Mainz: Schott's Söhne, 1958).

[13] Josef Rufer, *Musiker über Musik* (Musicians about Music) (Darmstadt: 1956).

Henze is one of the most serious talents of present-day Germany, although he has not yet found his identity.

Somewhat less well known, but gaining recognition, are two young avant-garde composers, Giselher Klebe (b. 1925) and Bernd Alois Zimmermann (b. 1918). Of the two, Klebe, a student of Blacher, is the more strikingly original. In 1950, at two different music festivals of contemporary music, two of his works, *Die Twitschermaschiene,* a short orchestral piece taking its title from one of Klee's paintings, and a string quartet, won enthusiastic reception. Other works include an opera, *Die Räuber* (1956), after Schiller's play, a Double Concerto, and a Piano Trio, entitled *Elegia Appassionata* (1955). Recently his opera, *Jacobowsky and the Colonel,* based on Werfel's famous play, scored a resounding success at its Hamburg premiere. The same work, however, received only a lukewarm reception in New York, despite the excellent performance of the Hamburg Opera Company.

Zimmermann, whose orientation is less advanced, writes primarily instrumental music. Schoenberg's influence is felt in his aphoristic piano pieces. Other works include a solo Violin Sonata, a solo Viola Sonata, and, most recently, a solo Cello Sonata (1963). In his recent opera, *Die Soldaten* (1958–1964), he fused various avant-garde tendencies into an intense, personal style.

The noted and easily the most controversial member of the postwar generation in Germany is Karlheinz Stockhausen (b. 1928), intellectual leader of the Darmstadt School and director of the Studio for Electronic Music at the Radio Station of Cologne. After studies with Frank Martin, Milhaud, and Messiaen, Stockhausen pioneered in all branches of experimental music. Thus, among his works one finds purely electronic compositions, such as the *Electronic Studies* I–II, (1953–1954); a combination of electronic and instrumental music in *Kontakte* (1960) for electronic sounds, piano, and percussion; chance music in *Klavierstück XI* (1956); and spatial music, that is, music which is based on certain spatial arrangement with regard to the origin of sound (player or loudspeaker), as in *Gruppen* (1957) for three orchestras and *Carré* (1960) for four orchestras and choruses.

Setting aside the esthetic problem of these compositional procedures per se (see Chapter 7), Stockhausen's music, judged on its own, affords a bewildering profile. The pointillistic approach is featured and seems to be found in all of his compositions. Here single tones are emphasized instead of connected groups of notes or phrases. The music is clearly athematical, following the tradition of Webern. The most problematic aspect of Stockhausen's music is form; despite the most rigorous organization of various parameters, the music seems shapeless, lacking any design. The apparent formlessness is intentional; the composer claims all archetypes of musical forms have become obsolete. He suggests each composition be perceived in small time units and not by its total architecture. His views are expressed in numerous articles in a language often incomprehensible even to the professional musician. His arguments are based on concepts taken from acoustics, mathematics, and Gestalt psychology. The following paragraph is fairly typical of the composer's writings:

> Differentiation of the intended permutation of timbres is obtained from the complexity resulting from the simultaneous combination of the six formant regions within one sound process, from the varying of the elements or groups of elements, in all their components, according to the series and of coordinating a special intervallic scale of partials or of medium frequency width ratios in each formant octave.[14]

Baffled professional musicians may feel somewhat relieved when a distinguished American physicist, John Backus[15] points out the pseudo-scientific aspect of Stockhausen's arguments. According to Backus, Stockhausen's favorite terms, such as "subharmonic series of proportions, statistical form criteria, quantum, formant, and so on" either lack definition, or are used incorrectly. In his summary Backus states:

> We conclude that Stockhausen's technical language is his own invention using terms stolen from acoustics but without their proper acoustical meanings, and that the technical jargon he has developed is designed mostly to impress the reader and to hide the fact that he has only the most meagre knowledge of acoustics.[16]

Incidentally, Backus is equally critical of the majority of the authors who contribute to *Die Reihe*. Their discussions, he states, do not make their reasoning clear, but rather the contrary, adding:

> If we boil down *Die Reihe* to see what solid content it has, we find first that the amount of valid scientific material vaporizes immediately; next, the technical jargon boils off, taking quite a time to do so, since there is so much of it; and finally, what remains is a microscopic residuum of nothing more than a mystical belief in numerology as the fundamental basis for music.[17]

The criticism of the last paragraph concerns Stockhausen too, at least indirectly, as Stockhausen, together with Herbert Eimert, is the editor of *Die Reihe*.

It is too early to tell whether or not the vulnerability of Stockhausen's

---

[14] Karlheinz Stockhausen, "Actualia," *Die Reihe,* **1** (1958), p. 47.

[15] John Backus, "Die Reihe: A Scientific Evaluation," *Perspectives of New Music,* **1**, No. 1 (1962), pp. 160–171.

[16] Backus, p. 169.

[17] Backus, p. 171.

theoretical writings applies to his music, since his music is not suffi-ciently familiar. On the whole, the composer's more recent works are less convincing than the earlier ones. For instance, the *Zyklus* (1959) for one percussion player—who hits and bangs at a carefully arranged battery of percussion instruments—fails to sustain interest. The com-poser attached the following explanation to the work:

> In *Zyklus* the primarily static, open form of my *Klavierstück XI*—which literally depends on the "Augenblick," the instantaneous glance of the eye—has been combined with the idea of a dynamic, closed form, re-sulting in a circular, curved form. Sixteen pages of notation have been spiral-bound to one another side by side; there is no beginning and no end; the player may start on whichever page he pleases, but he then must play a cycle in the given succession. During the performance the player stands in the center of a circle of percussion instruments and turns, from one playing position to another, once around his own axis, clockwise or counterclockwise, depending on the direction he has chosen to read. . . . Thus, one experiences a temporal circle in which one has the impression of moving constantly in the direction toward ever-increasing ambiguousness (clockwise) or certainty (counterclock-wise), although at the critical point at which the extremes touch, one of them imperceptibly turns into the other. The purpose is to close the open form through the circle, to realize the static state within the dy-namic, the aimless with the aimed, not to exclude or destroy one aspect or another . . . but rather to attempt again to eliminate the dualism, and to mediate between the seemingly incompatible, the utterly different.[18]

The composer's two most convincing works, both dated 1956, are *Zeitmasse* for flute, oboe, clarinet, bassoon, and English horn and *Ge-sang der Jünglinge*. In the first work there is brilliant writing for the in-struments, and an entirely new approach is used concerning the time element, while in the second, based on Chapter 3 of the Book of Daniel, fascinating sound effects are achieved with the help of electronic tape manipulations. The text, first sung and spoken by a twelve-year-old boy, was first taped and then all timbral components unique to the human voice were dissected, isolated, and "serialized" in the electronic sense. The work, originally designed for five loudspeakers surrounding the audience, has a compelling quality.

To round out the German contemporary music scene, one should know that German federal and municipal agencies subsidize the cause of modern music with great generosity. While one may disagree on the value of some of the compositions performed at these officially spon-sored festivals, modern music nevertheless occupies a vital position in the musical life of Germany.

---

[18] Karlheinz Stockhausen, program notes to the first performance at "Internationale Ferien Kurse für Neue Musik" (Darmstadt, 1959).

ITALY

In a letter dated 1883, to Julius Ricordi, Verdi voiced concern about the stagnation of Italian music, which he partially ascribed to the predominance of German musical influences. He pleaded for a renewal of Italian music based on the art of Italy's great masters such as Palestrina and Marcello. In the same year, two Italian composers were born, Alfredo Casella (1883–1947) and Gian Francesco Malipiero (b. 1883), whose destiny it was to carry out the master's wish. The need for a renewal became even more urgent in the decades following Verdi's death because the Straussian tone poems of Respighi (1879–1936) and the *verismo*[19] of the Puccini imitators brought Italian music to a complete standstill.

Casella and Malipiero, though different in temperament and outlook, derived their inspiration from the great Italian baroque masters. Drawing upon the tradition represented by Monteverdi and Vivaldi, they succeeded in establishing a new Italian instrumental style that emphasized clarity and balance. Next to Respighi's sensationalism, their music sounds almost austere and ascetic. Malipiero's operas, *Julius Caesar* (1935) and *Anthony and Cleopatra* (1938), stand in strong contrast to the *verismo* style. The purity of the melodic invention and the re-establishment of contrapuntal thinking are exemplified in Malipiero's seven quartets and in Casella's instrumental works. They were joined in their aim by Ildebrando Pizzetti (1880–1968), whose operas preserve the old Italian tradition.

Malipiero, Casella, and Pizzetti reached prominence in Italy's musical life; all three were recognized as outstanding composition teachers. Even if their music does hold only a tenuous place in the repertory, their contributions are significant because they recaptured the national ethos, reshaping it in terms of the twentieth century. In light of their achievements, a younger generation of composers, Dallapiccola and Petrassi, followed by Nono, Maderna, and Berio, were able to launch their careers with a firm point of departure.

Luigi Dallapiccola and Goffredo Petrassi, both born in 1904, have achieved international distinction; Dallapiccola especially has been gradually recognized on both sides of the Atlantic as one of the outstanding figures of twentieth-century music.

---

[19] *Verismo*—a literary term originally used as the equivalent for naturalism and referring to the depiction of life as seen, without any attempt to idealize it. As an operatic term it came to mean a music drama portraying a tragic love story which reaches some tragic climax, accompanied by lush, romantic music.

Dallapiccola was born in Istria, a section of Northern Italy that formed a part of the Austro-Hungarian empire before World War I. During the last years of World War I, Dallapiccola's family was suspected of irredentism and taken to a camp of internment in the interior of Austria. This detention left a scar on the young boy's development and when, many years later, as a result of Mussolini's anti-Semitic laws he faced persecution again, he resisted tyranny with his whole being. Freedom became a central concept in his thinking and in his music. In a moving article[20] the composer relates how his experiences led him to compose *The Songs of Captivity* (1938–1941) and *The Prisoner* (1944–1948), a one-act opera. The topics of both works are persecution, prison, self-examination, and inner freedom.

The Songs of Captivity is a prayer for freedom, written for mixed chorus, two pianos, two harps, xylophone, vibraphone, bells, six timpani, and ten large chimes. Divided into three parts, each section deals with the conscience and guilt of a famous prisoner, Boethius, Mary Stuart, and Savonarola. The examination of their conflicts is kept on an abstract level and no allusion is made to external circumstances. The vocal lines are highly expressive, supported by an imaginative instrumental accompaniment. In general, the music has the evocative power which is the hallmark of a great composer. Although by this time Dallapiccola was familiar with Schoenberg's atonal style, his own harmonic idiom consists of an original blend of the tonal and atonal.

In *The Prisoner* the composer employs the twelve-tone method bent to his own expressive needs. He once commented that "the twelve-tone method . . . must not be so tyrannical as to exclude a priori both expression and humanity." Listening to *The Prisoner,* one must conclude that the composer employed the twelve-tone technique with an entirely different purpose from that which originally prompted Schoenberg to formulate his method.

The Prisoner, based on a story by the French writer, Villiers de l'Isle Adam, was substantially rewritten by the composer. The story, in seven scenes is set in the milieu of the Inquisition under the rule of Philip II. A prisoner—called Brother by the guard—plans an escape in which he gains the aid of his guard. When the escape fails, the prisoner finds himself in the arms of the Grand Inquisitor, who turns out to be the same jail keeper who held out hope for his escape. The opera closes with the prisoner's last words before his execution: "What is freedom?" While *The Songs of Captivity* ends with an act of faith, as death meant the liberation of the spirit, *The Prisoner* ends without hope. Death is the final act of destruction.

---

[20] Luigi Dallapiccola, "The Genesis of the *Canti Di Prigionia* and *Il Prigioniero*: An Autobiographical Fragment," *Musical Quarterly, **39**,* No. 3 (1953).

The opera has some features in common with *Wozzeck;* the music is highly organized, employing the instrumental forms, such as ballata and ricercare. Yet, as in *Wozzeck,* it is the emotional impact of the music that matters. The powerful second choral intermezzo with tonal harmonies has a climactic effect not unlike the orchestral tonal interlude in Act III of *Wozzeck.* Dallapiccola's work is concerned with the emotional involvement of the listener, according to the instruction in the score:

> The sonority of the Second Choral intermezzo should be formidable; each listener should feel literally run through and submerged by the immensity of the sound. To effect this one should not hesitate to use mechanical aids, such as loudspeakers.[21]

The spiritual kinship between *The Prisoner* and *The Songs of Captivity* is unmistakable and is underlined in *The Prisoner* by a direct musical quotation from the earlier work: the "Prayer of Mary Stuart" is heard when the Grand Inquisitor leads the prisoner to the stake.

The music of *The Prisoner* has a language entirely its own, although the influence of the Viennese atonal school is perceptible. Yet, the suavity of the vocal lines and the luminous textures suggest a highly sublimated quality of the old Italian polyphonic style. An inexplicable euphoria pervades even the harshest dissonances.

Again in *Job* (1950) the subject is human suffering, spoken by a double chorus representing a dialogue between God and Satan.

Increasing interest in mysticism and a more rarified idiom in which canonic devices assume great significance indicate Dallapiccola's closeness to Webern's universe. In the divertimento for violin and orchestra, entitled "Tartiniana" (1951), a crab canon is the core of the work. Metaphysical references are made to a new conception of space in which effect can precede cause and the future anticipates the present.

The *Canti di Liberazione* (1955) for mixed chorus and orchestra suggests a more optimistic turn in the composer's outlook; the first and third songs emphasize faith in God, while the second expresses joy over the defeat of the Pharaoh's army, which represents the forces of evil (text: Exodus XV, 3–5).

An Mathilda (1955), a cantata, is based on Heine's poetry. A work commissioned by one of the leading German radio stations, it was premiered at the 1955 Donaueschingen Festival. The tone row of the work is organized with the same deliberate complexity that is seen in the work of Webern.

In the "Goethe Songs" (1957), based on the poems of the *Westöstlicher Divan,* the voice is accompanied by three clarinets, an instrument

---

[21]At the performance given by the Juilliard School of Music in New York loudspeakers were used.

for which Webern showed a predilection. Rhythmic complexities and a style that verges on athematic writing indicate that Webern's influence was not merely a passing one.

One of Dallapiccola's most recent compositions, *Preghiere* (1962), three songs for bass-baritone and chamber orchestra set to the verse of Murilo Mendez, a contemporary Brazilian poet, was given its premiere at the University of California, Berkeley, where the composer was visiting professor of Italian Culture. The text touches upon the central issue predominent in the Italian composer's art: humanity's desperate search for liberty. Arnold Elston's remarks about *Preghiere* sum up Dallapiccola's art as a whole:

> These songs approach the poetry with the greatest reverence, not simply as *matière sonore,* but as the embodiment of feeling and deep involvement in the human condition. The result is a music now impassioned, even violent in its anguish, and at other times most tender, luminous, with a sense of man's capacity for love and *caritas.* It is the music of a noble human being.[22]

Goffredo Petrassi's music, which showed an early leaning toward Casella and Hindemith, is more allied to neoclassicism. Petrassi's first instrumental works show a vital rhythmic sense which is particularly exemplified in the dance movements of *Partita* (1932), a work that made his name known outside his native country. After several minor instrumental works, Petrassi's interest turned to vocal music; two large choral works followed, *Psalm IX* (1936) and *Coro di Morti* (1940–1941). The first work is steeped in the Italian past and its polyphony recalls Palestrina's art, whereas the second work marks a crisis in the composer's development. The old and the new do not quite fuse; the vocal writing in a modal idiom recalls the past, while the instrumental accompaniment (consisting of three pianos, brass, percussion, and double basses) has an entirely modern sound. Significant advancement is shown in *Notte Oscura* (1951), a cantata composed ten years later. This work shows a mature, personal style in which serial construction is employed in a flexible manner.

Commissioned by the Boston Symphony Orchestra for the celebration of its seventy-fifth season, Petrassi composed his Fifth Concerto for Orchestra (1956), which was enthusiastically received at its premiere. The work is based on serial technique, employing a six-tone row in various permutations. More important, however, is the clarity of the musical ideas, their expressiveness, and the imaginative orchestral treatment.

A String Quartet (1958), also in serial style, was followed by the "Serenade" (1958) for flute, viola, double bass, harpsichord, and per-

---

[22]Arnold Elston, "Current Chronicle," *Musical Quarterly,* **49**, No. 2 (1963), p. 229.

cussion, commissioned by the Basel section of the ISCM. (International Society for Contemporary Music), and a String Trio (1959) commissioned by the Coolidge Foundation. All three works employ one-movement forms in which small motives are developed in harmonic contexts ranging from atonal to near diatonic simplicity.

In spite of their international reputations, Dallapiccola and Petrassi are little known in their native country. The same can be said of Luigi Nono (b. 1924), a composer affiliated with the Darmstadt School. His best known work, *Il Canto Sospeso* (1956) for chorus and orchestra, is a protest against tyranny. The text is based on letters of resistance fighters condemned to death during World War II. The music is more uncompromising than that of Dallapiccola, and the violence of the protest more frenzied. Nono also has a special affinity for the human voice; his choral works *Victory at Guernica* and *Sul ponte di Hiroshima* are among his best achievements. His opera *Intolleranza* (1960) met considerable success at its Boston performance in 1965.

Bruno Maderna (b. 1920) and Luciano Berio (b. 1925) are associated with the Darmstadt School. Maderna's *Composizione in tre tempi* for orchestra and his *Two-dimensional music for flute and electronic tape montage* show Stockhausen's influence. Berio's better-known works include his "Chamber Music" (1960) a setting of poems by James Joyce for female voice, clarinet, cello, and harp and his "Circles" (1960) for soprano, harp, and two percussionists, based on the poetry of e.e. cummings. The two percussion players are surrounded by fifteen instruments arranged in a circle, hence the title. The notation suggests entirely new effects; the singer has to speak, whisper, and change from one articulation to the other in the middle of a word or a syllable. She has to assume various positions in relation to the other players at different sections of the work, and, from time to time, she has to perform on chimes, finger cymbals, or clap her hands. On the other hand, the percussionists have to create vocal effects as an accompaniment to their performance on the instruments.

Berio, a teacher of composition at the Juilliard School of Music, writes in a style that comes closest to expressionism, as seen in the opera *Passaggio* (1963) and *Homage to Dante* (1965), a dramatic work for voices and instruments. Both works show tonal imagination and vitality.

Additional representatives of the Italian avant-garde are: Franco Evangelisti, Aldo Clementi, Camillo Togni, Sylvano Bussotti, and Franco Donatoni.

Evangelisti and Clementi are followers of Webern. In Evangelisti's two orchestral pieces, *Ordini* and *Random or Not Random,* the purity of timbres, the pulverized textures, and the use of silences point to the Austrian composer's style. In Clementi's *Ideogrammi* (1960) the referential meaning attached to intervals reminds one of Webern's influence. Togni seems to follow Stockhausen in correlating rhythmic values with interval sizes, while Bussotti and Donatoni are clearly using Cage's experiments as their point of departure. Best known among the traditionalists is Guido Turchi (b. 1916), whose music shows strong influences of Bartók.

ENGLAND

Compared to the high musical culture England had achieved in her earlier history, her musical attainments in the eighteenth and nineteenth centuries were negligible. The stagnation that began with Purcell's death in 1695 was still in evidence at the beginning of the twentieth century. In Mitchell's words:

> The musical scene in England after the turn of the century possessed all the immobility of a waxworks stacked with dummy composers and the effigies that they passed off as compositions . . . It had, as it were, to start all over again.[23]

The man who restored identity to English music was Ralph Vaughan Williams (1872–1958). He turned to the same source as Bartók, the folk treasure of the country. Although Vaughan Williams did not succeed in establishing a contemporary viewpoint, as Bartók did, he at least asserted the past and together with Gustave Holst (1874–1934) laid a foundation upon which a new generation could commence to build. Although celebrated and highly regarded in his lifetime, Vaughan Williams' nine symphonies have rarely been programmed since his death. His historical significance is greater than his accomplishments as a composer.

The leading composers of the next generation—all born prior to 1910 —are Alan Bush (b. 1900), Edmund Rubbra (b. 1901), William Walton (b. 1902), Lenox Berkeley (b. 1903), Michael Tippett (b. 1905), and Alan Rawsthorne (b. 1905). Best known to American audiences is Walton, the least adventurous in the group, while its most interesting member, Tippett, is familiar only to professional musicians.

Walton follows in the tradition of Edward Elgar and writes in a rather jaded romantic style, charting a familiar course. The orchestral effects of his First Symphony (1934) are fashioned after Sibelius. Among his more successful works are a Viola Concerto (1929), a valuable contribution to the neglected literature of the instrument; a Violin Concerto

---

[23] Donald Mitchell, *The Language of Modern Music* (London: Faber & Faber, Ltd., 1963), p. 110n.

(1939); and the oratorio *Belshazzar's Feast* (1931), a work of spontaneous spirit, also distinguished by fine choral writing. The works written after 1940, the Quartet (1948), the orchestral Partita, and the Second Symphony (1960), do not represent a new phase in the composer's development. Perhaps the most compelling of his later works is the opera, *Troilus and Cressida* (1953).

Tippett's music is difficult to classify; the steady growth of his style may be observed. The ornate melodic style of the early works such as the Double Concerto (1934) and the First Symphony (1943) suggest an interest in folk music. A fine work from this period is the Second Quartet (1942), in which—as pointed out by the composer in a prefatory note in the score—rhythms derived from madrigal techniques are used. Each part may have its own rhythm and the music is propelled by differing accents. The next phase in Tippett's development is marked by increasing textural complexities, as seen in his Piano Concerto (1955) and Second Symphony (1953). Recent works such as the opera, *King Priam* (1962), and the Concerto for Orchestra (1963) suggest that Tippett is a vital force on the current English musical scene.

The music of Bush is neglected in England, and almost totally unknown in this country. Better known, however, is Rubbra, a symphonist and author of a fine theoretical treatise.[24] Rubbra, a student of Holst, creates a luxuriant sound and rich polyphonic textures in his orchestral works. He speaks with a voice of greater authority, however, in his vocal compositions, such as the *Missa in Honorem Sancti Domini* and the Motets (1952).

The compositions of Alan Rawsthorne are entirely instrumental, which is unusual for his generation as most English composers felt closer to the heritage of the vocal tradition. Rawsthorne and others of this period often applied baroque forms, such as toccata, passacaglia, aria, and variation, to their instrumental works instead of the sonata form. When the sonata form is used, as in Tippett's First Symphony, the development section is based on the technique of baroque expansion rather than on the developmental processes of the classic-romantic tradition. Rawsthorne's idiom is the most advanced of the group and his works have been repeatedly performed at international festivals for contemporary music.

The dividing line between the older generation and the one born after 1920 is formed by England's most distinguished contemporary composer, Benjamin Britten (b. 1913). His attainments have been widely discussed. The comprehensive Mitchell-Keller Symposium on Britten's music[25] contains a bibliography of more than 350 items. Britten's ca-

---

[24]Edmund Rubbra, *Counterpoint* (London: Hutchinson University Library, 1960).
[25]Donald Mitchell and Hans Keller (Eds.), *Benjamin Britten: A Commentary on His Works by a Group of Specialists* (New York: Philosophical Library, Inc., 1953).

reer started auspiciously; first, he was fortunate in having Frank Bridge as his teacher for Bridge's wise guidance proved invaluable. Next, W. H. Auden played a considerable part in Britten's life from 1930 to 1939; the collaboration with the famous British poet certainly added to the young composer's stature. Finally, the composer's career was greatly helped by Ralph Hawkes, the noted publisher, who offered Britten a contract when he was barely out of school.

In 1939 Britten came to the United States; the trip was in the nature of a trial for eventual emigration. After a stay of three years, homesickness prompted the composer to return to his beloved Suffolk. The American visit produced *Les Illuminations* (1939), a song cycle for high voice and string orchestra based on the prose poems of Rimbaud. The work is an early example of Britten's poise in setting a foreign text to music and of his personal melodic gift. The *Michelangelo Sonnets* (1940), his last venture with a foreign language, and the *Sinfonia da Requiem* (1940), his first large-scale symphonic work, were additional products of the American sojourn.

Upon return to England, Britten devoted himself to the study of English folk songs; research into the works of Purcell followed, later expanding into a study of the entire Baroque period. This immersion in the music of the seventeenth century proved to be decisive for Britten's future development. In one commentator's view, Britten "brought the rhetorical tradition of the baroque to belated consummation in the twentieth century." It is not surprising that opera, a typically Baroque product, became Britten's favorite and highly successful form of expression.

The success of his first opera, *Peter Grimes* (1945), astonished the musical world. Derived from George Crabbe's poem, "The Borough," Britten collaborated with the librettist Montagu Slater to write a compelling and highly appealing work, thus founding a novel English operatic style. Its success is shown by the four operas that followed in as many years: *The Rape of Lucretia; Albert Herring; The Beggar's Opera,* a new realization of John Gay's ballad opera dating from 1728; and *The Little Sweep.* Britten achieved instant international fame; his operas were produced all over the world. Others soon followed: *Billy Budd* (1951) after Melville's story; *Gloriana* (1953); *The Turn of the Screw* (1954); *A Midsummer Night's Dream* (1960); and *Curlew River* (1964).

It is difficult to overestimate Britten's contribution to contemporary opera. Although not an innovator, he proved it was possible to produce original operas in a relatively conservative style. The deepest roots of Britten's style lie in the Baroque operatic tradition; his recitative technique and his use of the chorus point to Purcell and Handel. He undoubtedly learned from Verdi; it is easy to trace the influence of the Italian composer in the balance of recitatives and closed numbers, and in the pacing of his climaxes. At other times, traces of Mahler and Alban Berg are suggested. Despite such diverse influences, Britten's style is wholly English; it seems, however, that the over-all effect is much wider than the sum total of its parts.

Several English commentators drew parallels between Britten and Mozart, a comparison resented by most critics outside the English sphere. Although both composers have an impeccable sense of form, Keller's claim "that their art represents a synthesis of a similar order" seems grossly exaggerated. Next to Mozart's genius, Britten's limitations become apparent; compared to Mozart, Britten's procedures often seem calculated and his effects externalized. This is not to deny the English composer's unusual gifts: his melodic flair, his dramatic sense, the transparency of his scores, and above all, his literary acumen. Even his conservative harmonic style sustains a surprising freshness.

Basically, among the nonoperatic works, those in which instruments are combined with voices, are more successful than those that are purely instrumental. The charming but manneristic *Spring Symphony* (1949) for chorus and orchestra, based on Elizabethan poetry, and the "Serenade" (1953) for tenor solo, French horn, and string quartet enjoy considerable popularity. The moving *War Requiem* (1962) ranks among Britten's best compositions.

Britten's purely instrumental works, such as his two string quartets (1941 and 1945), *Lachrimae* (1950) for viola and piano, and a Cello Sonata (1961), remain below the level of his earlier works.

Among the middle generation of noted composers are Peter Racine Fricker (b. 1920), a twelve-tone composer, whose music is frequently performed in England and at festivals on the continent, and Malcolm Arnold (b. 1921).

Twelve-tone music before midcentury was not part of the English musical scene; the few composers associated with the method were Roberto Gerhard (b. 1886), a former student of Schoenberg; Humphrey Searle (b. 1915), who at one time studied with Webern; and Elisabeth Lutyens (b. 1905).

Summarizing England's position up to midcentury, it was found strongly conservative when compared to other European countries, or even to the United States. A new impetus became evident around 1950 when William Glock organized the Dartington Summer School of Music and invited members of the avant-garde, such as Berio, Nono, and Maderna, to lecture. As a result, young English composers went to the continent to study with Boulez, Messiaen, and others, and it was not long before a new generation, most of them born in the 1930s, appeared on the scene. Thus far, the new composers are merely names because their music is unknown in the United States; judged, however, from reports coming from England and music festivals on the continent, their names should be mentioned because they will undoubtedly give a new profile to British music. The first to be noted are the three composers who formed the Manchester group: Alexander Goehr (b. 1932); Peter Maxwell Davies (b. 1934), known in the United States in avant-garde circles; and Harrison Birtwistle (b. 1934). Also highly regarded are Richard Rodney Bennett (b. 1936), and, particularly, Nicholas Maw (b. 1936). According to a reliable English critic, Maw is one of the most promising of his generation.

All of these composers work with serial technique without being dogmatic. Their merit is that they established a new English idiom that does not lag behind the main currents of the continent, except possibly for electronic music, which as yet has no following in the British Isles.

SOVIET RUSSIA

Prior to World War I there were two schools of composition in Russia: the nationalistic school led by Rimsky-Korsakov, in St. Petersburg, and the Moscow Group, heirs to Tchaikovsky's Western tradition. Stravinsky, Prokofiev (1891–1953), and Miaskovsky (1881–1950) belonged to the first group, and Taneiev and Rachmaninoff (1873–1943) to the second. After the October Revolution in 1917 both groups lost their identity while Stravinsky, Prokofiev, and Rachmaninoff established themselves in Western Europe.

Initially, the new Soviet society appeared to encourage experimentation in the arts. The Association for Contemporary Music established contact with the modernists of the West; it was due to their efforts that *Wozzeck* received its first performance in Leningrad. Another sign of this spirit of experimentation was an orchestral performance without conductor, an attempt at collective musical expression produced by group effort. Also, the first electronic instrument, the theremin, was tried during these years. Soon this period of innovation came to an end as a countermovement, represented by the Russian Association of Proletarian Musicians, gained ascendancy. The members of this group literally accepted Lenin's teaching that the arts belong to the people, and demanded simplicity in music so that it could be understood by the masses at the first hearing. In the 1930s, Gorki's concept of social realism was applied to music. According to this principle, music should not only reflect life but also give it direction. In other words, music became the concern of the State, a means of ideological propaganda. Accordingly, music had to be optimistic, uplifting, and was expected to comment on the great issues concerning the people. Any work of art without such qualities was branded formalistic. The leadership of Soviet music encouraged those types of composition that lent themselves to topical representations, such as operas, cantatas, oratorios, and programmatic symphonic music.

At the same time, the new music of the Western countries was labeled bourgeois and decadent; atonality was decried and works of leading Western composers (Schoenberg and his school, Stravinsky, Hindemith, and even Bartók) were banned. Criticism was soon leveled at Soviet composers; in 1936 a highly critical article, "Chaos Instead of Music," appeared in the Communist Party organ *Pravda*, aiming its criticism at Shostakovich (b. 1906), the first Russian composer of distinction who was trained in the postrevolutionary period. More specifically, the criticism concerned Shostakovich's opera, *Lady Macbeth of Mtzensk*. The comments are typical of the Soviet criticism of the period:

> From the first moment, the listener is knocked over the head by an incoherent, chaotic stream of sounds. The fragments of melody, the germs of musical phrases, are drowned in a sea of bangs, rasping noises, and squeals. It is difficult to follow such "music"; it is impossible to remember it . . . . The music puffs and pants, groans and chokes, in order to present the love scenes in the most naturalistic way . . . . Such music can only appeal to esthetes and formalists who have lost all healthy tastes . . . .[26]

Twelve years later, Zhdanov, Stalin's cultural commissar, revived the criticisms of the *Pravda* article in an even stronger condemnation not only of the music of Shostakovich, but also of Prokofiev, Miaskovsky, and others. In a document, read at the Conference of the Central Committee, the leading Soviet composers were accused of formalism. The term was defined by a Soviet theoretician as follows:

> Formalism is usually considered to denote a lack of ideas, a lack of content, a complete concentration on form . . . with no reference to reality . . . . We feel that there is something in these works [works of Shostakovich, Prokofiev, Miaskovsky, and others] . . . that prevents them from penetrating simply and directly into our consciousness, and prevents us from seeing life and the world reflected in the feeling and consciousness of these composers.[27]

The composers were vindicated in 1958, when a public paper rescinded the earlier condemnation, placing the blame on Stalin. In recent years a fuller liberalization has taken place; exchange of artists between the East and West eventually led to Stravinsky's trip to Russia. The aged composer, long considered an arch enemy of the Soviet Union, was

---

[26]"Chaos Instead of Music," *Pravda*, January 28, 1936, quoted in Alexander Werth's *Musical Uproar in Moscow* (London: Turnstile Press, 1949), pp. 48-49.

[27]Composers' Meeting, Moscow, February 10, 1948, quoted in *Musical Uproar in Moscow*, by Alexander Werth (London: Turnstile Press, 1949), p. 87.

warmly received. Gradually his music, together with that of Bartók, Hindemith, and Milhaud was approved, although not the works of the serialists. Shostakovich's final vindication came in 1962, when his *Lady Macbeth,* renamed *Katerina Ismailova,* was revived after twenty-six years of banishment. Boris Schwarz, in his comprehensive account of Soviet music,[28] reports that the opera will be made into a film.

The government's pressure on composers may be chiefly responsible for the fact that the last thirty years have not produced an outstanding talent. However, additional factors must be weighed: the isolation of young composers from contacts with the Western world, the tremendous loss in manpower during the war, and the general terror of the Stalin era. While no composer achieved a reputation comparable to that of Shostakovich or Prokofiev—the latter returned to Russia from Paris in 1934—the excellence of Soviet performers (Gilels and Richter, pianists, Oistrakh and Kogan, violinists, Rostropovich, cellist) is well known. In fact, musical life in all other respects is flourishing. Boris Schwarz reports on the magnitude of Soviet music education which boasts of 2,000 music schools for children, among many other cultural organizations.

Turning to the music of Prokofiev and Shostakovich, it is a matter of speculation as to how their art may have developed in a different environment. Both composers showed unusual promise at the beginning of their careers. Prokofiev's *Scythian Suite* (1914) remains his boldest and most original work, and Shostakovich's First Symphony is still the most intriguing of his twelve symphonies. Thus far, his Thirteenth Symphony has been heard only in Russia. It is rather unexpected that the symphonic form remained so durable in Russia—to Shostakovich's thirteen symphonies Prokofiev's seven and Miaskovsky's twenty-seven should be added—as the official view advocated musical forms that lent themselves to concrete expressions of Soviet life, such as opera, oratorio, and program music. In order to satisfy this demand, many symphonies were dedicated to certain historic occasions or past events, such as the October Revolution, the siege of Leningrad, and others.

A comparison of the music of Prokofiev and Shostakovich reveals two musical personalities quite different in most respects. Common to their art is a trace of Russian folk music and a predilection for jest, mockery, and wit. Both are quite at home in the mood of the scherzo. Herbert Read's[29] formulation of state-controlled art seems particularly relevant in this context:

---

[28] Boris Schwarz, "Soviet Music Since the Second World War," *Musical Quarterly,* **51,** No. 1 (1965), pp. 253–281.

[29] Herbert Read (b. 1893), English art historian and philosopher.

> All attempts by authoritarian regimes to find a place for the artist in the modern industrial system have only turned the artist into a kind of clown, a jester, whose role is to amuse the industrial worker in his off-time (decorate the canteen) or keep his mind off disturbing problems.

Soviet music, born in a state-controlled society, was received in the United States, which represents the opposite ideological pole, with greater enthusiasm than in any other country abroad, a paradox that should challenge the cultural historian.

On the whole Prokofiev's music has a wider range of expression than that of Shostakovich. At its best Prokofiev's music has plastic lines, a clear texture, and is propelled by a strong rhythmic sense, while Shostakovich's compositions have the expressiveness of the late romantics, particularly Mahler.

Prokofiev's early works show bold originality. During the composer's stay in the United States in the years following World War I, he was unanimously condemned by American critics. The early works, in addition to the primitivistic *Scythian Suite,* obviously fashioned after Stravinsky's *Rite of Spring,* include the *Sarcasms* and *Visions Fugitives,* dating from 1912 and 1917, for piano; and an opera, *The Love for Three Oranges* (1921).

Prokofiev's career vaguely resembles Stravinsky's as both composers started in a daring and vehement style that soon gave way to a simplified and more detached mode of expression with classicizing elements in evidence. Prokofiev's change in style began with the *Classical Symphony* (1917), a work that has retained its freshness over the years. The parallel paths of Stravinsky and Prokofiev continued with the latter's stay in Paris and collaboration with Diaghilev, which resulted in a ballet, *Chout* (1920).

Among Prokofiev's seven symphonies, the Fifth (1944) has been praised as a masterpiece, a claim that seems exaggerated. Of the five piano concertos, the Third (1921) holds its place in the repertory. Also, the two violin concertos, two violin-piano sonatas, and several of the eight piano sonatas are valuable contributions to the literature. Considering the two quartets, the second provides greater interest even though the Central Asian folk songs do not thrive well in the chamber music setting.

Prokofiev's finest compositions are those written for ballet, film, and the like. These include the ballets, *Lieutenant Kije* (1934); *Romeo and Juliet* (1935); *Cinderella* (1945); and the *Stone Flower* (1950); the Cantata (1939), based on the film music to *Alexander Nevsky;* and above all the internationally successful and charming *Peter and the Wolf* (1936). All of these works contain the element that is so captivating in Prokofiev's music: skillful, fluent writing with a strong sense of characterization.

The composer's essentially lyric personality did not adapt itself well to the musico-dramatic demands; his operas are not among his most successful works. Highly regarded, however, is *War and Peace* (1942), although it did not make a strong impression in a cut television presentation in the United States. The earlier operas, *The Flaming Angel* (1925) and *Duenna* (1941), have all but disappeared from the repertory, while the last opera, *Story of a Real Man* (1947), was a total failure and was withdrawn after its first performance.

Shostakovich lived in his native country all of his life and had much less exposure to foreign contemporary music than Prokofiev. In his output, the symphony occupies a central position, which in Prokofiev's oeuvre is peripheral. Shostakovich's First Symphony (1925), a remarkable work from a nineteen-year-old conservatory student, established the composer's fame. Soon the work was introduced abroad by leading conductors, such as Toscanini, Stokowski, and Walter. The symphony shows a remarkable maturity both in the freshness of ideas and in the mastery of orchestration. The music never loses its momentum, and the textures remain transparent despite contrapuntal intricacies. The Scherzo movement is particularly brilliant and sets the tone for many scherzos to follow. In the slow movement long melodies are spun, their characteristic profiles recurring in later works.

Among the later symphonies, the Fifth stands out; the Seventh ("Leningrad") is almost completely void of interest if one disregards the stirring events that originally inspired the composer. The Eighth is less significant, and the Ninth received a lukewarm reception. The Tenth (1953), performed a few months after Stalin's death, created much controversy as it lacked any programmatic allusion, and was thereby charged with formalism. Perhaps to pacify the critics, the Eleventh and Twelfth were dedicated to the memory of the Revolutions of 1905 and 1917, respectively. Many of the later symphonies suffer from redundancy and a facile expression that lacks personal involvement. The harmonic style remains firmly tonal and unadventurous.

Strangely enough, in the concerto form, which by its very nature often invites a superficial, virtuoso approach, Shostakovich expressed himself with more depth than in many of his symphonies. This is particularly true of the Violin Concerto (1948) and the Cello Concerto (1959); both are works of serious musical purpose.

Shostakovich's chamber music (eight string quartets, piano quintet, and piano trio) remains below his best, notwithstanding the undeserved high praise bestowed on the quartets by I. Martinov in Cobbett's *Survey of Chamber Music*.[30] The string quartets fail to achieve the

[30] I. I. Martinov, "Russian Chamber Music," *Cobbett's Cyclopedic Survey of Chamber Music*, edited by Colin Mason (New York: Oxford University Press, 1963), pp. 130–150.

feeling of a foursome; the quartet technique used is rather elementary, whereby often one instrument takes the lead accompanied by three entirely subordinated lines. The Piano Quintet is perhaps his best essay in chamber music and the Piano Trio the most shallow.

Shostakovich's works include the popular oratorio, *The Song of the Forests* (1949); the cantata, *Over our Motherland Shines the Sun;* and two sets of preludes and fugues for piano (1951), in addition to assorted works, including music for several films.

Other composers who have earned reputations outside of Russia include Dmitri Kabalevsky (b. 1904), Aram Khachaturian (b. 1904), and Tikhon Khrennikov (b. 1913), all belonging to the older generation. Although all three hold powerful positions in Soviet musical life, their music is at best mediocre. Georgii Sviridov (b. 1915) has received high praise from Western commentators who have traveled in Russia. His *Pathetic Oratorio,* based on the text of the revolutionary poet Maya-kovsky, won the Lenin Prize in 1959.

Many names of the younger generation are cited in Boris Schwarz's account. Their music, he reports, follows the method of the nineteenth-century Russian school; it remained unaffected even by Debussy and the German expressionists, not to mention more recent trends.

Since 1960, however, the relaxation in Soviet cultural life gradually liberalized musical life too. The first sign came in 1964 when in New York at a New School concert a twelve-tone work written by a Soviet Russian composer was performed. His name, however, had to remain a secret.

It was only in 1967 that American audiences were to hear works written by avant-garde Soviet Russian composers at a concert given at Sarah Lawrence College, in Bronxville, New York. Compositions were heard, all scored for chamber ensembles, by Valentin Silvestrov, Andrei Volkonsky, Edison Denisov, all three from Kiev, and Vladimir Zagortsev. The style of these works resembled that of some post-Webernite com-posers, although the Russians, all four in their thirties, steered a more cautious course. Nevertheless, they adapted serial techniques and chance methods, a fact that may signal a new era in Soviet Russian music.

OTHER COUNTRIES

AUSTRIA

With the dissolution of the Austro-Hungarian monarchy after World War I, Vienna's significance as a political and cultural center diminished greatly. In the 1920s, Schoenberg and his school maintained the country's great musical tradition. After Schoenberg's move to Berlin and Berg's death, Webern remained the only representative of the so-called Viennese atonal school. When Austria was liberated at the end of World War II, Webern was the figure around whom a renewal of the musical life of the country would have naturally revolved. His tragic death, however, left Austria with no major creative personality to serve as a rallying point. While Vienna could still boast of its musical in-stitutions—the reorganized opera and the excellent Philharmonic Or-chestra—it could not muster any outstanding creative artist. The city that had once had a magnetic attraction for many of Europe's leading composers had lost all creative talent and become, in an Austrian critic's words, a "vast music museum." However, several prominent Austrian musicians established themselves abroad, among them, Ernst Křenek (b. 1900), Egon Wellesz (b. 1885), Hanns Jelinek (b. 1901), and Gottfried von Einem (b. 1918).

The most distinguished member of the group is Křenek, who in the 1920s achieved sensational success with his jazz opera, *Jonny spielt auf.* Few would have predicted at that time that twenty-five years later the composer would become one of the most uncompromising members of the avant-garde (see Chapter 7). His first twelve-tone work, the opera *Charles V* (1935), had to be premiered in Prague as its performance at the Vienna Opera was cancelled because of political opposition.

In 1938 Křenek emigrated to the United States, where he has made a rich contribution to the musical life of the country as a teacher, com-poser, and theoretician. Among the American works, the *Lamentatio Jeremiae Prophetae* (1942) for mixed *a cappella* chorus, in which medie-val *cantus firmus* technique and serial method are combined, deserves special mention. It preceded Stravinsky's *Canticum Sacrum* and *Threni,* both works conceived in the spirit of Křenek's *Lamentatio.* Among Křenek's later compositions his Seventh Quartet (1944) is one of his finest works; it is dedicated "in gratitude to the vivifying spirit of my American students." Next, an opera, *Pallas Athene weint* (1955), should be singled out of the composer's vast output. The story deals with the struggle between Athens and Sparta, but the conflict between freedom and tyranny has obvious contemporary allusions. The opera demonstrates Křenek's dramatic gift and his mastery of musical characterization; the work, a striking success at its Hamburg premiere, has yet to be per-formed in the United States. In his most recent works, the composer has turned to experimental music, including the electronic medium. The searching quality of his mind, which has characterized him throughout his life, remains fresh even as he approaches his seventieth year.

Another Viennese composer, Egon Wellesz,[31] at one time a student

---

[31]Wellesz is the author of a brief, but excellent, biography of Schoenberg.

of Schoenberg, was also forced into exile. He found a haven in England, where he has received high praise for his work as a musicologist.

Hanns Jelinek,[32] composer and theoretician, also left his native Vienna. He composed *Gebrauchsmusik* in twelve-tone style (some of it tonal) for educational use.

Gottfried von Einem (b. 1918), son of an Austrian diplomat, was born in Bern, Switzerland and spent most of his life in Germany. A student of Blacher, he won recognition for two operas, *Danton's Death* (1947), after Büchner's play, and *The Trial* (1953), based on Kafka's novel. A fine theatrical sense and a melodic gift rooted in tonal harmonies make his works easily accessible. Another Austrian exile, Johann Nepomuk David (b. 1895), who now resides in Stuttgart, is well-known for his organ and choral works.

Perhaps the only twentieth-century composer who became an Austrian by choice was the German-born Hans Erich Apostel (b. 1901), a follower of Schoenberg. His foremost achievements are songs, whose styles represents "conservative radicalism," a label furnished by the composer.

Among the younger Austrian composers Karl Schiske (b. 1916) stands out as a promising talent. On the whole, however, it seems as though the musical life of Austria is in a period of stagnation.

BALKAN COUNTRIES

Despite wars and the almost unceasing political tensions that have prevailed in Southeastern Europe during the twentieth century, composers from Greece, Rumania, and Yugoslavia have attracted international attention for the first time in history.

Of the three countries, the contribution of Greece stands out. The two leading personalities are Nikos Skalkottas (1904–1949) and Iannis Xenakis (b. 1922); their sophisticated musical culture stands in sharp contrast to the undeveloped musical tradition from which they emerged.

Skalkottas' musical talent manifested itself early, earning him a scholarship for study in Germany. The visit, planned originally for two years, was extended to twelve. During this time Skalkottas studied with Schoenberg for four years. Schoenberg considered him the most talented composer of the younger generation (after Berg and Webern, of course). After his return to Greece, Skalkottas lived a lonely existence; he produced more than 150 works which remained unpublished and unperformed during his lifetime. After his death, through the Skalkottas

---

[32] Hanns Jelinek, *Anleitung zur Zwoelftonkomposition* (Vienna: Universal Edition, 1952).

Archives in Athens, the scope and significance of the composer's rich heritage became known. His oeuvre includes a dozen symphonic works, fifteen concertos, and more than fifty chamber works. His style, analyzed in detail by Papaioannou,[33] has been compared to Alban Berg's because of its passionate intensity. The unique qualities in Skalkottas' music are his very personal use of serial technique and his long-spun melodies which are permeated with traces of Greek folk music. On the basis of the few published works, it is safe to predict that recognition of this serious artist cannot be long delayed.

Associated with Darmstadt avant-garde tendencies is Iannis Xenakis (b. 1922). His orchestral compositions include *Pithopracta* (1961)— already performed in the United States—and *Version,* a computer composition for string quartet. His conception of and methods for composition are summarized in his theoretical treatise.[34] In this study Xenakis shows the replacement of traditional compositional methods by what he calls a "stochastic" approach. This term, borrowed from the theory of probability, has a wide range of meaning; it may refer to serial procedures based on the formulas of the theory of probability; to the creation of antiphonal music for two orchestras by applying the two-person game theory; or to the use of an IBM digital computer.

Finally, Yorgo Sicilianos, a representative of a more traditional outlook, should be noted. During his visit to the United States he studied with Piston and Persichetti; his First Symphony was performed by the New York Philharmonic Orchestra in 1958.

Rumanian musical life is dominated by the spirit of the colorful violinist-composer George Enescu (1881–1955), whose main contribution consisted of the reorganization of the musical life of his country. During his later years he lived in Paris, as did his compatriot, Marcel Mihalovici (b. 1898), a student of d'Indy. Little is known about the young generation of composers, most of whom studied in Moscow, except for Anatol Vieru (b. 1926) whose Cello Concerto won first prize in 1962 at the International Competition in Geneva.

Little has been heard from Yugoslavia aside from reports about Josip Slavensky (b. 1895), whose folkloristic works have been performed abroad, and the younger Milko Kelemen (b. 1924), who studied with Wolfang Fortner. Kelemen's orchestral work, *Skolion* (1958), won the Beethoven Prize of the City of Bonn in 1963.

---

[33] John Papaioannou, "Nikos Skalkottas," *European Music in the Twentieth Century,* edited by Howard Hartog (New York: Frederick A. Praeger, Inc., 1957), pp. 320–331.

[34] Iannis Xenakis, *Musiques Formelles; nouveaux principes formels de compositions musicales* (Paris: La Revue Musicale, special edition, 1963), pp. 1–232.

CZECHOSLOVAKIA

In the latter part of the nineteenth century, Dvořák and Smetana established a Czech national school with a melodic-harmonic idiom that was folk oriented, but which otherwise followed the musical thinking of Western tradition. Despite this stylistic inconsistency, whereby a basically rhapsodic and improvisational musical culture was subjugated to a formal treatment based on entirely different premises, Dvořák and Smetana succeeded in achieving a satisfactory reconciliation of the disparate elements. The inherent weaknesses of their procedures became evident, however, when younger composers of lesser talent, among them Vitezslav Novak (1870–1949) and Josef Suk (1874–1935), were caught in the same dilemma, but without finding an adequate solution.

The man who recognized that Czech music must find its own path was Leos Janáček (1854–1928), an artist of courage and originality. He was not only a great musician, but also a great patriot who identified himself with the people instead of following the line of clerical nationalism. His love for his country was like that of Bartók; the Czech composer also dedicated himself to the course of Czech folk music, motivated by strong patriotic feelings. While Bartók's interest centered more on the musical characteristics of the folk songs, Janáček explored the texts—the language—with equal interest. He wrote:

> The inflections of human speech and indeed of the voices of all creatures became to me a source of profound truth—a life-necessity as it were— . . . Speech motifs are my windows into the soul . . . they are the expressions of a being's totality and of all phases of its activity.[35]

Based on these investigations, Janáček formulated a "theory of the melodic curve of speech" upon which he based his melodic invention. His fascination with the language explains his love for combining words with music; indeed, his vocal writing—operas, songs, and choral pieces— is superior to his instrumental works.

Well aware of the uniqueness of the speech pattern that inspired his music, Janáček realized that Western musical forms were not applicable to his art. Ideologically, too, he expressed his identification with the East:

> Our well-being lies with the East, not with the West. The Slavonic East needs us, while we are superfluous to the Germanic and Romanic West.[36]

[35] Hans Hollander, *Leos Janáček*, translated by Paul Hamburger (New York: St. Martin's Press, Inc., 1963), p. 54.
[36] *Leos Janáček*, p. 53.

In accord with this ideology, Janáček rejected the Western models of form and organized his music in a way that was entirely suited to the basic character of its elements. Melodically, he employed short phrases, rich in ornamentation, that were often molded into asymmetrical, rhythmical groupings. The architecture of his music is entirely original, uniquely designed for each composition. It is not surprising that a composer of such originality did not meet with success easily. At first, he encountered strong resistance in his native country, where local jealousies had temporarily suppressed the performance of his works in Prague.

A glance at Janáček's list of works shows that the majority of his outstanding compositions were written after 1918, the year of Czech independence, an event that thrilled the sixty-four-year-old composer and revitalized his creative energies.

Among his operas the following four are unquestionable masterpieces: *Jenufa* (1894–1903), *Kata Kabanova* (1921), *The Cunning Little Vixen* (1923), and *The House of the Dead* (1927–1928), after Dostoievski. Other vocal works include a song cycle, *Diary of One Who Vanished* (1919), *The Glagolitic Mass* (1927), and numerous choral compositions. Among the outstanding instrumental works are the Violin-Piano Sonata (revised in 1921), *Youth* (1924), a sextet for winds, and the Second String Quartet (1928). Since midcentury Janáček's works have been performed with increasing frequency and the composer is gradually receiving the recognition he so well deserves.

A compatriot, Alois Hába (b. 1893), also explored Czech folk music, particularly the East Moravian folk song, in which he discovered the subdivision of the half step into microtones. These small intervals, which sound natural in improvised embellishments, seem to have lost their evocative power in Hába's highly sophisticated music influenced by the Viennese atonalists.

The most popular and most widely performed Czech composer of the twentieth century is Bohuslav Martinu (1890–1959), who, after a long residence in Paris, emigrated to the United States. His large output includes operas and orchestral and chamber works. His music, on the whole, is fluid, amiable, and easily accessible.

Finally, a Slovak composer, Eugene Suchon (b. 1908), should be mentioned, whose opera, *The Whirlpool* (1949), has been successfully staged in several European countries.

HOLLAND AND BELGIUM

Holland and Belgium, together with a part of Northern France, formed at one time a geographical unit known as the Netherlands, which produced outstanding composers in the fifteenth and sixteenth centuries. In the centuries following, there was a musical decline. Music, however, has remained a part of everyday life. Evidence of this is seen in the works of the Dutch masters of the seventeenth and eighteenth centuries, in which musical activities often appear to accompany the everyday life they so vividly painted. The high level of musical culture in the nineteenth century is shown by the excellence of Holland's musical institutions (conservatories, opera, orchestras, and the like), and by the widespread participation of amateurs in musical performances.

Around the turn of the century, the excellent Concertgebouw Orchestra of Amsterdam contributed richly to the musical life of Holland. Their renditions of Mahler's symphonies, in particular, were enthusiastically received. Soon Mahler appeared as the interpreter of his own music, and his presence inspired the creative efforts of Dutch composers. Among the innovators was Alphons Diepenbrock (1862–1921), a personal friend of the Moravian composer. In Diepenbrock's symphonic songs, especially in *Die Nacht*, it is easy to trace the strong Mahlerian influence. In his later works, Diepenbrock was also affected by the French impressionists, and was the first among several Dutch composers to integrate Germanic and Latin elements into his style.

This double ancestry is found also in the music of Willem Pijper (1894–1947), Holland's outstanding musical figure of the twentieth century. Originally headed for a career in biology, Pijper applied his keen analytical mind to the problems of musical form. He developed a theory, known as the *Keimzelle* (germ cell) theory, whereby an entire composition is derived from a small melodic-harmonic unit. His first success was the Second Symphony in 1921, and from then on, until 1940, he was Holland's musical leader. His large output contains many piano works, among which his sonatinas have gained increasing popularity. Of the orchestral works, his Third Symphony has been the most successful. It is dedicated to Pierre Monteux, who made the work known in the United States. Pijper's style is forward-looking; he experimented with polytonality and with extremely complex rhythmic superimpositions. He was also a great admirer of Webern. As editor of *De Muziek*, Holland's leading music journal, he significantly influenced Dutch musical opinion, and as a teacher, he trained a whole generation of composers.

After Pijper, his former student, Henk Badings (b. 1907) became Holland's leading musical figure. His versatility is shown by twelve symphonies, chamber works, concertos for various instruments, oratorios, and operas. He also experimented with electronic music; his electronic ballet, *Evolutionen*, was warmly received in Vienna in 1960, and again in 1962.

Two composers of the serial camp also established international reputations: Kees Van Baaren (b. 1906), the director of the Conservatory in The Hague, and his former student, Peter Schat (b. 1935), who later studied with Boulez. Schat's compositions received high praise at recent festivals of the International Society for Contemporary Music (ISCM); his Septet was premiered in Strasbourg in 1958, and his *Signalement,* for six percussionists and three double basses, at the Donaueschingen Festival in 1962.

Belgium's outstanding composer and theorist of the twentieth century, Henri Pousseur (b. 1929), is identified with the Darmstadt group. His *Repons pour sept musiciens* (1962) is governed by chance procedures. At the Darmstadt premiere the audience was able to view a huge checkerboard that contained various musical possibilities. The piece began with a lottery, to determine who would start playing, and from then on, the information on the checkerboard and the players' free choices determined the outcome of the piece.

The *Caractères Ia and Ib* (1962), performed at the Los Angeles Contemporary Music Festival in 1963, contains new manners of pitch and metric notation, and also allows the player to choose between alternate versions.

The *Madrigal III* (1963) for clarinet, violin, cello, two percussionists, and piano introduces new, rhythmically indeterminate, notation. An occasional number over a note suggests duration but only with reference to the smallest unit, to be independently chosen by each musician between measures 120 and 240. Utmost rapport in performance is necessary, as each time the work is played it is recreated anew.

HUNGARY

Although Hungary has a rich cultural tradition, it failed to produce a composer of international renown until the beginning of the twentieth century, when, suddenly, a group of composers, led by Bartók and Zoltan Kodály (1882–1967), appeared on the scene.

Bartók and Kodály shared many phases of their career; they started as fellow students at the Royal Academy in Budapest, where both of them later held teaching positions. They also joined forces in folk music research and drew heavily on folk idioms. Kodály, however, stayed nearer the Hungarian roots, whereas Bartók's radius was wider. While Kodály immersed himself almost totally in Hungarian folk music, Bartók successfully integrated advanced Western European stylistic features as well (see Chapter 10). As a result, Bartók's music achieved a universality, next to which Kodály's style, however appealing and colorful, appears limited. Because of Kodály's closeness to Hungarian folk sources, his works are strongly tonal, emphasizing melody. His vein is lyric, and he was more at home in vocal music; choral works and songs occupy a central position in his output. The work that brought him international fame, *Psalmus Hungaricus* (1932), is essentially a vocal work, scored for tenor solo, chorus, and orchestra. Also active in the pedagogy of voice, Kodály contributed greatly to the present high level of choral singing in Hungary. His other works include a folk opera, *Háry János* (1923), from which the well-known orchestral Suite was excerpted; a solo Cello Sonata (1905); a Duo for Violin and Cello (1914); two string quartets (1908 and 1917); *Dances of Galánta,* an orchestral composition, and a late Symphony (1960).

Among the many Hungarian composers who left their country for political reasons, Tibor Harsányi (1898–1954) and László Lajtha (1892–1963), the latter known for his string quartets, found haven in Paris. Mátyás Seiber (1905–1960), a follower of Bartók, settled in England, where his Third Quartet (1950) was warmly received. Sándor Veress (b. 1907) established himself in Switzerland and achieved an independent and personal style. Among the younger expatriates, György Ligeti (b. 1923) is active in Germany and is highly regarded by the avant-garde. His orchestral composition *Atmosphères* (1961) was performed in the United States, and his recent *Requiem* (1965) received warm praise from European critics.

Prominent among the composers of the older generation who have remained in Hungary are Paul Kadosa (b. 1903), György Ránki (b. 1907), and Endre Szervánszky (b. 1911).

In the last decade, as a result of the liberalization following Stalin's death, Hungary re-established cultural contacts with the West. A new generation of composers emerged among whom György Kurtág (b. 1926) stands out; his quartet scored a great success at the 1964 ISCM Festival in Copenhagen. András Szöllösy (b. 1921) and Attila Bozay (b. 1939) are two highly gifted composers to be watched. Most recently Sándor Szokolay won high praise with his opera *Blood Wedding* (1965), based on Lorca's drama.

POLAND

In the first quarter of the twentieth century, Karol Szymanovski (1882–1937), the greatest Polish composer since Chopin, dominated Poland's musical scene. At first influenced by Debussy, Szymanovski established a subtle and refined harmonic style. After 1920 his music was enriched by Polish folk music and later by oriental (Hindu) influences. The effect of the first is seen in many piano compositions, mazurkas, songs, and in his ballet *Harnasie* (1926). The Far Eastern flavor comes through in the "Tagore" songs, the Third Symphony, and his opera, *King Roger* (1926), which centers on the philosophical and religious conflict between the East and the West.

In Poland, as in Germany, a whole generation seems to have vanished from 1930 until the end of World War II; political crises, military preparations, and then the destruction of the war all but stopped creative life. In 1949 a few young composers organized the *Group of '49*, dedicated to the cause of modern music. Most active in the group were Tadeusz Baird (b. 1928) and Kazimierz Serocki (b. 1922), both of whom occupy leading positions in Poland today. Two additional names have to be singled out among the numerous gifted young Polish composers, Witold Lutoslawski (b. 1913) and Krzysztof Penderecki (b. 1933), both of them well known to audiences of European contemporary music festivals.

Polish musical life is remarkably open-minded about advanced Western European musical currents. Accounts of the Warsaw Music Festivals (1958, 1962, and 1963) highly praised the broad spectrum of the programs and the amazing creative talent of the young Polish composers. The programs included not only the works of the Viennese atonal masters, but also music written by Boulez, Stockhausen, and Nono, including electronic music.

Of the composers mentioned, Baird's music is the most accessible; in reviewing the *Four Essays* for Orchestra (1958), a twelve-tone work, one critic observed that Baird's music sounds like Alban Berg's, reborn and rejuvenated in the Slavic world.

Serocki is interested in working with space as a structural element, as seen in his *Segmenti* for chamber orchestra (1962); the players are divided into one central and five peripheral groups. His *A piacere – Propositions for Piano* (1963) is fashioned after Stockhausen's *Klavierstück XI.* Serocki, too, allows chance to take a place in the shaping of the piece. The performer can decide in which order he wishes to play the ten ready-made fragments. The duration of the piece must not be longer than eight minutes or shorter than six.

Lutoslawski, somewhat older than his colleagues, is recognized as the leader. His *Funeral Music* for string orchestra, dedicated to the memory of Bartók (1958), is written in a highly personal twelve-tone idiom; it won the International UNESCO Prize in 1959 and has been included in the avant-garde series of the New York Philharmonic Orchestra. In *Jeux Vénitiens* (1961) Lutoslawski experimented with aleatory music, as a means of enriching rhythm. His *Trois Poèmes d'Henri Michaux* (1962–1963) for chorus and orchestra, commissioned by the Festival of Contemporary Music at Zagreb and performed there, is scored for a mixed chorus in twenty parts, winds, brass, and percussion. The tonal effects of the chorus ranging from whispering and moaning to wailing and shrieking, intensified by the instruments, have a terrifying impact, "an unforgettable experience" in one commentator's words. Lutoslawski, too, uses an alternating pattern of random and controlled passages.

Perhaps the most prominent Polish composer today is Penderecki. His first encounter with Western European audiences took place at the 1960 Donaueschingen Festival premiere of his *Anaklasis,* a work for strings and percussion. The composition was received with a mixture of applause and booing; Rosbaud, the conductor, decided to render a second playing of the piece, at the end of which the approval was unanimous. A British critic who reported on the 1963 Amsterdam ISCM Festival was so impressed with Penderecki's orchestral *Threnody for the Victims of Hiroshima* that he felt the whole ISCM gathering was a Penderecki festival. The Polish composer explores sound in a completely new way; in the *Threnody,* for instance, in addition to all the *sul ponticello* and like effects used by the Viennese atonal composers, he asks "for highest sound without pitch, play between the bridge and the tailpiece, arpeggio on four strings behind the strings," and so on. He also uses controlled slides; at times the string players tap the back of their instruments and the wind players blow air through their instruments without producing sound.

Poland's contribution to twentieth-century music is remarkable, and it is hoped that Polish composers will soon become known to the general public.

SCANDINAVIAN COUNTRIES[37]

In the first quarter of the twentieth century two prominent composers dominated the Scandinavian scene: the Finn, Jean Sibelius (see Chapter 8) and the Dane, Carl Nielsen, both born in 1865. Perhaps the awe in which these two towering figures were held in their native countries caused the new musical generation to assert itself rather slowly. Among the four Scandinavian countries, Sweden, which had no grand man to boast of, has made the most significant contribution to twentieth-century music.

Sweden   Sweden produced only minor musical figures in the nineteenth century. Its first composer of international reputation is Hilding Rosenberg (b. 1892), a central figure in Sweden's musical life today. When he visited Germany as a student, he became familiar with the modern Viennese methods of construction. Of his five symphonies, the last is most frequently played, and his recent quartets

[37] See the essay by Bo Wallner, "Scandinavian Music after the Second World War," *Musical Quarterly* (50th Anniversary issue), **51**, No. 1 (1965), pp. 111–143, for a comprehensive study of Scandinavian music.

show a flair for expressionism. His output suggests an artist with a wide range of interests; along with religious works and an oratorio based on Thomas Mann's *Joseph and his Brethren* (1948), he also wrote a bizarre ballet, *Orpheus in Town*. The title refers to a statue of Orpheus and Eurydice that stands in the center of Stockholm. Orpheus, animated, searches for Eurydice in the hectic traffic of the modern metropolis, accompanied by Rosenberg's jazzlike music.

Rosenberg has been the teacher of many promising composers, among whom the best known is Karl-Birger Blomdahl (b. 1916). Blomdahl's music attracted international attention in the 1940s at the ISCM festivals. In the 1950s his style became even bolder, veering toward Webern's pointillism. Blomdahl's *Facets,* an orchestral set of variations, received enthusiastic response. The space opera, *Aniara,* based on an epos of one hundred and three poems by the Swedish poet Henry Martinson, has been much publicized and has created considerable controversy. Aniara is the name of a spaceship headed toward Mars with eight thousand people aboard, fleeing the radioactive atmosphere of the Earth. In the opera the plight of modern man who is forced to leave Earth and face the awesomeness of unknown Space is portrayed. The rather traditional vocal line is embedded in a highly dissonant orchestral setting, studded with some sequences of electronic music, which, according to the composer, have a specific symbolic function "in the tension between technique and spirit, Space and Earth." The music of *Aniara* is the work of an original and imaginative composer.

Two composers with more conservative leanings, Lars-Erik Larsson (b. 1908) and Dag Wiren (b. 1905), whose music often turns up at international music festivals, should be noted. However, the most talented representatives of the avant-garde are Bo Nilsson (b. 1937) and Bengt Hambraeus (b. 1928). The former's *Szene I,* premiered at the Palermo Festival in 1963, has been cited for "the striking novelty of its aural effects and the fragile beauty of its cascades of crystalline sound,"[38] while Hambraeus' electronic works (*Doppelrohr II,* 1955) attracted attention in Germany.

Norway For some time the influence of Grieg (1843–1907) left its imprint on a group of Norwegian composers. Perhaps Harald Saeverud's (b. 1897) *Peer Gynt* (1948) should be looked upon as a sign of a new generation of composers. Saeverud's music is more appropriate to Ibsen's psychological drama than are Grieg's sweet melodies.

The music of two Norwegian composers, Bjarne Brustad (b. 1895) and Olav Kielland (b. 1901), has recently become available on a CRI recording in the United States. Brustad is the more versatile of the two

---

[38] John S. Weissmann, "Current Chronicle," *Musical Quarterly,* **49**, No. 2 (1963), p. 245.

composers; his Second Symphony (1951), which shows traces of the Bartókian influence, is the work of a serious and talented artist. Kielland in his *Concerto Grosso Norvegese* integrates Norwegian folk elements into a symphonic style.

Denmark   Carl Nielsen (1865–1931), like Sibelius, found the most receptive audiences in England, although the English public received Nielsen's music more slowly than that of the Finnish composer. Nielsen found a following in England in 1950, when his Fifth Symphony generated real enthusiasm at the Edinburgh Festival. On the whole, Nielsen's music has more *joie de vivre* and humor than that of the austere and brooding Sibelius. Both, however, remained unaffected by the revolutionary musical events that took place in Vienna and Paris in the pre-World War I years.

An internationally known Danish musician is Knud Jeppesen (b. 1890), whose study of Palestrina's style has become a standard work in music theory. A prominent figure in Denmark today is Knudaage Riisager (b. 1897), the present director of the Royal Danish Conservatory, a composer strongly influenced by French impressionism.

The other outstanding Danish composer is Vagn Holmboe (b. 1909). A student of Nielsen and Jeppesen, his travels took him to Germany where he studied with Ernest Toch, and to Eastern Europe where he fell under the spell of Bartók. Holmboe dedicated his First Quartet to the Hungarian composer. Several of his eight symphonies were written during World War II; the Fourth, the *Sinfonia Sacra,* expresses "the suffering of the suppressed peoples of the world." Holmboe's music is unknown in the United States, as neither the recordings nor the scores are available.

Finland   The overpowering influence of Sibelius (see Chapter 8) on the Finnish musical scene is obvious, and the only medium other Finnish composers ventured to tackle was opera, a field left untouched by Sibelius. Oscar Merikanto (1868–1934) is credited with having written the first Finnish opera, *Pohjan Nehti* (The Maid of the North). His son, Aare (1893–1958), who had studied abroad, identified himself with modern Western European tendencies, abandoning the romantic-nationalistic outlook. Another figure highly esteemed in Finland is Leevie Madetoja (1887–1947), who also distinguished himself in the field of opera.

SPAIN

The history of Spanish music shows a pattern similar to that of Holland and England: superior attainments in earlier centuries—in Spain the peak came in the sixteenth and seventeenth centuries—followed by a void in the eighteenth and nineteenth centuries.

A musical upsurge occurred at the threshold of the twentieth century, instigated by composers leaning heavily on Spanish folk sources. Isaac Albeniz (1860–1909) and Enrique Granados (1867–1916) were the first two representatives of this nationalistic style. Their music reflects the vital dance rhythms and the special color of their native folk music.

Their work was brought to fulfillment by Spain's outstanding composer of the twentieth century, Manuel de Falla (1876–1946). He achieved world fame with his two early ballets, *El Amor Brujo* (1915) and *The Three-cornered Hat* (1917), both inspired by the colorful Andalusian folk idiom. A turn to a more abstract and purified style is represented by the Harpsichord Concerto (1923–1926), written at a time when neoclassic tendencies swept through Europe. Gilbert Chase,[39] in his valuable book, sees a faint resemblance to the music of Domenico Scarlatti, although in a thoroughly twentieth-century syntax.

In the years that followed, de Falla produced little; he lived through the Spanish Civil War in seclusion in Granada. After Franco's victory, he left his country and settled in Argentina. In the last twenty years of his life, de Falla's chief creative efforts centered on a monumental work, *La Atlantida,* a scenic cantata based on the text of the Catalan poet, Jacinto Verdaguer. The unfinished work was completed by de Falla's former student, Ernesto Halffter, in 1961, and premiered in the same year in Barcelona with great success.

Although no later work has reached the popularity of de Falla's early ballets, his turn to a more cosmopolitan style in which Hispanic influences were sublimated pointed the way to a new generation of composers known as the Madrid Group. The group made an auspicious start in the early 1930s led by the two Halffter brothers, Ernesto and Rodolfo. Soon, however, the Civil War interrupted their activities and the majority of the group, associated with the Loyalist government, was forced into exile at the end of the war.

After more than two decades of stagnation, the *Grupo Nueva Musica* was formed in 1958 with the aim of bringing Spain back into the mainstream of modern European musical thought. Following an organizational crisis, the group was taken over by the *Aula de Musica* under the aegis of the *Ateneo de Madrid,* a state-supported center for contemporary thought in the arts.[40] Under its enthusiastic director, Ruiz Coca, Spanish audiences were exposed to works of Schoenberg, Webern, Stockhausen, and others. Soon a group of promising young composers sprang up, among whom Cristóbal Halffter (b. 1930), a nephew of Ernesto and Rodolfo, and Luis de Pablo (b. 1930) are best known.

[39] Gilbert Chase, *The Music of Spain,* 2d. ed. (New York: Dover Publications, Inc., 1959).

[40] The objectives of the group are ably summarized by Arthur Custer in "Contemporary Music in Spain," *Musical Quarterly,* **48**, No. 1 (1962), pp. 1–8.

Cristóbal Halffter first gained recognition when he won the UNESCO Award, at the age of twenty-six, with his *Two Movements for Timpani and String Orchestra*. His orchestral work, *Microformas* (1960), based on extremely complex serial operations, caused noisy demonstrations at its Madrid premiere. In the *Formantes for Two Pianos* (1961) duration and intensity as well as pitch are serialized, and a number of sections suggest improvisation by the performers.

De Pablo, also a member of the post-Webernite avant-garde, impressed audiences at the Palermo Music Festival in 1960 with his aleatory *Radial* for twenty-four instruments. His *Libro para el Pianista,* premiered at the Darmstadt Music Festival in 1961, gives a free choice to the performer in ordering and shaping the "sonorous objects," following the model of Stockhausen's *Klavierstück XI.*

SWITZERLAND

Although surrounded by three countries, Germany, France, and Italy, that are leaders in contemporary musical thought, Switzerland has remained conservative and almost completely unaffected by the musical currents of the last forty years. Nevertheless, it produced composers of distinction, among whom Frank Martin (b. 1890) is most prominent.

Martin, born in Geneva, matured slowly; almost all of the works upon which his reputation rests were written after 1940, when he was over fifty. His instrumental style is characterized by a fine sensitivity for texture and by clearly etched melodic lines. His approach to sound and instrumentation, and often his harmonies, point to Ravel as a distant source of inspiration. After 1930 Martin acquainted himself with the method of twelve-tone composition, but his use of the system has little to do with the method envisioned by Schoenberg. Martin's writings are always tonal and his motivic approach does not resemble the Viennese atonalists. Among his instrumental works, the *Petite Symphonie Concertante* (1945) for string orchestra, piano, harp, and harpsichord, achieved great popularity. Also, his Concerto for Harpsichord (1952) is frequently performed.

Martin achieved his best in the field of oratorio. Outstanding among his oratorios is *Le Vin Herbé* for solo voices, small chorus, strings, and piano. Written in 1939, the work has a curious history. Originally designed as an oratorio based on Joseph Bédier's literary adaptation of the Tristan story, the composer later reworked the idea into an opera. It was staged in 1949 at Salzburg and was revived in 1962 in Munich. The work is more successful as an oratorio because the operatic form fails to sustain one's interest for an entire evening despite the purity of style.

Two more oratorios, *Golgotha* (1945–1948), based on texts of St. Augustine recounting events of the life of Jesus, and *La Mystère de la Nativité* (1960) should be mentioned.

An opera, *The Tempest,* based on Shakespeare's play, failed to achieve success; the composer's rigid adherence to the words of the play resulted in a music-drama without any motion.

German influence may be detected in the works of Conrad Beck (b. 1901) and Willy Burkhard (1900–1955), although the former studied with Nadia Boulanger in Paris. Beck, primarily a symphonist, was at one time Koussevitzky's protegé, as a result of which his works became known to American audiences through performances by the Boston Symphony Orchestra. Burkhard, whose music shows affinities with Hindemith's style, is best known for his oratorio, *Das Gesicht Jesaja's* (1936).

Heinrich Sutermeister (b. 1910) and Rolf Liebermann (b. 1910) are noted for their stage works. Sutermeister, a student of Orff, achieved sensational success with his *Romeo and Juliet* (1939). An easygoing, melodic, and tonal style makes his music immediately accessible. More adventurous is Liebermann; his opera *Leonore 40/45* (1952), written with the literary collaboration of Heinrich Strobel, the well-known musicologist and biographer of Hindemith, was staged in many German opera houses after its Basel premiere. The story deals with the romance of a German soldier and a French girl, a music student, during World War II. The text is partly German, partly French; the shifts in language are accompanied by alternating musical styles. Another opera, *Penelope* (1954), with its elegant and virtuoso style brings Richard Strauss' later operas to mind.

Liebermann made an attempt in his Concerto for Jazz Band and Orchestra (1954) to combine jazz and symphonic styles; the work, written in serial style, is nothing more than a hodgepodge.

Of the younger generation, the name of Klaus Huber (b. 1924) is the only one among Swiss composers that occasionally appears at international festivals. His *Das Engels Anredung an die Seele* (1951), for tenor, flute, clarinet, horn, and harp won the ISCM prize in Rome in 1959.

MUSIC IN AMERICA

The musical achievements of the United States during the twentieth century cannot be brought into perspective without giving careful thought to the specific circumstances that were part of America's growth as a new country. America's rise as a nation was unique; as de Tocqueville pointed out, the United States had no infancy, but was born into a man's estate. Bypassing certain developmental phases had manifold and far-reaching consequences. The country was founded by settlers who brought with them many achievements of an advanced civilization—in terms of tools and techniques—but who left behind their cultural roots. With the exception of those immigrants who came from the British Isles, the newcomers soon gave up their native language and their songs. Also left behind were the art treasures, housed in the churches, museums, and castles of the old country, and the cultural institutions, libraries, universities, and opera houses. In the new country the hardships that had to be overcome drained the energies of the pioneers; little time was left for leisure. De Tocqueville reported in 1831:

> America has hitherto produced very few writers of distinction; it possesses no great historians and not a single eminent poet. The inhabitants of that country look upon literature properly so called with a kind of disapprobation. . . .[1]

The lack of a musical tradition, not even mentioned in de Tocqueville's report, was deplored some fifty years later by Frederic Louis Ritter, an immigrant musician from Alsatia, who in his book on American music, asked rhetorically:

> "How are we to account for this utter absence of national people's music and poetry in America?"[2]

In the beginning of the twentieth century, when America could boast of outstanding writers and architects, music still remained in a colonial state. It still had not become part of American life; it was also ignored in the school curriculum. In the Mosely Commission Report, dated 1903, we read:

> Nowhere in American schools did I find instrumental music forming a part of the instruction and in the few cases where vocal music was included, it was but poorly taught.

That music lagged behind the other arts should not be thought of as a specifically American phenomenon; this lag has been observed in other countries as well. In the United States, however, the circumstances were especially inauspicious for the emergence of a national musical tradition. Not only was the general cultural climate unfavorable, but there was no historical tradition in art music to hark back to. Musical institutions were almost nonexistent and music as a profession seldom attracted Americans. As a result the music teacher, the conductor, and most orchestral players were foreigners.

Another factor that hindered the development of a national musical culture was the diffuse state of folk tradition. Although there was a body of indigenous folk music (Negro and Indian) as well as some English, Irish, and Scottish songs that survived in the new environment, the immigrants, on the whole, did not have the same intimate contact with folk art as they had had in the old country. The melting pot

---

[1] Alexis de Tocqueville, *Democracy in America* (New York: Random House, 1945), p. 326.
[2] Frederic Louis Ritter, *Music in America* (New York: Charles Scribner's Sons, 1883).

that welded heterogenous elements to a cohesive society failed to achieve integration in the arts.

America's musical independence was not established until the 1920s when Aaron Copland (b. 1900) became the country's musical leader, representing in one person both the avant-garde and the "garde." About the same time musical organizations, such as the International Guild of Composers and the League of Composers, were formed for the purpose of promoting the cause of American music.

Seen in this light, the progress made in the last half century is truly remarkable. Today America boasts of more than twenty-five major symphony orchestras, half of which are among the world's best. American performers have gained worldwide recognition and each year hundreds of excellently trained musicians are graduated from American music schools and conservatories. In addition to a flourishing concert life that reaches every corner of the country, summer festivals have grown rapidly in the last two decades in such centers as Tanglewood, Massachusetts, Marlboro, Vermont, Ellenville and Saratoga Springs, New York, and Aspen, Colorado. The significance of music has been recognized by educational institutions on all levels. Colleges in particular have contributed significantly to the country's musical life; the artist-in-residence and string quartet-in-residence have become a part of American college life. Foundations also have come to the support of music, and federal and state aid to the arts has finally become a reality. A number of symphony orchestras receive financial aid from municipal or state sources. The recording industry has been instrumental in making both old and new music available to the mass audience.

While there is every reason for an optimistic outlook concerning the future of American music, there are many shortcomings in the country's musical life. For example, there are still only a handful of permanent opera houses in the country; concert life is highly commercialized and dominated by personalities; the level and quality of music education in many schools leaves much to be desired; and in many parts of the country radio stations allocate very little time to broadcasting "good" music. And finally, despite all the progress, America still has not produced a composer of a stature comparable to the leading European composers of the century.

STYLES AND SCHOOLS

It was only natural that the rising musical consciousness considered its first task the establishment of an American musical identity. The initiative was taken by Aaron Copland. After studies in New York, he went to Paris to establish a personal style, an aim he achieved with the help of Nadia Boulanger, the mentor of many American composers. After four years of study in France, Copland returned to the United States to found a truly American musical style that would be clearly different from European models. This nationalist movement, with which Roy Harris (b. 1898) is also identified, suggests a self-conscious attitude, but it defines at least one clearly recognizable tendency in the bewildering diversity that came to characterize American music. The diversity can be easily explained by the vastness of the country, the regional differences, and the different ethnic and cultural backgrounds of the composers. Diverse influences continued to dominate the American musical scene in the 1930s when so many leading European musical figures, among them Schoenberg, Stravinsky, Bartók, Milhaud, and Hindemith, found refuge in the United States. While their contributions to American musical culture were of the greatest importance, their towering personalities may have made it difficult for the young American composer to find his identity.

Despite the stylistic diversity in American music, the establishment of basic categories that encompass the total range of the spectrum of American music is very important, especially in a brief survey such as this that rules out an investigation based on individual composers.

Several attempts to stylistically classify American music have been made. Some writers (John T. Howard and Aaron Copland) discuss American composers on the basis of age groups, differentiating three generations: the "old" one, consisting of composers born around the turn of the century; the middle generation, those born between 1910 and 1920; and the young one, composers born after 1920. This chronological delineation does not necessarily reveal differences in musical styles; an "old" composer, such as Charles Ives, for instance, may show more stylistic daring than one of the young generation, or a young composer may write in dated idiom.

Two attempts have been made to create stylistic categories on the basis of musical orientation; one by Gilbert Chase in his valuable study on American music[3] and the other by Joseph Machlis.[4] While Chase established five categories—Americanists, eclectics, traditionalists, experimentalists, and twelve-tone composers—Machlis arrived at the following seven groups: impressionists, nationalists, classicists, romanticists, "new" expressionists, twelve-tone composers, and experimentalists. The two authors agree only in three instances: nationalists, experimentalists, and twelve-tone composers. (Both of them establish a separate category for composers of theater music.)

---

[3] Gilbert Chase, *America's Music from the Pilgrims to the Present* (New York: McGraw-Hill, Inc., 1955, second edition 1966).

[4] Joseph Machlis, *Introduction to Contemporary Music* (New York: W. W. Norton & Company, Inc., 1961).

While in agreement with the inclusion of the first two groups, this author has misgivings about establishing a category of twelve-tone composers (Machlis even establishes a subgroup of "partly" twelve-tone composers) since the twelve-tone method of composition does not constitute a specific style of writing (see Chapter 7).

In considering Chase's eclectics and traditionalists, it is difficult to see what constitutes the specific difference between the two groups; an eclectic—a composer, according to Chase who selects his material from various sources—may be a traditionalist too. In fact, almost all the composers mentioned among the eclectics could be considered traditionalists as well.

Fully aware of the danger of oversimplification and also of the inevitable overlaps that are part of any such stylistic distinctions, American composers will be grouped into the following four broad categories:

1) *Nationalists*   This group, led by Copland and Harris, includes composers who consciously and deliberately base their style on the American folk idiom (jazz or other folk sources).

2) *Traditionalists*   The majority of American composers included here represent a broad spectrum. On one end of that spectrum is the more conservative wing, whose style is rooted in the romantic tradition (hence often called neoromantic), distinguished by a firmly tonal approach and a melodic-harmonic texture. The other end of the spectrum is represented by composers whose style—loosely called neoclassic—is marked by a more dissonant harmonic idiom and a contrapuntal rather than harmonic texture. In terms of personalities Samuel Barber's style perhaps best exemplifies the first trend, and Walter Piston's the second. Caution should be exercised not to view rigidly the two subdivisions in this category; many composers may shift from one end of the spectrum to the other in different works.

3) *Progressives*   This category accommodates composers who write in a more advanced style (often atonal or serial or both) than the traditionalists, without being experimental. Ruggles, Sessions, Riegger, and Carter are representative of the group.

4) *Experimentalists*   Composers in this class (Ives, Varèse, Babbitt, Cage) break new ground employing novel methods in composition.

In summary, the spectrum of American music—using the terms of political parlance—shows the strongest representation, at least in numbers, in the center and to the right of center (nationalists and traditionalists), with additional strength coming from the left (experimentalists). The progressives are represented by a relatively small group and are the least well known to the general public, partly because their music is seldom performed, and partly because their achievements do not lend themselves to journalistic exploits. Despite this isolation, many of the most promising talents in America today are represented by the progressives.

NATIONALISTS

The two outstanding nationalistic composers are Aaron Copland and Roy Harris. Copland is, undoubtedly, the best known and most distinguished representative of the American school. One could state without exaggeration that the birth of American music dates from Copland's return from Paris to the States in 1925. As the founder and leader of modern American music, he has assured a permanent niche for himself in the history of American music. His importance lies in the fact that he gave direction to the country's musical life. He will also be remembered for his untiring efforts in promoting the music of his fellow composers; for his activities as a teacher, author, lecturer, organizer of concerts; and for the friendship and encouragement he extended to many young composers.

Copland's life is the most thoroughly documented of all American composers. Aside from his own charming *Autobiographical Sketch*,[5] the biographies of Arthur Berger[6] and Julia Smith[7] should be noted.

Copland's life story reveals a curious and unpredictable American destiny. Like Sousa—one of the most typically American figures—Copland was the offspring of newcomers to the country, the son of Jewish-Russian immigrants. He spent his first twenty years in a drab section of Brooklyn, inhabited largely by Irish, Italians, and Negroes. Copland himself comments that "It fills me with wonder each time I realize that a musician has been born in that street."

After studies with Rubin Goldmark, for whose taste the young student was soon too "modern," Copland enrolled at the Summer School in Fontainebleau as the first American student. Soon studies with Madame Boulanger commenced. Her admiration for Stravinsky's music consolidated the young American's affinities for the Russian composer's neoclassic outlook. The Stravinsky-Copland stylistic amalgam naturally influenced a host of young American composers.

Upon returning to New York, Copland carried a commission from Madame Boulanger for a symphony for organ and orchestra to be performed under Walter Damrosch with Madame Boulanger as soloist. The work, Copland's first major composition, was premiered in 1925 and won considerable acclaim. In the next year it was performed by the Boston Symphony Orchestra under the direction of Koussevitzky, who became an influence of great importance in Copland's life. The famed

[5] Aaron Copland, *Our New Music* (New York: McGraw Hill, Inc., 1941).
[6] Arthur Berger, *Aaron Copland* (New York: Oxford University Press, 1953).
[7] Julia Smith, *Aaron Copland* (New York: E. P. Dutton & Co., Inc., 1955).

Russian conductor should be remembered with gratitude for the friendship and help he extended to other young composers too, among them Harris, Schuman, and Bernstein.

Following the success of the Symphony for organ and orchestra (retitled as the First Symphony in a revised version), Copland wished "to write a work that would immediately be recognized as American in character." He embarked now on his *Music for the Theatre* in which he attempted to transplant the jazz idiom into a symphonic style. Copland must have been aware of Gershwin's similar attempts, although he does not mention this in his *Autobiographical Sketch*. Gershwin's *Rhapsody in Blue* was premiered in 1924 and was followed by his Piano Concerto in 1925. Perhaps it is more than a coincidence that Copland's next work was also a Piano Concerto (1926). In this work the composer felt "he had done all he could do with the idiom (jazz), considering its limited emotional scope." The *Symphonic Ode* (1929) for orchestra is a transition piece, partially inspired by jazz, but also pointing to the next stylistic period, referred to by his biographers as "esoteric" or "austere."

Copland's middle period is marked by rhythmic manipulation of short motives in a lean texture. The *Piano Variations* (1930) serve as a typical example. The work shows the surehandedness of a mature composer, and also the successful assimilation of Stravinsky's neoclassicism. The *Short Symphony* (1933) and the *Statements for Orchestra* (1934) also belong to this period of austerity.

In the mid-1930s, Copland found himself in a crisis, precipitated by doubts about his rapport with his audiences, a crisis similar to that which overcame Hindemith at about the same time. Copland felt, as did the German composer, that the average listener was estranged from contemporary music, and that a simplication of style was necessary to recapture the alienated public. He wrote:

> During these years I began to feel an increasing dissatisfaction with the relations of the music-loving public and the living composer. The old "special" public of the modern music concerts had fallen away, and the conventional concert public continued apathetic or indifferent to anything but the established classics. It seemed to me that we composers were in danger of working in a vacuum . . . I felt that it was worth the effort to see if I couldn't say what I had to say in the simplest possible terms.[8]

In the new simplified style Copland explored folk sources on a much wider basis now than he had in the early jazz period and produced his best known works. Through the ballets that followed, *Billy the Kid* (1938), *Rodeo* (1942), and *Appalachian Spring* (1944), Copland exerted

[8] *Our New Music*, pp. 228–229.

more influence on American folk music than it had exerted on him, as Berger wittily remarked. Berger was also correct in pointing out that Copland is more than a versatile folklorist; he shows an ability to sublimate and abstract the essence of American folk sources. Mexican folk tunes were skillfully employed in *El Salón México* (1936).

Soon the composer turned to abstract forms of composition, as exemplified by the Violin Sonata (1943), the Third Symphony (1946), and the Clarinet Concerto (1949). In these works folk melodies, whose declamatory character often suggest New England hymnody, receive a pandiatonic harmonic treatment.

With the Piano Quartet (1950)—the first work that employs some serial writing—and the *Twelve Poems of Emily Dickinson* (1950) for voice and piano, the composer reaches a new phase. His style, in which subjective processes of considerable intensity manifest themselves, has become introverted.

In his recent abstract instrumental works, such as the *Piano Fantasy* (1957) and the *Nonet* (1960) for three violins, three violas, and three cellos, Copland combines his traditional style with serial technique, although the latter always remains subservient to the essentially diatonic harmonic thinking. It is only in his *Connotations* (1962) for orchestra that serial logic became central. The composer himself pointed out in the program notes written for the first performance of the work that the "three four-voiced chords heard at the outset have primary meaning," and all implications and "connotations" are derived of them. The reaction to the work was mixed; while one reviewer judged it an uncongenial work that "lacked the honest strength and sheer power of Copland's earlier severe music," another commentator suggested that Copland had now found "a signal revivification of his talents through his own reading of the serial idea."

The composer's large oeuvre includes incidental music for films and an opera, *The Tender Land* (1954).

Another nationalist, Roy Harris (b. 1898), attained a leading position in the 1930s due more perhaps to his dynamic personality and vitality than to the quality of his music. His Third Symphony (1938), in one movement, has won more acclaim, more prizes, and more performances than any other American symphonic work. However, a rapid decline soon became apparent, and today few would consider Harris as part of the mainstream of American music. Copland implied twenty-five years ago that the music of his fellow-composer might not have lasting qualities. In his summation of Harris, he noted with acumen that "you can demonstrate to your own satisfaction that the man does not know the first thing about composing—but the fact will still remain that his is the most personal note in American music today."[9]

[9]*Our New Music,* p. 163.

An Oklahoman by birth, Harris moved to a suburban community in California, in his childhood, a fact that should dissipate the growing legend that Harris—born in a log cabin in Lincoln County—is a true representative of the open prairies of the Southwest. After making a late start in music, Harris followed Copland's example and pursued studies with Madame Boulanger in Paris. Upon his return to the States, he was even more fiercely determined than Copland to write American music. Harris' compositions achieved an immediate success with the public, and he was hailed as a genius in a burst of enthusiasm. The popularity of his music was also enhanced by his habit of furnishing patriotic program notes to his works, not unlike Soviet Russian composers who were required to do so by the State. Several of his eleven symphonies have programmatic connotations quite similar to the symphonies of Shostakovich. Thus, the Fifth Symphony (1942) endeavors to portray "qualities of heroic strength—determination—will to struggle—faith in our destiny." The Sixth Symphony (1945), based on the Gettysburg Address, is dedicated to the "Armed Forces of Our Nation."

His two major vocal works, *Song for Occupation* (1934) and *Symphony for Voices* (1935) both for *a cappella* chorus, based on texts by Walt Whitman, were criticized for flaws in the setting of the text. More felicitous are his chamber music works, particularly the Piano Quintet (1936).

Harris' style favors long spun-out melodies often accompanied by modal harmonies that flow for long stretches without being interrupted by cadences. The rhythmic component tends to betray the jazz influence and at times is heavily accentuated. Harris' musical thought processes were often found arbitrary and devoid of an inner consistency. Critics have noted a lack of coherence in his music. This has not been remedied in the composer's recent compositions, as evidenced in his *Rhythms and Spaces* (1965) for string orchestra.

Harris championed the cause of American national music in many articles and essays. His central theory was that it is the rhythmic component that distinguishes American music from European music. He wrote:

> Our sense of rhythm is less symmetrical than the European rhythmic sense. European musicians are trained to think of rhythm in its largest common denominator, while we are all born with a feeling for its smallest unit. . . . This asymmetrical balancing of rhythmic phrases is in our blood, it is not in the European blood . . . .[10]

Perhaps these generalizations tend to oversimplify matters. First, it is highly unlikely that a single component in music, such as rhythm, can successfully be singled out as the element that distinguishes the

---

[10] *American Composers on American Music,* edited by Henry Cowell (Palo Alto, Calif: Stanford University Press, 1933).

music of two continents. Secondly, and more specifically, the notion that asymmetrical rhythmic groupings are typically American cannot be maintained, for such groupings frequently appear in the music of European composers such as Stravinsky and Bartók. Actually, Harris was probably referring to a specific rhythmic style derived from jazz, in which a melody of asymmetrical rhythmic construction is superimposed on the regular pulsations of the bass line. This rhythmic effect was used by Harris as well as Copland. In general, the argument of whether or not there is an American musical style seems to be a futile one. If a composer stresses the folk element in his works, then the national affiliation will naturally become more apparent. In this sense, Mussorgsky is more Russian than Scriabin, just as Harris is more American than Barber.

Charles Ives and Henry Cowell were also prominent Americanists, but their music will be discussed with the experimentalists. Other composers who, in most of their works, remained close to a conscious American style include Randall Thompson (b. 1898), Ferde Grofé (b. 1892), and Morton Gould (b. 1913). Single instances of the nationalistic spirit may be observed in a number of isolated works (Ernest Bloch's *America,* for example) not typical of the composer's general style.

TRADITIONALISTS

The traditionalists are marked by their commitments to the past. Composers with such allegiance have also been labeled academicians, as many of them teach at universities and colleges and transmit the tradition as a professional concern. Two trends characterize the traditionalist outlook: the neoromantic and the neoclassic. The first usually represents a distinctly conservative outlook, one that is rooted in the subjective expressiveness of the nineteenth century and conveys a strongly tonal, melodic-harmonic style. The second trend is loosely related to the neoclassicism of Stravinsky or Hindemith. This style is involved with dissonant counterpoint, stressing the rhythmic component, and, on the whole, represents a universal rather than a personal approach.

NEOROMANTIC OUTLOOK

Of the neoromantics Samuel Barber (b. 1910) achieved the widest fame. His gift was recognized when he was still studying piano, composition, and voice at the Curtis Institute. Following his graduation from Curtis, Barber went to Italy, where he met Toscanini, who took a liking to the young composer. In 1938 Toscanini performed the twenty-seven-year-old composer's *Essay* for Orchestra, an arrangement for string orchestra of the *Adagio* for String Quartet. Barber's fame rose rapidly, as he was the only American composer whose music Toscanini ever conducted. By that time he had written his first Cello Sonata (1932), the overture, *The School for Scandal* (1933), and his First Symphony (1936). The lyricism and accessible melodic-harmonic idiom of these early works were also responsible for the quick rise of Barber's popularity.

The subsequent works, such as the Violin Concerto (1939), the Second Symphony (1942), the Cello Concerto (1945), and the ballet suite *Medea*, retained the same musical approach and methods of construction—both firmly rooted in the practices of the nineteenth century—although his harmonic language became somewhat bolder. The polytonal fugue of the "Second Essay," (1942), and *Medea's* "Dance of Vengeance" point to an expansion of the harmonic idiom. Barber is at his best in setting words to music; his song cycle *Mélodies Passagères,* based on five poems (in French) by Rilke (1951), shows that his sense of prosody even encompasses the idiom of a foreign language. Barber's gift of words is also apparent in his letters, several of which are quoted in Broder's biography.[11]

Barber's elegant craftsmanship and appealing style made him "safe" enough for the Metropolitan Opera to produce his *Vanessa* in 1958, an unusual honor for an American composer. The opera, based on Menotti's libretto, suffered, despite the competence of the vocal writing, from the clichés that pervaded both the harmonic texture and the orchestral style. An English critic, Mellers,[12] considers *Vanessa* "a failure because the composer sought to give it more weight than it could bear." Barber's more recent work, the Second Piano Concerto (1963), is a serviceable repertory piece, and his opera, *Antony and Cleopatra* (1966) was the commissioned curtain-raiser for the opening of the new Metropolitan Opera House at Lincoln Center.

Another "pure" type of the neoromantic orientation is Howard Hanson (b. 1896), for many years the head of the Eastman School of Music at the University of Rochester. Because of his prominent position, Hanson's influence affected a whole generation of American composers. The Eastman School became the stronghold of the traditionalist outlook and under its auspices several concert series were initiated to promote the works of young American composers.

[11] Nathan Broder, *Samuel Barber* (New York: G. Schirmer, Inc., 1954).

[12] Wilfrid Mellers, *Music in a New Found Land* (New York: Alfred A. Knopf, Inc., 1965).

The momentum Hanson gave the cause of American music transcends the significance of his own works. As a composer he is an avowed romanticist; he summarized his position in an interview given before the premiere of his Second ("Romantic") Symphony as follows:

> The symphony represents for me my escape from the rather bitter type of modern musical realism which occupies so large a place in contemporary thought. Much contemporary music seems to me to be showing a tendency to become entirely too cerebral. I do not believe that music is primarily a matter of intellect, but rather a manifestation of the emotions. I have, therefore, aimed in this symphony to create a work that was young in spirit, lyrical and romantic in temperament, and simple and direct in expression.[13]

Hanson wrote five symphonies between 1922 and 1955, a number of symphonic poems, and works for chorus and orchestra. His music, which follows the well-worn path of such composers as Liszt and Sibelius, found immediate acceptance.

The majority of the composers who received their training at Eastman achieved a high degree of professional competence, although they seldom ventured beyond the traditionalist orbit. Included among them are Peter Mennin (b. 1923), president of the Juilliard School of Music, Ulysses Kay (b. 1917), and Robert Ward (b. 1917). All three have definite romantic leanings, similar to a host of other composers, many of whom occupy important positions at universities, colleges, and conservatories.

Another distinguished representative of the romantic tradition is Ernest Bloch (1880–1959). Born in Geneva, Switzerland, he completed his musical training in Belgium and Germany. In 1916 he toured the United States as the conductor of a dance group. The tour unexpectedly turned into permanent residency. Active as a teacher first at the Cleveland Institute of Music, and later at Mills College in Oakland, California, Bloch exerted a powerful influence; among his students were such notable composers as Roger Sessions, Mark Brunswick, Douglas Moore, Frederic Jacobi, and Bernard Rogers.

A large number of Bloch's works express the spirit of Judaism without actually resorting to overt folklorism. The works that bear witness to his profound admiration of the Jewish cultural tradition include *Schelomo* (1916) for cello and orchestra; *Trois Poèmes Juifs* (1913) for orchestra; the symphony *Israel* (1916); *Baal Schem* (1923) for violin and piano; *Voice in the Wilderness* (1936) for cello and orchestra; and the *Sacred Service* (1933). The music of these works is marked by deep expressiveness with the mood ranging from philosophic to dramatic; the rich chromatic melodic-harmonic idiom is enhanced by brilliant

---

[13]*America's Music from the Pilgrims to the Present,* p. 550.

orchestration. Bloch, although essentially a romanticist, was not unaffected by the prevalent neoclassic currents, traces of which can be found in the two Concerti Grossi, dated 1925 and 1953; in the Violin Concerto (1938); and particularly in the Third and Fourth String Quartets (1946 and 1951–1952), both of which contain passacaglias and fugal writing. Strongly dissonant counterpoint is found in the *Sinfonia Brevis* (1954), in which some experimentation takes place with twelve-tone rows, although the technique bears little relation to Schoenberg's method. Even in these works, which reflect the influence of neoclassic trends, Bloch's style remains highly charged with emotion; the rhapsodic, improvisatory thought process is now more firmly controlled than in the earlier works. His oeuvre also includes five string quartets; two piano quintets, the first of which is a particularly successful work; three suites for solo cello (1956–1957); and two suites for solo violin (1958).

NEOCLASSICISTS

The purest representative of the classic ideology—universal expressive values and firm form consciousness—is Walter Piston (b. 1894). After studying with Nadia Boulanger, Piston joined the Harvard University music faculty where he taught composition until his retirement in 1960. His experiences as a teacher are laid down in four volumes: *Principles of Harmonic Analysis* (1933); *Counterpoint* (1947); *Harmony* (1948); and *Orchestration* (1955).

Piston's works show impeccable craftsmanship at all times; his care and ability in handling the materials of music are matched by very few American composers. Copland's appraisal of Piston's music, written twenty-five years ago, maintains its validity. On the whole Copland's criticism concerning a certain repetitiousness and lack of adventure remains valid as one scans through the eight symphonies and five string quartets, central to the composer's total work.

Piston's musical style is essentially tonal, although in this traditional harmonic framework there is a good deal of subtlety and intricacy. He almost invariably adheres to the classical forms (sonata and rondo forms are especially favored) in which he expresses himself with ease, though at times in a routine fashion. Textures are generally contrapuntal and rich in fugal involvements. Often two-part contrapuntal writing is pursued, supported by chords laid out in blocks. Original effects are frequently attained in rhythmic devices; although Piston never makes an attempt to be self-consciously "American," a subtle, sublimated use of jazz rhythms is felt. Such examples may be found in the syncopations of the first movement of the Second Symphony; in the second theme of the first movement of the Piano Trio (1935); and in the last movement of the Piano Quintet (1949), one of his best chamber works.

His output also includes the early ballet *The Incredible Flutist* (1938), two violin concertos (1940 and 1959-1960), the Violin-Harpsichord Sonata (1945), the expressive Woodwind Quintet (1956), and his recent String Sextet (1965).

Another neoclassicist who restricts himself to the medium of the string quartet is Quincy Porter (1897-1966); in addition to nine string quartets, he wrote a *Divertimento* for woodwind quintet (1960), a Quintet for harpsichord and string quartet (1961), and a Viola Concerto (1948).

Also active in the field of chamber music is Arthur Berger (b. 1912), an erudite writer on a variety of musical subjects. Among his best-known works, which show Stravinsky's influence, are the Quartet for Woodwinds (1941), the *Ideas of Order* (1953) for orchestra, and a string quartet (1958). Neoclassic tendencies also mark the work of Ross Lee Finney (b. 1906), the author of eight string quartets. Although employing twelve-tone devices his music is more conservative than the works written under the Stravinsky–Copland influence in the 1940s and 1950s by such composers as Lukas Foss (b. 1922), Irving Fine (1914-1962), Robert Palmer (b. 1915), David Diamond (b. 1915), Alexei Haieff (b. 1914), and others.

Finally William Schuman (b. 1910), the president of the Lincoln Center for the Performing Arts in New York, should be mentioned. As a composer, he is undoubtedly a traditionalist, incorporating romantic, classic, and nationalistic leanings. A student of Roy Harris, Schuman's early work had a good deal of conscious American associations. At all times his music has the buoyancy, restlessness, and crude strength that also characterizes the music of Harris. Schuman's compositions—including eight symphonies and four string quartets—are laid out on large canvasses and have considerable rhythmic momentum. The long-spun melodies and intense harmonies suggest romantic ties, while the frequent resorting to fugues, passacaglias, and other contrapuntal devices emphasizes the classic orientation.

PROGRESSIVES

Carl Ruggles (b. 1876), a mystic and an individualist, was a forward looking American composer who anticipated many future trends. The rich, chromatic counterpoint of the American composer shows a considerable likeness to the early works of Schoenberg. Ruggles' counterpoint is often dominated by the interval class of the minor second, a device observed in the music of Webern.

Ruggles, in his first mature work, *Angels* (1921) for six trumpets, abandoned tonality; his wide melodic skips are reminiscent of the Viennese atonal composers, with whose music he was unfamiliar at the time. One cannot but marvel at this composer's original creative mind and his uncompromising urge for clarity. He is just as astonishing a phenomenon as Ives, without the latter's eccentric diversity. Of the two, Ruggles is the "purer" musician, always faithful to his goal, a quality of beauty that he called "Sublime." His published works include *Men and Mountains* (1924) for chamber orchestra; *Portals* (1926) for string orchestra; *Sun Trader* (1933) for large orchestra; *Evocations* (1932–1945) for piano, and *Organum* (1945) and *Affirmations* (1957) for orchestra.

Another bold and original progressive American composer, ignored, by the larger audiences, is Wallingford Riegger (1885–1961). Trained in this country and later at the Berlin Hochschule, Riegger was one of the first American composers to adapt Schoenberg's twelve-tone method. He used it expressively, bending it to his own needs, and without the aridity found so often when employed by mediocre composers. Riegger himself posed the problem of construction in the program notes he wrote for a performance at Northwestern University of *Nonet:*

> What intrigues the composer about twelve-tone techniques is [their] severe restrictions. To keep within them is a challenge, as it is to a poet to stick to the rhyming scheme, once decided upon, of a sonnet. Cannot it be done without sacrificing plausibility, "spontaneity," or expressive content? To avoid clichés, yet to cover up traces of effort, is the goal of every artist, regardless of medium or technique. Has he succeeded? Only a second or third generation can decide.

Riegger's fondness for the brass sound prompted him to write the *Music for Brass Choir,* which has received more performances than any of his conventionally scored pieces. His works include five symphonies, two quartets, a Piano Quintet (1959), and the Duo for Piano and Orchestra (1960), in addition to choral works. Riegger's inventiveness and variety of musical solutions make it difficult to generalize about his style; perhaps one can define it in such negatives as never contrived, obvious, or clichélike.

Another uncompromising and solitary figure in American music is Roger Sessions (b. 1896), held in awe by the musical profession and unrecognized by the general public. To use Copland's description, there is something "titanic" about Sessions' music, titanic in its larger-than-life dimensions and in the depth of its thought. A philosophical quality may be added to this description; a seriousness and loftiness that seem almost unrelieved by lighter moments. These qualities are those that obviously do not lead to easy acceptance. The difficulty Sessions' music

encounters may be seen from the example of his First Symphony, composed in 1927 and published in full score in 1929, yet premiered only in
1949. It is the only one among the composer's five symphonies that is
currently available on discs; the second is out-of-print, and the other
three have not been recorded.

A descendant of a New England family, though born in New York,
Sessions received his musical training at Yale. Studies with Ernest Bloch
followed, and in 1921 Sessions accepted his first teaching position at
Smith College. Soon, however, the young composer was caught by
Wanderlust and went to Europe. His destination was not Paris where
so many young American composers gravitated, but Italy. He remained
in Florence for eight years, a stay interrupted occasionally by short
sojourns in Germany. Returning in 1933, he held teaching posts at
Princeton University, at the University of California, and since 1952,
again at Princeton. His profound musicianship and searching mind
guided a great many young composers. He is the author of two books:
The Musical Experience (1950) and *Harmonic Practice* (1951).

Sessions' music is difficult to characterize; to say—as some commentators have—that his style is a combination of Stravinsky and Schoenberg
is a gross oversimplification, one that would certainly be offensive to
the composer, who consciously avoids any *isms* or the utilization of
any system of composition. He defined his aims as a composer as
follows:

> I reject any kind of dogma or platform. I am not trying to write
> "modern," "American," or "neoclassic" music. I am seeking always and
> only the coherent and living expression of my musical ideas . . . I dislike
> rhetoric, overemphasis, vulgarity, but at the same time believe that per-
> fection in art is a sort of equilibrium which can be neither defined nor
> counterfeited . . . I have no sympathy with consciously sought originality.
> I accept my musical ideas without theorizing.[14]

This rejection of any consciously chosen "ism" does not imply that
Sessions did not painstakingly study all the musical currents of his
times. These studies, however, never led to a facile adoption of the
styles or methods of other composers. Sessions developed his art by
an almost unconscious accumulation of impressions. By sifting through,
accepting, rejecting, or refining his impressions, he made them part of his
musical language. The style that resulted "was not chosen" as Imbrie
points out in his perceptive study of the composer,[15] "any more than
an individual's handwriting or gait is chosen."

Thus, when one states that in the early works of Sessions certain

---

[14]"Roger Sessions," in Henry Cowell, ed., *American Composers on American Music* (Palo Alto, Calif.: Stanford University Press, 1933), p. 78.

[15]Andrew Imbrie, "Roger Sessions: In Honor of His Sixty-fifth Birthday," *Perspectives of New Music*, **1**, No. 1 (1962).

neoclassic trends are evident or that Stravinsky's influence is felt, as in the last movement of the First Symphony, it is not to imply that the composer used the mentioned stylistic current in a calculated manner. Rather, a certain interaction took place as Sessions examined Stravinsky's neoclassic music, as a result of which he enlarged his choices—his "repertory"—of compositional solutions. While rhythm plays a dominant part in the early works, as in the brilliant incidental music to the *Black Maskers,* a play by Andreyev, and in the First Symphony, after 1935 the long sustained melodic lines gain increasing emphasis. Harmonically, the well-defined tonality of the early works gives way to increasingly tenuous key centers. The works written after 1935 are also marked by great intensity of feeling, by rich chromaticism and by polyphonic textures. For these reasons many critics link this phase of Sessions' development to the music of Schoenberg; an example can be seen particularly in the slow movements (Second Symphony, Second String Quartet), where the composer's philosophical spirit asserts itself to great advantage. Here the listener can best perceive the intricate web of lines, the ambiguous harmonic destinations—which may or may not be reached—and the subtle interplay of motives. Elliott Carter aptly characterizes Sessions' music:

> During the progress of the over-all continuity pattern Sessions uses, there is usually an increase and decrease in definition and individualization of motif, of rhythm, or of some other feature, or group of features . . . . More and more the notion of extended, continuously flowing sections, during which ideas come to the surface, gain clarity and definition, and then sink back into the general flow, has characterized Session's unique style.[16]

In more recent works Sessions incorporates serial technique into his writing, again not as an ideology or platform, but as a means to a technical solution. The late works include the solo Violin Sonata (1953), *Idyll of Theocritus* (1956) for solo voice and orchestra, the Third and Fourth Symphonies (1957 and 1958), a String Quintet (1958) with added viola, the *Mass* (1958), the Fifth Symphony (1964), and the opera *Montezuma* (1947–1962).

Montezuma, according to reports from abroad, falls short of the composer's best. That opera is not a natural medium in which this inward composer expresses himself to best advantage can also be seen by the relative failure of the *Trial of Lucullus* (1947), an earlier opera based on Brecht's play. In summary, Session's output marks an outstanding achievement in American music and it is largely due to apathy and ignorance that his music remains unknown to larger audiences.

[16] Elliott Carter, "Current Chronicle," *Musical Quarterly,* **45**, No. 3 (1959), pp. 379–380.

Perhaps the most important musical event of recent years is the emergence of Elliott Carter (b. 1908) as a major composer, and also as a highly cultured spokesman for contemporary music.[17] Born in New York, Carter received a broad education at Harvard University, where he studied composition with Piston. After working with Nadia Boulanger for three years, the young composer accepted a position at St. John's College in Annapolis, teaching not only music, but also Greek and philosophy. After World War II, he joined the faculty of the Peabody Conservatory in Baltimore, and later that of Yale University.

Carter's early output consists mainly of choral compositions which, in retrospect, appear to lead up to his first three major works: the Piano Sonata (1945–1946), the Cello Sonata (1948), and the First Quartet (1951), which instantly assured his stature as a major composer. It was in these three works that his intricate use of rhythmic changes was first employed. The subtle rubato passages of the Piano Sonata, in which sixteenth notes appear in various groupings (predominantly 5 and 7) without a meter signature, give the music a swaying feeling. Some of the cross accents here, and also in earlier works, point to Copland's rhythmic style. In the Cello Sonata, a somber work, the composer's deeply personal style is unmistakable. Like Sessions, Carter is not a doctrinaire; he does not rely on the dogma or method of any particular school. His music is marked by a fresh and vivid imagination for sound, an admirable sense of balance, and an unusually flexible rhythmic pulse, made possible by such new devices as his metric modulation (see Chapter 3).

These qualities were further developed in three recent works, the *Variations for Orchestra* (1955); the Second Quartet (1959), winner of the Pulitzer Prize, the New York Music Critics' Award, and the UNESCO International Music Prize; and the Double Concerto (1960) for piano, harpsichord, and two chamber orchestras. Despite their complexities, all three works are transparent compared to the music of Sessions. Interestingly enough, Carter's works, although enormously taxing for the performer, are more accessible to the listener than Sessions' music, which is technically somewhat less demanding. Compositions by Sessions seem to form a closed universe based on an inimitable style; Carter's music, by contrast, has an openness—perhaps the word extroversion would characterize it properly—that provided a path for younger composers to follow.

The three later works show a novel and original approach to form in that each work is unified by a large plan of its own. Thus, in the

---

[17] Elliott Carter, "Shop Talk by an American Composer," *Contemporary Composers on Contemporary Music,* edited by Elliott Schwartz and Barney Childs (New York: Holt, Rinehart and Winston, Inc., 1967).

Variations, musical occurrences follow a sequence of events which starts with a strong definition of contrast and character. Followed by a decrease in the strength of characterization, the music reaches a point of neutrality in the central variation. Thereafter, stronger delineations again occur, until in the finale the pattern of strong contrasts with which the work began are resumed.

In the Second Quartet, described by the composer as an "auditory scenario," the individual roles of the performers are dramatized. According to the prefatory note to the score, the first violin is to exhibit the greatest variety of roles with emphasis on the bravura style. In turn, the second violin is to observe strictly its regular rhythms. The viola has a predominantly expressive role, while the cello is impetuous, similar to the first violin. An introduction and a conclusion provide a frame for the four movements which are separated by cadenzas. Although no conventional forms such as sonata or rondo are used, the sections stand in the most explicit relationship to each other. Structural differentiations are partly achieved by lending referential meaning to intervals and to rhythmic events, and partly by characterization of instrumental parts. It probably would be more appropriate to call the work a concerto for string quartet because of the virtuoso style. The parts are written with great sophistication, as if each instrument's musical and psychological role in the history of the string quartet were summarized from Haydn to Bartók. The events begin with an *allegro fantastico,* in which the first violin leads, proposing themes and developmental possibilities. Next, in the *presto scherzando,* the second violin rules with characteristically square rhythms. Gradually, the tendency is toward separateness that reaches its high point with the violin cadenza in the *andante espressivo* section. Here the other instruments respond with a stony silence. In the final *allegro,* noncooperation gives way to collaboration.

The Double Concerto is an antiphonal work in which two teams of instruments are linked to the piano and harpsichord, respectively. In addition to a division in space and timbre, each group follows assigned melodic and harmonic intervals and special pulsation. These features are not rigidly pursued; occasional overlaps and intersections appear between the two groups. In the composer's words, "the form is that of confrontations of diversified action patterns and a presentation of their mutual interreactions, conflicts, and resolutions, their growth and decay over various stretches of time."[18] The Double Concerto is a powerful and brilliant work; with the Second Quartet, it represents the apex of achievement in recent American music. Carter, beyond doubt, is a first-rate American composer.

[18]Program notes furnished by the composer.

More accessible than Sessions or Carter is the music of Leon Kirchner (b. 1919), born in New York and educated in California. Among his three teachers, Bloch, Schoenberg, and Sessions, Bloch left the strongest imprint, as is seen in Kirchner's rhapsodic ornamental style and in the exalted expressiveness of his music. Kirchner, presently a professor of composition at Harvard University, first commanded attention with his Piano Sonata (1948) and First Quartet (1949). The rhythmic style of the quartet shows the distinct influence of Bartók. Among the subsequent works which established Kirchner's reputation as an important composer, the following should be mentioned: *Sinfonia* (1950), the First Piano Concerto (1952), the Toccata (1955) for strings, winds, and percussion, the Piano Trio (1957), the Second Quartet (1959), the Double Concerto (1960) for violin, cello, ten winds, and percussion, and the Second Piano Concerto (1963).

Despite the obvious links to romanticism represented by an essentially conservative harmonic style, and even a touch of Lisztian virtuosity, Kirchner's music has a novel ring and communicates a feeling of contemporary sensibilities. Perhaps the strong intuitive aspect of Kirchner's personality gives a novel sound to his music, even though the parts that make up the whole are often identifiable in terms of their derivations.

Three additional musical personalities should be added to the list of progressive composers: George Rochberg (b. 1919), Ben Weber (b. 1916), and Salvatore Martirano (b. 1927). Of the three, Rochberg has gained increased recognition in recent years; his *Contra Mortem et Tempus* (1965) for flute, clarinet, violin, and piano shows interesting ways of accommodating musical quotations, such as a fragment of Ives' work.

EXPERIMENTALISTS

Of the composers who blazed new trails in American music Charles Ives (1874–1954) is the most astounding phenomenon. Called by Copland "a genius in a wasteland," Ives established a truly American instrumental musical style before 1910, foreshadowing many inventions usually credited to Schoenberg and Stravinsky.

Born in Danbury, Connecticut, Ives was first tutored by his father, a band leader and a musical explorer who experimented with microtones and sound-measuring devices. The young boy continued his composition studies at Yale, where, according to Cowell[19] he "got a little fed up with classroom counterpoint exercises."

[19] Henry Cowell and Sidney Cowell, *Charles Ives and His Music* (New York: Oxford University Press, 1955).

Choosing music as a profession presented a conflict for Ives; his ambivalent feelings regarding music as a full-time profession mirror not only a personal dilemma but also the tenuous position the arts held in the ideology of a new and vigorous nation. In his childhood Ives felt ashamed of music, an entirely wrong attitude, he admitted. Nevertheless, during vacations he felt guilty staying home and playing the piano when the other boys drove grocery carts or engaged in physical exercise. The childhood conflict led to a divided life. As it seemed wrong to him to be a composer "only," he entered the insurance business and became a part-time composer on evenings and weekends. He was convinced, perhaps driven by the puritanical sternness of his character, that an encounter with real life is more necessary for a composer than the isolation of the ivory tower. He believed with Emerson, who was his great idol, that "all things are One." Based on this principle, the composer explained the interrelatedness of business and art as follows:

> My business experience revealed life to me in many aspects that I might otherwise have missed. In it one sees tragedy, nobility, meanness, high aims, low aims, brave hopes, faint hopes, great ideals, no ideals, and one is able to watch these work inevitable destiny . . . . It is not even uncommon in business intercourse to sense a reflection of philosophy—a depth of something fine—akin to a strong sense of beauty in art . . . . I have experienced a great fulness of life in business. The fabric of existence weaves itself whole. You cannot set an art off in the corner and hope for it to have vitality, reality, and substance. There can be nothing *exclusive* about a substantial art. It comes directly out of the heart of experience of life and thinking about life and living life. My work in music helped my business and work in business helped my music.[20]

It was on the same basis that Ives, in his interesting *Essays before a Sonata*,[21] suggested that the content of Debussy's music "would have been worthier if he had hoed corn or sold newspapers for a living, for in this way he might have gained a deeper vitality and a truer theme to sing at night and of a Sunday." It was in the light of his beloved New England philosophers that Ives perceived all things; thus, in Debussy's attitude toward nature he found a rather *"sensual* sensuousness" as compared to Thoreau's *"spiritual* sensuousness."

Ives' entire philosophy and esthetic outlook was based on a moralistic, spiritual sturdiness; he felt that music is too often confused with something that lets the ears "lie back in an easy chair." He also condemned the notion that a sound should be called beautiful just because one is used to it. It seemed to him that the composer who uses

---

[20] *Charles Ives and His Music,* pp. 96–97.
[21] Charles Ives, *Essays before a Sonata,* edited by Howard Boatwright (New York: W. W. Norton & Company, Inc., 1961).

the same formulas is being drugged with an overdose of habit-forming sounds.

This philosophy earned Ives the nickname of a "raw genius" and it embodied the premises upon which his daring experiments were based. In complete isolation, without the benefit of hearing performances of his music and without the encouragement of an audience or a following, he continued on his lonely path. Most of his works were written before 1918, when a severe heart attack forced him to reduce his activities. The time span for the average Ives work from composition to premiere was about half a century; thus, the Second Symphony, written between 1897 and 1902, was premiered in 1951, and the Fourth Symphony, finished in 1916, was first performed in its entirety in 1965.

Ives was a more truly American composer than many who attempted to be so deliberately. His music is filled with indigenous tunes, such as minstrel songs, hymns, patriotic songs, and with the rich associations of the geography and history of his beloved New England. Thus, in his *Concord Sonata* (1909–1915), he pays tribute to Emerson, Hawthorne, the Alcotts, and Thoreau, and in his *Three Places in New England* (1903–1914) he refers to the Boston Commons, Putnam's Camp, and the Housatonic at Stockbridge.

Ives' bold innovations and experiments are too numerous to cite. Perhaps the most characteristic feature of his innovations is the simultaneity of different musical occurrences. These are often motivated by extramusical inspiration, as in the second movement of the *Three Places in New England,* where a boy dreams of two groups of soldiers walking at different speeds, one approaching, the other disappearing. Also, in *The Unanswered Question,* simultaneity is reached when the strings play quietly and undisturbed, while the "question" is posed with increasing urgency by the winds. At other times superimpositions of complex rhythms, tonalities, or melodies (known later as polyrhythms, polytonalities) appear in an abstract musical context. Ives also experimented with atonality, as in the *Soliloquy* (1907), before hearing the music of Schoenberg, whose music he heard for the first time in 1931.

Ives' melodic invention is the least striking aspect of his music. Mention should be made of the frequent quotations, ranging from the main theme of the first movement of Beethoven's Fifth Symphony to snatches of hymn tunes or college songs. The purpose of the quotations is often mystifying and they may have had their roots in the composer's private associations. The love for quotations is most likely linked to Emerson, who devoted an entire essay ("Quotation and Originality") to this topic. In the treatment of motives, Ives often uses inversion, retrograde forms along with rhythmic augmentation, and diminution. One is often amazed at the boldness of his harmonic procedures; tone clusters are followed by major sevenths and minor ninths and tritones.

The most revolutionary aspect of his music, however, is in the field of rhythm; there is hardly a contemporary rhythmic device—usually attributed to Bartók or Stravinsky—that does not appear in the composer's music. He uses unusual meters such as $\frac{5}{2}$, $\frac{11}{8}$ and even $\frac{6\frac{1}{2}}{2}$ (!), pulsations, such as $\frac{3 + 3 + 2}{16}$, as in Bartók's Bulgarian rhythms, as well as changing meters and music without bar lines. Complex superimpositions of meters also appear, as in the second movement of the Fourth Symphony where $\frac{6}{8}$, $\frac{5}{8}$, $\frac{7}{4}$, and $\frac{2}{4}$ occur simultaneously. Sometimes jazzlike rhythms are heard prior to the actual appearance of jazz.

Ives also anticipated spatial music (see Chapter 7); in several of his works two or more performing groups are used that require the assistance of several conductors (Fourth Symphony, *The Unanswered Question*).

In other works he capitalizes on "accidental" circumstances, such as the off-pitch tuning of the organ, the nervous violist who falls behind, and the like, thus foreshadowing aleatory music. He often preferred to postpone the final crystallization of a work; for instance, the "Emerson" movement of the *Concord Sonata* received its final form in print only ten years after it was first put on paper. An anticipation of Boulez' "work in progress" concept emerges from Ives' statement:

> Some of the passages now played have not been written out, and I do not know as I ever shall write them out as it may take away the daily pleasure of playing this music and seeing it grow and feeling that it is not finished and the hope that it never will be. . . .

He felt the same way about his last, unfinished work, the *Universe Symphony*, which was to represent an aspect of life "about which there is always more to say."

In other instances Ives allowed the performer certain liberties, such as the number of repetitions, the choice of dynamics, and in a few cases there are even instructions for improvisations. For example, in *Halloween* (1911), a bass drum player is instructed to improvise his part in the last repetition of the theme.

Ives also shunned conventionality in his treatment of form; he maintained that the relationships between parts should not be too obvious but should have the complexity of the individual's life experiences.

Ives' works include four symphonies; two string quartets; three piano sonatas, among which the *Concord Sonata* is outstanding; four violin and piano sonatas; a piano trio; and a number of additional orchestral selections, besides about two hundred songs.[22]

[22] Charles Ives, "Postface to 114 Songs," *Contemporary Composers on Contemporary Music*, edited by Elliott Schwartz and Barney Childs (New York: Holt, Rinehart and Winston, Inc., 1967).

In the last part of his life, long after he stopped composing, Ives received some degree of recognition. He was awarded the Pulitzer Prize and was made a member of the Institute of Arts and Letters. In 1939, when a whole evening of his music was presented for the first time, Lawrence Gilman, the noted critic wrote:

> The greatest music composed by an American . . . music of breadth . . . profoundly stirring in its intensity and nobility of expression . . . astounding ability to fluctuate, combine and invent rhythms.[23]

Perhaps the greatest recognition came from Arnold Schoenberg, whose widow found the following note among his papers:

> There is a great man living in this country—a composer. He has solved the problem how to preserve one's self and to learn. He responds to negligence by contempt. He is not forced to accept praise or blame. His name is Ives.[24]

This is a most fitting tribute to the uncompromising American composer who once said: "If you want something played, write something you do not want played."

Another experimentalist, who earned fame both in the United States and abroad, was Henry Cowell (1897–1965), Ives' friend and biographer. A Californian by birth, Cowell's career began with a style that was sensationally novel, turning gradually to the comparatively conventional. Cowell took a vital part in promoting contemporary music as a teacher, performer, editor, critic, and concert organizer.

In his early music, he introduced tone clusters, that is, three or more, up to twelve, adjacent tones on the keyboard performed with the palm of the hand or with the forearm. This new pianistic device (also applicable to orchestral writing) impressed European composers, among them Bartók, who shortly after a personal meeting with Cowell, used tone clusters in his First Piano Concerto.[25] Cowell also developed, in collaboration with Theremin, the rhythmicon, an instrument designed to reproduce the most intricate rhythmic combinations. His later innovations included the "prepared piano," a manipulation of the strings of the piano (a device further developed by John Cage) by applying various kinds of metal and wooden objects, such as thumbtacks, nails, coins, and wooden bars. Percussion instruments were another object of Cowell's interest; he wrote for various percussion combinations, as seen in his *Concerto for Percussion* (1958–1959). Cowell explored theoretical

---

[23] *Charles Ives and His Music,* p. 113.

[24] *Charles Ives and His Music,* p. 114n.

[25] Henry Cowell, "New Musical Resources," *Contemporary Composers on Contemporary Music,* edited by Elliott Schwartz and Barney Childs (New York: Holt, Rinehart and Winston, Inc., 1967).

problems too; the results of his investigations are summed up in his book, *New Musical Resources.*[26]

The composer also delved into folk music research; his interest in this field ranged from native American folk music to Oriental sources. Elements of folklore derived from Japanese, Indian, and Persian sources are an integral part of his style. From the American scene he explored the hymn-and-fuguing-tune combination. Cowell's very large oeuvre includes sixteen symphonies, six quartets, and numerous choral and instrumental works. In a summation of his work as a composer, Hugo Weisgall[27] aptly states that "despite the diversity of musical impulses, Cowell has achieved a remarkable consistency in his style."

While both Ives and Cowell remained, in their experimentation, within the boundaries of the traditional musical vocabulary, Edgar Varèse (1885–1965) precipitated a complete break with established musical practices. The French-born composer, who settled in New York in 1916, liberated the sound material of music from what Sessions called "the musical train of thought." In Varèse's music sound complexes or densities create musical continuity instead of the traditional context in which melodic phrases supported by harmonic progressions established musical logic and continuity. Varèse's densities, delineated by differentiations in timbres and intensities, yielded a type of music that is more spatial than temporal in character. The composer himself confirmed the notion that his densities should be perceived as asymmetric spatial configurations. He explains that his composition, *Intégrales,* "was conceived as a spatial projection constructed according to certain acoustical principles which had not existed previously, but which I knew could be realized and made use of sooner or later."[28]

Varèse's music leaves the impression of self-contained entities and sonorous bodies with mass and density propelled by their own weight rather than by rhythmic pulsation.

Marc Wilkinson, in a penetrating study[29] of Varèse's style writes:

> . . . his music seldom relies on a mounting kinetic impulse to create a mood or a feeling of excitement, but is like large and imaginative precision instruments made to be admired for their inherent beauty and their complex self-sufficient workings.

[26]Henry Cowell, *New Musical Resources* (New York: Alfred A. Knopf, Inc., 1930).

[27]Hugo Weisgall, "The Music of Henry Cowell," *Musical Quarterly,* **45**, No. 4 (1959), pp. 484–507.

[28]Edgar Varèse, "The Liberation of Sound," *Contemporary Composers on Contemporary Music,* edited by Elliott Schwartz and Barney Childs (New York: Holt, Rinehart and Winston, Inc., 1967).

[29]Marc Wilkinson, "An Introduction to the Music of Edgar Varèse," *Score and I.M.A. Magazine* (March 1957).

Varèse's output falls into two phases. In the first phase are the purely instrumental works such as the *Intégrales* (1923), *Octandre* (1923), *Ionization* (1931) for percussion instruments, *Density 21.5* (1936) for solo flute. In 1937 Varèse stopped composing because he felt that without electronic means he could not achieve his objective.

After a silence of sixteen years he resumed composing, combining electronic and nonelectronic sounds, as in *Déserts* (1953). This work is divided into seven sections, of which sections 1, 3, 5, and 7 are played on wind and percussion instruments, and sections 2, 4, and 6 are interpolated on magnetic tape. The passages linking the sections together are conceived as "bridges from the human being to the industrial machine and back again." One of Varèse's late works, *Poème Electronique* (1958), was written for the Philips Radio Corporation's pavilion at the Brussels World's Fair.

In more recent years, American experimental music shows a bipolar tendency, as represented by Milton Babbitt (b. 1916) and John Cage (b. 1912), both mentioned in Chapter 7.

Whereas Babbitt's point of departure was Schoenberg's twelve-tone method of composition, Cage started with a re-examination of the raw material of music, that is, sound. Babbitt, a trained mathematician, set out to investigate the theoretical implications of serial music and arrived at total organization before the European experimentalists. Cage, on the other hand, enlarged upon the freedom of creating almost *any* sound, often verging on incoherence. Despite their utterly different approaches, the two composers arrived at a common ground in producing music by electronic means. Both men are considered "way-out" figures in American musical life, and as a perceptive British visiting composer, Peter Maxwell Davies[30] stated, it presents a difficult problem for the young American composer "to come to terms with and even replace such paradoxical father figures." Davies adds that "one can out-Cage Cage by indulging in more and more aleatory stunts, or one can out-Babbitt Babbitt by spinning even more complex mathematical-musical nets, but this hardly amounts to establishing a distinct musical identity." While Babbitt's following is actually small, for the intellectual discipline is too forbidding, Cage has gained ground in recent years, backed by patrons of the visual arts, by dancers, and by those who easily join any new fad, particularly if it is embedded in pseudo-Zen philosophy.

Babbitt is actually more widely known for his theoretical writings than for his compositions.[31] He is now a professor of composition at

---

[30] Peter Maxwell Davies, "The Young Composer in America," *The American Scholar,* **33,** No. 4 (1964).

[31] Milton Babbitt, "Who Cares if You Listen?" *Contemporary Composers on Contemporary Music,* edited by Elliott Schwartz and Barney Childs (New York: Holt, Rinehart and Winston, Inc., 1967).

Princeton University, his former alma mater, where at one time he studied with Roger Sessions. His earlier compositions include piano music, *Composition for Viola and Piano* (1950), *Du* (1951) a song cycle, and *Composition for Four Instruments* (1948). These are rather inaccessible and convey the impression of an order governed by severely cerebral operations. Curiously, the more recent electronic works, such as *Vision and Prayer* (1961) for soprano and synthesized accompaniment, based on a text by Dylan Thomas, and *Philomel* (1963) for soprano, recorded soprano, and synthesized sound, based on a text by John Hollander, both show an expressiveness and tonal imagination seldom encountered in electronic works.

Cage, who studied with Cowell, and for a short while with Schoenberg, followed in Varèse's path at first. Cage was fascinated with Varèse's enlargement of the raw material of music and the combination of musical sound with noise. Cage's theory[32] was that, whereas in earlier music consonance and dissonance achieved reconciliation, now noise and musical sounds should gain a synthesis. In order to attain this goal, Cage experimented with percussion instruments, and works such as the *Construction in Metal* (1939) for orchestral bells, eight cowbells, three Japanese temple gongs, four automobile brake drums, four Turkish and four Chinese cymbals, four muted gongs, and eight anvils, and the *Quartet for Twelve Tom Toms* (1943) followed.

Next, in his *Duo* (1943), the composer's attention turned to the prepared piano, an invention of Henry Cowell. By the late 1940s, Cage achieved such respectability that he received an award from the National Academy of Arts and Letters "for having extended the boundaries of musical art."

In the early 1950s, Cage immersed himself in Oriental philosophy, and particularly in Zen Buddhism. Aided by the formulations of a Hindu philosopher, Coomaraswamy, that "all arts should imitate Nature in her *manner of operation*," Cage concluded that music, instead of communicating thoughts or feelings, should become "an unending process without any inherent design." He claimed that as man has no control over nature—or even over his own destiny—he should give up his control over musical sounds. At this point Cage turned to the ancient Chinese Book of *I-Ching*, or Book of Changes, whose intricate chance operations from then on directed his choice of sounds (see Chapter 7).

Another feat of random music was reached in *Imaginary Landscape No. 4* (1951); here, the musical material consisted of the chance combination of twelve radios, "manned" by two performers, one handling

[32] For details see John Cage's "Interview with Roger Reynolds" in *Contemporary Composers on Contemporary Music,* edited by Elliott Schwartz and Barney Childs (New York: Holt, Rinehart and Winston, Inc., 1967).

the station selector, the other the volume controls. Cage described their activities as "fishermen catching sounds."

Cage was also preoccupied with the relationship between sound and silence; the composer considers silence simply as "sounds not intended." Based on this premise, he composed 4'33" (1952), a piece for piano, composed entirely of not-intended sounds—silence. Divided into three movements of silence, at its first performance the pianist David Tudor opened and covered the keyboard to separate the movements. Aside from this he did nothing but sit at the keyboard, silent but intent. Cage's most recent work, the *Atlas Eclipticalis with Winter Music* (electronic version, 1962), a composition worked out on the basis of astronomical charts, met with strong resistance from the performing members of the New York Philharmonic Orchestra.

It is difficult to assess Cage's experimentations since 1950. Even his friend and former teacher, Henry Cowell, felt compelled to write about Cage's more recent music that "if one must decide whether genuine value is or is not to be found in this music, a last throw of the coins of *I-Ching* will have to determine that for us too." It often seems as if the creative emphasis lies in the methods applied to the composition, but not in the music itself.

Among the followers of Cage, Lou Harrison, Morton Feldman, and Earle Brown are best known. Other composers interested in aleatory processes include Lukas Foss, whose earlier works were mentioned among those of the neoclassicists.

Since the mid-1950s Foss achieved a leading role among the avant-garde. In 1957 he founded his Improvisation Chamber Ensemble,[33] consisting of clarinet, cello, percussion, and piano. Highly original works were forthcoming, such as *Time Cycle* (1960) and *Echoi* (1963). In these works, Foss "neoclassicizes a certain avant-garde idiom," according to Eric Salzman. Foss' recent works include a Cello Concerto (1965) written for the Russian cellist Rostropovich, and *Fragments of Archilocos* (1966), an open form, chance-and-choice setting of translations of scraps of ancient Greek texts.

Another avant-garde group, consisting of Charles Wuorinen (b. 1938), Mario Davidovsky (b. 1934), and Harvey Sollberger (b. 1935), draws considerable attention with their concert series at Columbia University.

Two more names should be added to the experimenters: Gunther Schuller (b. 1925) and Henry Brant (b. 1913). Schuller is known for his "third stream" music—an attempt to integrate jazz combinations with traditional music.

---

[33] Lukas Foss, "The Changing Composer-Performer Relationship," in *Contemporary Composers on Contemporary Music*, edited by Elliott Schwartz and Barney Childs (New York: Holt, Rinehart and Winston, Inc., 1967).

Schuller's opera, *The Visitation* (1965), based on Kafka's *The Trial,* was received enthusiastically at its Hamburg premiere, but met with luke-warm reception in New York. Brant is the leading explorer of spatial music.

OPERA IN AMERICA

Music-drama is perhaps the most neglected branch of music in the United States. The general neglect of operatic tradition and the almost insurmountable difficulties of staging a new opera discouraged composers from being active in this field. Even some outstanding composers (Copland and Sessions) have failed to produce their best in this medium.

Chronologically, the first contribution is Gershwin's *Porgy and Bess* (1935), often called a folk opera. Despite its various shortcomings, it shows the composer's dramatic gifts. Next, Marc Blitzstein (1905–1964) and the German-born Kurt Weill (1900–1950) should be mentioned, both of whom distinguished themselves in the socially conscious musical play. From the viewpoint of audience success and fame, Gian Carlo Menotti (b. 1911) undoubtedly holds a leading position. Although his operas, such as *The Consul* (1950), *The Saint of Bleeker Street* (1954), and *Amahl and The Night Visitors* (1951) show a fine sense of stage craftsmanship, musically they have little to offer but clichés borrowed from Puccini and Mascagni.

Among the composers who achieved their best in opera are Virgil Thomson (b. 1896), Douglas Moore (b. 1893), and Hugo Weisgall (b. 1912). Thomson's *Four Saints in Three Acts* (1928) and *The Mother of Us All* (1947); Moore's *The Ballad of Baby Doe* (1956); and Weisgall's *Six Characters in Search of an Author* (1953–1956) represent their outstanding achievements. Finally, the recent premiere in 1967 of an American opera at the Metropolitan Opera House, *Mourning Becomes Electra,* by Marvin David Levy, received critical acclaim, although it was praised more for the brilliancy of its staging than for its musical substance.

MUSIC IN LATIN AMERICA

In recent years, through the Inter-American Music Festival, a fairly large number of Latin American composers have been brought to the attention of American audiences, but only three have become widely known. They are the Brazillian, Heitor Villa-Lobos (1887–1959); the Mexican, Carlos Chávez (b. 1899); and the Argentinian, Alberto Ginastera (b. 1916). All three composers have employed their native folk idiom in their music—the source material for rhythmic originality and unusually interesting coloristic effects.

Villa-Lobos, after trips to Europe and the United States, returned to his native country and became its musical leader. He reorganized all phases of music education and sponsored new concert series; as a conductor, he greatly improved the level of orchestral performance. At the same time he immersed himself in the study of the Brazilian folk music that later became the dominant ingredient of his music. His works, consisting of more than two thousand compositions, include symphonies, a dozen tone poems, eight string quartets, operas, numerous ballets, and piano and vocal compositions. He is best known for the *Chôros* and the *Bachianas Brasileiras.* In the *Bachianas* he attempted to blend the spirit of Bach with the flavor of his native folk music. Both groups of works are distinguished by melodic appeal and richness of sound. In the series of nine *Bachianas,* the fifth, scored for soprano and eight cellos, is best known. The fourteen *Chôros,* a type of modern serenade, are based on Brazilian and Indian folk sources and show the composer's flair for improvising forms of expression and also his tonal imagination. The special appeal of the *Chôros* lies in their rhythmic intricacies executed by augmented percussion sections which include native percussion instruments.

Nearer to the mainstream of contemporary musical thought stands Carlos Chávez, the Mexican counterpart of Villa-Lobos. Chávez, too, after visits to Europe and the United States, took charge of the musical life of his native country, first as the founder and leader of the Orquesta Sinfónico de México, and later as the director of the National Conservatory. Chávez has close ties with the United States: he frequently appears as guest conductor with leading orchestras; he taught at the Berkshire Music Center and, in 1959, delivered the Charles Eliot Norton lectures at Harvard University. In addition, a number of his works have been commissioned by American organizations.

Like Villa-Lobos, Chávez also found inspiration in the folk music of his country, as seen in the primitive violence of his early *Sinfonia India* (1935–1936). Perhaps closest to the folk roots is *Xochipilli Macuilxochitl* (the name of the Aztec god of music) (1940), a piece scored for an ensemble of Mexican instruments. American audiences are quite familiar with his ballet, *Hija de Colquide* (1944), performed under the title of *Dark Meadow* by Martha Graham. In the 1950s the folk idiom became less pronounced and Chávez turned to a more controlled brand of neoclassicism, as his Violin Concerto (1950) illustrates.

Chávez' late music has become increasingly dissonant; his *II Inven-*

tion (1963), performed at the 1965 Inter-American Music Festival, is a one-movement atonal work in which color and timbres are used as organizational devices.

More advanced than Chávez is the music of Ginastera, who represents the younger generation of Argentinian composers and the Latin American avant-garde. In his early works the folk idiom, namely the foot-stamping dance of the *gauchos,* is evident, as in the Scherzo movement of the First Quartet and in the *Pampeana No 3* (1953), commissioned by the Louisville Symphony Orchestra. His interest in and identification with Latin American history is exemplified, too, in the *Cantata para America Magica* (1960) for dramatic soprano and a percussion orchestra of fifty-three instruments, based on six settings of poems from Mayan, Aztec, and Indian literary sources. This work together with the Violin Concerto were the outstanding successes of the 1961 Inter-American Music Festival.

A deep impression was made by his opera *Bomarzo* at the 1963 Coolidge Festival in Washington, D.C. The work deals with three Kafkaesque episodes taken from the life of the Italian Renaissance figure, the Duke of Bomarzo, and is scored for narrator, baritone, and chamber orchestra. The voice is occasionally cast in *Sprechstimme,* and aleatory elements are introduced frequently, allowing the performer to determine pitch and duration.

Mention should also be made of Ginastera's opera, *Don Rodrigo* (1964), staged by the New York City Center Opera in 1966; in one critic's opinion it is a curious blend of "romantic primitivism and avant-garde sophistication."

RÉSUMÉ

The twentieth century, of which only one-third is left, has witnessed two major musical upheavals, separated by a period of consolidation. The first, taking place around 1910, had two determinants: one was Schoenberg's renunciation of tonality, and the other, the impact of Asiatic and East European influences that swept Western music in the wake of Stravinsky and Bartók. Previous conceptions of melody, rhythm, harmony, and form were shattered by these occurrences.

The explosive forces soon receded and gave way to a period of consolidation which lasted from 1920 to 1950. This period was marked by a search for a new equilibrium seen in the neo-classical tendencies of Stravinsky, Hindemith, and *Les Six;* in

Bartók's quartets and concertos based on the cohesive forces of earlier traditions; and finally, in Schoenberg's twelve-tone method that attempted to impose a new order on the unbound forces of atonality.

This period came to an end in the years following World War II when music underwent a less spectacular, but even more drastic, change than in the first decade of the century. The avant-garde, drawn to Webern's athematic style, to his method of serialism, and to his emphasis on timbre and register, turned to the serialism of duration, tone color, and type of attack.

Music soon became too complex to be performed and the electronic production of sound became inevitable. The exclusion of the human element in performance seemed in line with the new ideology that music was no longer considered a vehicle by which to communicate thought and feeling. As interest turned to the manipulation of sound material, electronic or spatial, either according to a rigorously planned serial scheme or left entirely to chance procedures, the traditional aspects of melody, rhythm, harmony, and principles of form were abandoned.

Although the described currents were not uniformly followed, they were prevalent enough to be seriously reflected upon. Seen in a historical light, they represent an entirely new musical and esthetic outlook. At midcentury a dividing line in the history of music seems to have emerged, signifying the end of the last vestiges of the classic-romantic tradition, or perhaps of the era of sonata form. Whether the short period that has passed since 1950 is a period of transition, or whether the new ideas are here to stay, is impossible to determine from this vantage point.

In a larger framework one cannot help but wonder what the complete repudiation of tradition and of history as a continuous process means. Is it the symptom of the crisis that engulfs the other arts too, perhaps pointing to man's plight and, in general, to his uncertainty about his fate? The questions must remain rhetorical; all one can hope for is that when a new phase in human consciousness is reached, music will again become a testimony of man who takes a stand through his art.

In the meantime, the reader is urged to familiarize himself with the new music. To facilitate this process concrete suggestions are made in the Discography for building a record library of twentieth-century music.

APPENDIX
Texts and Translations of Vocal Works

SELECTIVE BIBLIOGRAPHY

DISCOGRAPHY

INDEX

A) L'APRÈS-MIDI D'UN FAUNE*

STÉPHANE MALLARMÉ

ECLOGUE

I would perpetuate those nymphs.
                              Their rosy
Bloom's so light, it floats upon air drowsy
With heavy sleep.
                    Was it a dream?
                                    The mound
Of my old dark uncertainty was crowned
By subtle boughs and leaves which, still remaining
Woods, alas, persuade me that the feigning
Roses shaped my fleeting dream for me.
Reflect . . . . . .
                    Are then those nymphs that came to thee
Desires that from thy fabled senses rise?
Illusion wells forth from the chaste blue eyes
Of the first, cold as weeping springs: and she,
The second, made of sighs, O can she be
The sultry breeze that stirs thy fleece at noon?
Ah no! Athwart the still and weary swoon
That stifles the freshness of the struggling breeze,
No water murmurs, save what dews the trees
In sound poured from my flute. Amid the hush
The only puff of wind to stir's the gush
That from my twin pipes blows an arid rain
Of music, save that where upon the plain
The skyline circles tranquilly there floats
The breath that artifice transmutes to notes,
Seeking at length the home it left on high
When inspiration called it from the sky.

Calm mere, whose shores are pillaged by my pride
That with Sicilian suns has more than vied,
But now is mute 'neath flowering sparks, tell how
"I here cut reeds that I did then endow
With genius; how, upon the distant wold
That wreathes its limpid springs with green and gold,
A wave of white flesh resting idly stirred:
How, when the first slow notes I piped were heard,
The swans, no! naiads, flew off helter-skelter,
Or swiftly dived" . . . . . .
                    Around this woodland shelter

*Revised translation by Alexander Cohen. Used by permission of Musical Opinion Ltd., London.

500

The tawny hour is burning fiercely, so
That all things lie inert, and none doth know
How that great rout of hymen fled from me,
Whose all consuming quest is for the SHE.
Let me then wake old ardours and, upright
And lone, lilies, flooded neath ancient light,
Let me be one of you for artlessness!

In no wise like the lips' lightsome caress
—The kiss with which false love calms doubt and fear—
My breast attests a mystic imprint here,
Although no mark of queenly teeth it bears.
—Enough! such secrets must be told in airs
Played by the confidant who sings my fires,
Twin-reed that, fluting of languor and desires,
Dreams, in an arabesque, we were amusing
The beauty hereabout by falsely confusing
Its charm with the illusion art creates:
Scaling the heights to which love modulates,
My music veils those forms, naked and white
—Through closed eyes I pursue the flock in flight—
Blurring the starkness of the tedious line.

Essay then, instrument of flight—malign
Syrinx—to bloom again beside our lake!
I'll paint adored goddesses and make
The girdle fall from many a shadowy shape:
Proud of my fame, their forms I shall undrape.
Thus, when the grape's radiance I drain,
To quench regret I fill the globes again,
Laughingly puffing the empty grape-skins tight
And gazing through the glowing spheres till night
Athirst for drunkenness and ecstasy.

O, nymphs, let's plump the grapes of MEMORY!
"Piercing the reeds, mine eye speared each immortal
Bosom that slakes a rage unknown to mortal
Within that lake, and cries from wood to sky;
In a sun-shot flash of shuddering jewelry
The glitter of their tresses sinks from view!
I run: when, at my feet outstretched, lo two
Maidens with languor laden I see sleeping,
Wounded with love, each in their other's keeping,
Their arms twined in a casual fond embrace.
I pick them up, not seeking to unlace
The pair, and bear them to this rosebush where
Sweet sun-drained perfume fills the ambient air
And where our play and sun-drunk pleasure may
Be rose-flecked like the heavens of burnt-out day."
I love thee, virginal fury, shrinking rapture
Of sacred naked burdens that I capture
Fleeing my fiery lips that drink like quivering

Lightning the secret terror of the shivering
Flesh. From the elder's feet my kisses dart
Their fire to the younger's timid heart,
And both together with their kindling sense,
Forsaken are by erstwhile innocence,
Wild tears, or some less piteous dew, in eyes
From which the old ingenuousness dies.

"But herein lay my trespass and my guilt;
Quelling their traitor fears I did exult,
And the tangled tuft of kisses I unwound
That gods about the guileless pair had bound.
By her hand I held the younger of the twain
So that her sister's quickened sense might stain
Her dove's unblushing whiteness: straight thereafter,
Seeking to suppress my burning laughter
In the happy bosom of the elder one,
I felt as though some vague death had undone
The prison of my drunken arms. My prey,
Ingrate, deaf to my sobbing, slipped away."

No matter! Others will drag me to caresses,
Blinding my horns with bonds of amorous tresses.
Desire, thou knowest, that to quench the thirst
Of murmuring bees, the pomegranates will burst
Their ripe and purple fruit; and that our blood,
In love with all that seeks it, is in flood
For all the everlasting swarms of passion.
At evening, when this wood grows gold and ashen,
The dying foliage blazes festively.
Etna! 'tis then that Venus visits thee,
Withdrawn as is her wont from her retreat,
To tread thy lava with her artless feet
When thy flames die in slumbrous thunder, spent.
I hold the goddess!

O sure chastisement! . . . . . .

Quelled at length by conquering silent noon,
My speechless soul and heavy body swoon.
On thirsty sand be now my sin in sleep's
Oblivion stilled. I'd drain with parted lips
Dream's starry wine. Farewell! I go to see
O Nymphs, the shades that ye already be.

B) OEDIPUS REX*

Text by Jean Cocteau translated into Latin by J. Daniélou
English translation of the opera-oratorio by M. D. Calvocoressi
English translation of the narration by e. e. cummings

PROLOGUE

NARRATOR:

You are about to hear a Latin version of King Oedipus.

This version is an opera-oratorio; based on the tragedy by Sophocles, but preserving only a certain monumental aspect of its various scenes. And so (wishing to spare your ears and your memories) I shall recall the story as we go along.

Oedipus, unknown to himself, contends with supernatural powers: those sleepless deities who are always watching us from a world beyond death. At the moment of his birth a snare was laid for him—and you will see the snare closing.

Now our drama begins.

Thebes is prostrate. After the Sphinx, a plague breaks out. The chorus implores Oedipus to save his city. Oedipus has vanquished the Sphinx; he promises.

ACTUS PRIMUS	ACT ONE
Chorus	Chorus
Caedit nos pestis,	The plague slayeth us,
Theba peste moritur.	By the plague Thebes is dying.
E peste serva nos	From the plague save us, Oedipus,
qua Theba moritur.	From the plague wherewith Thebes
Oedipus, adest pestis;	is dying,
a peste libera urbem,	Oedipus, the plague is upon us,
urbem serva morientem.	Save the dying city.
Oedipus	Oedipus
Liberi, vos liberabo a peste	My children, I will deliver you from
Ego clarissimus Oedipus vos diligo,	the plague,
ego Oedipus vos servabo.	I, the far-famed, I Oedipus
	I, Oedipus, love you.
Chorus	Chorus
Serva nos adhuc,	Save us, save the city,
serva urbem, Oedipus;	What must be done, that we may be
serva nos, clarissime Oedipus!	delivered?
Quid faciendum, Oedipus	
ut liberemur?	
Oedipus	Oedipus
Uxoris frater mittitur	The brother of the Queen is sent,
oraculum consulit,	he consulteth the oracle,
deo mittitur Creo;	To the God Créon is sent,

oraculum consulit,
quid faciendum consulit.
Creone commoretur.

He, he is asking what must be done,
May Créon make haste.

Chorus
Vale, Creo! Audimus.
Vale, Creo! Cito, cito.
Audituri te salutant.

Chorus
Good befall Créon—
We give the greeting,
We hearken.

NARRATOR:

Créon, the brother-in-law of Oedipus, has returned from Delphi, where he consulted the oracle.

The oracle demands that Laius' murderer be punished. The assassin is hiding in Thebes; at whatever cost, he must be discovered.

Oedipus boasts of his skill in dealing with the powers of darkness. He will discover and drive out the assassin.

Creo
Respondit deus:—
Laium ulcisci,
sce¹us ulcisci;
reperire peremptorem.
Thebis peremptor latet.
Latet peremptor regis,
reperire opus istum;
luere Thebas,
Thebas a labe luere,
caedem regis ulcisci,
regis Laii perempti,
Thebis peremptor latet.
Opus istum reperire,
quem depelli deus iubet.
Peste inficit Thebas.—
Apollo dixit deus.

Creon
The God answereth:
Avenge Laius, avenge the guilt:
In Thebes the slayer lurketh,
The slayer of the king lurketh;
There is need to find him, to find
    him,
To purge Thebes from the stain,
To avenge the slaying of the king.
Laius the King is slain,
In Thebes the slayer lurketh,
The God biddeth that the slayer be
    driven from among us.
With the plague he infecteth Thebes.
Apollo the God has spoken:

Oedipus
Non reperias vetus scelus,
Thebas eruam.
Thebis incolit scelestus.

Oedipus
Nay, if ye find not out the ancient
        guilt,
Thebes will I destroy.

Chorus
Deus dixit, tibi dixit.

Chorus
So the God has decreed.

Oedipus
Tibi dixit.
Mici debet se dedere.
Opus vos istum deferre.
Thebas eruam,
Thebis pellere istum.
Vetus scelus non reperias.

Oedipus
My friends, he must give himself up.
He must give himself up.
You must denounce him.

Chorus
Thebis scelestus incolit.

Chorus
[The villain dwells in Thebes.]

Oedipus
Deus dixit . . .
Sphynga solvi, carmen solvi,
ego divinabo.
Iterum divinabo,
clarissimus Oedipus,
Thebas iterum servabo,
ego Oedipus carmen divinabo.

Chorus
Solve! Solve, Oedipus, solve!

Oedipus
Polliceor divinabo.
Clarissimus Oedipus,
polliceor divinabo.

Oedipus
I read the riddle of the Sphinx,
Once again will I prophecy, I,
    Oedipus the far-famed.
Once again will I save Thebes,
I pledge my word to read it.

Chorus
Read it, O Oedipus!

Oedipus
I promise to divine it.
I, the famed Oedipus,
shall divine it.

NARRATOR:

Oedipus questions that fountain of truth: Tirésias, the seer.

Tirésias will not answer. He already realizes that Oedipus is a plaything of the heartless gods.

This silence angers Oedipus, who accuses Créon of desiring the throne for himself, and Tirésias of being his accomplice.

Revolted by the injustice of this attitude, Tirésias decides—the fountain speaks.

This is the oracle: the assassin of the King is a King.

Chorus
Delie, exspectamus.
Minerva filia Jovis,
Diana in trono insidens,
et tu, Phaebe
insignis iaculator,
succurrite nobis.
Ut praeceps ales ruit malum
et premitur funere funus
et corporibus corpora inhumata,
expelle, everte in mare
atrocem istum Martem
qui nos urit inermis
dementer ululans.
Et tu, Bacce, cum taeda
advola nobis urens infamem
inter deos deum.
Salve, Tiresia,
homo clare, vates!
Dic nobis quod monet deus,
dic cito, sacrorum docte, dic!

Chorus
God of Delos, we are waiting,
    Minerva, daughter of Jove,
Diana seated upon thy throne,
And thou, Phoebus, O splendid
    Archer, help us.
For headlong the winged evil rusheth
    upon us, death followeth
    hard upon death, and the dead
    lie a-heap without burial.
Drive forth and hurl into the sea the
    dread
Slaughter which burneth us helpless,
    madly howling.
O Bacchus, come swiftly with thy
    brand, burning the god
    infamous among gods.
Hail, Tirésias, hail! Thou who
    knowest the mysteries of the
    gods, speak quickly.
Hail, Tirésias, thou great one, thou
    prophet: tell to us what the god
    biddeth;

Tiresias
Dicere non possum,
dicere non licet,
dicere nefastum,

Tirésias
I cannot speak, I may not speak,
Oedipus, it is not lawful that I
    should speak;

Oedipus, non possum.
Dicere ne cogas,
cave ne dicam.
Clarissime Oedipus,
tacere fas.

I cannot speak; compel me not;
    beware lest I should speak
Most noble Oedipus, I must keep
    silence.

Oedipus
Taciturnitas te acusat:
tu peremptor.

Oedipus
Thy silence accuseth thee;
Thou art the slayer.

Tiresias
Miserande, dico,
quod me acusas.
Dicam quod dixit deus;
nullum dictum celabo;
inter vos peremptor est,
apud vos peremptor est,
cum vobis, vobiscum est.
Regis est rex peremptor.
Rex cecidit Laium,
rex cecidit regem,
deus regem acusat;
peremptor rex!
Opus Thebis pelli regem.
Rex scelestus urbem foedat,
rex peremptor regis est.

Tirésias
Unhappy man, I speak, because thou
    accusest me;
I will tell what the god hath told.
    No word will I conceal.
The slayer is amongst you, in your
    city is the slayer.
The King is the slayer of the king.
The God accuseth the king.
He must be driven from Thebes,
A guilty king polluteth the city.

Oedipus
Invidia fortunam odit,
creavistis me regem.
Servavi vos carminibus
et creavistis me regem.
Solvendum carmen,
cui erat solvendum?
Tibi, homo clare, vates;
a me solutum est
et creavistis me regem.
Invidia fortunam odit.
Nunc, vult quidam munus meum,
Creo vult munus regis.
Stipendarius es, Tiresia!
Hoc facimus ego solvo!
Creo vult rex fieri.
Quis liberavit vos carminibus?
Amici! Ego Oedipus clarus, ego.
Invidia fortunam odit.
Volunt regem perire,
vestrum regem perire,
clarum Oedipodem, vestrum regem.

Oedipus
Envy hateth fair fortune. You made
    me king.
I saved you, I saved you from the
    riddle, and you made me king.
By whom should the riddle have
    been read?
By thee, thou famous man, thou
    prophet.
It was read by me, and ye made me
    king.
Now there is one that desireth my
    office,
Créon would be king.
Thou workest for pay, Tirésias! the
    riddle of this crime I read,
Créon would be king.
Who freed you from the spells?
Friends, it was I, Oedipus the famed.
They wish the king to perish,
Famed Oedipus, your king.

Chorus
Gloria!
Laudibus regina Jocasta
in pestilentibus Thebis
Laudibus regina nostra.
Laudibus Oedipodis uxor.
Gloria!

Chorus
Glory, glory, glory!
Jocasta is queen in stricken Thebes,
Sing praises to our queen.
Sing praises to the wife of Oedipus.

ACTUS SECUNDUS   ACT TWO

NARRATOR: (*The act begins with a repetition of the final chorus.*)

The dispute of the princes attracts Jocasta.

You will hear her calm them, shame them for raising their voices in a stricken city.

She proves that oracles lie. For example, an oracle predicted that Laius would perish by the hand of a son of hers; whereas Laius was murdered by thieves, at the crossing of three roads from Daulis and Delphi.

Three roads . . . crossroads—mark well those words. They horrify Oedipus. He remembers how, arriving from Corinth before encountering the Sphinx, he killed an old man where three roads meet. If Laius of Thebes were that man—what then? Oedipus cannot return to Corinth, having been threatened by the oracle with a double crime: killing his father and marrying his mother. He is afraid.

Jocasta
Nonne erubescite, reges,
clamare, ululare in aegra urbe
domesticis altercationibus?
Nonne erubescite in aegra urbe
clamare vestros domesticos clamores?
Coram omnibus clamare,
coram omnibus domesticos clamores
clamare in aegra urbe, reges,
nonne erubescite?
Ne probentur oracula
quae semper mentiantur.
Oracula—mentita sunt oracula.
Cui rex interficiendus est?
Nato meo.
Age rex peremptus est.
Laius in trivio mortuus.
Ne probentur oracula
quae semper mentiantur.
Cave oracula.

Jocasta
Are you not ashamed, O princes,
To cry aloud, to howl in a city that
    is stricken with your domestic
    broils?
Let not the oracles be proved true,
The oracles which ever lie.
The oracles have lied.
By whom was the king to be slain?
By my son.
The King was slain. Laius at the
    crossroads was slain,
Let not the oracles be proved true,
    the oracles which ever lie.

Chorus
Trivium, trivium . . .

Chorus
The crossroads, the crossroads . . .

Oedipus
Pavesco subito, Jocasta,
pavesco maxime. Jocasta, audi:
locuta es de trivio?
Ego senem cecidi,
cum Corintho excederem,
cecidi in trivio,
cecidi, Jocasta, senem.

Oedipus
On a sudden I am afraid, Jocasta,
I am afraid with a great fear,
Jocasta, Jocasta, hearken; didst thou
    speak of the corssroads?
I slew an old man, when I was
    coming from Corinth,
I slew him at the crossroads, I slew
    an old man, Jocasta.
Always the oracles have lied;
Quickly let us return to our house.
I am afraid with a great fear; on a
    sudden I am afraid, Jocasta,
Jocasta, my wife, I am afraid.
For at the crossroads I slew an old
    man.

Jocasta
Oracula mentiuntur,
semper oracula mentiuntur,
Oedipus, cave oracula;
quae mentiantur.
Domum cito redeamus.
non est consulendum.

Oedipus
Pavesco, maxime pavesco,
pavesco subito, Jocasta;
pavor magnus, Jocasta,
in me inest.
Subito pavesco, uxor Jocasta.
Nam in trivio cecidi senem.
Volo consulere,
consulendum est, Jocasta,
volo videre pastorem.
Sceleris superest spectator.
Jocasta, consulendum
volo consulere. Sciam!

Jocasta
Consult not the oracle,
Oedipus, let us return with speed to
    our house.
Beware of the oracles which ever lie.
It is my will to consult the oracle; it
    must be done.

Odeipus
Jocasta, I would see the shepherd; he
    liveth yet, the witness of the
    crime.
Let me know!

NARRATOR

*The witness of the murder steps from the shadows. A messenger, announcing
    that king Polybus of Corinth is dead, reveals to Oedipus that he is only an
    adopted son of the king.*

Jocasta understands.

She tries to draw Oedipus back—in vain. She flees.

Oedipus supposes that she is ashamed of being the wife of an upstart.

*O, this lofty all-discerning Oedipus: He is in the snare. He alone does not
    know it.*

And then the truth strikes him. He falls. He falls headlong.

Chorus
Adest omniscius pastor
et nuntius horribilis.

Chorus
The shepherd who knoweth all is
    here and a messenger with
    dread tidings.

Nuntio
Mortuus est Polybus.
Senex mortuus Polybus
non genitor Oedipodis;
a me ceperat Polybus,
ego attuleram regi.

Messenger
Polybus is dead. Polybus was not the
    father of Oedipus.
From me Polybus took him; I
    brought him to the king.

Chorus
Verus non fuerat pater Oedipodis.

Chorus
[He was not the real father.]

Nuntio
Falsus pater per me!

Messenger
A false father, through me he was
    his father.

Chorus
Falsus pater per te!

Chorus
[You only feigned that Polybus was
    his father!]

Nuntio
Reppereram in monte
puerum Oedipoda,
derelictum in monte
parvulum Oedipoda
foratum pedes,
vulneratum pedes,
parvulum Oedipoda.
Repereram in monte,
attuleram pastori
puerum Oedipoda.

Messenger
I found Oedipus, a baby abandoned
    upon the mountain
His feet wounded with a thong,
I brought him to the shepherd.

Chorus
Resciturus sum monstrum,
monstram resciscam.
Deo claro Oedipus natus est,
deo et nympha montium
in quibus repertus est.

Chorus
I am soon to discover a wonder;
Oedipus is born of a God, of a
    great God and the Nymph of
    the mountains whereon he was
    found.
Will you not find out the wonder,
    find it out?

Pastor
Oporbetat tacere, nunquam loqui.
Sane repperit parvulum Oedipoda,
a patre, a matre
in monte derelictum.
pedes laqueis foratum.
Utinam ne diceres;
hoc semper celandum
inventum esse in monte
derelictum parvulum,
parvum Oedipoda,
in monte derelictum.
Oportebat tacere, nunquam loqui.

Shepherd
Silence was better, not speech,
Indeed, he found the child Oedipus
By his father and his mother
    abandoned on the hills, his
    feet pierced with the thong.
Would thou hadst not spoken, this
    should ever have been hidden
That the child was found left alone
    on the mountain.

Oedipus
Nonne monstrum rescituri
quis Oedipus, genus Oedipodis sciam.
Pudet Jocastam, fugit.
Pudet Oedipi exulis,
pudet Oedipodis generis.
Sciam Oedipodis genus;
genus meum sciam.
Nonne monstrum rescituri,
genus Oedipodis sciam,
genus exulis mei.
Ego exul exsulto.

Oedipus
Will you not find out the wonder;
    let me know the birth of
    Oedipus, the birth of my exile.
I, an exile, rejoice.
Jocasta is ashamed, she fleeth away;
    she is ashamed of Oedipus the
    exile,
She is ashamed of the birth of
    Oedipus.
Let me know of the birth of Oedipus
Let me know of my birth.

Pastor et Nuntio
In monte reppertus est,
a matre derelictus;
a matre derelictum
in montibus repperimus.
Laio Jocastaque natus!
Peremptor Laii parentis!
Coniux Jocastae parentis!
Utinam ne diceres,

Shepherd and Messenger
On the mountain he was found, left
    by his mother;
He is the son of Laius and Jocasta,
He is the slayer of Laius, his father!
The son of Laius and Jocasta;
Husband of Jocasta his mother.
Would that thou hadst not spoken.

oportebat tacere,
nunquam dicere istud:
a Jocasta derelictum
in monte repertus est. (Exeunt)

Silence had been better, never
To speak, never to speak, never to
speak that word.

Oedipus
Natus sum quo nefastum est,
concubui cui nefastum est,
cecidi quem nefastum est.
Lux facta est! (Exit)

Oedipus
Against my father I have sinned:
in my marriage I have sinned;
In my slaying I have sinned.
All now is made plain!

NARRATOR:

And now you will hear that famous monologue "The Divine Jocasta Is Dead,"
a monologue in which the messenger describes Jocasta's doom.

He can scarcely open his mouth. The chorus takes his part and helps him to
tell how the queen has hanged herself, and how Oedipus has pierced his
eyeballs with her golden pin.

Then comes the epilogue.

The king is caught. He would show himself to all: as a filthy beast, an incestuous
monster, a fatherkiller, a fool.

His people drive him (gently, very gently) away.

Farewell, farewell, poor Oedipus! Farewell, Oedipus—we loved you.

Nuntio
Divum Jocastae caput mortuum!

Messenger
Jocasta the Queen is dead,

Chorus
Mulier in vestibulo
comas lacerare.
Claustris occludere fores,
occluldere, exclamare.
Et Oedipus irrumpere,
irrumpere et pulsare,
et Oedipus pulsare, ululare.

Chorus
Women in the palace entrance tear
their hair.
With bars they make fast the doors,
And Oedipus is bursting in, and
beating on the doors with bitter
crying.

Nuntio
Divum Jocastae caput mortuum!

Messenger
Jocasta the Queen is dead,

Chorus
Et ubi evelit claustra,
suspensam mulierem
omnes conspexerunt.
Et Oedipus praeceps ruens
illam exsolvebat, illam collocabat;
illam exsolvere, illam collocare.
Et aurea fibula et avulsa fibula
oculos effodire;
ater sanguis rigare.

Chorus
And when they plucked the bars
away, hanging there they saw
the queen.
And Oedipus rushing headlong was
loosing the cord, and laying her
down; her, the queen was he
laying on the ground,
And with a brooch plucked from her
dress, he dug out his eyes,
The black blood was flowing

Nuntio
Divum Jocastae caput mortuum!

Messenger
Jocasta, the Queen, is dead.

Chorus
Sanguis ater rigabat,
ater sanguis prosiliebat;
et Oedipus exclamare
et sese detestare.
Omnibus se ostendere.
Aspicite fores pandere,
spectaculum aspicite,
spectaculum omnium atrocissimum.

Nuntio
Divum Jocastae caput mortuum!

Chorus
Ecce! Regem Oedipoda,
foedissimum monstrum monstrat,
foedissimam beluam.
Ellum, regem Oedipoda!
Ellem, regem occeaetum!
Rex parricida, miser Oedipus,
miser rex Oedipus carminum coniec-
    tor.
Adest! Ellum! Regem Oedipoda!
Vale, Oedipus,
te amabam, te miseror.
Miser Oedipus, oculos tuos deploro.
Vale, Oedipus,
miser Oedipus noster,
te amabam, Oedipus.
Tibi valedico, Oedipus,
tibi valedico.

Chorus
The black blood was flowing
And Oedipus crying aloud and
    cursing himself
To all he showed himself . . . it is
    his will to show this horror.
Behold the doors, see, they are
    opening, behold a sight of all
    sights most horrible.

Messenger
Jocasta, the Queen, is dead.

Chorus
Lo! Oedipus the King; he showeth a
    monstrous thing most foul, a
    portent horrible.
Behold the King with blinded eyes!
    Oedipus the King ill-starred, the
    slayer of his father, Oedipus the
    King, ill-starred, the reader of
    riddles.
Lo, he is here, Oedipus the King!
Lo, Oedipus the King; the King with
    blinded eyes,
The slayer of his father, Oedipus the
    King, ill-starred, the reader of
    riddles.
Oedipus, farewell, Thou wast dear
    to me; I pity thee,
O unhappy one; Thou wast dear to
    me, I pity thee.
Hapless Oedipus, for thine eyes I
    weep,
Farewell, Oedipus;
Thou wast dear to me, Oedipus.
I bid thee farewell.

LITANEI and *ENTRÜCKUNG**

Text by Stephan George to the third and fourth movements of the String Quartet, No. 2, by Arnold Schoenberg

LITANEI

Tief is die trauer,
    die mich umdüstert,
Ein tret ich wieder
    Herr! in dein haus . . .

Lang war die reise,
    matt sind die glieder,
Leer sind die schreine,
    voll nur die qual.

Durstende zunge
    darbt nach dem weine.
Hart war gestritten,
    starr ist mein arm.

Gönne die ruhe
    schwankenden schritten,
Hungrigem gaume
    bröckle dein brot!

Schwach ist mein atem
    rufend dem traume,
Hohl sind die hände
    fiebernd der mund

Leih deine kühle,
    lösche die brände,
Tilge das hoffen,
    sende das licht!

Gluten im herzen
    lodern noch offen,
Innerst im grunde
    wacht noch ein schrei . . .

Töte das sehnen,
    schliesse die wunde!
Nimm mir die liebe,
    gib mir dein glück!

LITANY

Deep is the sadness
    which doth enfold me
Lord I return now
    unto Thy house . . .

Long was the journey
    weary my body,
Empty the shrines are
    grief's only full.

Tongue that is thirsting
    for the communion
Hard was the struggle
    tired my arm.

May rest be granted
    to trembling footsteps
For hungry palate
    break Thou, thy bread.

Weak is my breathing
    troubled in dreaming
My hands are empty
    feverish my mouth

Lend of Thy coolness
    quench all the fires,
Banish the longing
    O send the light!

Heart full of embers
    sullenly flaming
Innermost bosom
    guarding a cry . . .

Consume the craving
    Bind up the bruises
Free me from passion
    Grant me Thy joy.

*Translated by Carleton Sprague Smith. Used by permission of Carleton Sprague Smith and Helmut Küpper, Düsseldorf, publisher.

ENTRÜCKUNG	TRANSPORT
Ich fühle luft von anderem planeten.	I feel an air from other planets streaming
Mir blassen durch das dunkel die gesichter	Through darkness, faces which but now turned toward me
Die freundlich eben noch sich zu mir drehten.	In friendly fashion, ghostly white are gleaming.
Und bäum und wege die ich liebte fahlen	Dear groves and paths their colors do relinquish
Dass ich sie kaum mehr kenne und du lichter ·	So that I scarcely know them and thou Glimmer
Geliebter schatten—rufer meiner qualen	Rapturous shadow—summoner of anguish.
Bist nun erloschen ganz in tiefern gluten	In a more glowing radiance art released
Um nach dem taumel streitenden getobes	Bringing to me a new most sacred wonder.
Mit einem frommen schauer anzumuten.	After the clamorous frenzied din has ceased.
Ich löse mich in tönen, kreisend, webend,	Through circling, weaving harmony comes relief
Ungründigen danks und unbenamten lobes	With thanks unending and praise beyond compare
Dem grossen atem wunschlos mich ergebend.	Wishless I pledge myself to the awesome breath.
Mich überfahrt ein ungestümes wehen	A storm sweeps by me carrying all before
Im rausch der weihe wo inbrünstige schreie	With fervent cries transfixed by consecration
In staub gewofner beterinnen flehen:	Worshipping women, bowed in the dust, implore.
Dann seh ich wie sich duftige nebel lüpfen	Then I behold how nebulous mists can lift
In einer sonnerfüllten klaren freie	O'er a transparent sun-drenched wide horizon,
Die nur umfängt auf fernsten bergesschlüpfen.	Only remaining by hidden crags to drift.
Der boden schüttert weiss und weich wie molke . .	The earth shakes, quivering white and soft as whey
Ich steige über schluchten ungeheuer.	I step across celestial, fearful chasms
Ich fühle wie ich über letzter wolke.	Touching the final clouds over which I sway
Ich einem meer kristallnen glanzes schwimme	In a sea of crystal brilliancy rejoice
Ich bin ein funke nur vom heiligen feuer	For I am but a spark of the Holy Fire
Ich bin ein dröhnen nur der heiligen stimme.	Only an utterance of the Holy Voice.

SELECTIVE BIBLIOGRAPHY

THEORETICAL

Abraham, Gerald. *This Modern Music* (New York: W. W. Norton & Company, Inc., 1952).

Basart, Ann Phillips. *Serial Music.* A classified bibliography of writings on twelve-tone and electronic music. (Berkeley, Calif.: University of California Press, 1961).

Blades, James. *Orchestral Percussion Technique* (New York: Oxford University Press, 1961).

Cage, John. *Silence* (Middletown, Conn.: Wesleyan University Press, 1961).

Carner, Mosco. *A Study of Twentieth-Century Harmony* (London: Williams & Norgate, Ltd., 1942).

Copland, Aaron. *Music and Imagination* (Cambridge, Mass.: Harvard University Press, 1952).

———— *What To Listen For In Music,* rev. ed. (New York: McGraw-Hill, Inc., 1957; Mentor, 1951).

Cross, Lowell M. *A Bibliography of Electronic Music* (Toronto: University of Toronto Press, 1967).

Crowhurst, Norman H. *Electronic Musical Instruments* (Indianapolis, Ind.: Howard W. Sams & Co., 1962).

Edwards, Arthur C. *The Art of Melody* (New York: Philosophical Library, Inc., 1956).

Erickson, Robert. *The Structure of Music* (New York: The Noonday Press, 1957).

Eschman, Karl H. *Changing Forms in Modern Music* (Boston: E. C. Schirmer, 1947).

Forte, Allen. *Contemporary Tone Structures* (New York: Columbia University Press, 1955).

Graves, William L. *Twentieth-Century Fugue* (Washington, D.C.: The Catholic University of America Press, 1962).

Hanson, Howard. *Harmonic Materials of Modern Music* (New York: Appleton-Century-Crofts, 1960).

Hindemith, Paul. *A Composer's World* (Cambridge, Mass.: Harvard University Press, 1952).

―――. *A Concentrated Course in Traditional Harmony* (New York: Associated Music Publishers, 1943).

―――. *The Craft of Musical Composition* (New York: Associated Music Publishers, 1945).

―――. *Elementary Training for Musicians* (New York: Associated Music Publishers, 1946).

Kauder, Hugo. *Counterpoint* (New York: The Macmillan Company, 1960).

Křenek, Ernst. *Studies in Counterpoint: Based on the Twelve-Tone Technique* (New York: G. Schirmer, Inc., 1940).

Lang, Paul Henry. *Problems of Modern Music: The Princeton Seminar in Advanced Musical Studies* (New York: W. W. Norton & Company, Inc., 1960).

Leibowitz, René. *Thinking for Orchestra* (New York: G. Schirmer, Inc., 1960).

Messiaen, Olivier. *The Technique of My Musical Language* (Paris: Leduc, 1956).

Meyer, Leonard B., and Grosvenor Cooper. *The Rhythmic Structure of Music* (Chicago, Ill.: Chicago University Press, 1960).

Perle, George. *Serial Composition and Atonality* (Berkeley, Calif.: University of California Press, 1962).

Persichetti, Vincent. *Twentieth-Century Harmony* (New York: W. W. Norton & Company, Inc., 1961).

Piston, Walter. *Counterpoint* (New York: W. W. Norton & Company, Inc., 1947).

―――. *Harmony,* 3rd ed. (New York: W. W. Norton & Company, Inc., 1962).

————. *Orchestration* (New York: W. W. Norton & Company, Inc., 1955).

Reti, Rudolph. *Tonality, Atonality, Pantonality* (New York: The Macmillan Company, 1958).

Rochberg, George. *The Hexachord and Its Relation to the Twelve-Tone Row* (Bryn Mawr, Pa.: Theodore Presser Company, 1955).

Rogers, Bernard. *The Art of Orchestration: Principles of Tone Color in Modern Scoring* (New York: Appleton-Century-Crofts, 1951).

Rufer, Josef. *Composition with Twelve Tones* (New York: The Macmillan Company, 1954).

Sachs, Curt. *Rhythm and Tempo* (New York: W. W. Norton & Company, Inc., 1953).

Schoenberg, Arnold. *Models for Beginners in Composition* (New York: G. Schirmer, Inc., 1943).

————. *Structural Functions of Harmony* (New York: W. W. Norton & Company, Inc., 1954).

————. *Theory of Harmony* (New York: Philosophical Library, Inc., 1948).

Searle, Humphrey. *Twentieth-Century Counterpoint* (London: Williams & Norgate, Ltd., 1956).

Sessions, Roger. *Harmonic Practice* (New York: Harcourt, Brace & World, Inc., 1957).

Szabolcsi, Bence. *The History of Melody,* translated by Cynthia Jolly and Sari Karig (New York: St. Martin's Press, Inc., 1965).

Toch, Ernst. *The Shaping Forces in Music: An Inquiry into Harmony, Melody, Counterpoint, and Form* (New York: Criterion Books, Inc., 1948).

Ulehla, Ludmilla. *Contemporary Harmony* (New York: The Free Press, 1966).

Vincent, John. *The Diatonic Modes in Modern Music* (Berkeley, Calif.: University of California Press, 1951).

Books on and by individual composers from Part II*

STRAVINSKY, Igor

Ledermann, Minna (Ed.). *Stravinsky in the Theatre* (New York: Pellegrini & Cudahy, 1949).

Stravinsky, Igor. *An Autobiography* (New York: Simon and Schuster, Inc., 1936).

————. *Poetics of Music* (New York: Random House, Inc., 1956).

————, and Robert Craft. *Conversations* (Garden City, N.Y.: Doubleday & Company, Inc., 1959).

————. *Dialogues and a Diary* (Garden City, N.Y.: Doubleday & Company, Inc., 1963).

*The theoretical works of the composers are listed in the first group.

————. *Expositions and Developments* (New York: Doubleday & Company, Inc., 1962).

————. *Memories and Commentaries* (New York: Doubleday & Company, Inc., 1958).

————. *Themes and Episodes* (New York: A. Knopf, 1966).

Stravinsky, Igor. A complete catalogue of his published works (London: Boosey & Hawkes, Ltd., 1957).

Strobel, Heinrich. *Stravinsky: A Classic Humanist* (New York: Merlin Press, 1955).

Tansman, Alexandre. *Stravinsky* (New York: G. P. Putnam's Sons, 1949).

Vlad, Roman. *Stravinsky* (New York: Oxford University Press, 1960).

White, Eric Walter. *Stravinsky: The Composer and His Works* (London: Faber & Faber, Inc., 1966).

White, Eric. *Stravinsky* (London: Lehmann, 1947).

BARTÓK, Béla

Bartók, Béla. *Hungarian Folk Music* (New York: Oxford University Press, 1931).

————, and Albert B. Lord. *Serbo-Croatian Folk Songs* (New York: Columbia University Press, 1951).

Béla Bartók Archives. Victor Bátor (Ed.) (New York: Bartók Archives Publication, 1963).

Seiber, Mátyás. *The String Quartets of Béla Bartók* (London: Boosey & Hawkes, Ltd., 1945).

Stevens, Halsey. *The Life and Music of Béla Bartók,* rev. ed. (New York: Oxford University Press, 1963).

Suchoff, Benjamin. *Guide to the Mikrokosmos of Béla Bartók* (Silver Springs, Md.: Music Service Corp., 1956).

Szabolcsi, Bence (Ed.). *Weg und Werk—Béla Bartók.* A compilation of letters and documents (Budapest: Corvina, 1957).

Tempo, "Bartók Memorial Review" (New York: Boosey & Hawkes, Inc., 1950).

Traimer, Roswitha. *Béla Bartók's Kompositionstechnik dargestellt in seinen sechs Streichquartetten* (Regensburg: G. Bosse, 1956).

SCHOENBERG, Arnold

Schoenberg, Arnold. *Letters.* Selected and edited by Erwin Stein (New York: St. Martin's Press, Inc., 1965).

————. *Style and Idea* (New York: Philosophical Library, Inc., 1950).

Gould, Glenn. *Arnold Schoenberg: a Perspective* (Cincinnati: University of Cincinnati Press, 1964).

Leibowitz, René. *Schoenberg and His School* (New York: Philosophical Library, Inc., 1949).

Meyerowitz, Jan. *Arnold Schoenberg* (Berlin: Colloquium Verlag, 1967).

Newlin, Dika. *Bruckner, Mahler, Schoenberg* (New York: King's Crown Press, 1947).

Rufer, Josef. *Das Werk Arnold Schoenberg.* A complete bibliography. Translated into English by Dika Newlin as *The Works of Arnold Schoenberg* (Kassel: Bärenreiter, 1959).

Stuckenschmidt, H. H. *Arnold Schoenberg* (New York: Grove Press, Inc., 1960).

Welles, Egon. *Arnold Schoenberg* (Leipzig: E. P. Tal, 1921).

Wörner, Karl. *Schoenberg's Moses und Aron* (New York: St. Martin's Press, Inc., 1964).

BERG, Alban

Redlich, Hans F. *Alban Berg* (London: Calder, 1957).

Reich, Willi. *The Life and Works of Alban Berg* (London: Calder, 1965).

WEBERN, Anton

Demar, Irvine (Ed.). *Anton Webern: Perspectives* (Seattle: University of Washington Press, 1966).

Kolneder, Walter. *Anton Webern: Einführung in Werk und Stil* (Rodenkirchen/Rhein: P. J. Tonger, 1961).

Webern, Anton. *The Path to New Music,* edited by Willi Reich (Bryn Mawr, Pa.: Theodore Presser Company, 1963).

Webern, Die Reihe, No. 2 (Bryn Mawr, Pa.: Theodore Presser Company, 1957).

HINDEMITH, Paul

Strobel, Heinrich. *Paul Hindemith,* 3rd ed. (Mainz: Schott's Söhne, 1948).

Westphal, Elizabeth. *Paul Hindemith: eine Bibliographie seit 1922* (Köln: Greven Verlag, 1957).

EUROPE

CZECHOSLOVAKIA

Gardavsky, Cenek. *Contemporary Czechoslovak Composers* (Prague: Panton, 1966).

Hollander, Hans. *Leos Janáček* (New York: St. Martin's Press, Inc., 1963).

Janáček, Leos. *Letters and Reminiscences* (Prague: Artia, 1955).

Vogel, Jaroslav. *Leos Janáček* (London: Hamlyn, 1963).

FRANCE

Cooper, Martin. *French Music* (New York: Oxford University Press, 1951).

Debussy, Claude. *Monsieur Croche, the Dilettante Hater* (London: Noel Douglas, 1927).

Demuth, Norman. *Albert Roussel* (London: United Music, Ltd., 1947).

————. *Ravel* (London: J. M. Dent & Sons, Ltd., 1947).

Hell, Henri. *Francis Poulenc* (New York: Grove Press, Inc., 1959).

Honegger, Arthur. *I am a Composer* (London: Faber & Faber, Ltd., 1966).

Lockspeiser, Eduard. *Debussy: His Life and Mind* (2 vols.) (New York: The Macmillan Company, 1962 and 1965).

Manuel, Roland. *Maurice Ravel* (London: Dobson, 1947).

Milhaud, Darius. *Notes Without Music: An Autobiography* (New York: Alfred A. Knopf, 1953).

Myers, Rollo. *Debussy* (New York: A. A. Wyn, Inc., 1949).

————. *Ravel* (London: Gerald Duckworth & Co., Ltd., 1960).

Schmitz, Robert. *The Piano Works of Claude Debussy* (New York: Duell, Sloan & Pearce-Meredith Press, 1950).

Vallas, Léon. *Claude Debussy* (New York: Oxford University Press, 1937).

GERMANY

Busoni, Ferruccio. *The Essence of Music* (New York: Philosophical Library, Inc., 1957).

Cardus, Neville. *Gustav Mahler. Vol. I.* (New York: St. Martin's Press, Inc., 1965).

Del Mar, Norman. *Richard Strauss* (London: Rockliff, 1962).

Dent, Edward J. *Ferruccio Busoni* (New York: Oxford University Press, 1966).

Liess, Andreas. *Carl Orff: His Life and his Music.* English translation by Adelheid and Herbert Parkin (London: Calder and Boyars, 1966).

Mann, William. *Richard Strauss: A Critical Study of His Operas* (London: Cassell & Co., Ltd., 1964).

Mitchell, Donald. *Gustav Mahler: The Early Years* (London: Rockliff, 1958).

Redlich, Hans F. *Bruckner and Mahler* (New York: Philosophical Library, Inc., 1957).

Strauss, Richard. *A Working Friendship: Correspondence Between Richard Strauss and Hugo v. Hofmannsthal* (New York: Random House, Inc., 1961).

———— *Recollections and Reflections,* edited by Willi Shuh (New York: Boosey & Hawkes, Inc., 1957).

Wörner, Karl. *Stockhausen* (Radenkirchen/Rhein: Tonger, 1963).

GREAT BRITAIN

Beecham, Sir Thomas. *Frederick Delius* (New York: Alfred A. Knopf, 1960).

Day, James. *Vaughan Williams* (New York: Farrar, Straus & Giroux, Inc., 1961).

Dickinson, Alan E. *Vaughan Williams* (London: Faber & Faber, Ltd., 1963).

Howes, Frank S. *The Music of Ralph Vaughan Williams* (New York: Oxford University Press, 1954).

————. *The Music of William Walton* (New York: Oxford University Press, 1965).

Kemp, Ian (Ed.). *Michael Tippett.* A symposium on his sixtieth birthday (London: Faber & Faber, Ltd., 1965).

Mitchell, Donald, and Hans Keller (Eds.). *Benjamin Britten* (New York: Philosophical Library, Inc., 1953).

HOLLAND

Reeser, Eduard (Ed.). *Music in Holland: A Review of Contemporary Music in the Netherlands* (Amsterdam: J. M. Meulenhoff, 1959).

HUNGARY

Eosze, László. *Zoltán Kodály* (London: Collet, 1962).

Kodály, Zoltán. *Folk Music of Hungary* (London: Rockliff, 1960).

"Kodaly Memorial Issue," *The New Hungarian Quarterly,* 1962.

Young, Percy. *Zoltán Kodály* (New York: Dover Publications, Inc., 1964).

POLAND

Jarocinsky, Stefan (Ed.). *Polish Music* (Warsaw: Polish Scientific Publisher, 1965).

RUSSIA

Bakst, James. *A History of Russian-Soviet Music* (New York: Dodd, Mead and Co., 1966).

Nestyev, Israel. *Sergei Prokofiev* (New York: Alfred A. Knopf, 1946).

Olkhovsky, Andrey. *Music Under the Soviets* (New York: Frederick A. Praeger, Inc., 1955).

Seroff, Victor. *Dimitri Shostakovich* (New York: Alfred A. Knopf, 1943).

Swan, Alfred. *Scriabin* (London: John Lane, The Bodley Head, Ltd., 1923).

Scandinavia

Abraham, Gerald (Ed.). *The Music of Sibelius* (New York: W. W. Norton & Company, Inc., 1947).

Horton, John. *Scandinavian Music* (New York: W. W. Norton & Company, Inc., 1963).

Johnson, Harold E. *Jean Sibelius* (New York: Alfred A. Knopf, 1959).

Lange, Kristian. *Norwegian Music* (London: Dobson, 1958).

Layton, Robert. *Sibelius.* (London: J. M. Dent & Sons, Ltd., 1965).

Ollen, Olaf (Ed.). *Sweden in Music* (New York: American Scandinavian Foundation, 1949).

Spain

Chase, Gilbert. *The Music of Spain* (New York: Dover Publications, Inc., 1959).

Pahissa, Jaime. *Manuel de Falla* (London: Museum Press, 1954).

UNITED STATES

Barzun, Jacques. *Music in American Life* (New York: Doubleday & Company, Inc., 1956).

Berger, Arthur. *Aaron Copland* (New York: Oxford University Press, 1953).

Broden, Nathan. *Samuel Barber* (New York: G. Schirmer, Inc., 1954).

Chase, Gilbert. *America's Music from the Pilgrims to the Present,* rev. ed. (New York: McGraw-Hill, Inc., 1966).

Cowell, Henry (Ed.). *American Composers on American Music* (Stanford, Calif.: Stanford University Press, 1933).

————. *New Musical Resources* (New York: Alfred A. Knopf, 1930).

————, and Sidney Cowell. *Charles Ives and His Music* (New York: Oxford University Press, 1955).

Goldberg, Isaac. *George Gershwin* (New York: Frederick Ungar Publishing Co., 1958).

Graf, Herbert. *Producing Opera for America* (Zurich/New York: Atlantis Books, 1961).

Hoover, Kathleen, and John Cage. *Virgil Thompson* (New York: Thomas Yoseloff, Inc., 1959).

Howard, John T. *Our American Music* (New York: Thomas Y. Crowell Company, 1946).

————. *Our Contemporary Composers* (New York: Thomas Y. Crowell Company, 1948).

Ives, Charles. *Essays Before a Sonata,* edited by Howard Boatright (New York: W. W. Norton & Company, Inc., 1962).

Mellers, Wilfrid. *Music in a New Found Land* (New York: Alfred A. Knopf, 1965).

Reis, Claire. *Composers in America* (New York: The Macmillan Company, 1947).

Scheiber, Flora, and Vincent Persichetti. *William Schuman* (New York: G. Schirmer, Inc., 1954).

Schwartz, Elliot and Barney Childs (Eds.). *Contemporary Composers on Contemporary Music* (New York: Holt, Rinehart and Winston, 1967).

Sessions, Roger. *The Musical Experience* (Princeton, N.J.: Princeton University Press, 1958).

Smith, Julia. *Aaron Copland* (New York: E. P. Dutton & Co., Inc., 1955).

Waters, Edward N. *Victor Herbert* (New York: The Macmillan Company, 1955).

GENERAL

Abraham, Gerald. *A Hundred Years of Music* (London: Gerald Duckworth & Co., Ltd., 1949).

Austin, William W. *Music in the Twentieth Century* (New York: W. W. Norton and Co., Inc., 1966).

Bauer, Marion. *Twentieth-Century Music* (New York: G. P. Putnam's Sons, 1937).

Bernstein, Leonard. *The Joy of Music* (New York: Simon and Schuster, Inc., 1959).

Collaer, Paul. *A History of Modern Music* (New York: Grosset & Dunlap, Inc., 1961).

Copland, Aaron. *Our New Music* (New York: McGraw-Hill, Inc., 1941).

Demuth, Norman. *Musical Trends in the Twentieth-Century* (London: Rockliff, 1952).

Hansen, Peter. *An Introduction to Twentieth-Century Music* (Boston: Allyn and Bacon, Inc., 1961).

Hartog, Howard (Ed.). *European Music in the Twentieth Century* (London: Routledge & Kegan Paul, Ltd., 1957).

Hodeir, André. *Since Debussy: A View of Contemporary Music* (New York: Grove Press, Inc., 1961).

Lambert, Constant. *Music Ho!* (London: Faber & Faber, Ltd., 1948).

Lang, Paul Henry (Ed.). "Contemporary Music in Europe," *Musical Quarterly,* **51,** No. 1 (1965).

Machlis, Josef. *Introduction to Contemporary Music* (New York: W. W. Norton & Company, Inc., 1961).

Mellers, Wilfrid. *Caliban Reborn: Renewal in Twentieth-Century Music* (New York-London: Harper & Row, Publishers, 1967).

————. *Studies in Contemporary Music* (London: Dobson, 1947).

Mitchell, Donald. *The Language of Modern Music,* enlarged ed. (London: Faber & Faber, Ltd., 1966).

Pleasants, Henry. *The Agony of Modern Music* (New York: Simon and Schuster, Inc., 1955).

Salazar, Adolfo. *Music in Our Time* (New York: W. W. Norton & Company, Inc., 1946).

Salzman, Eric. *Twentieth-Century Music: An Introduction* (Englewood Cliffs, N.J.: Prentice-Hall, Inc., 1967).

Schwartz, Elliott, and Barney Childs (Eds.), *Contemporary Composers on Contemporary Music* (New York: Holt, Rinehart and Winston, Inc., 1967).

Slonimsky, Nicholas. *Music Since 1900,* 3rd ed. (New York: Coleman-Rose, 1949).

Wörner, Karl. *Neue Musik in der Entscheidung* (Mainz: Schott's Söhne, 1954).

Yates, Peter. *Twentieth-Century Music* (New York: Pantheon, 1966).

Zillig, Winfried. *Die neue Musik* (München: Nymphenburger Verlag, 1963).

DISCOGRAPHY

This list of records has been compiled for the reader who wishes to build a library of contemporary music. The list, totalling about one hundred items, emphasizes the works of the leading composers mentioned in the text. In addition, considerable prominence has been given to American compositions; representing a part of the American consciousness, they are valuable documents for the American student of contemporary music.

The list is divided into two parts: Group A contains the music of the forerunners to new music (Chapter 8), and the more accessible works of the "classics" of contemporary music. Added to these are selections by secondary composers whose music yields rather easily to the listener.

Familiarity with the works in the first group will prepare the listener for the more demanding works of Group B. This group, representing a broad stylistic spectrum, includes the more difficult works of the leading composers, along with some advanced and avant-garde works.

When a choice had to be made between two or more recordings of the same composition, preference was given to the more authentic performance. In a few instances, however, the choice favored the disc that offered a particularly advantageous pairing of works.

GROUP A

BARBER, SAMUEL: *Medea* Ballet Suite, Capricorn Concerto, Hanson, Eastman-Rochester Orch., Mer. 50224; *90224**

BARTÓK, BÉLA: *Bluebeard's Castle,* Dorati, Mer. 50311; *90311*
  Concerto for Orchestra, Karajan, Berlin Phil. DGG 39003
  Mikrokosmos (Excerpts), Bartók, Col. ML-4419
  Piano Concerto No. 2 and No. 3, Farnadi, Scherchen, West. 18277

BERG, ALBAN: Violin Concerto, Krasner, Rodzinski, Col. ML-4857
  Wozzeck, Mitropoulos, 2 Col. SL-118

BLOCH, ERNEST: *Schelomo,* Rose, Ormandy, Phila. Orch., Col. ML-5653, *MS-6253*

BRITTEN, BENJAMIN: *Peter Grimes,* Britten, Royal Op. House, 3 Lon. 4342; *1305*

COPLAND, AARON: *Appalachian Spring, El Salón México,* Bernstein, N.Y. Phil., Col. MI-5755; *MS-6355*

DEBUSSY, CLAUDE: *La Mer,* Munch, Boston Symph., Vic. 1041; *Vics-1041*
  Afternoon of a Faun, Nocturnes, Ormandy, Phila. Orch., Col. ML-5112
  Quartet, Loewenguth Quartet, Vox 12020; *512020*

HARRIS, ROY: Symphony No. 3., Hendl, Vienna Symp., Desto 404; *6404*

HINDEMITH, PAUL: *Kleine Kammermusik,* Op. 24, No. 2, Phila. Quintet, Col. ML-5093
  Mathis der Maler, Symphonic Metamorphosis of Themes by Weber, Ormandy, Phila. Orch., Col. ML-5962; *MS-6562*

HONEGGER, ARTHUR: *King David,* Utah Symp., 2 Van 1090/1; *2117/8*

JANÁČEK, LEOS: *Diary of One Who Vanished,* DGG-18904; *13894*
  Jenufa, Prague Nat'l Theatre, 3 Artia 80

KODALY, ZOLTAN: *Psalmus Hungaricus,* Kodály, Hung. Orch. & Chorus, Artia 152

MAHLER, GUSTAV: *Das Lied Von der Erde,* Walter, Vienna Phil., 2 Lon. 4212

MARTIN, FRANK: *Vin herbé,* West. 2232-232

MILHAUD, DARIUS: *Création du Monde* (for number see Honegger's *King David*)
  La Cheminée de Roi René, N.Y. Woodwind Quintet
  Pastorale for oboe, clarinet, and piano, EMS 6

ORFF, CARL: *Carmina Burana,* Ormandy, Phila. Orch., Col. ML-5498; *MS-6163*

PISTON, WALTER: Symphony No. 4, Ormandy, Col. ML-4992

POULENC, FRANCIS: *Les Dialogues des Carmélites,* Nat'l Opera, Paris, 3 Ang. 3585

PROKOFIEV, SERGE: Violin Concerto No. 1 and No. 2, Stern, Ormandy, Phila. Orch., Col. ML-6035, *6635*
  Symphony No. 5, Leinsdorf, Boston Symp., Vic. LM-2707; *LSC-2707*

RAVEL, MAURICE: Quartet, Loewenguth Quartet (for number see Debussy's Quartet)
  Daphnis et Chloé, Rhapsodie Espagnole (for number see Debussy's *La Mer*)

SCHOENBERG, ARNOLD: Concerto for Violin (for number see Berg's Violin Concerto)
  Five Pieces for Orchestra, Dorati, London Symph., Mer. 50316, *90316*
  String Quartet No. 2 and No. 3, Juilliard Quartet, Col. ML-4736
  Verklärte Nacht, Galimir Ensemble, Col. ML-5644; *MS-6244*

*Italicized numbers indicate stereo recordings.

SCRIABIN, ALEXANDER: Sonata No. 9 for Piano, Horowitz, Vic. D-7021
SESSIONS, ROGER: *The Black Maskers* (for number see Harris' Third Symphony)
SHOSTAKOVICH, DIMITRI: Symphony No. 6, Boult, London Phil., Ev. 6007; *3007*
SIBELIUS, JEAN: Symphony No. 6 and No. 7, Karajan, Phila. Orch., Ang. 35316
STRAUSS, RICHARD: *Salomé*, Solti, Vienna Phil., 2 Lon. 4247; *1218*
   Till Eulenspiegel, Don Juan, Ormandy, Phila. Orch., Col. ML-5177
STRAVINSKY, IGOR: *Firebird, Petrouchka, The Rite of Spring*, Stravinsky, Columbia Symph. 3 Col. D-3 L-305, D 3S 705
   Les Noces, Symphony of Psalms, Ansermet, Orch. Suisse Romande, Lon. 9288 *6219*
VAUGHAN WILLIAMS, RALPH: Symphony No. 4, Boult, Lon. Phil., Lon. 9094
WEBERN, ANTON: *Five Movements*, Op. 5 Juilliard Quartet, Col. ML-4737

GROUP B

BARTÓK, BÉLA: Violin Concerto, Menuhin, New Phil. Ang. *S-36360*
   Music for Strings, Percussion, and Celesta, Byrns, Los Angeles Chamber Symph., Cap. P-8299
   String Quartets 1-6 (complete), Végh Quartet, 3 Ang. 35240/2
BERG, ALBAN: *Three Pieces for Orchestra*, Rosbaud, SW German Orch., West. 9709
   Lyric Suite, Juilliard Quartet, Vic. LM-2531; *LSC-2531*
   Lulu, Steingruber, 3 Col. SL-121
BERIO, LUCIANO: *Differences*, Time 58002; *8002*
BLOCH, ERNEST: Fifth Quartet, Fine Arts Quartet, Con.-Disc. 1225; *225*
BOULEZ, PIERRE: *Marteau sans Maître*, Boulez, Ang. *S-36295*
BRITTEN, BENJAMIN: *War Requiem*, Britten, London Symph. 2 Lon. 4255; *1255*
BUSONI, FERRUCCIO: Sonatinas, *Elegies* for piano, Steuermann, Contem. 6501; *8501*
CARTER, ELLIOTT: Second Quartet, Juilliard Quartet, RCA LM-2481
   Double Concerto for harpsichord, piano, and two chamber orchestras, Epic LC-3830; *BC-57*
COPLAND, AARON: Third Symphony, Copland, London Symph. Ev. 6018; *3018*
DALLAPICCOLA, LUIGI: *Songs of Liberation*, Ang. 35228
   Goethe Songs, *Liriche Greche, Cinque Canti, Concerto per la Notte di Natale dell'Anno 1956*, Epic LC-3706; *BC-1088*
DAVIES, PETER MAXWELL: *O Magnum Mysterium*, Lon. Argo 327; *5327*
DEBUSSY, CLAUDE: *Jeux*, Bernstein, N.Y. Phil., Col. ML-5671; *MS-6271*
EGK, WERNER: *Abraxas*, ballet suite, Lon. 643
HENZE, HANS WERNER: *Elegy for Young Lovers*, Henze, Berlin Radio Orch., DGG-18876; *138876*
HINDEMITH, PAUL: Third Quartet (for number see Bloch's Fifth Quartet)
   Requiem "for those we love," Hindemith, N.Y. Phil., Col. ML-5973; *MS-6573*
IVES, CHARLES: *Central Park in the Dark, Hallowe'en*, CRI-163
   Piano Sonata No. 2 ("Concord"), Time 58005; *8005*
KIRCHNER, LEON: Concerto for violin, cello, ten wind instruments and percussion (for number see Carter's Double Concerto)
   Quartet No. 1, Col. ML-4843
KODALY, ZOLTAN: Sonata for Solo Cello, Starker, Per. 510
LUENING, OTTO, and VLADIMIR USSACHEVSKY: *Poem in Cycles & Bells*, Tape Recorder & Orch., CRI-112
MADERNA, BRUNO: *Serenata* (for number see Berio)

MESSIAEN, OLIVIER: *Trois Petites Liturgies de la Présence Divine,* Bernstein, N.Y.
Phil., Col. ML-5982; *MS-6582*
MILHAUD, DARIUS: Concerto for Percussion and Orchestra (for number see
Bartók's *Music for Strings, Percussion, and Celesta*)
NEW ELECTRONIC MUSIC (Babbitt, Pousseur, etc.): Col. MS-7051.
NONO, LUIGI: *Polifonica* (for number see Berio)
ORFF, CARL: *Die Kluge,* 2 Ang. 3551; *S-3551*
ROUSSEL, ALBERT: Symphony No. 3 (for number see Messiaen)
RUGGLES, CARL: *Evocations, Lilacs, Portals,* Col. ML-4986
SCHOENBERG, ARNOLD: *Moses und Aron,* 3 Col. K-3 L-241
 Piano Music; complete (Steuermann), Col. ML-5216
 Pierrot Lunaire, Erwartung, Craft, 2 Col. M-2 L-279; *M-2 S-679*
SESSIONS, ROGER: Quartet No. 2, New Music Quartet, Col. ML-5105
STOCKHAUSEN, KARLHEINZ: *Gesang der Jünglinge,* DGG-38811
 Zeitmasse for five woodwinds, Col. ML-5275
STRAVINSKY, IGOR: *Mass,* Col. ML-5757; *MS-6357*
 Agon (for number see Berg's *Three Pieces for Orchestra*)
 Canticum Sacrum, Stravinsky, Col. ML-5215; *MS-6022*
 Oedipus Rex, Stravinsky, Cologne Radio Orch. and Chorus, Col. ML-4644
TIPPETT, MICHAEL: *Magnificat,* Lon., Argo 340; *5340*
VARESE, EDGAR: *Intégrales, Density 21.5, Ionization, Poème électronique,* Col.
ML-5478; *MS-6146*
WEBERN, ANTON: Complete Works, 4 Col. K-4 L-232

INDEX

Compositions are listed under their composers; works, however, which are merely mentioned in the text, do not appear in the index. In alphabetization of titles, articles are disregarded.